Living the Policy Process

Living the Policy Process

Philip B. Heymann

Including extended case studies written by John Buntin,
Kirsten Lundberg, and Esther Scott

OXFORD
UNIVERSITY PRESS
2008

OXFORD
UNIVERSITY PRESS

Oxford University Press, Inc., publishes works that further
Oxford University's objective of excellence
in research, scholarship, and education.

Oxford   New York
Auckland   Cape Town   Dar es Salaam   Hong Kong   Karachi
Kuala Lumpur   Madrid   Melbourne   Mexico City   Nairobi
New Delhi   Shanghai   Taipei   Toronto

With offices in
Argentina   Austria   Brazil   Chile   Czech Republic   France   Greece
Guatemala   Hungary   Italy   Japan   Poland   Portugal   Singapore
South Korea   Switzerland   Thailand   Turkey   Ukraine   Vietnam

Published by Oxford University Press, Inc.
198 Madison Avenue, New York, New York 10016

www.oup.com

Oxford is a registered trademark of Oxford University Press.

Library of Congress Cataloging-in-Publication Data

Heymann, Philip B.
Living the policy process / Philip Heymann.
p.   cm.
ISBN 978-0-19-533538-5;   978-0-19-533539-2 (pbk.)
1. Policy sciences—Case studies.   2. Political planning—United States—Case studies.
3. Military assistance, American—Afghanistan.   4. Stinger (Missile)   5. Iran-Contra Affair,
1985–1990.   6. Tobacco use–Government policy—United States.   I. Title.
JK468.P64H49 2008
320.6—dc22   2007029031

9 8 7 6 5 4 3 2 1

Printed in the United States of America
on acid-free paper

Dedicated to my brother-in-law, Dr. Joseph Ross,
who has taught us what living is all about.

Preface: The Logic of Governmental Policy Choice

When we think about the decisions of a government official, we often imagine a decision maker who has all the information she needs in order to apply her own set of values to the situation at hand. Conversely, we often deduce the decision maker's values by imagining what values, when applied to predictions based on the best set of facts available, would have led to a particular decision. All of that was described decades ago by Graham Allison in his splendid book, *Essence of Decision*, as "Model One." Allison also reminded us that decisions are not really owned and made by a particular official; they are also organizational (his "Model Two") and the product of political contests within bureaucracies ("Model Three"). Nor are the values that inform both decision making and the assessment of outcomes necessarily shared.

Moreover, the information relevant to applying her values to a situation does not come to any decision maker (or player in a political contest) complete or without bias. No one has shown the distorting effects of systematic flows of partial information in a government (or any) bureaucracy better than Mort Halperin did long ago in his book *Bureaucratic Politics*.[1] The flow is not merely subject to inevitable distortions; often it is carefully manipulated. Supporters lobby, legislators threaten, subordinates shape reports, and much more. Finally the information is processed by each individual—in other words, is placed to be analyzed—within a context of assumptions about the world and the people in it that result from a lifetime of particular experiences, different from others' understanding of the same situation.

Despite these complexities, and others almost as serious, there is in fact a logic to policy choice that is intuitive and familiar. That is the subject of this book. I use richly detailed and, as far as humanly possible, accurate accounts of real decisions to illustrate that logic in highly concrete situations. What makes this form of argument—and in particular its reliance on case studies—possible is that it builds on what we all know about the concerns and influences at work when individuals are making more familiar group decisions. In government, the institutional and democratic context reshapes that massive body of everyday experience in ways that are not so familiar to us.

The argument of the book, illustrated by the case studies, is intended to bring what the reader already understands from his daily life to bear in the special governmental context. The case studies involve both foreign and domestic policy decisions. I have worked for years in each area. The differences, while real, are not critical. In each area the crucial and special characteristics of the setting to which an individual must relate are:

- a stream of decisions over time
- to be made by a shifting but overlapping group of players, largely defined by rules
- each of whom has responsibility to the organizational units she heads or to which she belongs
- as well as concern for her influence over future decisions.

The First Three Parts: How Are Policy Choices in Fact Made in This Bafflingly Complex Setting?

The argument that follows has a number of pieces that connect in complicated ways. It may help to state it in summary form at the beginning, providing a blueprint before describing the more detailed specifications.

The politics of policy choice—deciding what actions the government will take on proposals for government action—involves the rich relationships among, as well as the individually held beliefs and values of, a group of people. So as good a starting point as any is to identify who participates. There are, essentially, two subgroups: First, there are those who are given a right and obligation to participate because of their assigned positions, that is, in order to establish an orderly and consistent process of group choice. Second, there are those who have resources to influence the first group. The second group is wide enough to include everyone from interested constituents to the person who deferred to your strong preferences last week and expects reciprocal concern now. In the middle are the press, organized interest groups, legislators, those who furnish cooperation or money, and more.

Fortunately, not all of these potential participants will want to become involved in every decision; but, if they do, it will be important to know what will motivate them. The content of the proposal, the proposal's salience and the timeliness of it, and exercises of influence by others can all affect the members of either of these groups. Such matters will affect a player in the game of policy choice if she sees the matter as related (in an important way, for they are busy) to the good of society, the welfare of her organization, her influence on future decisions, her moral commitments, or her personal welfare.

Note that what is important for prediction is not so much what the proposal and those using influence for or against it actually mean to an actor, but what she perceives they mean. That requires us to also examine differences among players in their very understandings of the significance of the shared situation in which the group is choosing a policy.

There are only six or seven ways that one individual can influence the position that another will take in governmental choice. These range from authority and persuasion to bargaining and changing the situation by a fait accompli (with several others in between). Each of these ways of exercising influence has certain prerequisites; persuasion, for example, requires trust. Building and storing these prerequisites—which are the resources of influence—so that influence can be exercised over time and not just now is a central part of living the policy process. Using the resources effectively, designing and choosing a proposal that influential players will like, and timing the proposal for when it will seem responsive to a particularly salient demand, need, or opportunity are the three major tactics of a policy maker.

Thus, Part I of this book is devoted to a careful description of the bureaucratic politics of decision making. That requires examining who takes part in any decision, what concerns them as they take a position, what options there are for the positions they can take on a proposal, what enters into their understanding of the relationship between their concerns and the situation that confronts them, and finally how they can seek to influence others in the structured process that will produce a government decision. Merely making that list suggests that the politics of bureaucratic decision making is a subject worthy of a book of its own. It has in fact generated several very distinguished books, taking a more descriptive, less intuitive and action-oriented approach than mine.

The description in Part I is largely of the interaction of individuals whose relationships within the executive branch are occasional or, at most, somewhat regular, but hardly intimate. The motivations of these individuals need not, therefore, be examined in psychological terms; considering their interests or concerns is enough. Although the framework in Part I is broad enough to include loyalty and reciprocity as ways of influencing others, that is no substitute for a richer psychological examination of one critically important and pervasive relationship. Therefore, Part II moves deeper into the emotionally charged relationships between superiors and the few subordinates who interact with them personally on a regular basis. Multiple, connected instances of this type of relationship forms the skeleton of any hierarchical organization. And this relationship is held together or shattered apart by hopes and fears, by trust and suspicion, in a way that is not characteristic of dealings with players far less tied to each other's past, present, and future.

Thus, to the complicated subject of Part I (Missiles for the Mujahideen), Part II (Loyalty and Respect) adds an important reminder. The currency of policy decisions within a government is not simply resources. It is simultaneously loyalty and respect—in particular, respect. Whether for political or policy reasons, the members of a decision-making group or team want to perform effectively. They, therefore, come to defer to the advice of anyone who earns their respect. Having more or less respect among the members of the team thus creates its own hierarchy that can compete with the hierarchy of formal authority. Like authority, and unlike resources that are specific to the relationship between two players, the hierarchy of respect may be recognized and deferred to even by members of the group who have had no personal interaction on the basis of which they could develop trust.

The good side of respect is that it provides a check on the ease with which mistakes may be made by those occupying positions of considerable authority. The bad side is that competition for respect, more than anything else, disrupts relationships in a decision-making group, as we shall see in discussing Secretary of State George Shultz's experience during the Iran-Contra affair. Giving loyalty generally depends upon receiving respect.

Bureaucratic politics takes place against a background of legislative and electoral politics. In Part III the interaction among the three must finally be considered. The third part (Nicotine for Teens) moves the leader into the politics of winning and using political and legislative support for a particular policy. Often the effect of public support for a proposal reaches executive decisions through an intermediary: elected representatives in the legislature. Sometimes dangers to (or opportunities for) public support directly affect the President. The relations are reciprocal; both the President and Congress can, and make substantial efforts to, greatly affect the attitudes of the public.

In Part III's first case, David Kessler must work his way through all these factors in deciding whether, when, and how to proceed by an administrative regulation, rather than congressional action, in an attempt to limit the lethality of smoking by teenagers. For most policy decisions, legislation is one alternative, even if the executive has been delegated the power to decide the matter. When to go to the legislature—with all the benefits and risks that accompany that choice—must be addressed. Matt Myers, the protagonist of a second case on smoking, has the same objective. But his case, involving the difficulties of obtaining a fiercely contested, legislative policy choice, displays three differences from what has come before: a new type of player, the public or private interest group; new techniques to form a coalition of influential players; and a new and important tactic for legislative or executive action, trying to prevent the formation of rival coalitions.

Having explored how governmental choices are made and how successful policy entrepreneurs influence them, I turn in Part IV, the concluding section, to address the quality of the resulting decisions. Players differ in ultimate values, so the quality of decisions cannot be judged by how well we like particular results. But everyone wants a process that considers the full range of widely valued consequences, intangible as well as tangible; that carefully predicts outcomes along these dimensions; and that, in making those predictions, considers the consequences of all plausible assumptions about the likely results of our actions, not just hoped-for ones. Nothing in the political processes of choice that I describe in the first three parts promises decisions that satisfy these criteria. A final critical job of those individuals whose positions make them responsible for policy choices is to develop and insist upon processes that do satisfy these criteria.

Looking in detail at the handling of the decisions to authorize highly coercive interrogation of suspected terrorists and at the unconsidered and unwanted consequences of those decisions, we will examine what went wrong and will compare the processes used on this occasion to those used for other decisions that far better satisfy almost everyone's minimal criteria. This aspect of management is comfortably within the boundaries of my subject: policy making. But the case study is also a useful reminder of other responsibilities of many officials that are not included in this volume.

The decisions on highly coercive interrogation were not only poorly considered; their implementation was also poorly managed as their implications spread confusingly as far as the Abu Ghraib prison, creating a scandal that President George W. Bush called perhaps the greatest mistake of a war with many competitors for that title. Implementation is part of the responsibility of policy makers; sharing in policy making is only part of what the players in a complicated contest over government activities have to think about.

Graham Allison describes a famous moment during the deliberations over the Cuban Missile Crisis, when President Kennedy discovered that his earlier decision to remove missiles pointed at the Soviet Union from Turkey had never been executed or implemented. He had conveyed it to the military, but they had done nothing. Obviously, there may be little importance to an initial policy decision if it is ignored, or misconstrued, or assigned to an organizational unit incapable of carrying it out. One important political maneuver in the game of government choice is, for example, to deny adequate resources to those who must carry out a decision one opposes.

Implementation over time, not only of new policies but also of policies largely determined in the past, is a large part of management. (Other major parts would include obtaining the needed external support for the organization and building its capacity and willingness to carry out policies.) Some players, with important resources of influence, particularly trust, may have no sizable organization under their control and no significant responsibilities for implementing the previously agreed-upon policies. But many, perhaps most, major policy players within the executive branch have management responsibilities at the same time. That these are not discussed in the present volume should not suggest that they are of lesser importance or difficulty. Results can be as much determined by how a set of previously decided policies are carried out as by winning a contest for a new policy statement.

Being effective in managing the processes that carry out policies, largely chosen long ago, is a very big part of the role and opportunity of many who are simultaneously engaged in making new policies.

Protecting their independence and effectiveness in playing the former role is one of such players' basic concerns. Developing a reputation for effective management of past policies is also important to being entrusted with management of new policies and the array of resources and choices of outcomes that come with that.

A Caution about Differences in Evaluating Outcomes

Giving any appraisal of outcomes and processes of policy choice is of course a function of values. A final reminder, by way of preface, is that not only do values differ among the players we shall consider, but they often differ along two particularly fundamental fault lines. The first, liberal versus conservative perspectives, is very familiar. The second—a dichotomy between "value-based" expressive goals and "cost/benefit-based" instrumental goals—is not, although it too is pervasive in our society. The two fault lines do not coincide.

Both officials and ordinary citizens care greatly about their share of the goods and services, and of the powers and liberties, that people enjoy in their society; but they care equally about the respect that society shows for them, for how they work, for how they live their lives, and for their associations and group identifications. There is every reason why a person should care greatly about his relation to the values and beliefs of the society, for that relationship determines the respect he gets and the nature of his social relationships—matters just as important to him as goods and services. Since the symbolic judgments about values and beliefs that are implicit in the choices and actions of government are major determinants of a society's beliefs and values, he has to be concerned about the expressive, as well as the instrumental, consequences of policy choice.

These are also powerful determinants of one's sense of security and well-being; to feel pride in the group to which one belongs and which is part of one's identity is the frosting on the cake of expressive concerns and values. Even in terms of goods and services themselves, an individual has reason to believe that how his neighbors and government will act and react in commercial and professional dealings with him will be shaped by widely shared values and beliefs about the society and the understanding its citizens live by.

Not only do values and beliefs shape governmental action. The reverse is also true. People recognize that governmental action and law are major forces in shaping and ratifying shared normative and descriptive beliefs about social reality. Emile Durkheim noted the importance of criminal convictions as an authoritative stamp of social disapproval, defining a boundary around what is permissible. The Civil Rights Act of 1964 changed attitudes toward segregation in privately owned public settings. The Reagan revolution brought about an end not only to many government programs supporting the poor but also to much public support for these programs. President George W. Bush declared that the surprisingly massive damage from a terrorist attack on the World Trade Center launched the beginning of twenty-first-century "war," a description that shaped, by government action, American attitudes pervasively. In each of these instances the values of our society have been defined and shaped by government action, and the new definition is important to citizens and officials.

Expressive goals involve a variety of relationships that are important to us and that always involve what economists call externalities. I care what my neighbor believes and values, particularly about me and what is important to me. Those values are taken as seriously as a separate accounting of more concrete benefits and harms for each individual and then a summing of the results as if each individual were concerned only with these, not relationships. A focus on medical treatment of drug addicts might most effectively reduce crime, but it downplays a moral message of the importance of assuming personal responsibility for one's behavior that many citizens want repeated to their community. Similarly, medical use of marijuana for some cancer patients might be helpful, as many doctors believe, but making it available as a medicine might have the expressive effect of obscuring the relationship of marijuana to hard drugs.

There are risks to taking expressive values seriously. Because they are built on relationships and a desire to affect how others see the world, they are inherently intolerant and therefore divisive. Expressive values tend to be simplistic. They often substitute symbols for action and so may leave the harms and benefits of a situation largely unaffected by the expressive actions. Yet they are the major alternative that citizens have for making choices in situations in which they are unwilling to accept the judgments of experts who identify and then add up costs and benefits. In that sense, expressive values are profoundly democratic, and policy actors must include them in their calculation of goals.

Where We Go from Here

This book that follows is not primarily intended to teach individuals what is good public policy or a desirable goal, although Part IV moves some distance in that direction. Most of the lessons lie, rather, in how to accomplish objectives in a world where power is shared—the politics of policy choice. Many of the protagonists are government officials; some are private individuals. Sometimes the setting is legislative; more often it is executive. My aim in all these variations is different from that of those whose interest is focused on how governments behave—the causes and nature of governmental choices and outcomes. Instead, each of my examples focuses on an individual navigating, for better or worse, in a crowded sea of other players, each of whom has his own set of resources and can throw more or less of them into the game of policy choice. I want the reader to think rigorously, with that individual, to consider his options for tactics and strategy.

To convey this, I saw three great advantages to using the work of remarkably talented case writers at the Kennedy School of Government, rather than rewriting it in my own more conclusory words. First, I could not describe the interactions nearly as well. The case writers are fine and accurate story tellers. Second, for me to recount the case histories would inevitably involve my selection of facts to support the arguments that I set out. I want to demonstrate that there is a way of thinking that organizes a rich and complicated political reality—a method that successful policy entrepreneurs know and use. If the reader only had a set of facts chosen by me to illustrate my point, she could not assess for herself how valid my argument is. If I rewrote the cases to remove the complexity, the reader would have no way of testing whether I am correct as I set forth a way of thinking that I claim organizes the complexity in a very useful way.

A third advantage of using rich case histories is that it conveys the world as it is. Political reality is in fact extraordinarily rich in potentially relevant details. The reader should get used to seeking opportunity—a path towards a desired outcome—in a forest of relationships, beliefs, and pressures. The price to the reader for these three advantages is that the cases are necessarily long, intricate, and detailed. I think it is a price well worth paying.

The result of this is that extended parts of this volume were written by others, generally at my request, as case studies to be taught at Harvard and elsewhere. Neither the remarkable studies by Kirsten Lundberg in chapters 2, 4, and 9, nor the wonderful work by Esther Scott in chapters 10, 11, 12, 14, 15, nor the account by John Buntin in chapter 1 are my creations. The credit for that superb work goes to them and to Howard Husock, who managed the case program at the Kennedy School of Government when they were produced. I have noted where the writing and the credit belongs to someone else by attaching to the title of the section the comment "a case history by ——." They have my profound thanks.

There is, of course, no schematic that can, in a few hundred pages, fully describe the psychological, social, and political complexity of governmental decision making. What can be done is to furnish a description and, hopefully, an understanding, of 80 percent of the critical variables and of 65 percent of their interactions. But that requires the reader "living the policy process" vicariously through the detailed accounts of actual events that follow.

The task I have set could not have been done without the research and editing assistance of Alex Blenkinsopp; the patience and thoughtful commentary of my wife, Ann; the wise suggestions of my daughter, Jody Heymann, when I felt stumped; the almost daily comparisons of our experiences with bureaucratic life with my son, Steve Heymann, also a long-term observer of government at work; the quiet but unmistakable brilliance of the writers of the cases I have used (particularly Kirsten Lundberg, Esther Scott, and John Buntin), and far from least important, the tireless help with the manuscript of Jane Reader and Ben Lambert.

Contents

Living the Policy Process

1

Introduction

This book is about the process of making policy decisions. All policy decisions are shared decisions in the sense that they are subject to powerful influences from multiple sources. In the federal government, a decision made by anyone short of the President is shared with those serving in positions above the decision maker, those who must inform and advise, and then accept and follow that act of judgment or discretion and those who will appraise the formal decision maker on the basis of her decisions. It is also shared by any peers whose areas of responsibility are likely to be significantly affected and who are therefore protected by well-understood rules, enforceable by various forms of retaliation, that forbid unilateral determinations affecting that area of overlapping responsibilities. Every decision is also shared with the legislature. Law trumps policy; executing policy requires appropriations.

Even the President's decisions are shared, not only with the Congress, but also with others who can influence his choice by threatening to withhold electoral support. Indeed, the President's decisions, like those of any superior official, are also shared with subordinates who provide the information and analysis about any areas of his concerns—advice he needs for an informed decision. And his decisions are shared with any subordinates whose wholehearted support in executing his decisions he cannot monitor and thus whose loyalty he must win, and with those to whom he has delegated responsibilities for the areas that the decision affects because he needs to support and reinforce a sense of responsibility for matters he cannot decide or even monitor himself.

For these reasons, as well as others that I will describe, the picture of an individual with sole authority for deciding a policy question by calling on subordinates or perhaps peers to provide the necessary facts, predictions, and analysis, and then consciously choosing, from among an adequate set of alternatives, which societal outcome is "best" is far from realistic. Even the decisions that are formally "made" by a particular decision maker are subject to the influences that I have just described. I had not yet arrived at the Department of Justice when Attorney General Janet Reno had to decide whether to authorize the FBI to storm the Waco compound in 1993. To her great credit, Reno always accepted full responsibility for the tragic consequences of the decision, but I assume that while the final decision was formally hers, she had to be very aware indeed of the influential views of the President, his staff, the FBI, and others. In that sense, the decision was ultimately shared. When strong influences point in one direction, deciding to proceed in a very different direction is costly and risky.

In addition to sharing in this way the decisions he formally makes, the President or any other decision maker knows that there are a multitude of yet unanticipated decisions that have to be made by others in the vast governmental bureaucracy. The same is true at most levels of government. Even many levels down, officials face far too many decisions to be made by any single individual. To obtain the immense advantages of specialization of knowledge and experience, and of clear placement of responsibility for governmental activities and concerns, a superior almost always divides up her responsibilities among a number of subordinates according to areas of knowledge, activity, and concern. The understanding is always that, even having been delegated responsibility, each subordinate must assess whether, in light of the prominence or importance of a matter, the superior would want to spend the time to make that decision herself. But that will be true of only a small portion of the delegated decisions. It is simply not possible for an official with a broad area of responsibilities to attempt to make more than a few of the needed decisions in that area. Many matters must be decided by subordinates.

Very few of such delegated issues will fall entirely within one area of assigned responsibility. For all the others, a system that involves "working it out" between those in different jurisdictions is highly desirable. Indeed, it is necessary. Such a "clearance" system, requiring for action a negotiated agreement among the players whose responsibilities are affected by a proposal, could only be dispensed with if, instead of "working it out," each could (and would) "reason it out" in an identical way based on authoritative premises—if the superior could announce a strategy, a set of goals, or a culture that was specific enough for each subordinate to resolve all conflicts in the same way. But this is not remotely practicable in most instances.

Most decisions will bear on the assigned responsibilities of several subordinates either because what is proposed will significantly affect each of their spheres of activity or because the underlying problem raises several governmental concerns for which different subordinates have been made responsible. Critically, differences must be resolved even though most shared issues are not important enough to take to a common superior. Sometimes the first common superior of subordinates whose areas of delegated responsibility would be affected by a proposal may be many layers up. For example, if the issue involves food assistance to an African nation and there is disagreement between a section chief in the Department of Agriculture and a desk officer in the Department of State, their first common superior would be the President or, perhaps less formally, one of his aides on the National Security Council (NSC) staff in the White House. But even the relatively large NSC staff does not have time to resolve many such disagreements.

For one thing, statements of strategy, goals, and culture are, and must be, far too general to resolve close cases. And in these, players with different fields of expertise, different responsibilities, and different concerns, will not even agree as to what types of consequences are "truly" relevant. Predicting consequences is contentious. Worse, the very allocation of responsibilities within the organization will guarantee that the values assigned to consequences are not shared. If the manager wants one set of subordinates to focus on our agriculture interests, he cannot expect them to bring the same values to the predicted results of a possible decision as another set of subordinates whom he has charged with emphasizing our relations with Nigeria (which may be affected by the sale of farm products).

Nor can a shared cost/benefit analysis provide the magic bullet to reconcile competing views. For most problems this way of deciding is simply impossible—even assuming complete abandonment of loyalties and suppression of policy views by subordinates.[1] Indeed, it is not at all clear that a superior dividing up the responsibilities for attending to a number of policy concerns would even want to direct subordinates to put aside their special responsibilities and instead assess occasions in terms of the overall welfare of all those affected. For, if each player focuses on her area, the consequences for that area will be explored and evaluated more fully and carefully; and a well designed process of group decision making may assure that nothing important is left out.

All that the President or any superior can in fact do about the many decisions he cannot handle himself is: to decide how influence over policies should be shared within the organization by creating areas of responsibilities; to determine whom to place in charge of each area; to make as clear as he can general categories of matters he wants to be brought to him personally; to promulgate rules for the process of choice when he is not involved; and, finally, to convey and reward adherence to a combination of goals and culture he expects to bound disagreements within the rather wide area he will learn to tolerate. That is our subject.

How then are policy decisions made, if not by a single decision maker considering an adequate range of alternatives with a reasonable prediction of the consequences of each and not by conveying and monitoring a well-designed preference function for subordinates to use to choose among the sets of consequences? In fact, policy decisions are made of six parts, which function together to produce an outcome. Consider the following example.

The 1998 Needle Exchange Decision: The McCaffrey-Shalala Confrontation
A Case History by John Buntin

In the spring of 1998, AIDS activists and public health specialists saw their best opportunity in a decade to roll back a ban on the use of federal funds for needle exchange programs, which provide drug addicts with clean needles.[2] The shared use of dirty needles was a major contributor to the spread of HIV, the virus that causes AIDS; according to the Department of Health and Human Services (HHS), by the end of 1997 nearly 40 percent of the 652,000 cases of AIDS reported in the United States were linked to intravenous drug use. Many AIDS activists and public health specialists had long believed that programs to provide intravenous drug users with clean needles would retard the spread of HIV. However, critics had countered that the government had no business handing out needles, and in 1998 needle exchange opponents had persuaded Congress to impose a ban on federal funds for needle exchange programs. At the end of March, that ban on needle exchange programs was due to expire, and powerful players within the administration of President Bill Clinton seemed willing to overturn the ban and support federal funding for needle exchange programs.

One major obstacle stood in their way—General Barry McCaffrey, the head of the Office of National Drug Control Policy (ONDCP), better known as the nation's drug czar. McCaffrey was adamantly opposed to federal funding for needle exchange programs. Such a step would, in McCaffrey's opinion, muddy the government's message that drug use was unequivocally bad and would very possibly lead to an increase in heroin use, which already killed 4,000 people a year. During the spring of 1998, McCaffrey waged an unusually dramatic, no-holds-barred battle with needle exchange advocates within the administration over the fate of the needle exchange ban.

A Decisive Edge?

McCaffrey's arguments against needle exchange were not new, but in the spring of 1998, needle exchange advocates, led by Sandra Thurman, the White House AIDS czar, felt increasingly confident that they could prevail over the objections of McCaffrey and other critics. Advocates of needle exchange programs in 1998 had an advantage that they had not enjoyed ten years earlier—a growing body of scientific evidence that supported their contention that needle exchange programs could reduce the risk of HIV infection without resulting in increased rates of drug use.

The flow of good news for advocates of needle exchange had been unceasing. In February 1998, Donna Shalala, Secretary of Health and Human Services (HHS), reported to Congress that a review of scientific studies indicated that needle exchange programs "can be an effective component of a comprehensive strategy to prevent HIV and other blood borne infectious diseases in communities that choose to include them." However, Shalala directed the Department's scientific agencies to continue to review research findings regarding the effect of needle exchange programs on illegal drug use. In March 1998, the National Institutes of Health published a report that concluded that needle exchange programs "show a reduction in risk behaviors as high as 80 percent in injecting drug users, with estimates of a 30 percent or greater reduction of HIV." As the scientific evidence supporting their position accumulated, AIDS activists and others intensified the pressure on the White House and HHS to provide federal funding for needle exchange programs.

In mid-March, President Clinton's own Presidential Advisory Council on HIV/AIDS issued a statement condemning the administration's refusal to spend federal money on needle exchange programs. "Lack of political will can no longer justify ignoring the science," said the council in a letter to Shalala. "Every day that goes by means more needless new infections and more human suffering."

The Clinton administration seemed to be listening. In early April, rumors began to circulate within the AIDS community that the Clinton administration was moving toward a decision to lift the ban on federal funding for needle exchange programs.[3] However, within the White House an intense battle had broken out between Thurman and McCaffrey about whether or not the ban should be lifted. A letter that McCaffrey had written to Thurman criticizing needle exchange programs had been leaked to conservative members of Congress, prompting a fusillade of Republican criticism. Efforts were made to patch over the differences between Thurman and McCaffrey, and they soon agreed to a common line: the Secretary of HHS would make the decision as soon as all the science was in.

Communicating His Position

McCaffrey and his advisers, however, had no intention of waiting passively for the science to come in. In early April, ONDCP dispatched several specialists from its office to go up to Vancouver to check out a thoroughly studied needle exchange program that was often adduced as evidence that needle exchange programs could be successful. The ONDCP team was horrified by what they found: HIV infection among intravenous drug users had skyrocketed since Vancouver's needle exchange program had been put in place. This finding confirmed McCaffrey's suspicion that much of the so-called "science" supporting needle exchange programs was bogus.

McCaffrey lost no time in sharing this horrifying discovery with others, including conservative opponents of the administration in Congress, law enforcement agencies, and the conservative *Washington Times*. (Indeed, so widely were these findings disseminated that the original authors of the Vancouver study ultimately challenged ONDCP's interpretation of their study in a *New York Times* Op-Ed.[4]) Republicans responded by stepping up their attacks on the Clinton administration and floating the idea of passing a permanent ban on needle exchange programs.

Advocates of needle exchange programs within the administration were angered by what they saw as McCaffrey's willingness to mobilize Republicans against a course of action being considered within the administration. Officials at ONDCP, however, insisted that the agency was merely fulfilling its statutory duty to keep Congress apprised of its viewpoint on drug policy issues.

In mid-April, McCaffrey and Thurman again patched up their breach over the needle exchange issue. McCaffrey and Thurman reiterated that they would agree to disagree on whether or not the federal government should fund needle exchange programs until the science was in. McCaffrey came away from this meeting with the belief that no decision was imminent.

McCaffrey Leaves, a Decision Arrives

On the evening of Wednesday, April 15, McCaffrey left with President Clinton for a long trip to Chile and several other South American countries. Aboard Air Force One, McCaffrey made a strong argument against federal funding for needle exchange to the President, who seemed receptive.

Then, on Thursday night, Jim McDonough, the director of strategy at ONDCP, got a startling phone call from a reporter at the *Washington Times*. The reporter told McDonough that he had heard reports that the administration was moving ahead with a decision to lift the ban on federal funds for needle exchange, perhaps as early as the coming Monday. McDonough expressed his surprise and reiterated ONDCP's belief that "needle exchange is not the way to go."

The next morning McDonough was tipped off to the fact that a meeting was currently underway in the Roosevelt Room of the White House to determine exactly when HHS would announce the decision to provide federal funds for needle exchange programs. McDonough arrived at the Roosevelt Room midway into the meeting. There he found Thurman, several officials from HHS, and a White House aide discussing how the decision to fund needle exchange would be "rolled out" on Monday. An unsuccessful attempt was made to shift the topic of conversation. McDonough, however, had only one question: had the President made a definite decision to fund needle exchanges? The answer to this question was no. In that case, McDonough informed the gathered officials, ONDCP would continue to speak out on the issue until a decision was made.

McDonough's discovery that planning for a rollout was underway came at an awkward time. McCaffrey himself was in South America and was difficult to contact; therefore, it was impossible for him to talk to the principal decision makers and find out what was going on.[5] The ONDCP staff would have to take on that task. Janet Crist, the chief of staff at ONDCP, spent the afternoon attempting to ascertain if a decision on needle exchange had been made or if a decision was imminent. After a round of phone calls with officials at HHS, Crist concluded that no immediate decision was in the works. HHS was still waiting for the science to come in.

On Saturday morning, the senior staff at ONDCP managed to make contact with McCaffrey. They updated him on the situation as they understood it: there seemed to be movement toward a decision to proceed with needle exchanges, but no decision had been reached. McCaffrey reiterated his opposition to the proposal and urged his staff to hold the line.

The Endgame

Early Monday morning, ONDCP staff learned that Secretary Donna Shalala, the head of HHS, had scheduled a ten o'clock press conference on needle exchange. ONDCP staff were officially notified that the science was in and that it supported needle exchange programs, and that HHS was going ahead with the announcement that federal funds would be available for needle exchange programs. This was followed by a series of calls from Erskine Bowles, the White House Chief of Staff, Shalala, and others, who wanted to talk to McCaffrey. However, attempts to get McCaffrey on the phone were unsuccessful. Still, it appeared that at ten o'clock Shalala would announce the federal government's intention to fund needle exchange programs.

Then, shortly after nine o'clock, ONDCP got another call from the White House with still more startling news: President Clinton had come out against federal funding for needle exchange. Subsequent accounts of Clinton's decision identified two decisive factors behind the President's last-minute reversal—his discussion with McCaffrey on the trip to Chile and his concern that needle exchange would only provoke a Congressional onslaught. If Clinton had endorsed federal funds for needle exchange, predicted presidential adviser Rahm Emanuel, funding efforts "would have been voted down immediately and you would have scared off local people."[6]

President Clinton's unexpected decision threw HHS into complete disarray. The nation's most prominent AIDS activists and public health specialists were already gathered in Washington to celebrate the administration's decision to recognize, at last, the role that needle exchanges could play in reducing the transmission of HIV via dirty needles. Shalala's press conference was pushed back until one o'clock and restricted to the print press.

At one o'clock, Shalala, surrounded by a grim-faced gathering of the nation's top public health officials, appeared to announce that the government now had decisive evidence that needle exchange programs did not lead to an increased rate of drug use and could reduce rates of HIV transmission via dirty needles—and that the administration would not provide federal funding for such programs.

"This nation is fighting two deadly epidemics—AIDS and drug abuse," said Shalala. "A meticulous scientific review has now proven that needle exchange programs can reduce the transmission of HIV and save lives without losing ground in the battle against illegal drugs." Creating needle exchange programs, Shalala went on to say, "offers communities that decide to pursue needle exchange programs yet another weapon in their fight against AIDS."

There was no mention of federal funding for needle exchange programs. When asked why the federal government should not itself fund needle exchange programs given their documented effectiveness, Shalala responded, "We had to make a choice. It was a decision. It was a decision to leave it to local communities."

The Aftermath

The fallout was instantaneous. AIDS activists were outraged by the President's decision. "At best, it's hypocrisy, and at worst, it's immoral," said Scott Hitt, the chairman of the President's Advisory Council on HIV/AIDS. "It's like saying, 'We acknowledge the world is not flat, but we are not going to give Columbus the money for ships,'" said Daniel Zingale, executive director of AIDS Action.[7]

Many representatives from the African American community were also outraged. (Though African Americans comprise just 13 percent of the population, they accounted for 36 percent of all AIDS cases reported through 1997.) Several days later, Eleanor Holmes Norton, the Congressional delegate from the District of Columbia, called for

McCaffrey's resignation. "In the face of compelling evidence, Barry McCaffrey has used brutal tactics with the administration to subvert a decision to fund needle exchange programs," charged Norton.[8] Rep. Maxine Walters, D-Calif., the head of the Congressional Black Caucus, who had already taken a dislike to McCaffrey, seconded Norton's call.

Republicans also condemned Shalala's announcement. Determining that needle exchange programs could work, said Sen. John Ashcroft, R-Mo., a presidential hopeful, "is an intolerable message that it's time to accept drug use as a way of life."[9] Sen. Paul Coverdell, R-Ga., immediately introduced a bill that would forbid the HHS Secretary from ever lifting the ban. On April 29, the House of Representatives passed similar legislation.

McCaffrey had triumphed but at a considerable cost. Needle exchange proponents within the administration were infuriated at McCaffrey's tactics. HHS officials were reportedly livid at the way in which McCaffrey's office had apparently urged Republicans in Congress to speak out against lifting the ban. "It's one thing to have a view on a policy decision and argue for it internally. It's quite another to go to the Hill and Republican members and get them to do something that's still being discussed internally," an unnamed HHS official told the *Washington Post* soon after the decision was made.

McCaffrey, however, was unrepentant. "Let me be absolutely blunt now. By law, I am a nonpolitical officer of government. And the president of the United States told me to work these issues with a bipartisan approach."[10] Said Jim McDonough, ONDCP's strategic planning director: "General McCaffrey constantly keeps Congress informed of where he stands on the drug issue. He is not reticent in defining his concerns."[11]

McDonough, however, acknowledged that McCaffrey's stance against needle exchange hurt him in some quarters. "He's making enemies within the administration; he's making enemies in the AIDS community; he's making enemies in the Congressional Black Caucus. This isn't great politics for him," says McDonough. "My view is that he took a very principled stand on this one. He didn't think it would be without cost, but he figured out where he wanted to stand and that's where he stood."

Shared Policy Decisions

Now let's review the six parts of any shared policy decision as illustrated in the Needle Exchange Case.

1. There is a partial structure that is in fact imposed from above. It consists of several pieces that are put beyond the bargaining realm for all participants in the process of choice. Most importantly, the given structure describes the rules for who can make what decisions, who must (and who must not) participate, and when one of the participants can insist on a different decision maker by appealing the decision. The structure also contains necessarily vague and incomplete but authoritative statements of goals and objectives. Finally, it conveys certain uncontestable understandings within the organization about its factual setting, such as who are friends and who are opponents or enemies.

The Needle Exchange Case is unusual in the willingness of several of the major participants to ignore the normal structure of rules. Secretary of DHHS Donna Shalala has tried to bypass a rule requiring her to consult with Barry McCaffrey, the director of OMDCP, on a matter so fundamental to his responsibilities. He, in turn, ignored common rules forbidding the inclusion, within the executive decision-making process, of influential players from the opposing political party and from hostile media. The dispute itself was made possible, indeed likely, because it occurred along a divide where there had been—and could be—no authoritative statement of goals. The divide reflected a conflict between an expressive goal (that Senator Ashcroft voiced) of demanding self-reliance and responsibility, even from addicts, and a harm reduction goal (stated by Hitt, the chair of the President's Advisory Council on HIV/AIDS) of reducing the health consequences to addicts of using dirty needles.

2. Each of the set of players required to participate in the decision, plus any others who are invited or invite themselves into the decision making, is sensitive to a set of quite distinct types of concerns, only one of which is her view of the overall social welfare on this particular occasion. Building personal capacities and enhancing organizational capacities to influence future decisions are two others. Moral and personal concerns complete the set. Having or being expected to have an effect on those concerns of another player generally defines the exercise of influence.

Shalala's resources of influence—her moral authority and standing—is weakened by an obvious attempt to bypass accepted rules. McCaffrey's resources with the President are debited for violating rules of exclusion. In both cases the cabinet member is motivated not only by a view of what is desirable for the United States, but also what is necessary to maintain his or her standing with Congressional and private groups who can influence future decisions. The point is simply this: to understand

McCaffrey's or Shalala's actions you have to consider not just the outcomes they publicly seek in the world of policy, but also how one or another course of action will affect his or her ability to influence future decisions, the strength and morale of his or her organization, and his or her personal concerns and sense of moral imperatives.

3. More than concerns are involved in reacting to the initiatives of others. Each player has an understanding of the significance of the occasion that includes not only her concerns but also her factual beliefs about the predicted relationship between any proposal and her concerns. Concerns need to be linked to a proposal by predictions of the consequences of possible changes brought about by adoption of the proposal or by the efforts of its proponents and opponents to exercise influence. Central to these predictions are views about the motivations of other players and the players' sense of whether they can be trusted.

McCaffrey predicts that federal funding of needle exchange will undermine the sense of individual responsibility (even of addicts) that both he and Shalala value as a condition of a healthy society. Shalala predicts there will be no such effect. McCaffrey also probably believes that his own resources of influence with conservative Republicans in the Senate and House will be reduced if the administration goes forward with needle exchange. If Shalala could convince him that this prediction was wrong, he would be less opposed to needle exchange.

Such predictions by a player flow from an organized set of beliefs—an understanding of the significance of the occasion—that must be combined with his concerns if he is to develop a position on the issue. Donna Shalala believes that needle exchange will significantly reduce disease and resulting death, and she believes that the federal government playing a role in needle exchange may be critical to its widespread adoption. She also believes that she would lose support from a powerful health constituency if she did not press forward with needle exchange. Her understanding of the significance of the occasion bridges for her the gap that would otherwise exist between the proposal and her concerns.

4. Our protagonist player will see that both the terms of a particular proposal—and its timing (for the concerns of any player and his predictions of consequences will change as time moves on and the situation he faces changes)—will help determine what benefits are promised and what costs are threatened in terms of the concerns felt by many of the other players. Thus there will be bargaining over its terms and over the timing of its introduction.

A needle exchange proposal that followed soon after a report of a shocking increase in HIV positives, particularly among the young, would have a quite different reception than a needle exchange proposal that was not brought forth against that background. Substantive differences in the scope of the proposal—such as whether it involves federal finding or instead relies on state or local funding or on income tax deductions for charitable contributions—will create political differences in the amount of support and opposition. Less obviously, changes in the proposal that appear to be totally symbolic may change the expressive valence. Professor Mark Kleiman of UCLA suggested at the time that the opposition to needle exchange could be presented as a bumper sticker saying, "Now we're furnishing the equipment needed for addiction." He argued that this expressive, thematic concern could be addressed by an instrumentally insignificant change in the proposal: having the government buy dirty needles from addicts (thus symbolically removing needles from circulation) combined with arranging that new needles could be legally purchased, perhaps with the proceeds, by anyone certified to be addicted.

5. The concerns of any player are not just triggered by the predicted consequences of a proposal. They can also be affected by the calculated use of influence by others in any of several forms, ranging from authority to reciprocity, with persuasion in between. Whether the others will attempt to influence a player depends upon their understanding of how significant the occasion is to their concerns. Whether they will have the capacity to influence others depends on their "resources of influence," a concept we will explore in some detail.

President Clinton's position on the merits of the proposal alone may well have been to favor federally funded needle exchange, and the rules of the game entitled him to decide, at least subject to Congressional review. To deal with that likely presidential preference, McCaffrey brought to bear the political resources of Congressional opponents of that decision and of the conservative media. Each of these groups would be motivated to use the resources of influence they have, and each had substantial capacity to "punish" a presidential decision to fund needle exchange.

6. Finally, the choice of better or worse tactics and the commitment of more or less energy to exercise influence, to build coalitions, and to shape and time the proposal also have an effect on the outcome. Skill and energy are the last of the working pieces that players can use, within the rules, goals, and understandings set by superiors for the organization, taking advantage of resources they have earned or have been given, to

further or block initiatives affecting their concerns. The Stinger missile case that follows in Chapter 2 is a detailed proof of that point.

Goals

In broad outline, this is the set of issues I will explore. One final warning is necessary. That the sole subject of this book is the politics of shared policy decisions must not lead us to lose sight of the other managerial aspects of the roles and responsibilities of many players who must manage organizations while they also engage in policy battles.

Secretary Shalala and General McCaffrey each headed an important organization with responsibilities that flowed from those management roles. In carrying out these responsibilities, each had to develop and convey some sense of goals to large numbers of people. By goals I mean priority activities, expressive themes, and alliances that would not only reflect the policy values of McCaffrey or Shalala but would also be designed to elicit the support they each would need from those they could not control, such as the President, the Congress, and constituency groups. I have written about this in *The Politics of Public Management* (Yale University Press, 1987). Each also had to see to it that the organization understood, responded to, and had the capacity to carry out these goals. That required each to direct, supervise, and inspire as they made decisions about hiring, discipline, information systems, assignments, organizational culture, and much more. They also had responsibility for indirectly influencing others who did not have to obey their orders. Thus, each had substantial control over funding decisions that they were expected to use to affect activities of independent public and private agencies—another major facet of management.

Carrying out their management responsibilities well would increase the political resources of Shalala and McCaffrey in making shared decisions. The political consequences of appearing unable to manage their organization effectively would include debilitating Congressional hearings, statutory interventions, reduced budgets, and political consequences for the President. The converse is also true. Effectiveness in making shared policy decisions would bring support to the job of management. It would affect the morale of subordinates, the predictions of those whose cooperation was needed, and the resources of money and authority made available by the President and Congress.

The Two Quartets

As we move into the first major case, it will be convenient to rearrange our pieces and place each in one of two closely interrelated quartets of issues that any policy entrepreneur must address.

First, he must recognize that a very high proportion of his possible tactics fall into one of four categories. (1) He can shape the proposal in a way that will make it more appealing to those whose support he needs or wants. (2) He can time the proposal so that it becomes responsive to a situation demanding some form of action that is at least somewhat like his proposal. (3) He can use a variety of forms of relationships among the players who may influence either the decision maker or other players who can themselves influence the decision maker. (4) And he can take measures to prevent opponents from making effective use of their influence or counter it in some way.

But using these four tactics depends upon filling out the answers to four sets of questions—the second quartet. (A) What do the rules say about who must or may make the decision or be consulted in the process leading up to the decision, and who and what tactics are excluded? (B) What are the types of concerns that may motivate these players (C) in light of their somewhat unique understandings of the significance of the occasion? (D) And finally, what resources of influence, carefully defined, does each of them have to influence others, creating a promising chain leading to the decision maker?

It is now time to illustrate and apply these two quartets.

Part I
Missiles for the Mujahideen

2

The Stinger Missile Case

Well before September 12, 2001, it was very clear that the Islamic jihadists (the "Mujahideen") who had fought successfully against the Soviet Union in Afghanistan regarded themselves as now at all-out war with the United States and its Western allies. High on the list of dangers the United States faced was the use of sophisticated surface-to-air missiles against our civilian airlines. For, beginning in 1986, we had provided 2,300 such missiles (the highly sophisticated Stinger missile) to what would become our newest enemy at a time when, without our knowledge, Gorbachev was already planning to pull the Soviet Union out of its misadventures in Afghanistan and shortly before the collapse of this rival superpower.

The Stinger missiles were furnished after a meeting with President Reagan, during which he was assured there were no objections from the Department of State, the Department of Defense, the Joint Chiefs of Staff, or the CIA (which had, for a number of years, been secretly supplying the Mujahideen with far less dangerous weapons). Presidents are far too busy to question most unanimous recommendations of their senior advisors, especially when, as in this case, many members of Congress are pressing for the same decision. While fears had earlier been expressed that the Stinger might find its way to unfriendly governments, such as the USSR or Iran, no one seems to have spent time on the possibility that today's jihadists harassing our superpower opponent might be tomorrow's lethal adversary attacking the United States.

As these risks became more apparent after the collapse of the Soviet Union, the United States scrambled and paid premium prices to recover as many of these missiles as it could. Still, many hundreds more were never found or were too valuable to their new owners (such as the Taliban sup-porters of Osama bin Laden) to be sold. But that is a separate story.[1] Here, our concern is how we arrived at the decision to furnish a likely enemy with 2,300 missiles that were dangerously effective against U.S. aircraft. To answer that question is to understand the political process behind a great majority of governmental decisions at all levels and in every field.

Answering the question persuasively requires, first, an extremely detailed look at what processes led up to a unanimous recommendation, without serious reservations or cautions, to a President most of whose time had to be spent on matters where his advisors disagreed—not where they all agreed. These processes and the possibility of winning policy advan-tage by using them are inherent in the operation of any large bureaucracy and are indeed necessary to its efficient functioning. Their effect on the decision maker is also predictable, for agreement offers him the social reassurance of consensus and the personal calm of an absence of friction among valued advisors at the same time that it provides the convenience of a sorting device that allows him more time for addressing contested decisions. Only a combination of an unusual character on the part of the decision maker and, at his behest, a carefully maintained structure for developing information about, and political consideration of, matters that all the principal advisors would rather ignore, can compensate for the processes that led to providing missiles for the Mujahideen.

The Politics of a Covert Action: The United States, the Mujahideen, and the Stinger Missile
A Case History by Kirsten Lundberg

The Soviet Union invaded Afghanistan on December 24, 1979.[2] Standing in the way of speedy success stood the Afghan rebels, or Mujahideen. While no one doubted the courage of the Afghan fighters opposing the Soviets, their ability to hold at bay the far greater invading force was largely due to generous international assistance. Among the friends of the Mujahideen was the U.S. Central Intelligence Agency.

The Mujahideen swore to wage a jihad, or holy war, to oust the Sovi-ets, and the United States was happy to help. CIA aid came in the form of weapons—all of Communist bloc manufacture—and other supplies. These were given to the Pakistani military intelligence service, which operated the distribution network.

For years, the CIA's program achieved the U.S. policy aim of making life difficult for the Soviets without costing the Americans anything more than money. It was a perfect covert action, according to the time-honored rule of the CIA: no U.S. weapons, allowing for "plausible deniability" that the United States was involved.

But in 1984 and early 1985, the Soviets introduced two new elements into the war: Spetsnaz special troops, and a more intensive deployment of armored helicopters known as Hinds. The helicopters could go with impunity into the mountain redoubts where the Mujahideen lay concealed and slaughter them. With only the Soviet-made SA-7 and a few British Blowpipe antiaircraft weapons, the rebels had proved increasingly impotent against the new attacks. It seemed possible the rebels would lose.

Within the Defense Department, the Office of Policy and Planning revived a solution originally put forth by the Mujahideen themselves: give the rebels state-of-the-art U.S.-made Stinger missiles, and the Soviet Hinds would be blown out of the skies. Undersecretary of Defense Fred Iklé and his deputy, Michael Pillsbury, thought this a logical and achievable undertaking.

The Directorate of Operations (DO) of the CIA, which ran the Afghan operation, disagreed vehemently. While there were powerful voices within the CIA—notably Director William Casey and the head of the DO, Clair George—who found the Stinger option attractive, key officers close to the program opposed it vigorously. Their reasons were many. Deployment of the U.S.-made weapon would violate an agreement with the Pakistani government that American involvement remain untraceable. It would put "paid" to "plausible deniability." It would risk provoking retaliation from the Soviets against host country Pakistan—and such an attack could plausibly escalate into World War III. The Stingers might easily fall into the hands of terrorists. The Soviets might capture a weapon and thus the technology to produce it.

But the CIA had another fear, less geopolitical but equally compelling: introducing the Stinger would expose a small, well-run operation to meddling from the Department of Defense (DOD). Covert actions are the most hallowed of all CIA undertakings. They are unacknowledged, leave almost no written trail, and are discussed on a strictly need-to-know basis. Covert actions are approved by the President, but the CIA's job is to keep hidden the hand of the U.S. government. Allow in the Stinger, and DOD would stand at the door. Covert would be overt and the operation destroyed.

The contest over the Stinger had many phases. As the dispute caught fire, the Defense Department and the CIA fought a battle royal for the support of the U.S. foreign policy establishment leadership—the Joint Chiefs of Staff, key members of Congress, the State Department's top officials, and the director of central intelligence. Ultimately, they would have to win over the one man who could issue the order—President Reagan.

Phase One: A Model Covert Action

By the time the Stinger missile became an issue in 1985, the CIA's Afghan program already had five years of considerable success under its belt. The CIA had moved into Afghanistan in force in January 1980 and had set up what it considered a model covert action. By and large, the Afghan program enjoyed widespread and bipartisan support and was given ever more generous funding.

So when in the spring of 1985 the Defense Department, notably Iklé's Office of Policy and Planning, floated the idea of providing Stingers to the Afghans, the CIA could hardly decide on what grounds to fight the suggestion first. The history of the covert action alone, felt CIA officials, would explain why introducing the Stinger would be a gross and perhaps fatal error.

Soviet Invasion

On Christmas Eve of 1979, the Soviet Union sent troops pouring across its southern border into the mountainous country of Afghanistan. The Soviets came at the invitation of Afghanistan's Communist regime, which in April 1978 had toppled the former right-wing government in a coup but then proved unable to consolidate its hold on power.[3] Western reaction to the invasion was swift and decisive. The U.S. boycotted the 1980 Olympic Games in Moscow. It also imposed economic sanctions, including a grain embargo.

Carter's Reaction

President Jimmy Carter's reaction to the invasion of Afghanistan was widely thought at the time to be naïve; many believed he was caught unawares by the aggression.[4] But Carter's administration had begun nonlethal covert assistance to the Afghan rebels under a secret presidential finding that Carter had signed six months before the invasion.[5] The CIA, charged with managing the details of the program, had spent some $500,000 on propaganda, medicine, and so forth.[6] All of it was sent into Afghanistan via neighboring Pakistan.

Immediately following the Christmas invasion, Carter signed a second presidential finding. This finding substantially altered the nature of the covert action by allowing the CIA to provide the rebels with weapons. Carter's directive called specifically for "harassment" of the Soviet forces, rather than their defeat.[7] In part, this modest goal reflected the fearsome reputation of the Red Army at the time. In addition, the Brezhnev Doctrine called for eternal Soviet support to neighboring Communist regimes.[8] Any withdrawal, reasoned U.S. analysts, would put at unacceptable risk the USSR's dominant position in its client states of Eastern Europe. Carter's finding would govern U.S. policy for the next five years.

Pakistan: The Linchpin

Within two weeks, the first U.S.-funded arms shipment (mostly rifles) arrived in Pakistan. In February 1980, National Security Advisor Zbigniew Brzezinski flew to Pakistan to formalize with President Muhammad Zia-ul-Haq the establishment of a reliable supply line to the Afghan rebels.[9] Pakistan and the United States had a reasonably good relationship based on mutual interest. From the U.S. standpoint, Pakistan was a strategic buffer between the Soviet Union and China (with whom Pakistan had, however, warm relations). For Pakistan, the United States offered the world's best weaponry, and insurance against incursions from India. For the United States, there was not much choice—Afghanistan's remaining neighbor, Iran, was rabidly anti-American. Secrecy was, from the start, paramount. Zia was willing to be seen as helping the Afghan rebels in their jihad, but he feared repercussions if the U.S. role were to be openly acknowledged. Domestically, Pakistan's masses were vehemently anti-American. In addition, neither Zia nor the United States wanted to substantiate the communist propaganda—that capitalist imperialists were responsible for instability in Afghanistan, which had necessitated the Soviet intervention.

Finally, there were appearances to consider. As one CIA officer pointed out, "this is a Jihad [holy war], and within the Islamic context, you can't get a bunch of blue eyes in there running a Jihad."[10] Therefore, the operation on the ground, the actual delivery of weapons to the Mujahideen, would be turned over to the Pakistani military intelligence service, the Inter-Services Intelligence Directorate (ISI).[11]

That suited the CIA just fine. The Agency had a good working relationship with ISI, dating back decades. A former intelligence official says, "The CIA relationship was very strong in Pakistan and went on for decades." The ISI role appealed to the CIA for another reason: the Pakistani service supplied the paramilitary resources CIA lacked. John McMahon was a career CIA officer who in June 1982 was named second in command in the Agency. Explains McMahon: "The Agency years and years ago lost its paramilitary capability. What we did in Afghanistan is we let the Mujahideen fight the war. We relied very heavily on the Pakistanis to be the interface to run it, and we were the implementers of the supply chain."[12]

In their February 1980 meeting, Brzezinski discussed with Zia the proposed expansion of the covert action program.[13] He then flew to Saudi Arabia, which was already funding the Afghan rebels. There he cemented a deal that the Saudis would match, dollar for dollar, U.S. contributions to the Afghan resistance effort.[14]

The CIA's next step was to set up the covert arms pipeline.

Maxims of a Covert Action

A covert action, broadly defined, attempts to influence events in a foreign country to the advantage of the United States. By definition, such an operation should ideally involve only a very small number of people. Covert actions are run out of the CIA's Directorate of Operations (DO).[15] Even within the DO, only a handful of officers are aware of any single covert action, and only a couple of those are privy to the complete lineup of current covert operations. Robert R. Simmons, former chief of staff for the Senate Select Committee on Intelligence (SSCI), says CIA covert action operatives "didn't write memos. They wanted to talk [to superiors]. They didn't want to write it down."[16]

Those within the CIA with a "need to know" about Afghanistan included the chiefs of station in Islamabad, Beijing, and Cairo, the members of the DO Near East/South Asia Division in Washington, the Deputy Director for Operations (DDO), the Director of Central Intelligence (DCI), and the Deputy Director of Central Intelligence (DDCI). At no time were more than 100 Americans assigned to the Afghan covert action.

It was directed by the Near East/South Asia Division. For military expertise, the division borrowed a couple of Defense Department weapons experts—officers seconded to the CIA—for a limited period of time.

The CIA set up its supply line to the Afghan rebels according to what one former senior intelligence officer calls "a few axiomatic, near-sacred assumptions, one of which was that they would never be broken."[17] This meant one cardinal rule: no identifiable direct U.S. involvement. The weapons provided had to be non-American—preferably of Eastern European, Soviet, or Chinese manufacture—and obtainable from third parties.

Plausible Deniability

The rationale for insisting on non-American weapons could be traced back to a larger principle: plausible deniability—the idea that U.S. involvement could be plausibly denied even if suspicions were strong. The CIA's covert actions were taken at the behest of the President; each one had to be personally approved by a presidential finding. But that did not mean the United States wanted its hand in the operation to be visible. On the contrary, disclosure of the CIA's role could undermine or even destroy its effectiveness. Discovery could cause at a minimum severe embarrassment—if the target happened, for example, to be a U.S. ally. At the worst, it could spark an outbreak of hostilities or even war, as an aggrieved enemy moved to recover prestige and redress its injury.

In this case, there were a few additional rules imposed by the Pakistanis. No American government representative could cross the border into Afghanistan. All the operational logistics would be handled by ISI. All the training would be done by ISI, though the CIA could train the trainers. The CIA would be the paymaster and the overseer. But Zia would remain the authority of last resort on any changes to the pipeline arrangement. Under him, operational responsibility rested with ISI Director Lieutenant-General Akhtar Abdul Rahman Khan.

This was, from the CIA viewpoint, an ideal covert action.

According to Simmons, "the Afghan program had all the elements you would normally want in a covert action." He specifies: "It had a little group of people defending their country or their interests against a superpower. It had a superpower invading a third or fourth-world country. It had a spirited resistance which simply needed help, which is something that we could provide. So the politics were good for us."

The Covert Pipeline

While it took years for the pipeline to develop the capacity to absorb the volume of weapons it would eventually carry, the outlines of the system were visible from the start.[18] Weapons for the Afghan effort were bought from arms merchants and middlemen around the world. They included rifles, mines, grenade launchers, and Soviet-designed SA-7 light antiaircraft weapons (modeled on the American Redeye missile). The idea was to make it appear as likely as possible that the rebels were using captured Soviet weapons. So the CIA bought arms in Eastern Europe.[19] They purchased stock from Egypt.[20] They bought weapons from China. Some arms even came from Pakistan.

Weapons were loaded onto non-U.S. ships and delivered, irregularly, into the port of Karachi. From Karachi, ISI took over. Mohammad Yousaf, the ISI brigadier who ran the day-to-day operation of the pipeline from 1983 to 1987, described ISI's control system. He wrote: "ISI decided who got the weapons, how many, and what types....No one outside the ISI, including President Zia, had any say or control over the allocation of arms, ammunition and allied logistic stores from our warehouses."[21]

ISI transported the weapons by freight trains to warehouses in the cities of Rawalpindi and Quetta. Occasionally, planeloads were also flown directly to Rawalpindi. At the ISI base in Rawalpindi, the weapons were divided into consignments for the seven recognized Afghan political parties and the commanders under their control. From there, some 200 trucks, chosen to look inconspicuous, moved the weapons 150 kilometers to Peshawar, the capital of the North-West Territory bordering Afghanistan.[22] In every truck a man rode shotgun to protect the shipment. It was in Peshawar that the rebel leaders had their headquarters, and the bulk of the Afghan refugees lived in camps.

At Peshawar, the Afghan political parties took over the distribution job, allocating weapons to their commanders in the field. Arms were loaded onto mules and the backs of fighters for transport into the rugged Afghan mountains. While there were recurring charges of corruption in the pipeline, Yousaf denied vehemently that any arms went astray under ISI. He maintained that "the middle section of the pipe was virtually corruption-free."[23] A senior CIA operations officer agreed that ISI was the most efficient and the least corrupt organization in Pakistan.[24]

The pipeline operated at a fairly low level from 1980 to 1983. In 1980 the CIA purchased about $30 million of arms, matched by the Saudis.

That level of assistance doubled in 1981 to $60 million, but then held steady through 1983.[25] This was not enough, however, to make a real difference in the fighting. In 1981 and 1982, the Soviets had increased their troop strength in Afghanistan from 75,000 to 108,000.

The Reagan Administration

A number of U.S. politicians and policy makers were starting to wonder why the United States did not do more. In January 1981, President Carter turned over the White House to incoming President Ronald Reagan. A new team was running U.S. foreign policy: Alexander Haig as Secretary of State (replaced in July 1982 by George Shultz); Caspar Weinberger at the Defense Department; William Clark and then (in October 1983) Robert "Bud" McFarlane as National Security Advisor; and William Casey as director of the CIA.

Nuclear Caveat

Zia moved early to consolidate his own interests with the new administration. In July 1981 he traded on his newly critical position in U.S. strategic policy to conclude a five-year, $1.5 billion military assistance package, plus another $1.7 billion in economic aid.[26] The United States attached only one condition to this assistance—that the Pakistanis adhere to an agreement not to develop nuclear weapons. This agreement was honored in the breach, and more so as the Afghan aid program mushroomed. The United States turned a blind eye to some Pakistani developments; the Pakistanis continued to maintain for the record that they had no nuclear program. This tacit arrangement suited both sides.

No one in the U.S. government wanted to risk the Afghan program. Among its most enthusiastic supporters was the new director of central intelligence. Casey wanted to do more for the Afghans—not the least because it would help rebuild the CIA.

Casey and the CIA's Afghan Program

Casey inherited a weakened and demoralized CIA. The Agency had, in the mid-1970s, been subjected to withering scrutiny by the congressional Pike and Church committees. The Directorate of Operations had taken a particular beating. The committees had expressed outrage at the involve-ment of (admittedly former) CIA officials in President Richard Nixon's Watergate break-in. The DO had followed orders to conduct surveillance of Vietnam War protesters and—on instruction from the Kennedy White House—tried to assassinate Cuban leader Fidel Castro. In the wake of the congressional investigations, DCI Stansfield Turner organized panels to review the performance records of all DO officers. The lowest-rated 700 members of the clandestine service were fired—including a significant number of the senior leadership.[27] DO veterans, while conceding that their activities had overstepped the bounds, felt unjustly sacrificed for doing their job—carrying out directives from the President of the United States. Many in DO retained lasting scars from the investigation, includ-ing a permanent abhorrence for any activity not clearly and concisely spelled out as within the CIA's purview.

Casey wanted to rebuild the Agency's capacity to mount covert actions. Casey had worked for the Office of Strategic Services (OSS) during World War II and relished his memories of rule-bending derring-do from those days. A congressional official once commented that "Casey loves covert operations. He'd mount a covert operation in the Vatican if he could."[28]

Casey was not happy with the state of the DO, believing it to be too cautious. For this, some CIA officers did not trust Casey. Thomas Twet-ten, deputy chief in 1983–1986 of the DO's Near East/South Asia Divi-sion, says that during the Reagan years "there was a concern between what I call the sensible bureaucrats, having been one of them, and the rabid right. You had these strange people developing strange ideas. We had this uneasy suspicion that Bill Casey was one of them on more than some occasions. So we were worried about being undercut."

But in the Afghan program, Casey thought he perceived an oppor-tunity to restore the DO's luster. Moreover, the Afghan cause appealed to him ideologically. As one Pakistani officer put it, Casey was "ruthless in his approach and he had a built-in hatred for the Soviets."[29] The DCI also, says former National Intelligence Officer Graham Fuller, "perceived that the Soviet Union was a totally failing operation....In the end, [he] was extraordinarily prescient in a way that more sophisticated thinkers missed."[30] Casey's interest took on more urgency, however, after an April 1982 visit to Pakistan and his first meeting with Zia. The two men met on April 6 in Zia's residence, a bungalow in the Rawalpindi Cantonment.

The Zia-Casey Relationship

During their conversation, Zia said he believed that the Soviet strategic aim in the region was to reach the Persian Gulf with its warm water ports and oil deposits.[31] Zia and Casey hit it off immediately. DO's Near East/South Asia chief at the time, Charles Cogan, says "Zia made a great impression on" Casey.[32]

Casey became Zia's closest contact in the Reagan administration. This mirrored the relationship that often develops between a CIA chief of station and his host government—to the detriment of the State Department. Compared to a U.S. ambassador, a CIA officer is practically a free agent. Elaborates SSCI's Simmons: "In a lot of instances, the CIA station chief can deliver resources faster, can provide useful information, and can have what I call a no-bullshit relationship. The ambassador is the President's representative, but he has a lot of policy baggage he has to carry....The CIA station chief doesn't have to worry about any of that [and can provide] a pipeline, a channel with no encumbrances."

Keep the Pot Boiling

Zia must have responded to Casey's can-do attitude. Author and journalist Robert Woodward wrote: "When Zia wanted assistance from the United States or just needed someone to listen, his avenue was Casey."[33] Casey and Zia met four or five times in 1982–1983. Their second encounter was in 1982 (after Brezhnev's death and Yuri Andropov's succession). At that second meeting, Zia expressed his intent—in words which became his Afghan policy mantra—that the Afghan support program "keep the pot boiling, turn up the heat, but don't let the pot boil over." In other words, irritate and undermine the Soviets, but don't provoke them to massively escalate the level and intensity of their commitment. Make them pay for their incursion, but don't drive them to retaliate against the Pakistanis.

As the military conflict gathered steam, diplomats took their own steps to see whether the parties could reach a diplomatic solution. In June 1982, UN-sponsored peace talks got underway in Geneva. But while Pakistan and Afghanistan sent representatives to negotiations in Geneva, no one expected the talks would be anything but window dressing.

The Geneva Talks

The Geneva talks convened formally between the governments of Afghanistan and Pakistan, as the ostensible belligerents. It was an odd arrangement, attributable to the Soviet claim that it had sent troops to Afghanistan in response to "outside interference"—implicitly from Pakistan. Moscow said it could not withdraw until the "interference" ceased and demanded direct talks between Pakistan and Afghanistan.

But Pakistan refused to recognize the Soviet-supported Kabul government as legitimate. An imperfect but serviceable compromise resulted: the Soviets agreed to UN mediation, and the Pakistanis agreed to deal with Afghanistan indirectly in so-called proximity talks. This meant that the parties never actually met in the same room, but had their negotiating demands carried back and forth by a third party (in this case the UN special envoy). Both the Soviet Union and the United States stood as silent and unofficial partners to the negotiations. An additional peculiar aspect of the talks from the start was that the Mujahideen had no representation whatsoever.

The agenda items at Geneva were: a withdrawal of all non-Afghan military; noninterference by other parties in Afghan affairs; international guarantees of a peace settlement; and the voluntary return of refugees to their homes.[34] The trickiest matter proved to be crafting a link between a withdrawal of Soviet troops (and how long that would take), and the point at which others would cease assistance to the Mujahideen. The Soviets wanted aid to the rebels to cease as soon as withdrawal began, but they contemplated stringing out withdrawal over as long as four years. This would leave the Mujahideen unacceptably exposed in the interim.

Within most of the U.S. policy establishment, the talks were met with utmost indifference. Few expected them to lead anywhere. Those who wanted to turn Afghanistan into a Soviet Vietnam did not want the talks to succeed. They worried that a diplomatic settlement would amount to a "sell out" of the Afghan fighters and give the Soviets a "cheap" way out of the conflict. But there were those, particularly within the State Department, who felt strongly that military pressure on the Soviets could not be divorced from diplomatic measures aimed at achieving a permanent settlement for Afghanistan and the region. Historian and journalist Selig Harrison has termed this the standoff between the "bleeders"—those who wished to pin down the Soviet Union in Afghanistan—and the "dealers"—those who wanted through a combination of diplomatic and military pressure to compel its withdrawal.

Despite brief optimism, the talks early took on a static, stalemated quality that remained little changed by 1985.[35] But by then, the Afghan program had taken on a life of its own thanks, in no small part, to Texas Democratic Congressman Charles Wilson.

Oerlikon: Stinger Dress Rehearsal

Congressman Wilson had represented the East Texas district of Lufkin since 1973. He became a powerful politician, with expertise in military finance, foreign intelligence, and energy policy. Among the committees on which he sat was the Subcommittee for Defense Appropriations of the House Appropriations Committee, where he was a senior Democrat. Wilson, almost uniquely among the subcommittee's members, did not have a defense installation in his home district. This gave him unusual leverage over other members who had to be concerned about meeting constituents' demands.

In 1981, Representative Wilson visited Pakistan for the first time, met with the Mujahideen, and returned to Washington determined to advance their cause. Wilson was impressed. He says, "[P]eople this brave shouldn't sell their lives too cheaply."[36]

Wilson made no secret of his anti-Soviet sentiments. Like many Americans, Wilson blamed the Soviets, who had supported the North Vietnamese, for the humiliating U.S. defeat in Vietnam in the early 1970s. In urging support for the Mujahideen, he hoped to turn the Afghan war into a Vietnam-type quagmire for Moscow. Robert Gates, who would rise to become DCI, wrote that "Wilson's motives were fairly uncomplicated— in circumstances where the United States had international opinion and a good cause going for it, he wanted to kill Soviets."[37] Wilson himself said: "There were 58,000 dead in Vietnam and we owe the Russians one…."[38]

CIA Courts Wilson

At the same time that Wilson was looking for ways to help the Mujahideen, Casey—with Zia's support—wanted to expand the Afghan covert action. In 1983 Casey's new congressional affairs director was veteran CIA officer Clair George, with Norman Gardner as deputy. At the time, recalls Gardner, the CIA was "looking for money" to build up the Afghan program, which stood at about $60 million a year. Wilson was one of the congressmen who seemed receptive. Importantly, says Gardner, Wilson enjoyed a warm relationship with the chairman of the Defense Appropriations Subcommittee, Representative John Murtha. In fact, Wilson would become a friend of the CIA and, according to the CIA's Anderson, "the single most effective legislator on the subject" of Afghanistan.

In August 1983, Representative Clarence D. Long, D-Md., then chair of the Foreign Operations Subcommittee of the Appropriations Committee, led a bipartisan delegation to Asia. Wilson—hoping to build support for increased aid to the Afghans—insisted that the group stop in Pakistan, where he arranged an interview with President Zia as well as a visit to Afghan refugee camps just inside the Pakistani border.[39] Long later reported that Zia and the rebel leaders described the Afghan fighters as desperate, in particular, for antiaircraft weapons. The Soviet-designed SA-7s had proved disappointing. But, Long told the *Washington Post*, Zia did not want U.S.-manufactured arms: "If it was American made, the Soviets would trace it to Pakistan and he [Zia] didn't want that. He suggested we get foreign-made guns.... He was perfectly willing to take a chance if it couldn't be traced back to him."[40]

By a twist of fate, the Soviets on September 1, 1983, shot down a Korean airliner that had strayed into Soviet airspace (KAL-007). The Soviets insisted it had been a spy plane; the West declared it an act of deliberate state terrorism. The incident sparked a firestorm of anti-Soviet sentiment among U.S. citizens and prepared fertile ground for any action that would hurt the Kremlin.

With Long's support, Wilson sponsored a secret amendment to the annual appropriations bill that would shift $40 million from the Defense Department to the CIA's budget for the Afghan effort.[41] Wilson not only sat on the crucial appropriations subcommittee, but also was a member of the House-Senate conference committee that reconciled the two bodies' versions of the defense appropriations bill. He was able, therefore, to argue for his $40 million at key stages of the legislative process. He recalls: "I didn't have too much trouble once they realized I was serious because most of those guys have bases in their districts to protect and what they are concerned about is the spending in their districts. None of them really opposed helping the Afghans, and I was able to trade off—you know, 'I'll support those tanks, I want my money for the Mujahideen.' It only took me about a month to turn around the subcommittee."[42]

Once the money was in hand, it turned out that Wilson had very definite ideas about how to spend it.

The Oerlikon

Wilson had heard repeatedly from the Afghans that they were unable to bring down Soviet MI-24 Hind D helicopters. The congressman felt he had found just the antiaircraft weapon: the Swiss-made Oerlikon. The 22-mm gun weighed 1,200 pounds, and required 20 mules to transport it. Nor was it cheap. Each gun cost $1 million, while the shells were $50 each. But the Oerlikon could bring down helicopters.

Wilson's was not the only suggestion. Among those mentioned was the state-of-the-art Stinger, confirms SSCI's Simmons. But the Stinger was ruled out in no uncertain terms—it was U.S.-made and would violate the "plausible deniability" principle of a covert action.

The CIA felt the Oerlikon was also a mistake. Although it was not U.S.-made, its deployment would constitute a retreat from "plausible deniability" because it was not of Soviet manufacture and could not have been captured on the battlefield. The CIA station chief in Islamabad at the end of 1983 was Howard Hart.[43] Hart reviewed the Oerlikon's utility in the mountainous, roadless terrain of Afghanistan and pronounced it "tactically stupid."[44] He urged its rejection.

In Washington, the CIA paramilitary experts were also skeptical about the Oerlikon. DDCI McMahon recalls: "They said the Oerlikon is a great weapon. But it's too heavy, too difficult to move in mountainous terrain, and also it's extremely expensive, particularly the shells. So our guys were against it."[45]

But Wilson did not abandon his campaign, despite the pressure from the CIA. Even when the congressional intelligence committees expressed skepticism, he simply redoubled his efforts. Under standard procedure, the intelligence committees would make a budget request, which the appropriations committees would approve.[46] It was highly unusual for the authorization request to come from the budget committee. So Wilson himself lobbied the intelligence committees. Former SSCI staff director Simmons remembers: "In my seven years in Washington, I never saw an individual congressman lobby an issue as aggressively and as personally as Congressman Wilson lobbied this effort to supply the Afghan resistance with Oerlikon guns."[47]

When the intelligence committees were asked to approve the reprogrammed $40 million, the House committee complied but the Senate committee resisted. Chair Senator Barry Goldwater, R-Ariz., not only thought that the Oerlikon was the wrong weapon, but also resented Wilson's assumption of intelligence committee responsibilities. Goldwater relented after McMahon, by now a convert to the Oerlikon, wrote him a letter supporting its use. McMahon's about-face was not hard to understand. Wilson's project was, from the CIA's standpoint, a windfall.' "[48]

Twetten in DO explains that "we got the agreement to do the Oerlikon partly to satisfy Charlie." He elaborates: "Once we realized that we were going to get their money whether we wanted it or not, even McMahon decided that there was no sense fighting."

By the late spring of 1984, the relevant committees in Congress approved a limited test of Oerlikons in Afghanistan. They were on the ground later that summer. Wilson did not rest on his laurels. In July 1984 the Texan successfully rechanneled another $50 million from DOD to the CIA for the Afghans.[49] That brought the total for 1984 to at least $120 million.[50]

Congress Gets with the Program

Meanwhile, Congress—not only the intelligence committees but the general membership—was taking an unprecedented interest in the CIA's covert actions, both in Afghanistan and Nicaragua (where the CIA was supporting counterrevolutionary insurgents, or "Contras," against the Marxist Sandinista government). Thanks to plentiful press leaks, the covert actions were becoming anything but.[51] Politically, the two arenas contrasted sharply.

One did not have to look far to understand the appeal of the Afghan program, with its heroic, barefoot "freedom fighters," as opposed to the Nicaraguan operation, whose murky goals had induced Congress, as early as December 1982, specifically to forbid funding of groups "for the purpose of overthrowing the Government of Nicaragua." Congress treated the two insurgencies accordingly. In 1984, Congress capped the funding available to the CIA for the Contras and sought to confine aid to nonmilitary, humanitarian assistance.[52] Yet the 1984 Nicaraguan assistance—$24 million a year supporting 15,000 contras—was only one-tenth the size of the 1985 budget for the Afghan program.

By contrast, the Afghan operation enjoyed broad bilateral support. In 1982, Senator Paul Tsongas, D-Mass., founded a congressional Afghan

Task Force to coordinate political activity on behalf of the rebels. In May 1983, Tsongas and ninety other senators cosponsored a resolution calling for expanded aid to the Afghan rebels. It criticized the Reagan administration for providing insufficient aid to the Mujahideen. While the resolution did not pass on that attempt, it reflected growing U.S. discomfort with an arguably immoral policy of "fighting to the last Afghan." The resolution finally passed in October 1984, with its wording changed—in deference to objections from the State Department and the CIA—from providing "material assistance" to pledging to "effectively support" the Afghan resistance. "It would be indefensible," read the resolution, "to provide the freedom fighters with only enough aid to fight and die, but not enough to advance their cause of freedom." Sixty-nine senators and 161 representatives from both parties cosponsored the resolution. Not coincidentally, 1984 was a campaign year for many senators, and the vote fell shortly before the November elections.

Part of the appeal was that, for the first time, the United States was championing a resistance group that was fighting the Soviets directly. In most conflicts across the globe, a U.S. client confronted a Soviet surrogate. But here was the Red Army itself. The administration was delighted at the bipartisan support. There was material support as well as moral backing for the Mujahideen. What Charlie Wilson had begun, Senator Malcolm Wallop, R-Wyo., continued. Wallop had access to the nation's intelligence secrets, thanks to his position as chair of the Senate Intelligence Committee's budget subcommittee. At his urging, the committee raised the Afghan program funding for 1985 to $250 million, which made the Afghan program the largest CIA military support operation since Vietnam. At $250 million, Afghanistan was consuming a reported 80 percent of the CIA's annual covert operations budget.[53] For the moment, the challenge for the covert action pipeline was not how to raise funds, but how to manage physically the increased volume of supplies.

Congressmen interested in Afghanistan began to travel to the area in considerable numbers. If Congress, and the average U.S. newspaper reader, knew so much about the Afghan covert action, its details were surely even more familiar to the Soviet Politburo. So far, however, there was no indication whether, or how, Moscow would react to the U.S. escalation. The uncertainty was enhanced by the rise to power in March 1985 of an unknown General Secretary, Mikhail Gorbachev.

Changes in Moscow

Gorbachev succeeded the short-term Konstantin Cherneko, who had replaced Yuri Andropov in February 1984. The world had reason to believe the new Soviet leader would have a different attitude toward Afghanistan from his predecessors. In 1980 he had objected to increased defense spending. In 1983, during a trip to Canada, he characterized the Afghan invasion as "a mistake." But such tea leaves were not enough to predict a policy.

In fact, Gorbachev's early actions provided only discouragement for those promoting a political solution to the conflict.[54] In April 1985 he ordered a secret Politburo reappraisal of Afghan policy. In May he authorized the military to proceed with ambitious offensives against rebel positions in the Kunar valley. He approved the transfer to Afghanistan from East Germany of the highly respected General Mikhail Zaitsev as new commander of the Afghan forces. All this came on the heels of a steady buildup throughout 1984 of some 2,000 Soviet Spetsnaz, or "special forces," in Afghanistan. The Soviet troops already in the country were distinguished by their absence from the battlefield. Afghan Army soldiers were sent into any hot engagement, while the Soviets remained quartered in their strongholds, venturing out only in large numbers when the threat was minimal.

The Spetsnaz were different. They were fighters, and proved particularly successful in their helicopter attacks on Afghan rebel supply lines. They could take the war to the remote valleys and mountain fastnesses where the Mujahideen had established base camps. In their MI-24 Hind D helicopter gunships with armored belly and cockpit, they attacked with impunity from above, at a distance beyond the range of most anti-aircraft weapons, and escaped.

In August 1985 the Soviets launched their largest offensive of the year against the eastern region of Afghanistan bordering Pakistan. The Soviet military advances increased the worries of the Mujahideen's supporters in the United States. At the same time, it strengthened their hand in arguing for more aggressive U.S. involvement in the Afghan conflict.

U.S. Ratchets Up Aims in Afghanistan

It was high time, DOD Undersecretary for Policy Fred C. Iklé felt in early 1985, to update the presidential finding governing U.S. policy in

Afghanistan. The finding authorizing the covert action had been signed in 1980, under a Democratic president. It was five years old. The aims of the CIA's enterprise had to be sharpened. Simply "harassing" the Soviets was no longer adequate. Carter's goal should be explicitly upgraded—to winning. Now the time was ripe, Iklé said, "for the president to put his stamp and imprimatur on this important operation instead of just relying on the old decision memorandum [sic] of the Carter Administration."

But Iklé had in mind something more than simply issuing a new presidential finding. A finding tells the CIA what to do in covert actions. Iklé wanted to rethink U.S. policy toward Afghanistan. For that, a more appropriate vehicle would be a new presidential National Security Decision Directive (NSDD), which defines policy. One element of any new policy on Afghanistan would, of course, concern the CIA covert action. But to reach consensus on a new presidential directive would involve persuading first the foreign policy establishment, and then the President.

Iklé knew how government worked and how policies were made and unmade. One of Iklé's deputies, the assistant undersecretary for policy planning, was Michael Pillsbury. Pillsbury came to the DOD job in October 1984 from the Senate Republican Steering Committee, where he had served as national security advisor to the twenty-five senators on the committee.[55] Pillsbury was known within government circles as a Republican operator, a smart and able wheeler-dealer. He had strong ties to conservative Republican Senator Orrin Hatch, R-Utah, a member of the Steering Committee.[56] Iklé asked Pillsbury to work on the NSDD project.

Iklé relied on his staff to draft the language and lay the groundwork for a new NSDD. As he recalls, "my covert action staff worked this in the working level groups. And they consulted with me. I didn't go [to a discussion] until maybe the final meeting at my level." The goal was to "improve the intelligence support we would provide, its timeliness. [Also] not just the weaponry, but the training, the strategy that could be more effective."

In drafting the proposed NSDD, Iklé and his staff were well aware of the five pillars of the Reagan administration's national security strategy. As one scholar summarizes, they were: military modernization; expanded military spending by U.S. allies; economic pressure on the USSR and its allies; propaganda; and covert actions to split client governments from Moscow.[57] This campaign to face down the Soviet Union more aggressively worldwide gained renown as the Reagan Doctrine.

Iklé had worked on NSDD 32, as well as on subsequent directives setting policy toward the Soviet Union. NSDD 66's (November 12, 1982) title was self-explanatory: "Protracted Economic Warfare Against the USSR." NSDD 70 (undated, probably November 1982) established a Defense Technology Security Administration to monitor and restrict trade with the USSR in sensitive information technology. Finally, NSDD 75 (January 17, 1983) defined "U.S. Policy on the USSR." It further refined NSDD 32's goals of putting multifaceted pressure on the Soviet system. Cumulatively, says Pillsbury, these presidential directives provided clear evidence of President Reagan's intention to "impose costs on the Soviet Union's 'empire' and its access to Western credit and technology."[58]

Pillsbury hoped the draft directive on which he was working would bring U.S. policy on Afghanistan into line with the existing NSDDs. His thinking was further influenced by U.S. intelligence in early 1985 that the Soviet General Staff had plans to sharply escalate their Afghan engagement.[59]

So in March 1985, President Reagan issued National Security Decision Directive 166 ("Expanded US Aid to Afghan Guerrillas").[60] In contrast to Carter, Reagan called for challenging the Soviets "by all means available."[61] But the NSDD did not mention the covert action. That was addressed in an even more highly classified sixteen-page annex, signed by National Security Advisor Robert McFarlane. NSDD 166 endorsed direct attacks on Soviet military officers in order to demoralize them (thereby walking a fine line between appropriate military action and assassination). The annex called for significant technical assistance to the Mujahideen in the form of satellite photographs, communications equipment, and so forth.[62] NSDD 166 also established a subcommittee, or working group, operating out of the National Security Council, to review implementation of the directive, including the CIA's covert action.[63]

Only the originators of the new NSDD recall it provoking much debate. Iklé recounts that "it did take pushing from my people." Pillsbury remembers "quite a little struggle about that document... [It] involved efforts for the first time to define our goal." Moving from "harassment" to "all means available" represented, suggests Pillsbury, a "pretty big jump." Pillsbury elaborates: "The purpose of this NSDD was to have a strategy involving State, AID [Agency for International Development], Defense, the U.S. mission to the UN, USIA [United States Information Agency] and, in the name of that process, to also review the CIA program for the first time."

The NSDD had, emphasizes Pillsbury, "changed the management structure. Instead of a presidential finding of the President to the House and Senate Intelligence Committees to carry out a CIA covert action program, it had now been changed to an NSC program in which all agencies had a part, including the CIA. There would be a subcommittee to oversee the CIA's compliance with the NSDD. This is a huge change. Now the DO had to answer questions to the subcommittee."

Representatives of other agencies recall little dispute over the new directive. Pillsbury maintains there is cause for memories of comity. The NSDD 166 debate, he says, initiated a new model of interagency cooperation under which "everybody gets to do what everybody wants to." A State Department request that more pressure be brought to bear on the Soviets in the UN General Assembly was included. A U.S. Information Agency (USIA) desire to launch a media-training program for the Afghan rebels was in there. The U.S. Agency for International Development (USAID) got an Afghan refugee aid program. "We would kind of go around the room," says Pillsbury. "Everybody got what they wanted into this document and, in return for all this harmony, the goal got changed."

Whether or not it generated heated debate, the new directive represented a clear shift in the thinking of U.S. policy makers, many of whom had for years assumed that the Soviets could not be defeated. As Vince Cannistraro, a CIA officer seconded to the NSC staff as Director of Intelligence, elucidates: "The goal now changed. It wasn't just to bleed the Soviets in stalemate. It was actually to force the Soviets out of Afghanistan, and everything else followed." Richard Armitage recalls that the new U.S. objective in Afghanistan was twofold: "to eject the Soviets, but also to remind them very specifically that they had a very soft underbelly"—the Central Asian, predominantly Muslim republics of the Soviet Union.

CIA in Accord

The CIA seemed to embrace the new directive. After all, it meant extra money for the Agency's pipeline. In accordance with the classified annex, CIA began in 1985 to supply the Afghans (through the Pakistanis) with reconnaissance photographs of Soviet targets in Afghanistan, plans for military operations, intercepts of Soviet communications, delayed timing devices for plastic explosives, sniper rifles, a targeting device for mortars, wire-guided antitank missiles, and other equipment.[64]

William Piekney, who represented the CIA in Pakistan at the time of NSDD 166, did not even consider the new directive much of a change. But changing the policy toward Afghanistan was seen in Iklé's office as only a first step. To change the situation on the ground required a different kind of commitment. Satellite photographs and radio intercepts were well and good, but they couldn't kill more Soviets. Only better weapons could do that. And only more dead Soviets would persuade the Kremlin to pull its troops out of Afghanistan.

The Stinger Proposal

Iklé's deputy Pillsbury arrived at the Defense Department in October 1984 unsure of what policy area he wanted to concentrate on. As he puts it: "I needed something to do."[65] Pillsbury had long found the Afghan cause a compelling one. One of Pillsbury's first assignments after joining Iklé's staff was to formulate a series of memorandums detailing the issues facing the second Reagan administration. One of his memos dealt with the anti-Communist resistance forces in places such as Afghanistan, in which he argued that U.S. policy makers were not taking the rebel causes as seriously as they should. Pillsbury proposed some specific remedies, such as better military support and assistance to countries providing sanctuary for the fighters.

In October, Pillsbury also drafted a memo from Iklé to Weinberger requesting authority to explore supplying high-tech U.S. weapons to insurgents, including the Afghan rebels.[66] It happened to be the same month that Congress passed the Afghan support resolution. Iklé's memo did not mention the word "Stinger." But it did float the idea that better weaponry could turn the tide of war in Afghanistan.

Opinions differed on how the war was going. But all could agree that the Soviet Spetsnaz forces, with their armored helicopter attacks, had given the Soviet military new tactical advantages that should be neutralized. While the Mujahideen were bringing down helicopters and even occasional aircraft with the old SA-7 antiaircraft missiles, the Soviet-style weapons were not the best to be had.

The best would be the Stinger. Giving the rebels Stingers was not a new idea. It originated in the State Department with then-Ambassador to Pakistan Ronald I. Spiers in mid-1983.[67] But his suggestion came to nothing. The CIA had dismissed it out of hand as unnecessarily violating the "plausible deniability" principle of covert actions. Pillsbury had never understood why the "plausible deniability" principle was so sacred. To him, the purpose of the CIA's covert action was to win the war against the Soviets. To do so, one exploited all potential resources. Given the state of the war, the current ascendance of the Soviet Spetsnaz forces, the amount of U.S. funds already invested in the Afghan effort, and the proportions of the eventual payoff, it seemed sheer foolishness to withhold from the war anything that might tip the balance.

The Stinger Weapon

The Stinger was one of the U.S. military's prize possessions, a state-of-the-art antiaircraft missile. It had a range of up to five miles, which compared favorably with the two-mile range of the SA-7. Its super-cooled sensor could lock onto aircraft infrared emissions, making it impervious to the heat flares that Soviet aircraft used as decoys to fool other antiaircraft weapons (such as the SA-7, which was heat-seeking). General Dynamics Corporation manufactured the Stinger, which had been made available to a few NATO allies, plus Israel. Each missile cost about $30,000.[68] It was shoulder-mounted like a shotgun for firing, but with less recoil. It weighed 34 pounds and measured 5 feet long. Despite that considerable length, Afghan rebels could port it with the help of mules.

Pillsbury, with Iklé behind him, decided to try to pilot his Stinger idea through Washington's decision-making channels. Winning approval would require the endorsement of some of Washington's most powerful political figures. The two that counted most, however, were groups that operated out of the National Security Council.

The Committees

Afghan policy was made by two committees of the National Security Council. One was the Policy Review Group (or Deputies' Committee), which oversaw policy aspects of the Afghan assistance program. The Policy Review Group was an interagency group of undersecretary-level officials from the foreign policy community: the State Department, Joint Chiefs of Staff (JCS), Defense Department, National Security Council, and the Central Intelligence Agency.

In 1985 its core members were Michael Armacost from State (who chaired the committee), Fred Iklé from Defense, a representative from JCS, and National Security Advisor Bud McFarlane or his deputy, Don Fortier. The CIA's deputy director for intelligence analysis (the DDI), or his deputy, also came to meetings. In 1985 the DDI was Robert Gates. The CIA's job was not to recommend policies but to communicate the latest intelligence reports. The Policy Review Group did not specifically discuss covert actions, since not all its members had the clearance to know about such operations. But the debate over and the decision to recommend NSDD 166, for example, took place within the Policy Review Committee.[69]

The PCG

A separate committee, also chaired out of the NSC, dealt with covert actions. It was known in the Reagan years as the Planning and Coordination Group (PCG). This committee was secret, and public details about it are sketchy. Confusingly, its membership overlapped heavily with that of the Policy Review Group.[70] As Armacost puts it: "It was kind of a floating game because the people were, for the most part, the same. That's why I don't remember who chaired what. Basically we were just the same people operating the same mandate."

The chief difference between the Policy Review Group and the Planning and Coordination Group lay in which CIA officers attended meetings: the intelligence analysts (DI) were on the policy review committee, whereas the clandestine service (DO) sent officials to the covert action committee.[71] The covert action committee met every three to four weeks. Its existence was not officially acknowledged, although such a committee had operated in every administration since Eisenhower. In the Kennedy administration, for example, it was known as the Forty Committee.

PCG was formally established by NSDD 159, a top-secret review of covert action policy dated January 18, 1985. The review was undertaken to clarify day-to-day management of covert operations, given the legal requirement to notify congressional intelligence oversight committees. Any information on covert actions was protected under a compartmentalized security system given the name VEIL.

PCG met regularly in the White House or in the Old Executive Office Building.[72] The committee, says Pillsbury, "controlled access to the nonroutine use of the CIA overseas." He characterizes it as an "interagency consulting group with no name, no official existence." Adds DO's Twet-ten: "It is a deputies' meeting that considers national security matters, including covert actions. It is the principal committee by which covert actions are drawn up and approved on an interagency basis. And it gets a new name every four years."

Its members, stipulated NSDD 159, were: a representative from the office of the Vice President, the Undersecretary of State for Political Affairs, the Undersecretary of Defense for Policy, the Deputy Direc-tor of CIA for Operations, the Assistant to the Chairman of the Joint Chiefs of Staff; the chair was the Deputy Assistant to the President for National Security Affairs. Others could attend by invitation.[73] In 1985 these officials included Fortier (who chaired it), Armacost, and Iklé. Vice President Bush's representative was his national security adviser, Donald Gregg. JCS sent Lt. Gen. John H. Moellering.[74] The CIA's representative in 1985 was DDO Clair George, who often dispatched his special assis-tant, Norman Gardner. As occasion warranted, other DO officials such as the head of the Near East/South Asia Division, Bert Dunn, or his deputy Thomas Twetten, attended.[75] Typically, fewer than twenty-five people in U.S. government would have the necessary security clearance to take part in committee discussions.

NSDD 166 had established a working group of staff assistants to the undersecretaries to monitor implementation of the directive. This group—only one of some thirty working groups at the NSC, each inves-tigating a discrete issue—was chaired by NSC intelligence liaison Vin-cent Cannistraro. The working group was formed, says Cannistraro, "to coordinate the actual assistance envisaged by the NSDD; to supervise the implementation of the NSDD and to make recommendations to the deputies." In fact, says Pillsbury, meetings were infrequent and few people attended.

The NSPG

Riding above all these committees, and meeting on an as-needed basis, was the National Security Planning Group (NSPG). It stood at the Cabi-net level, a "shrunken version" of the NSC, as one insider characterizes it. It was chaired by the President along with the Vice President and included the Secretary of State, Secretary of Defense, Counsellor to the President, Chief and Deputy Chief of Staff to the President, National Security Advisor, Chairman of the JCS, and Director of CIA.[76] As with the PCG, others such as the Attorney General could attend by invitation as needed.

Typically, Cabinet members also met regularly, and more informally, outside the NSPG or the NSC at breakfasts and luncheons. Casey, for example, had breakfast with Weinberger once a week to reconcile the demands of military intelligence with those of the CIA and State Department. He lunched, separately and less often, with Shultz (the two Cabinet officers had developed a keen personal and professional antipathy) to discuss intelligence collection and foreign policy goals. Shultz and Weinberger, for their part, had Wednesday breakfasts to which Casey was invited a couple of times a year.[77]

Going to Zia

Pillsbury and Iklé knew that, before they could hope to win the approval of the Planning and Coordination Group or the National Security Planning Group to send Stingers to Afghanistan, they had to obtain Pakistani President Zia's assent. So on April 30, 1985, the two Defense Department officials visited Islamabad.[78]

Pillsbury says their first conversation was with the ISI director, Lieutenant General Akhtar Abdul Rahman Khan. The men discussed how best to increase assistance to the Mujahideen. The Americans sought Akhtar's views on the CIA support program and proffered their own suggestions. "Dr. Iklé wanted to convey the thrust of the President's new decision directive," remembers Pillsbury. "And General Akhtar was saying words to the effect of 'this is music to my ears.'"

Akhtar proved quite willing to put Stingers on the annual "shopping list" he provided to the CIA. This attitude was in marked contrast to his reaction in early 1984, some sixteen months earlier. Pillsbury was now so struck by Akhtar's about-face that he persuaded the CIA chief, William Piekney, to cable Casey directly with the news of Akhtar's request.[79]

Pillsbury and Iklé also took the opportunity to sit down and talk to Piekney himself about the operation under his charge.[80] To their surprise, they discovered that the CIA had a very small presence in Pakistan—as best they could make out, two people.[81] "I had assumed mistakenly that there must be some sort of huge CIA presence in Pakistan," says Pillsbury. "I remember Dr. Iklé and I were astonished....This was our first big clue to what I later thought of as a scandal—that the DO had handed over everything about the program to the ISI, and had not told anybody about this back at the NSC."

The two also remember hearing that Piekney did not consider the Afghan supply operation his highest priority in Pakistan, although Piekney himself says the program consumed "75 percent of my day—every day—and 100 percent of every day for several others."[82] Pillsbury amplifies: "For Dr. Iklé and myself, the 'Eureka!' moment in all of this is in those meetings with the station chief. We begin to understand that what to us is a very big deal back in Washington, from the point of view of the President, is a second order priority handled by one GS [civil service officer]."

Then Pillsbury and Iklé went on to a meeting with Zia. It was a large group meeting whose participants did not have clearance to discuss the covert action. Nonetheless, the issue of Stingers was raised. But the president was not as unequivocal as Akhtar had been. Said Iklé afterward: "He hemmed and hawed."[83] Among Zia's objections was the fact that Pakistan itself did not have Stingers.

The Stinger—Why Not?

On their return from Pakistan, Iklé and Pillsbury were determined to see how far they could get with the idea of sending Stingers to the Mujahideen. There were two separate decision-making structures for such a step. One was internal to the Pentagon—the two Defense Policy officials had to persuade their boss, Secretary of Defense Weinberger. When approached, Weinberger asked his assistant, Colin Powell, to ascertain the views of the Joint Chiefs of Staff and CIA Director Casey on the subject.[84] The second was through the Planning and Coordination Group (the covert action committee).

Congress

The two Defense Department officials knew they had Congress on their side. Surely the bipartisan support in Congress for a popular cause should weigh heavily in any administration decision. More critically for Iklé and Pillsbury's arguments, key members of the congressional intelligence committees were growing impatient with the limited nature of the CIA's covert action. Senate Intelligence Committee member Malcolm Wallop,

R-Wyo., was "troubled," he remembers, "by what I thought was a very meek U.S. response to something that we were publicly saying was an outrage and privately tolerating." To arguments about plausible deniability, he responds, "some of us thought that the worst possible thing we could do was to continue to deny, while feebly assisting....That was offensive foreign policy to me and to [conservative Senator] Gordon Humphrey and to others."

But Congress did not have a representative to the Planning and Coordination Group. The State Department, the CIA, and the Joint Chiefs of Staff did. Iklé and Pillsbury knew that those institutions came to the DOD proposal with skepticism.

Leading the charge to stop the Stinger idea dead in its tracks was the Directorate of Operations at the CIA. Yet that opposition was not unanimous, even within the DO. Clair George had left his position overseeing legislative liaison to become chief of the directorate (DDO) in July 1984. George supported the Stinger proposal. Representative Wilson recalls the divided ranks within CIA: "One camp was the old boys, the old Ivy League guys, who were very cautious and did not want to do anything that might provoke the Russians into a more serious attack on Pakistan. On the other hand, there were some of the younger, more stridently anti-Communist types, who wanted to defeat the Russians."

Nonetheless, institutionally the DO presented a united front. The directorate marshaled what arguments it could against deployment. The first person the operations folks had to convince was their boss.

The CIA

Casey, always in favor of causing pain to the Soviets, found in principle no objection to the Stinger. But he also practiced institutional loyalty. On this issue, he listened to his DO and to DDCI McMahon. McMahon had begun to worry that the Afghan covert action was becoming a substitute for a U.S. policy toward the Afghan conflict. He reminisces: "My objection was that we didn't have a foreign policy to back it up. I made it clear at the highest levels throughout 1983 and afterward that I felt we had to have a political settlement...."[85]

Introducing the Stinger, worried CIA officials, was not part of a larger, carefully conceived foreign policy strategy. What about, for example, the risks to Pakistan? Introducing the Stinger could trigger reprisals against Pakistan more deadly than the transborder incursions that had become a standard feature of the war. McMahon and DO officials also emphasized the U.S. obligation to honor Zia's desire to keep U.S. weapons out of the subcontinent.

Pakistan's fears, adds Piekney, were widely shared in Washington. "The congressional delegations, the Department of State and the Agency were all of the view that there ought not to be U.S. weapons in Afghanistan, primarily because that's the way the Pakistanis wanted it and two, we were—through attrition and over time and distance—causing the Soviets to lose a great deal."

Others in the CIA concurred that the Mujahideen were, contrary to the laments of the Afghan lobbyists in Washington, performing rather creditably. After all, in 1984 specially trained units had for the first time targeted members of the Soviet high command and killed fourteen senior officers. They had successfully infiltrated anti-Soviet propaganda over the border into Central Asia. In early 1985 the Mujahideen managed for the first time to fire rockets directly into Kabul.[86]

And there were other concerns. Chief among them was that the U.S. weapon would nullify the CIA's principle of "plausible deniability" for covert actions. Were a Stinger to be captured by the Soviets, there could be no illusion that the weapon came from anywhere but the United States.

But the CIA did not need to be the spokesperson for all of the arguments against the Stinger. In some cases concerns felt at the CIA were eloquently expressed by other speakers, such as diplomats or generals. In part, the wider opposition to the Stinger proposal was personal. While Pillsbury was not yet well-known at the DO, he had a reputation in Washington's foreign-policy circles as a wheeler-dealer. Pillsbury's role as champion of the Stinger cause was reason enough to undermine it in the eyes of many. Notes DOD's Armitage: "There was a lot of distrust of Pillsbury.... Had it been Joe Jones that was Fred Iklé's point person on the Stinger issue, then it would have gone down a little easier." Undersecretary of State Armacost adds that Pillsbury "had a kind of reputation for being a loose guy who was out playing for himself."

State Department

But the State Department had substantive objections unrelated to Pillsbury. The Senior Deputy Assistant Secretary for Near East and South Asian Affairs was Arnold Raphel. His deputy was Robert Peck.[87] The fact that Zia appeared unwilling to request the Stingers on behalf of the rebels weighed heavily with Raphel. Raphel and Peck felt strongly about protecting Pakistan in its delicate role as arms conduit to the rebels.

Among his other duties, Raphel headed the U.S. team monitoring the Afghan proximity peace talks in Geneva. The diplomat felt the time was wrong for escalating the U.S. military presence in Afghanistan. He believed that the Geneva talks were, in the spring of 1985, making some headway. Raphel did not wish to jeopardize their progress.[88]

The Soviet desk at the State Department also opposed the Stinger option. The desk officers, like their boss, Secretary Shultz, had come to feel that Gorbachev offered the best chance for improved U.S.-Soviet relations in decades. The Foreign Service had no wish to see the United States provoke the Soviets, derailing painstaking efforts to forge a new relationship with the other superpower. Representative Wilson underlines that "there was immense opposition in the State Department."

Joint Chiefs

Other concerns of the CIA were also voiced by the Joint Chiefs of Staff, who represented the military services of Navy, Army, and Air Force. While the political figures in DOD approved of, were even promoting, the idea of sending Stingers to Afghanistan, the military harbored grave doubts. They focused on the threat to technology. The generals worried that, in the case of capture, the Soviets could reverse engineer the weapon, thereby eliminating the technological advantage that the Stinger provided.

The Joint Chiefs also argued that the weapon could fall into the wrong hands. Afghanistan was an unstable place, with a thriving arms market, bordering Iran. There could be no guarantee that the Stinger would not end up among the weapons of the Islamic revolutionaries in Iran, for example, where it could be used for terrorism.

Finally, the military was dubious about the Mujahideen's ability to use such an advanced weapon effectively. The Stinger had never been fired in anger, making it in a sense an untested battlefield weapon. Giving it to barefoot rebels for its maiden application would not, the generals reasoned, constitute the best use of the Stinger. The training program alone, they maintained, would be difficult to implement, with Americans training the Pakistanis who would train the Mujahideen. The CIA's Piekney reiterates the military worry that "any complicated program for a training sequence like that, you've got to consider what you lose in the translation."

Press Reaction

Somewhat surprisingly, the CIA found a powerful, albeit unwitting, ally in the press. Some commentators felt that the CIA was being misused and even maltreated. As early as August 1984, when reports of U.S. covert assistance to the Afghan rebels were plentiful in the U.S. press, a *Washington Post* opinion piece deplored the risk posed to U.S. policy, the Mujahideen, and Pakistan by "a leaky U.S. intelligence community,... congressional sources with no great care for classified information, and...politicians who cannot afford not to pledge their allegiance to Afghan freedom fighters."[89] In February 1985, the *Los Angeles Times* worried that "a \$250 million 'covert' aid program cannot really be covert." The editorial argued that "the CIA should not be drawn into the business of effectively managing a large-scale guerrilla war virtually on the border of the Soviet Union."[90]

"No!" to the Stinger

Despite this line-up of opponents, Pillsbury and Iklé felt that the Stinger proposal had obvious and cogent merits. But they found no one to agree with them. Powell reported back to Weinberger that the Joint Chiefs and CIA's Casey were firmly opposed to the idea.[91] Iklé told Pillsbury, presumably after a meeting of the PCG, that the concept was dead in the water. He gave his subordinate, remembers Pillsbury, direct orders to cease and desist. "He said: 'We don't have the votes. Zia doesn't want Stingers. NSC is against it. State is against it. CIA is against it. Stop working on this.' "

Pillsbury heeded Iklé and turned his attention to other problems: India, Angola. "I just stopped working on the Stinger," he recalls. "I didn't have the authority to raise it in the interagency meeting."

But while Pillsbury may have stopped actively promoting the Stinger, he did not stop thinking about it. And when his old mentor, Senator Hatch, called asking where to spend the upcoming congressional recess, Pillsbury lost no time in recommending Pakistan.

3

Categories of Concerns and the Set of Beliefs That Connect Actions to Them

A policy player such as Michael Pillsbury may have absorbed many of the critical rules of the game of shared policy choice without even thinking of them as rules. But they are, and they should be, our starting place.

I argued in Chapter 1 that, while dividing responsibilities among agents and agencies is necessary for specialization and focused attention, it leaves the problem of how to coordinate actions that affect the responsibilities of a number of agencies. That problem is far too common to expect each occasion to be resolved in a written or oral debate before a common superior. It is equally unreasonable to allow the decision to be made independently by any of the people who have some responsibility in the area, leaving superiors and peers simply to react to the change. The solution, which is absorbed by players as part of the culture of any bureaucracy in which they work, is a set of rules that binds all the players; these rules are enforced by making compliance a condition for good standing in the organization and for reciprocal cooperation by others.

What is covered by the rules? They specify, less than precisely, who has formal and informal authority to make a decision or announce a policy. They give a right to consultation (and an opportunity to bring up the issue at a higher level) to any peer whose responsibilities or activities may be significantly affected by the decision. And they specify when a player may, or may not, furnish an opportunity to "weigh in" on the decision to other influential parties who care about the issue but, lacking an immediately affected area of responsibility, are not automatically given a "right" of consultation and participation. A leak to the press or a tip to an interested Senator would be examples. By regulating these matters, the rules go far toward specifying who can play certain roles and who can exercise influence in the decision.

The Stinger missile case illustrates the importance of all this. Pillsbury cannot even begin to try to sell his proposal for the Stinger missile without having some idea of what player or alternative players might make the final decision. He knows that his boss—Undersecretary of Defense for Policy Planning, Fred Iklé—has no authority to direct a new weapons system to the Mujahideen. The project is a "covert action" run by the CIA. William Casey, Director of the CIA, could theoretically make this decision, with the concurrence of other Cabinet-level officials whose responsibilities would be affected, but not if providing Stinger missiles was obviously of such importance or political prominence that the President would want to decide. This decision is obviously of that character for several reasons. If approved, we may be furnishing a terrifying weapon to a present or future enemy. There is a small chance that we will encourage dangerous forms of retaliation by the Soviet Union. Even the shift from a "plausibly deniable" covert action to the open support of a guerrilla force fighting the Soviet Union would raise issues in Congress that the President would want to consider in light of his staff's advice.

Of course, even this rule for moving the decision to a higher level is less than clear. Presidents can differ in the extent to which the President is prepared to trust particular Cabinet secretaries to decide different matters. The relationship between Cabinet secretaries and their assistant secretaries or between the latter and their section chiefs can similarly differ. Still, the first rule that Pillsbury and everyone else must follow is that any official who knows that his superior may well not have meant to delegate a decision cannot make the decision without checking back with that superior. For example, an Assistant Secretary of the Department of Homeland Security, in February 2006, himself approved a transfer of management of major U.S. ports to a company based in an Arab Emirate that had been the home of some of the suicide attackers on 9/11; in so doing, he was violating implicit rules that require the participation in any such politically charged decision of his boss, Secretary Michael Chertoff, and his boss's boss, President Bush.

As we have seen, Undersecretary Iklé and his assistant Pillsbury persuaded Reagan to promulgate a Presidential Decision Directive, forming a new group to supervise U.S. activities in support of the Mujahideen in Afghanistan. A new level of supervision by a committee means that each of its members is entitled to be consulted by those who propose any significant action within the supervising body's area of responsibility. Here the committee members are entitled to notice and have an opportunity to challenge a proposal by the CIA before it takes any action to accept or reject Pillsbury's Stinger missile proposal, so long as this appears to be a decision that bears importantly on the committee's responsibilities. The committee can also direct the CIA to consider or take action on a particular matter. Thus the creation of the committee affects the designation of those who have procedural rights as necessary parties under the rules.

The second set of critical rules is that no decision should be made by one official to whom authority has been delegated without consultation with, and opportunity to appeal to higher levels by, any peer who also has responsibility for results likely to be affected by the decision (or whose activities will be affected by that decision). Casey, the Director of the CIA, could see that the responsibilities of the Department of State for diplomatic relations with the Soviet Union and its negotiating activities with regard to Afghanistan could be substantially affected by the furnishing of Stinger missiles to those fighting the Russian troops in Afghanistan. Similarly, a proposal risking Soviet capture of the Stinger missile would have significant effects on the responsibility of the Department of Defense and its Secretary for maintaining the superiority of U.S. arms. The Joint Chiefs must thus also be consulted; so we see Secretary of Defense Weinberger seeking their judgment on the proposal. He also seeks the views of the CIA because the furnishing of arms to the Mujahideen has so far been a set of activities carried out by the CIA. Those activities would change dramatically if the supply were no longer covert—an inevitable consequence of furnishing a state-of-the-art U.S. missile to the Afghan rebels.

Consider, next, the rules that describe whom a player is *allowed* to consult. Many people and organizations may care greatly about a decision, and some of these will have the power to make life better or worse for those to whom the rules give more direct responsibility for that decision. From the group of influential and interested parties without a "right" to participate, Pillsbury will want to select and bring into the action those favorable to his positions. But those opposing his proposal will not want to be subject to the pressure that such outside supporters can bring to bear. The conflict is generally resolved by an appeal to understood practices and rules that will tell Pillsbury when he may call on the influences of particular "outsiders" and when that is sharply discouraged.

Pillsbury openly includes Congressman Wilson (and will include Senator Hatch), each of whom can make it costly for executive officials to seek to enforce a bureaucratic rule that excludes him. Pillsbury cannot, however, openly take the matter to the press. That rule is, in this particular case, enforced by statutes protecting classified information. Still, the account of the decision process suggests that someone is keeping the press regularly informed about what is supposed to be a covert action. Even clear rules as to participation may be broken at some risk of detection.

Identifying Factors That Affect a Decision Maker or Other Players

Obviously, whoever will be the decision maker will base his acceptance or rejection of any proposal on how *he* imagines the proposal (and its timing) will affect the aspects of the situation, as he understands it, that are important and salient *for him*. So the steps that someone like Pillsbury must take to persuade or influence a specific decision maker will be tailored to all those special characteristics of that person.

The decision maker will also be influenced by the actions or anticipated reactions of a certain number of other players who either must or may become involved. Advice from some will inform him about the impact of the proposal on the situation as he perceives it; and the attitudes of others will make a difference to him as he contemplates what he will need from them during their longer term relationships. So Pillsbury will want to understand these relationships and the attitude of these other players toward his Stinger proposal. Of course, the persuasive beliefs and influential attitudes of still other players will in turn affect the beliefs and attitudes of those just described who are persuasive or who can influence the decision maker.

Thus, in the Stinger missile case, President Reagan's decision will depend on how he thinks the furnishing of Stinger missiles will affect what he cares about in the diplomatic, national security, and political world as he sees it; at the same time, his decision will also depend on his concerns about the longer-term effects of his actions on his relationship with other players who are important to him. Every one of those players—who may affect Reagan's decision—is herself subject to the persuasion or influence that policy entrepreneurs can bring to bear on her as well as to her judgment about the important effects of the proposal on her world as she sees it.

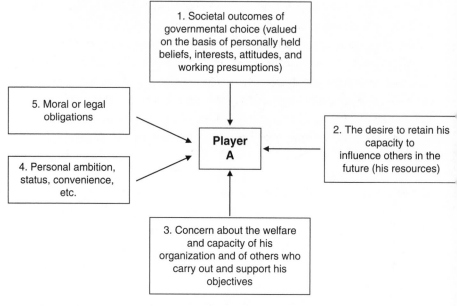

Figure 3.1.

Identifying a set of categories that captures the great majority of the concerns of any official taking part in shared governmental choice is just a small part of this complicated picture, but it is one logical starting place for further enriching our understanding of group decision making. It is these types of concerns that motivate each player's actions. So they are the categories within which an entrepreneur like Pillsbury looks to review what are in fact likely to be the concerns of a particular player. No less important, activating them is how Pillsbury or other players seek to influence her choices.

Figure 3.1 captures the major categories of concerns for any player.

1. Societal Outcomes

The first category includes convictions about what is good or bad for the citizen constituency in whose name the player's organization and the player will choose and act. These are often stated as a set of goals. For one player, these might be as conceptually precise but instrumentally difficult as maximizing the excess of carefully counted and very concrete benefits over carefully counted and very well specified costs. In dealing with illicit drug use, such a player might, for example, consider her objective to be minimizing the combined harms flowing from both drug use and the costly steps we take to reduce that use.

For another player, the objective might be grounded in often symbolic relationships between the proposal and spreading or maintaining deeply held beliefs about one or another of the conditions of having a healthy and productive society. The relationship is likely to be expressive, morally based, and intuitive; thus, it is hard to measure or even compare to other goals. He might believe that the non-therapeutic use of drugs degrades the user's humanity and thus is, like torture, unequivocally wrong.

Some concerns about societal outcomes are shared; some differ among players. In the Stinger missile case, the President, the Secretary of State, the Secretary of Defense, the Director of the CIA, and each of their subordinates is concerned that the Soviet Union not triumph (whatever that might mean) in Afghanistan; that the Soviet Union not take some form of military action against Pakistan; and that the conflict not escalate to one in which the United States and the USSR are confronting each other openly and directly. More broadly, each is concerned that the United States benefit from some form of constructive coexistence with the Soviet Union, so long as it exists and is powerful; and that the United States maintain its military superiority over the Soviet Union. Each of the parties is also concerned about hostile action by Iran and should, although perhaps they do not, fear the direction that jihad may next take.

But Pillsbury must, and does, see that some parts of the desired future for the United States are contested. The Department of State wants constructive coexistence with the Soviet Union; Pillsbury and Iklé contemplate severely weakening the Soviet Union as their ultimate goal. As Pillsbury argues, to some extent that difference, insofar as it bears on Afghanistan, has been resolved by a formal decision of the President—the presidential directive that we shall work to defeat the Soviets in Afghanistan. The central concern of Representative Wilson is of the most expressive/symbolic type—retribution. He wants to get even for the assistance the Soviets gave the Viet Cong and the North Vietnamese against the United States. It is only a slight stretch to say that he wants to create a world that is more just, from his point of view, than one in which the harm that the USSR did to us goes unpunished.

2. Personal Resources of Influence

Any particular occasion when policy is being made is, for a particular player, just one of many such occasions that are richly related to each other over time. What he does on this occasion may build or diminish his personal capacity to influence others in future policy decisions. For example, any resentment that his actions generate on this occasion will threaten his hopes for success if he comes to need the other (now resentful) player on a future occasion. Several powerful players in the Departments of State and Defense will prove reluctant to cooperate with Pillsbury because of prior bad experiences.

I shall call what is needed to create or maintain the capacity to influence others a player's "resources of influence." As we shall see in Chapter 4, having resources of influence means having those attributes or capacities (such as trust or authority) that allow one to exercise influence with specific other players in any of the limited number of ways such influence is used. Here it is enough to emphasize that concern about outcomes of future policy decisions, as they bear on the player's goals or objectives (and more), is very relevant to her decisions and actions on any particular occasion.

3. Organizational Resources

One of the ways that many players can bring about goals that they consider important is by building, maintaining, and shaping the capacity of an organization or unit they head and whose objectives they very generally share. Director Casey thus seeks to encourage and enable covert actions to be taken by the CIA. His doubts about Pillsbury's proposal are attributable, in major part, to his recognition that furnishing a highly valued, complex, and easily traceable Department of Defense weapon system to those fighting Soviet troops in Afghanistan will undermine the unique role and capacity of the CIA in the area of covert actions. To the extent that an organization's leader can make valuing a particular objective or activity part of the institutionalized culture of the organization, she can even project her personal influence into periods when she is no longer in office. Thus, as we will see in the next chapter, Casey is also trying to make the agency conform more to his image of a risk-taking intelligence organization.

The capacity of an organization depends on its morale, culture, internal systems, and the skills and knowledge of its people. Maintaining morale has motivated Casey to support his subordinates on the Stinger issue, even when he may disagree personally. Capacity also depends to a large extent upon the support that the leader's goals and objectives for the organization elicit among those who provide it with funding, authority, people, and cooperation. Preserving such external support and using it to build the capacity of the organization is a regular concern of the organization's leaders. Casey is thus reluctant to disagree with his funders and authorizers in the Senate and the House, and his deputy, McMahon, supports powerful Representative Wilson's very foolish project to send Oerlikon missiles to Afghanistan.

It may not be immediately clear how a particular proposal for a change in policy might affect the resources of an organization and thus raise this third type of concern for a player. In the most obvious case, the proposal may be to transfer authority, responsibility, and accompanying appropriations or powers from one organization to another. The risk of that happening (with Defense taking over from the CIA) with regard to our national operations in Afghanistan was an important concern of the CIA in the example of the Stinger missile case.

A far more frequent example of a particular policy or action affecting the resources of an organization arises whenever a particular decision or action of the organization would appear to confirm the suspicions of large segments of the public or its elected representatives about the dangers or weaknesses of that organization. In an earlier book, *The Politics of Public Management*, I have described this as the importance of a manager recognizing the "political vulnerabilities of his organization." In fact, the American people have always been suspicious that the efficiency, lawfulness, fairness, and restraint that they think are essential in government may be missing in practice. Thus, fear of governmental overreaching explains the felt necessity of adding the Bill of Rights to achieve ratification of the Constitution more than two hundred years ago. The political payoff of oversight activities to Congress and to individual political careers reflects the fact that the public has long been suspicious of the fairness and effectiveness of executive use of power. Partisan politics also focuses here. The party that does not control the White House has always found that attacks on the manner in which the powers of the executive were being used—with what energy, efficiency, fairness, and restraint or lack thereof—constitute a major weapon against the administration.

Many of these suspicions come to be sharply focused on particular activities of specific organizations. The FBI, since September 11, 2001, has been scrutinized for its unwillingness to share information. Homeland Security has been made the subject of ridicule for its color-coded warning system and its response to Hurricane Katrina. The CIA is suspected of abusing terrorist suspects. The leader of each of these organizations will pay special attention to—will be particularly concerned about—the effects of any policy that might appear to confirm the particular public and congressional suspicions that focus on his organization. The public suspicions of an organization (its "vulnerabilities") constitute tinder for political attack. Its leaders are wise to avoid carefully any decision that may ignite this tinder, undermining needed support for the organization.

4. *Personal Interests*

It would be foolish to ignore the self-interested or personal aspects that sometimes play a large role, and often play at least a small role, in reaching a position on a policy. It matters to many players whether carrying out the policy will bring them credit or resentment; whether it is likely to lead to promotions or other valued opportunities, rather than to place these out of reach; and whether the work involved will complicate their daily work lives, reduce their free time, and diminish their capacity to do other things they value. Every civil servant or military officer who holds a management position at the discretion of his political superiors must choose his policy positions and actions with this dependence in mind. The President, at the very top of the hierarchy, chooses with the next election in mind.

5. *Moral Obligations*

Every job comes with a set of moral obligations. Some are personal, like a Cabinet member's loyalty to the President who appointed him or the loyalty that Casey feels toward those under him in the organization. Other obligations are process-oriented and more general and demanding: to obey the law that surrounds the activities of the position he occupies; to act with enough honesty and transparency to satisfy the minimum conditions of democratic control of that area; and to show fairness to those entitled to rely on unbiased decisions by the occupant of the role he has accepted. Still others involve powerful claims of justice. Some of the players in the Stinger case are primarily motivated by a passionate belief in fairness: that if we are encouraging the Afghan attacks on the Soviet occupation, we must provide the equipment that would make victory possible. Assistant Attorney General Jack Goldsmith and Deputy Attorney General Jim Coney refused to follow President Bush's wishes as to the legality of certain measures to combat terrorism because of a felt moral obligation to law.

The Role of a Player's Understanding of the Situation in Relating Actions to Concerns

Knowing the broad areas of concern that any player is likely to think about when he is presented with a proposal or confronted with another player's efforts to influence his decision is not sufficient to predict how that person will act. Concerns may or may not be activated by the situation as he sees it. The player's beliefs about critical facts and relationships and his predictions about how various interventions will change the world and build or diminish his influence will determine how relevant a particular type of concern seems to his decision. More broadly, such beliefs determine what is important to the player about the situation he faces, *as he sees it.*

For example, every player is interested in building her resources to affect future policy choices; but, in any particular case, understanding the impact of a proposal on her resources may require knowing, among other things, what she thinks the role of particular players are likely to be in future policy decisions and how she predicts they will be affected by her actions now. Similarly, what she does to maintain and enhance her organization's capacities may depend upon there being, and her recognizing, a relationship between various proposals and the home district of the chairman of an appropriations committee. And her sense of moral obligation on one occasion may depend on how she feels a person who is now making a moral claim on her loyalty has treated her in the past. For example, Casey's sense of obligation to support the views of his subordinates in the Directorate of Operations is rooted in their prior demonstrations of loyalty to him.

Of course, part of a player's understanding of the significance for her concerns of a particular event or proposal in its setting is imposed on the members of the organization and thus not idiosyncratic to particular actors. The views of superiors or funders about the dangers of the Soviet Union cannot be ignored.

Other beliefs are idiosyncratic but predetermined: Even without externally imposed concerns and beliefs, she cannot afford to figure everything out anew on every occasion. At its most thoughtful, the beliefs about the impact of a particular action in a specific situation may reflect a previously developed and articulated organizational strategy that goes far toward defining a preferred path once the situation is categorized.

Less formally, she may have adopted any number of possible shortcuts to address quickly and cheaply the ways that events and occasions inspired by others are likely to affect her concerns. Some organizing concepts may be purely descriptive and very general, ranging from rules about how others behave, such as, "No one does favors without expecting something in return," to historical lessons such as, "Domestic intelligence policy alternates between reform periods and periods of heightened demands for information." Other shortcuts may be prescriptive. A player may have certain rules of thumb, such as, "Never sacrifice any part of my jurisdiction or responsibilities." He may have far more specific tactics for particular situations. Pillsbury describes himself as operating on the theory that he should always try to prevent opponents from seeing in advance his efforts to develop a coalition.

Finally, part of the set of preprocessed beliefs will be far more specific understandings as to how particular individuals, with whom she regularly engages, act and interact. For example, "What is Pillsbury likely to do if we tell him he isn't invited to a particular meeting with the Pakistanis?"

The Effects of Self-Image and Reputation

As a last step in predicting how another player will react, a policy entrepreneur of course must recognize that the player whose reactions he is predicting will have to integrate the impact of a proposal or of an interaction across all five dimensions of her concerns. A proposal might, for example, be good for her in terms of resources of influence but bad in terms of her favored policies. And she must do this integration with some consistency from one occasion to another. It is the relative weights of different concerns, when applied consistently to different fact situations, that form most of a player's self-image and, closely related, her reputation among players, including her superiors. This is, quite simply, her character as an official. Indeed, to create a valuable reputation—or a "character" she can feel good about—she may decide to put a thumb on the scales as she weighs some of her concerns. She may want to be considered hard-nosed and "nobody's fool"; she may, instead, want to be thought generous and even indulgent. She will need moral excuses if she is going to lie to someone personally or professionally important to her, because she will want others to continue to think of her as a reliable partner. Thus—while most of what she does can be captured by a description of how she makes decisions as to how much time to devote to a problem, how she processes information within those constraints, and how she evaluates her various concerns as they are implicated by an occasion of interaction with a proposal, an individual, or a group—the player is often also aware that others are judging her as part of their own calculations. Developing an image that is comfortable in the present and will be useful in the future is an inevitable part of the process of dealing with her concerns.

4

The Action Resumes

The Politics of a Covert Action: The United States, the Mujahideen,
and the Stinger Missile
A Case History by Kirsten Lundberg

In early June 1985, Senator Orrin Hatch arrived in Pakistan to see President Zia-ul-Haq.[1] On the plane with Hatch was his former associate from the Republican Steering Committee, Michael Pillsbury.[2] Hatch had become a member of the Senate Select Committee on Intelligence (SSCI) in January 1985. He brought along three fellow committee members, a visibly bipartisan group. The group had two items on their agenda. The first was to learn directly from the Mujahideen what assistance would be most helpful. The second was to hear from Zia, unambiguously and without misunderstanding, whether he would sanction the delivery of Stinger missiles to the rebels. There was considerable confusion on this point.

So What Does Zia Want?

Over the years, Zia had been frustratingly circumspect about whether he would endorse giving the advanced weapon to the Afghan rebels. The Pakistani president had left different impressions with different people.

The CIA's contacts conveyed the clear impression that Zia believed that providing the Mujahideen with Stingers would pose an unacceptable security risk to Pakistan. Recounts one former CIA official involved in the Afghan operation: "It was well understood by the U.S. mission in Islamabad that it was Pakistan's very, very firm policy from the very beginning that no American weapons would ever end up in Afghanistan....The Pakistanis felt that the Americans are here right now because it's in their global, geopolitical strategic interests to do so. But the American, they felt, is not a long-term friend."

Zia, amplifies the official, "was very, very worried about introducing at that time blatant, undeniable evidence of superpower involvement and rivalry into the subcontinent by allowing American weapons or American personnel....Zia was very keen on ensuring that this thing looked like a home-grown insurrection, with obvious support from Pakistan."

CIA Lies?

Within the U.S. government, however, there were powerful voices maintaining that the CIA was censoring Zia, failing to pass on requests for Stingers. Undersecretary of Defense Fred Iklé, for one, contends that Zia did ask the CIA repeatedly for Stingers but that the Agency misreported or failed to report the request. Pillsbury sees the situation darkly. "My own view...is that several mid-level DO officers were openly defying President Reagan's signed directives and most likely belonged to the opposition political party....These officers acted in a near-mutiny by exploiting their monopoly on access to ISI and Zia about the sensitive Afghan program to deny information to their own DCI, and to DOD and the NSC."[3]

Others do not recall such obfuscation. Richard Armitage, Assistant Secretary of Defense for International Security, says "I don't remember enormous pressure for [Stingers] from Zia ul-Haq. I remember this being much more a debate in the United States than it was between Pakistan and us. For his part, Piekney denies "categorically that I ever received or withheld any request from President Zia or General Akhtar for Stinger missiles to be introduced into Afghanistan...."[4]

Norman Gardner, who in 1985 became special assistant to CIA Director for Operations Clair George, confirms that "every goddamn word that Zia ever uttered to anybody was reported in excruciating, nauseating detail. Believe me." Gardner attributes the confusion to Zia himself. He contends, "Zia wasn't telling the same story to everybody...."

The Senator and the President

But the Hatch delegation would now not have to take anyone else's word for it. They were to meet on June 6 with Zia in person, and could hear his response for themselves. General Akhtar Abdul Rahman Khan, the head of Pakistani military intelligence (ISI), was also scheduled to attend. Pillsbury, in particular, could not help hoping that Akhtar might be able to sway Zia, if that proved necessary. Akhtar in April had told Iklé and Pillsbury that he would welcome Stingers for the Mujahideen.

At the last moment, however, it seemed that Pillsbury might not have the chance to monitor the proceedings in person. The CIA's William Piekney had orders to bar him from the meeting. "Casey had forbidden Pillsbury from attending the principals' discussions in Pakistan," recalls Piekney. "Our instructions—and I had verified them the night before in a telephone satellite conversation with Washington—were that the only people to go were the ambassador, myself, and Senator Hatch." Only after Hatch personally called Casey did the DCI relent.[5]

The meeting took place in Rawalpindi. During the talks, the Pakistani leader emphasized—repeating what he had told Pillsbury and Iklé in April—that his country needed Stingers for its own defense. He noticeably did not request Stingers for the Afghan rebels. But Zia did hint that, were Pakistan to get Stingers, a few might well end up in the "right hands," that is, the Mujahideen. Pillsbury says he had to explain to Zia that this would be illegal under U.S. law. Instead, Hatch suggested that Zia put his request in writing and send a letter to President Reagan. Zia did so, and in July the United States sold Pakistan twenty Stingers on the understanding that the weaponry was for Pakistani use exclusively.[6]

The Hatch trip had failed, however, to advance the aims of Pillsbury and others who wanted to secure Zia's permission to give Stingers to the Mujahideen. Lacking Zia's unequivocal support, Pillsbury felt he could only follow Iklé's instruction to abandon the Stinger effort and devote his energies elsewhere. Nonetheless, he was disturbed to learn in August that the Geneva talks might, according to Deputy Assistant Secretary of State Arnold Raphel, yield a preliminary agreement.

Diplomatic Breakthrough?

The new Soviet leadership had raised diplomatic hopes that the proximity talks in Geneva might become productive. The chief UN negotiator, Diego Cordovez, was working hard to reach acceptance on the format of a draft comprehensive settlement. The Soviet Union, in the summer of 1985, had signaled a new readiness to be, along with the United States, a guarantor of any eventual settlement.

Raphel wanted the United States to approve this role as guarantor before the sixth round of UN negotiations, scheduled for August 27, 1985. Others in the State Department, however, expressed considerable anxiety about consenting to guarantee an agreement that did not yet exist. Nonetheless, on August 23 Raphel secured permission from Undersecretary of State Michael Armacost to convey conditional oral approval "in principle."[7]

But that was not the end of it. There was an outcry at the NSC and at DOD as details of this assent leaked out. Supporters of the Afghan rebels already had a quarrel with the format of the UN talks because they lent de facto legitimacy to the Kabul government. Worse, the Geneva talks accorded the Mujahideen no standing at all. Any Geneva agreement, they felt, would betray the rebels and contravene the intent of NSDD 166. Pillsbury, who tried in vain to obtain a copy of the proposed settlement from the State Department, spoke for the opposition. "We heard rumors and we also got reports through intelligence channels. We were outraged. In March we had finally succeeded in getting the President to make a real military commitment to win the war by adopting NSDD 166, and now here it was, only month six of escalation, and we found that some people at State were getting ready to sell us out behind our backs."[8]

Abramowitz Goes to Pakistan

In September 1985, Morton Abramowitz joined a Defense Department trip to the Middle East and Pakistan. Abramowitz, widely regarded as a liberal, was the director of the Bureau of Intelligence and Research (INR) at the State Department.[9] During the stop in Pakistan, the delegation met with Akhtar. The Americans also went to the border area to meet with Afghan fighters. There, General Mirza Aslam Beg, Pakistan's vice chief of army staff, told them outright that he thought the rebels were losing the war. Abramowitz remembers "a lot of complaints about helicopters." Abramowitz was also impressed by the "extraordinary determination" of the Mujahideen leaders and a "sense that the mechanism was failing them, leaving them hanging out." He became convinced that the United States was not doing enough for the rebels. On his return to Washington, "I began to beat the drums for it." The argument that introducing the Stingers would enrage the Soviets, notes Abramowitz, "struck me as ridiculous, since we were carrying on a huge supply campaign." He also thought that raising the level of Soviet casualties by going after helicopters might persuade Gorbachev—possibly already dubious about the war—to change his policy in Afghanistan.

Abramowitz took every opportunity to raise the issue of giving Stinger missiles to the Afghan rebels. But repeatedly, through the fall of 1985, Abramowitz discovered, as Iklé and Pillsbury had in May, that there was plenty of opposition within the foreign policy establishment to sending Stingers to the Mujahideen.

Cannistraro at the National Security Council remembers Abramowitz arguing that "if we were going to do this, we either did it right or got out of it altogether, because at the present time we were encouraging brave people to go and get themselves killed. He looked at it in very moralistic terms." Cannistraro contrasts Abramowitz's attitude with that of Iklé and Pillsbury, who saw "Afghanistan as a theater of confrontation with the Soviets, looked at it in big-power terms."

Aid Escalates

The administration clearly had no quarrel with increasing the magnitude of the CIA's covert action. The White House had managed to add $200 million to the existing $250 million Afghan appropriation by reprogramming unused funds in a secret DOD account.[10] Some members of the congressional intelligence committees were insulted by the end-run, as they had been over the $40 million reappropriation for the Oerlikon. A few key members of the intelligence committees were beginning to worry about the growing scope of covert paramilitary operations. Not only had covert actions become a substitute for a foreign policy, charged the critics, but congressional overseers learned of new developments only after the fact. As SSCI vice chair Senator Patrick J. Leahy, D-Vt., would later say, "Can a democracy like the United States engage in large-scale, so-called 'covert paramilitary operations,' using our intelligence agencies as instruments in waging proxy wars against the Soviet Union or its clients?"[11]

Gorbachev's Secret Decision

What no one outside the Kremlin could know was that, as the Stinger option circulated for debate in U.S. policy circles, Gorbachev's Politburo was making up its mind to withdraw from Afghanistan. On October 17, 1985, Gorbachev asked the Politburo to make it clear to Afghan President Babrak Karmal that "with or without Karmal, we will firmly carry out policies that must lead to withdrawal from Afghanistan in the shortest possible time."[12] The Politburo chose a policy of trying to get out of Afghanistan by forcing the enemy to sue for peace. In other words, the new policy combined political carrots with military sticks.

There were hints of the changed Soviet attitude when Reagan and Gorbachev held their first, get-acquainted summit in Geneva on November 19–21, 1985. Reagan felt that Gorbachev was trying, among other things, to seek a solution to the Afghan conflict. Secretary of State Shultz also detected a new tone from the Kremlin and told Iklé that "it sounds as if they're going to change their policy on Afghanistan."[13]

The new Soviet rhetoric was not enough, however, to persuade key hard-line U.S. policy makers of any genuine Soviet change of heart. As they saw it, there had been plenty of unfulfilled Communist promises before. Indeed, Soviet military pressure was increasing. So, they reasoned, if Gorbachev *was* looking for an excuse to get out of Afghanistan, how better to help him than by making the situation on the ground untenable?

Bringing Around State

Despite his early discouragement, INR's Abramowitz pursued the campaign to get Stingers into the hands of the Afghan rebels. The "strongest articulate opposition," as he terms it, came from within the State Department. Raphel's Near East and South Asian Affairs Division continued to mount a spirited resistance to the Stinger on the grounds that

Zia did not want it and that its deployment could derail the Geneva talks. But Abramowitz felt that Raphel had it wrong. Arguing against Raphel, Abramowitz convinced Undersecretary Armacost that the Mujahideen should have Stingers. "I tended to get my counsel from INR," says Armacost. Abramowitz "was impressed by the potential [of the Stinger], and that made a big impression on me." Armacost remembers that Pillsbury, too, was advocating the Stinger, but adds that "I wouldn't have taken his view if it was only coming from him....My views were more influenced by Mort."

Armacost in turn persuaded Shultz to support the Stinger.[14] Shultz, says Abramowitz, "was never out in front on this issue. But I never felt he was opposed to it. I just felt he had to be brought along." Shultz referred in his memoirs to Abramowitz's persuasive argument that "we are not putting significant pressure on the Soviets. We should put in an American weapon: the Stinger."[15]

But at the time, it was not so clear that Shultz was fully behind the Stinger decision. He wanted to play the diplomatic card with the same energy as the military card. Certainly in the wake of the Reagan-Gorbachev summit, the State Department was treating the Geneva talks with new seriousness. In a speech on December 13, 1985, Deputy Secretary of State John Whitehead made it public that the United States had accepted one of the key demands in Geneva—that a withdrawal of Soviet troops would trigger a cutoff (*when* remained a matter of dispute) of outside aid to the rebels.

Once again, news of a possible diplomatic breakthrough angered those who saw the proposed agreement as wholly inadequate, sacrificing the Afghan freedom fighters for a face-saving compromise with the Soviets. Pillsbury, who had by now returned openly to his advocacy of the Stinger, redoubled his efforts. DOD's Armitage gives him full credit. "The question of the Stingers is quite simple," he posits. "It was a matter of primarily Fred Iklé, helped in the main by Pillsbury....They felt they could dramatically escalate the cost to the Soviet Union by the introduction of Stingers."

That Abramowitz had brought around the State Department was only the first step. There still remained the CIA and the Joint Chiefs of Staff, not to mention Secretary Weinberger.[16] But by the end of 1985, CIA opposition felt spongy—especially its plea for preserving "plausible deniability." "The real problem," recalls Abramowitz, "was in the Agency....I could never really understand the Agency negativism on it....Deniability was a joke. It was an open, overt covert program. Here we're giving them a couple of hundred million a year, and then if we're going to send them 200 Stingers, that was going to suddenly get the Soviets to attack the United States or Pakistan? Nonsense."

For his part, Pillsbury was frankly angry at the disproportionate influence that a few CIA officers seemed able to exert over national policy. He recalls with exasperation, "their military equivalent rank was that of colonels, not deputy cabinet secretaries [ranked as a four-star general]....Their experience in long-range strategic planning was zero....[Yet] even low-ranking DO staff had a monopoly on access to the ISI and to Zia that put them in an omnipotent position to claim to Raphel and to DOD that Zia did not want the Stingers....They really had no business arrogating to themselves the right to make presidential decisions."[17]

Pillsbury decided that his best bet for overcoming CIA intransigence lay in isolating the DO by persuading the holdouts in other agencies. Hardly the first government employee to transfer from the legislative to the executive branch, Pillsbury nonetheless felt he had acquired lobbying skills as a congressional staffer that were little used, even looked down upon, by administration officials. He decided to put these skills to use in the service of the Stinger. "I had to go 'underground' as it were," comments Pillsbury, "and meet in private with each objector to unravel the knot....That meant preventing the formation of a coalition, which would have happened if each had all the others' objections."[18] He elaborates: "As a former Senate staffer, I was used to how one passes legislation. You have to work with the different groups....Instead of raising an issue at [interagency] meetings, I held off-line meetings with each of the participants. I tried to find out: What are your objections? What might be incentives? How could I sweeten this? What should I take out?...I applied these techniques, which were not familiar to the executive branch. They were not used to lobbying."

Pillsbury says that Armitage, for one, criticized him because "this is not up-front." But Iklé applauded his deputy's tactics. They appeared to be working. There were signs that the pro-Stinger campaign was yielding dividends. Even the Agency was split on the merits. But what Iklé and Pillsbury may not have fully appreciated was that the CIA perceived itself as engaged in a two-front war. One was against the Stinger. The other was against encroachments from the Office of the Secretary of Defense (OSD) on CIA business. In some ways, the turf issue was the more worrisome because it was more enduring.

CIA versus OSD

It was, at the least, troubling. It seemed to CIA officials more than possible that the Stinger proposal was a stalking horse, meant to wrest control of the Afghan operation from the CIA and give it to the Defense Department. Given its recent comeback from disgrace, the CIA was not inclined to sacrifice any of its hard-won standing.

A Restored CIA

The CIA, and especially the Directorate of Operations (DO), had gained immensely under Casey's leadership. Since 1979, the overall intelligence budget had more than doubled from $10 billion to $24 billion, while the CIA's share of that had climbed an estimated $2.5 to $3 billion and represented some 15 percent of the total.[19] The budget for covert actions exceeded $500 million, the highest level since the Vietnam War. The *Washington Post* wrote that "Casey has rebuilt the CIA into a lethal and controversial instrument for carrying out covert operations."[20]

But it was the CIA's renewed capability in a field—paramilitary operations—arguably belonging to the military that fueled a turf war between the CIA and the Defense Department. The immediate battle was for the control of covert actions. In part, the CIA's leadership felt that the DOD could not do the job properly. The DO's Gardner, who started his career in the military, was among those who felt any formal military participation would be a disaster. He says: "One of the things the Agency can do is to put something together like this. If you take the fetters off and let them go ahead and do it, they can do it. Where they have the problem is with people.... So they can go to the military and get the people. But the military just couldn't. I mean it would take them thousands and thousands of people and it would be a big goddamn project, and it'd just be awful. They can't do it quietly and on the sly and on the cheap. They just can't get it done."

The DO's Frank Anderson says that someone outside the Agency once explained to him why the CIA could be so effective at what it did: less bureaucracy. An examiner from the Office of Management and Budget (OMB) defined for Anderson the difference between the CIA and other federal departments. At the CIA, said the OMB examiner, from the time an authorizing official signs a document until something happens takes an average of 42 days. At USAID, by way of comparison, it takes an average of 444 days.

But the greater worry had to do with power and control. The CIA simply did not want the Defense Department reaching down into CIA operations and trying to call the shots.

At one point, says Piekney, Iklé wanted the Agency to consider sending US C-130 military transport planes to make direct drops of supplies and weapons into Afghanistan "without this costly and time consuming and inefficient process that we were using." DDCI John McMahon was dismayed at this effort to circumvent the Pakistani ISI. He felt the existing arrangement worked fine. McMahon says: "I did my utmost to keep it that way—where we didn't try to run the war. We weren't going to bring American ingenuity into the hills of Afghanistan because few people have ever been there and knew what it was like. I wanted the people that knew what ground truth was to call the shots....It was a very simple operation that was very effective."

The Stinger contest was, in many ways, only another skirmish in the ongoing and larger turf war.

Obstructing the Stinger

But the CIA did not intend to forfeit even a skirmish. Institutionally, the CIA continued to present a united front against the Stinger in any interagency discussions. Casey certainly spoke out against it, whatever his private views may have been. But in fact, Agency officers—even within DO—were divided on the merits of the Stinger, along much the same lines as had existed the previous May. The director of DO, Clair George, endorsed the Stinger idea. His assistant, Norm Gardner, was also not opposed. But critical members of the Near East/South Asia Division, such as deputy chief Twetten, remained adamant against it, as did the chief U.S. intelligence officer in Pakistan, Piekney.

Piekney was concerned above all with the impact on Pakistan, and the threat that the weapons could quickly end up in the arsenals of terrorists. Comments Piekney: "You put a number of Stingers into Afghanistan and you have no way of knowing where they'll end up....Once you gave it to them, essentially you kissed it goodbye and hoped they would do the best they could with it. When you put a highly sophisticated, technologically advanced weapon like a Stinger into Afghanistan, the high side is you can start knocking down more planes; the low side is you don't know where it's going to end up."

DOD's Armitage, too, "thought there was a fair chance of this falling into other hands that we didn't want." He gave credit to the CIA for understanding—as well as anyone in the U.S. government—the psychology of the Mujahideen, who "like money, weapons, and their women." As he puts it: "They [CIA] worked a little bit more closely with the 'muj' than anyone....They were right in there cheek-by-jowl. They knew these characters were pretty bad guys."

McMahon Takes the Heat

DDCI McMahon had become the CIA's chief public proponent of the anti-Stinger view. During the fall of 1985, McMahon testified repeatedly to the intelligence committees that providing the Afghan fighters with Stingers would be a mistake. He opposed the provision of U.S. weapons, he said, because the Soviets might retaliate against Pakistan.[21] McMahon stresses that he was no longer concerned about the issue of plausible deniability. "Non-attribution to the U.S. [had gone by] the boards a long time earlier," he says.

Casey's View

There are mixed reports as to how Casey stood on the Stinger issue which, absent his personal account, are impossible to reconcile. McMahon says Casey supported his views fully—"On Afghanistan, we had no question whatsoever. He knew that there was good and sufficient reason not to send the Stinger in." But DO's Twetten remembers Casey as impatient with DO recalcitrance—"Bill Casey's attitude on anything like this was always 'Why is the DO being so conservative? What's wrong with giving it a try?'"

In interagency meetings, however, Casey remained studiously lukewarm on the proposal, citing the concerns of the DO. INR Director Abramowitz was never convinced that Casey's opposition was heartfelt—"I didn't feel his opposition had any real depth or any steam. I thought he was reflecting the company view rather than being deeply committed to it." But Anderson feels this was consistent with Casey's management style. He explains: "Most of the time, Casey worked awfully hard to get the system behind him. It wouldn't be at all out of character for him to have gone into an NSC meeting with an Agency position."

McMahon Concedes

But by December 1985, even McMahon began to stoop under the weight of the mounting pressure on the CIA to bow to the inevitable and endorse the Stinger proposal. On December 6, 1985, he decided to throw in the towel. That morning Casey, Secretary of Defense Weinberger, and McMahon met for breakfast with Iklé. In the course of the conversation, Iklé wondered out loud whether the CIA could use any Stingers. Recalls McMahon: "I decided then and there that I had had enough of carrying the water for the Joint Chiefs, and I said 'Fred, I'll take every Stinger you can send me.' "[22]

A week later, there was a meeting at the State Department of Armacost, Abramowitz, Casey, and McMahon. During the conversation, Abramowitz urged those present to support the dispatch of Stingers to Afghanistan.[23] McMahon offered no objection. Piekney says he can understand why. "John did not think that we should be doing these things....But at the end of the day, the DCI and the DDCI are no match for the Secretary of Defense and the Deputy Secretary of Defense....The Agency can't stand up against heavy political pressure.."

McMahon had become, not coincidentally, the target of a letter-writing campaign by two arch-conservative groups, Free the Eagle and the Federation for American Afghan Action. The groups were lobbying for McMahon's dismissal on the grounds that he was trying to limit the quality of U.S.-financed arms going to the rebels. They also accused McMahon of encouraging the CIA to formulate U.S. policy. At public meetings, they went so far as to throw ripe fruit at him.[24]

McMahon's apparent capitulation in the Stinger struggle did not, however, constitute formal CIA acceptance of the proposal. The predominant concern for the CIA continued to be Zia's unwillingness to endorse Stingers for the rebels. If Pillsbury was to adhere to his strategy of satisfying the objections of each individual institution in turn in order to reach agreement, it was clear that his next move had to address the Zia enigma.

Lining up the Ducks

Once again, Pillsbury packed his bags for a trip—once again led by Senator Orrin Hatch. The trip was billed as a fact-finding mission to seven nations, including Pakistan. This time, the guest list included key members of the House and Senate intelligence committees. But unlike Hatch's June trip, this was not a bipartisan delegation. Its members were Senators Hatch and Chic Hecht, R.-Nev., along with Representatives Michael DeWine, R-Ohio, Robert Lagomarsino, R-Calif., and James Courter, R-N.J.[25]

The Senator and the President, Take Two

The group set out from Washington in the first week of January. In addition to the congressmen, on the plane were Mort Abramowitz and Charles Dunbar (Afghan coordinator) from State, Vince Cannistraro from the NSC, Pillsbury from DOD, and Norm Gardner, special assistant to the deputy director for operations at the CIA. "Hatch and Pillsbury wanted me to go," remembers Gardner, "because they knew my relationship with Clair [George] and they just figured that would give a Directorate of Operations stamp to the effort."[26]

The first stop was Beijing. Hatch asked whether the Chinese would have any objection if the United States sent Stingers to Afghanistan. If not—as turned out to be the case—he suggested the Chinese might communicate this directly to Zia. Such support would carry weight, coming from Pakistan's closest ally.[27]

The party then continued on to Islamabad, where they were to meet with Zia. The Pakistani leader received the Americans at his residence. General Akhtar was also present. Senator Hatch spoke bluntly to the Pakistani leader about the need to approve Stinger anti-aircraft weapons for the Mujahideen. The senator emphasized that a lot of planes that could be brought down were not being brought down. He stressed Zia's moral obligation to obtain advanced weapons. Zia "kind of hesitated for a moment," remembers one meeting participant, "and sort of looked up, and reflected for what might have been 10 seconds or so, and he said 'Okay.' This was not something that he was gunning for."

Abramowitz felt the message was unambiguous. "He made it crystal-clear 'I want the Stinger.' Having that unequivocal request for the first time was very important," reported Abramowitz.[28] Gardner affirms that Zia "embraced it. I think that was the first time he really felt as though it was time to do it and that they could stand it."

Riaz Khan, a Pakistani diplomat who served from 1984 to 1986 as a member of the negotiating team in Geneva, points out that Zia was equally under pressure from numerous domestic factions. The ISI and General Akhtar, for example, had made no secret of their **wish** for the Mujahideen to have Stingers. "In Pakistan," says Riaz, "there was a strong lobby for helping these Mujahideen and giving them an effective weapon." Zia, he adds, spent at least a year deliberating the merits of giving Stingers to the rebels.

So it was incontestable. Zia endorsed the Stinger option, and representatives of all the major Washington players were witnesses to his acquiescence. Pillsbury had his most important card in hand.

CIA Informed

Senator Hatch personally called DCI Casey to assure him of Zia's support for the Stinger. Given that DDO Clair George had long favored the Stinger option and that, in addition, Gardner had witnessed Zia's acceptance of the Stinger proposal, Pillsbury assumed that Agency compliance would be automatic. The chief task remaining was to convince the military. But that would have to be undertaken simultaneously with an equally important effort—overcoming the scruples of Defense Secretary Weinberger.

The Generals

The Joint Chiefs of Staff had not been persuaded in May of 1985. Nor were they converted in the fall of 1985 when Weinberger, at Iklé's behest, raised the Stinger option with them in a "tank" meeting held in a secure meeting room underneath the Secretary of Defense's office in the Pentagon.[29] At that stormy meeting, assistant to the chairman of the JCS, General John Moellering, had registered his views. A later report says Moellering "was initially opposed to the possible release of the [Stinger] weapons to Third World countries for reasons of technology loss, accountability problems and depletion of a finite and small, strategic stockpile."

Now, in late January 1986, the generals were still deeply concerned that the technology could be lost to the Soviets, and that the weapons themselves could fall into the hands of terrorists.

The Joint Chiefs remained apprehensive regarding "the possibility that the Stingers would be lost and could get into the hands of terrorists, and be used against airliners or against U.S. army helicopters or other civilian aircraft," says General Wickham. "The second concern I had was technology...that [the Stingers] could be sold trying to raise money." Raising a third objection, the military argued that, with only 3,000 Stingers in its own arsenals, the Pentagon could ill afford any for the Afghans.

Weinberger's Doubts

Significantly, it was not just the Joint Chiefs who were opposed. Secretary of Defense Caspar Weinberger continued to harbor grave reservation. As Weinberger later recounted: "In general I felt we should not let our technology out." He also worried about Pillsbury's role, considering Iklé's deputy "a loose cannon who was really in the department on sufferance because of his political friends."[30] General Wickham sensed that Weinberger "was somewhat neutral....He wanted to be sure that the Joint Chiefs of Staff were supportive." McMahon considers it telling that Weinberger never formally asked him, "Why don't you get Stingers over?" Notes McMahon: "If he had said that, I would have moved then to put it on the agenda for the NSPG [National Security Planning Group] to consider."

To overcome such steadfast and well-founded opposition, Pillsbury knew he would have to find utterly convincing counterarguments. That seems only to have spurred him on. As Abramowitz puts it: "Pillsbury was very eager to see this happen." To Pillsbury's delight, he found what he wanted, thanks to the CIA's Directorate of Intelligence (DI).

The Greek Leak

Approaching an analyst on the DI/Near East desk for any information on the Stinger, Pillsbury was handed a full folder of raw material on the weapon. Among the documents, Pillsbury discovered one that established that the Soviets had already obtained a microfiche copy of the Stinger blueprint. A GRU (Soviet military intelligence) double agent in Greece had warned the CIA that the Stinger technology was on its way to Moscow.[31] The United States was unable to stop it for fear of exposing the source.[32]

Iklé says Pillsbury's discovery of the espionage leak was a key element in a February 1986 memo Iklé prepared for Secretary Weinberger. The memorandum, submitted to Weinberger in advance of an upcoming meeting of the Planning and Coordination Group, set forth the objections raised by the JCS and answered them one by one. It listed the advantages of the Stinger. It persuaded the Secretary. Remembers Iklé: "Weinberger might have hesitated. [After all] the chiefs had said this could compromise our technology. The Secretary of Defense was responsible. I could say it's already been compromised."

To address the military's objection that it had an inadequate supply of Stingers, Pillsbury then put in a call to General Dynamics, manufacturer of the Stinger. He learned that the production line for the basic Stinger was about to be phased out to make room for an upgraded model. There would be no problem making up the extra basic-model Stingers. Pillsbury asked Hatch to request that Casey inform Weinberger that the military's last concern—or excuse—had been laid to rest.[33] Iklé, who had felt the JCS consideration was rather far-fetched, was relieved. Given Pillsbury's discoveries, plus assurances from Casey that the Agency would ensure control over the Stingers by putting in place an exchange system of live launchers for expended ones, the JCS capitulated. Says General Wickham: "The chiefs finally signed off on it. They finally bowed to the persuasion that this was important, that the essentiality of these systems to the success of the war was uppermost."

Making It Official

With all parties to the decision apparently won over, a meeting was scheduled in mid-February of the Planning and Coordination Group (covert actions) to approve the Stinger proposal. Invited participants that day were the deputy chief of the DO's Near East/South Asia Division, Thomas Twetten, and Pillsbury. Regular committee members Iklé, Abramowitz, and General Moellering, among others, were in attendance in the White House situation room.[34] Iklé proposed the Stinger matter for discussion, saying that Secretary Weinberger had changed his mind and now endorsed the proposal.

At this juncture, however, Twetten reintroduced previous concerns based on Zia's objections and declared that the Agency was still opposed to deployment.[35] Twetten's demurral constituted a veto to the decision the other participants at the meeting intended to make. Abramowitz, according to one account, "reacted with outrage and the meeting broke down without consensus."[36] Whatever the reason for Twetten's stand, it was soon reversed. During a second meeting on February 26, 1986, the PCG adopted a unanimous recommendation that the United States make Stingers available to the Afghan rebels.[37] Next, the decision would be rubber-stamped by the Cabinet-level National Security Planning Group. There was little doubt that the Undersecretaries' recommendation would meet with a warm reception by their superiors. In his February 4th State of the Union address, Reagan had spoken directly to U.S.-supported freedom fighters throughout the developing world. "You are not alone, freedom fighters," he declaimed. "America will support…with moral and material assistance, your right not just to fight and die for freedom but to fight and win freedom."[38]

Meanwhile in Moscow

Meanwhile, on February 25, 1986, Gorbachev, in a published report to the Central Committee of the Communist Party Congress, said he harbored doubts about continued Soviet involvement in Afghanistan, and that "counterrevolution and imperialism have turned Afghanistan into a bleeding wound." He expressed the hope that Moscow could bring home its troops "in the nearest future" under a "phased withdrawal" to be agreed upon in Geneva.

Shultz's Cold Feet

Secretary of State Shultz, however, developed last-minute anxieties. Providing the Stinger to the Afghans could, he worried, seriously damage U.S.-Soviet relations. He conveyed his concern to the White House. On March 5, Senate Majority Leader Robert Dole and other conservatives, including Senator Wallop, convened a meeting with Shultz in Dole's office. Shultz, remembers Wallop, "was adamant against" the Stinger.

Wallop sensed that the Secretary did not want to shatter a tacit U.S.-USSR understanding on who wielded influence where. Pakistani diplomat Riaz Khan mentioned an additional implicit agreement—that neither superpower would provide advanced, shoulder-mounted anti-aircraft weaponry to guerrilla groups.

But during the 70-minute meeting, the senators were relentless. Four times they pressed Shultz to provide Stingers to Afghanistan (as well as to rebels in Angola). Each time, Shultz asked, "Are you sure you want me to go back to Bill Casey and tell him you want Stingers?" The answer was always yes.[39] The Secretary was persuaded.

In mid-March, the PCG recommendation went for approval to the National Security Planning Group. President Reagan chaired the meeting. Sometime within the next week (details remain classified), he issued a secret order authorizing the transfer of Stingers to the Afghan freedom fighters. Two weeks later, the congressional intelligence oversight committees were informed of the administration's decision.

Coda

On March 29, John McMahon retired "for personal reasons" from the CIA after thirty-four years of service.[40] On March 30, the last shreds of any fiction that the CIA was operating a covert action in Afghanistan were ripped away when the *Washington Post* reported "U.S. sends new arms to rebels; Afghans, Angolans get Stinger missiles in change of policy." Stingers in the hands of Afghan rebels began shooting down Soviet aircraft in September 1986. The rebels considered the weapons extraordinarily effective. What the Soviet government thought is less clear.[41] But it is known that Gorbachev and his colleagues were reevaluating their Afghan policy, culminating in a Politburo discussion in November 1986.[42] All agreed that the military path had failed, and the best they could achieve would be an indefinite, draining stalemate. In December 1987, at a summit in Washington, Gorbachev announced that his government had decided to withdraw all its forces from Afghanistan (although it would continue to lavish military aid on "Afghan comrades"). On February 9, 1988, he promised that Soviet troops would begin their departure in May and would be entirely gone within a year.

Political accords were signed in Geneva. The last Soviet ground forces quit Afghanistan in February 1989, leaving behind a country in the throes of civil war. Decades later, the embers of that war were still burning.

5

An Individual's Understanding of the Situation

For two reasons, the notion of an individual's understanding of a situation—her understanding of the significance of an occasion or proposal ("USO") for her concerns in light of the situation as *she* understands it—is a critical concept for understanding policy choice. First, in order for any player to help shape a policy choice to further her own concerns, she must develop her own understanding of the bearing of the particular occasion or situation on those concerns. Second, knowing concerns alone is not enough to intelligently seek to influence others and to anticipate how others will seek to influence her. She will also need a refined notion of their understandings of the situation in terms of the effects of the situation on those concerns. Indeed, much of the value of experience in government is captured by these two uses of the notion of a USO.

Thinking about what goes into your own USO is a good introduction to understanding the USOs of other players. So let's begin there.

Shared Constraints: Goals, Rules, and Roles

Your USO begins its life subject to certain socially imposed constraints dictated by the organization, history, and superiors. Sociologists might call this part the socially accepted "definition" of the situation. At the organizational level, the boundaries limiting how a player can define a situation's implications for her concerns include: accepting any goals or objectives announced by her superiors; following generally accepted rules for, and knowing the demands of established roles in decision making; honoring the expectations created by long-established organizational activities; and using organizationally accepted assumptions about the nature of the outer world the government is seeking to influence. Accepting particular assumptions as not contestable is a condition of being taken seriously in an organization's discussions of what to do.

The moral and practical importance of the goals of hierarchical superiors to any player is obvious. Even without articulated goals, how the decision affects the social, political, and organizational concerns of one's superiors (and, more broadly, those who select those superiors) generally "trumps" a player's own concerns and must be taken extremely seriously. Conversely, certain types of a player's own concerns cannot be used to persuade peers or superiors. Speaking frankly to other players about what one action or another would mean for an individual's personal resources and her influence in the future, or for the welfare of an organization to which the other party does not belong, or for the person's personal interests and ambitions, is frowned upon. Such concerns of another player can be ignored or rejected by simply reminding that player of the "higher" or broader goals. In the Stinger missile case, the CIA cannot be frank about its concern that it will lose a treasured part of its jurisdiction to the military; that frankness would undermine the credibility needed for its role in any policy debate about the Stinger.

The whole set of "rules" that form a critical part of a player's understanding of the situation is often less obvious than her superior's goals. The predictability needed for sophisticated coordination requires many rules operating as constraints on one's complete independence. We have already observed this requirement with regard to the bureaucratic rules applicable to the processes of policy choice. More fundamentally, with very few exceptions, laws must also be obeyed and promises must also be kept, even by presidents.

The special obligations accepted by agreeing to occupy a particular role in a network of roles must be respected if an organization is to divide responsibilities and yet function effectively. So accepting a particular role in a process of choice may impose a significant constraint. The acceptance of a position forces him to partially define the weight of relevant concerns by reference to the expectations of legislators, superiors, and subordinates that came with that role. A prosecutor, for example, will be widely and historically expected to focus his time and resources on the need for punishment of wrongdoers, not on the social conditions that make crime more likely—whatever his personal views on the relative importance of each approach.

On other occasions, one may have far more leeway to define one's role and thus to shape the constraints under which he may work. Consider a particularly dramatic example. In early 2002, at the request of the CIA (whose officers were already interrogating individuals captured in Afghanistan), the White House Counsel, Alberto Gonzales, asked the Justice Department's Office of Legal Counsel what the laws permitted and prohibited in terms of coercive interrogation. The Assistant Attorney General, Jay Bybee, could have adopted any one of several roles in responding. The choice was critical, for it would determine what facts and concerns others would accept as legitimate parts of his understanding of the significance of the occasion, and which should be disregarded as not legitimate for that role. Consider six possibilities.

1. Bybee could have—and seems to have—decided that, much like an Assistant Secretary of Defense, his role and responsibility was to give as much support as possible to his Commander in Chief in a global war against terrorism. That would lead him to make every argument that was somewhat plausible to support maximum presidential power, even in the face of relatively clear prohibitions in international conventions and U.S. statutes. The mere acceptance of this conception of his role—without regard to concerns for the personal benefits of loyalty and support—might have dictated that type of response.

2. Alternatively, Bybee could have seen his role as requiring him to assess, introspectively, where the weightier legal arguments lay in his own mind, ignoring the President's desires or needs. The benefits to the United States of one ruling or another and the effects on his own resources and those of his division and department would be irrelevant to that role. With only a slight modification, he could have added to his statement of personal judgments an honest description of his own uncertainties and their reasons—thus enabling the President to give more weight to the law in the areas where Bybee was more certain.

3. Using a subtly, but importantly, different interpretation, Bybee might have felt his role obligated him to note that many respectable views differed from his and on what basis. The President would need to know this if one of his concerns was

the reputation of the United States or his administration for
lawfulness.

4. Bybee might have thought that anticipating the predictable
reactions of powerful groups—domestic critics of the war on
terrorism, foreign allies, or those in Muslim states likely to
feel some sympathy for the terrorists—should be part of his
responsibility. That would have included an assessment of how
lawful or unlawful highly coercive interrogation would be likely
to appear to various audiences. Still, this role would not in
itself entitle him to discuss resources, personal hopes, or moral
qualms.

5. According to the Code of Professional Responsibility for lawyers,
the role of counsel includes calling to the client's attention
the moral, economic, social, and political (as well as legal)
consequences of various actions. This role would have required,
among other matters, a frank statement to the President of
any moral qualms Bybee might have had about torture. It
would also include assessing what benefits and what costs
would probably flow from presidential authorization of highly
coercive interrogation, in light of how the authorization would
likely be implemented by untrained, inexperienced, frightened
interrogators, some of whose friends or colleagues may have
recently been maimed or killed. In hindsight, the administration
might well have been willing to pay billions of dollars to avoid the
worldwide effects of the pictures and accounts from Abu Ghraib
of degrading and cruel treatment, even in light of whatever was
learned through these methods that could not have been learned
otherwise.

6. Finally, Bybee could even have thought that the historic
organizational expectations of his role required him to add to the
wide-ranging advice in the fifth option the effects of his decision
on the trust the Department of Justice and his Office of Legal
Council would enjoy with the Congress and the American people.

The point is that, even when a player has some choice in adopting a
conception of his role, the role he chooses to accept will carry with it
obligations to consider or ignore certain facets of a situation. A conception of one's role is therefore a particularly powerful ingredient of any
understanding of the significance of a particular occasion.

The Stinger Missile Case: Illustrating the Sources of Congruence in Understandings of the Significance of a Particular Occasion

Established goals, rules, and roles are centripetal forces tending to create common elements in each player's understanding of the significance of an occasion. Nevertheless, each player is likely to have a somewhat idiosyncratic understanding of the significance of the occasion—creating a diversity of views, concerns, and roles that raises powerful centrifugal forces. Consider both centripetal and centrifugal forces in a single instance.

Let me start by acknowledging the shared part of each individual's USO in the Stinger missile case—the part that corresponds roughly to what sociologists have called a social "definition of a situation." Some shared understandings in the Stinger missile case derive from statements of goals by a superior, up to the President himself. Thus Iklé invests in getting a new, more militant, NSDD signed by the President and a new council to control our activities in Afghanistan. That situation-defining mandate is reinforced by remarks in President Reagan's State of the Union address.

Superiors are entitled to demand common understandings of some aspects of a situation. When President George W. Bush created a new Director of National Intelligence and placed him over the Director of Central Intelligence, everyone knew they had to accept the new hierarchy. When he gave the Department of Homeland Security a mandate to increase inspections of aliens seeking to enter the United States from certain countries, no player could argue that this should not be an important part of any shared decision involving immigration issues. Similarly, parts of the forest of factual assumptions that will shape any later, shared decisions are authoritatively put in place by the decision of superiors. When the government adds Hezbollah to its list of terrorist organizations or when the President announces that democratization is our goal in Iraq, those decisions must be accepted by all players involved in those policy arenas.

All the players know that a certain set of rules are necessary for coordinated policy making. To make management manageable, a superior delegates broad areas of government activity, responsibility, and concern to different organizational units. Nevertheless, he will still want to decide personally some unanticipated matters that fall in delegated areas; and many real world problems will have implications for the activities and

concerns of more than one unit. For these reasons, it is generally understood that no one should unilaterally decide a matter, even if it is within
the authority that appears to have been delegated to her, if she knows
that her boss would not have intended to delegate it, or if her decision
will affect the activities or concerns of others who could be consulted.

President Reagan would want to make, personally, any decision to ship
Stinger missiles to the Mujahideen. Because such a decision would have
profound effects on the CIA (ending plausible denial), the State Department (redefining our relation to the USSR), and the U.S. military (whose
valued weapon system will be at least depleted and, at most, compromised)—each of them would have to be consulted by any one of them
who are considering making a significant decision in this area. No one
short of the Secretaries of State and Defense and the Director of the
CIA would, for reasons similar to those that explain Reagan's personal
role, make a decision as to the positions of their departments regarding
deployment of the Stinger missiles.

These rules of consultation define the categories of mandatory players
in any policy choice. There is also a variety of rules intended to specify
the occasions in which it is, or is not, appropriate to invite in additional,
optional players—like Senator Orrin Hatch or Representative Charlie
Wilson—who would be willing to use their influence on a player's behalf.
Michael Pillsbury does this openly in the Stinger missile case, but the violation of widely understood rules is often most dramatically manifest in
the form of secret leaks to the press or to Congress. Finally, law generally
trumps any bureaucratic rules, although it is rarely applicable or effective
in these situations. Still, it leads Pillsbury to caution Pakistan's President
Zia that, much as Pillsbury might like the result, Pakistan cannot legally
divert to the Mujahideen the Stingers that we furnish to Pakistan.

Like all rules, rules of process are vague in a number of areas, and players may be more or less aggressive in exploiting the vagueness. Whether
Pillsbury should be bringing Senator Hatch so far into U.S. diplomacy is
far from clear; Pillsbury can, at some cost in trust, exploit that vagueness.
One particular uncertainty about the rules is especially important. If
one set of players believes that an action is forbidden because the courts
would consider it illegal, but another set of players believes the action
is required by legitimate orders of superiors or is dictated for national
security, the rules will have become uncertain in a very fundamental way.
When CIA Director Richard Helms was called to answer questions before
the Senate Foreign Relations Committee about the CIA's involvement in

the overthrow of the Allende government in Chile, he lied because he felt it was necessary to protect the national security interest. Many agreed with this understanding of the rules. The lie was nonetheless illegal, and he was convicted in court. When, on the other hand, in order to prevent profound political embarrassment, President Nixon's staff asked CIA Director Helms to lie to the FBI about whether their Watergate investigation would interfere with some pending CIA project, he refused. Law trumps politics but not, for all players, national security.

Finally, as we have seen, common understandings about roles in the decision-making process filter a player's understanding of the situation and give prominence and weight to particular concerns intimately related to the player's role. In the Stinger missile case, only the Joint Chiefs of Staff could, in the final analysis, decide whether the military costs of giving the Stinger missiles to the Mujahideen were too great. On the other hand, no one was interested in their views of the effect of the decision on State Department negotiations with the Soviets. When your role is less than clearly defined, as it was for Jay Bybee in 2002, conceptualizing your role is the first step in deciding which of your views can claim weight in the process and which cannot.

The Stinger Missile Case: The Predictable Ways in Which USOs Differ

Still, the critical point to observe is not how similar a variety of players' viewpoints are, but how often and importantly they diverge, even when the players are likely to have a very similar view of most of the operative facts. In most situations, despite working for the same government and sharing the same information, various players, within any set of players charged with a shared policy responsibility, are likely to have very different individual understandings of the significance of the occasion (USO). Let me illustrate.

As we have seen, in the early and mid-1980s, the United States was providing military and other equipment and assistance to the Mujahideen fighting the Soviet occupation of Afghanistan. This was all done in the form of a "covert action," a class of intelligence activity entrusted to the CIA and intended to affect political and military events in a different part of the world without revealing the hand of the United States. At a minimum, the U.S. role in the Afghan-Soviet conflict had to be subject to "plausible deniability."

Having been battered for some time at the hands of the Mujahideen, the Soviet Union responded by sending in new and more effective helicopters and its own equivalent of our Special Forces. Some believed that this move could tilt the battle in favor of the Soviets; all knew that it would make the cost in lives to the Mujahideen far greater.

One possible response was to furnish the Mujahideen with U.S. Stinger missiles. Readily transportable, these surface-to-air missiles could bring down the feared Soviet helicopters. But plausible deniability depended upon the United States furnishing only weapons it had purchased in Eastern Europe—weapons that "could" have been taken on the battlefield in Afghanistan by the Mujahideen themselves. The state-of-the-art Stinger missile would change all this. The United States would no longer be able to deny involvement. Let's look at the understandings of various players as to the significance of the occasion. Consider the USO for each.

The Undersecretary of Defense for Policy Planning, Fred Iklé, and particularly his Deputy, Pillsbury, were pressing for the delivery of Stinger missiles. They saw the occasion as one in which we could impose a devastating defeat on our superpower rival. The Joint Chiefs of Staff, whose support was critical to the Secretary of Defense and the President for a number of reasons, saw less to be gained from providing the Stinger than would be lost in terms of both the risk that the Soviets would be able to copy the technology and the chance that our own missiles would be turned against us by the Mujahideen or their allies. A major and prominent figure on the Defense Subcommittee of the Appropriations Committee of the House of Representatives, Representative Wilson, understood the significance of the occasion as an opportunity to get even with the Soviets for their support of the North Vietnamese. After all, many players have what we might think of as a morality play or movie playing in their heads as they consider the meaning of a situation—not just more prosaic policy concerns. Revenge is a powerful theme in such movies; it was for Wilson.

For the CIA and its Director, William Casey, a large part of the significance of the occasion was that openly supporting the Mujahideen would end a very successful demonstration of the importance of the capacity of the CIA for conducting covert actions—a responsibility of the CIA that Casey and many members of Congress greatly valued. Ending plausible deniability was also a major concern for his staff in the Directorate of Operations; to maintain personal and organizational resources, Casey wanted to support the staff, although he may have personal sympathized with the views of Iklé and Pillsbury. Finally, the Secretary of State and his Department were addressing a larger question with a different focus, based on their responsibilities. One relevant part of the issue for them was the impact on our relations with Pakistan, which might resent any revelation of its role in covertly supplying the Mujahideen, hand in hand with the United States, given all the potential domestic and foreign consequences of such a revelation. A much bigger part of the picture was the USSR. Gorbachev had just become Secretary General of the Communist Party in the Soviet Union, and he showed promise of adopting a policy of radical transformation that could, and did, grandly affect all aspects of our foreign relations in a bipolar world. This hardly looked like the time to strengthen the hand of those in the Soviet Union who were hostile to any form of détente.

Different forms of organizational self-interest account for many of these differences. Sociology also explains the differences. Within each organization or even any informally allied group of players, there is likely to be a comparatively uniform or shared understanding of the significance of the occasion. Members of groups that work together constantly understand, instinctively, the importance of a coordinated viewpoint and will organize themselves and recruit new members around that viewpoint. Purposely encouraging a particular shared understanding of the significance of the occasion—a shared culture—is much of what we mean by the term "leadership." So is the development and protection of particular sets of valued skills: covert action (CIA) or negotiation (State) or fighting wars (Defense).

Thus, for a variety of reasons—ranging from the organizational interest of the CIA to a very broad worldview at State—this set of major players would adopt very different understandings of the significance of this occasion. A good player in the game of shared policy making has to see as many of the complete set of understandings of the significance of the situation as possible, for his actions must be addressed to those concerns of each player that are made prominent by this situation as they see it.

Some Far Less Obvious Sources of Differences in USOs

It is only necessary to explore one final piece of the puzzle: the reasons for and results of particularly serious misunderstandings about the other's USO.

It is relatively easy for Player A to appreciate some of the reasons that Player B is likely to define the relevant situation differently from Player A. For example, it was easy for Pillsbury to see that the Department of State's USO with regard to the proposed sale of the Stinger missile went far beyond relations in Southwest Asia. Player A can also notice concerns that are related specifically to Player B's organization, as in the case of the CIA's desire to preserve its primacy in dealing with covert actions. Finally, Player A should, and is likely to, expect that players who work together on many occasions will not only recognize each other's USO but will also develop reciprocal interests in accommodating their different perspectives.

Moreover, if a difference in USO is recognized by the relevant players, discussion and persuasion grounded on any of three bases may help solve the problem: (1) relating particular factual arguments to the other's concerns (as Pillsbury does when he reveals that the Soviets already have the secrets that the Joint Chiefs had hoped to preserve); (2) far more broadly, convincing the other that the world is likely to respond to the proposal in one way rather than another (as Pillsbury does when he argues that this will speed rather than delay the Soviet's departure from Afghanistan); and, (3) hardest of all, leading the other to understand that several very different understandings of the significance of the occasion are at work and that only by each of the players simultaneously recognizing and respecting each other's USO can they avoid the cost of disagreement and lack of cooperation. But all this depends on one player recognizing the different way in which another player views the same situation.

Some bases of differences in USOs are far more idiosyncratic and therefore are harder to anticipate; and, unseen, they are far more difficult to reconcile. History teaches different lessons to different players. Representative Wilson is thinking about Vietnam. Secretary of State Shultz may be thinking about the Cuban missile crisis. When President Nixon fired Archibald Cox as Special Prosecutor, Cox's USO involved fears of a president, like Andrew Jackson, greatly weakening the rule of law by ignoring a Supreme Court decision; Nixon's undoubtedly involved a sense of the prolonged enmity of liberals since his days as a fiercely anti-Communist Congressman.

Players may have a variety of understandings of how binding are the rules intended to encourage cooperation among players or how compelling are other parts of an authoritative definition of the situation. Pillsbury doubts the importance of the rules of process that limit access to pending executive decisions; at the same time, he thinks the CIA Station Chief in Pakistan is impermissibly ignoring President Reagan's situation-defining decision that our objective is to drive the Soviets out of Afghanistan. These differences are hard to spot, for no one who is prepared to bend or break the rules or ignore the President's announced goal will want others to know of this readiness. Based on their life experiences, different players will have different predictions about the likely responses of other individuals, organizations, or governments to various strategic moves. Iklé may believe that generosity toward the USSR will be taken as weakness; Shultz, that aggressiveness only generates reciprocal aggressiveness. They are likely to choose their actions based on such beliefs in ways that are unpredictable by others.

An understanding of character is needed to anticipate how players will individually understand a situation, shaping the actions of each in the decision-making process. This, too, can be a critical part of understanding the significance of an occasion. One player may be suspicious and therefore easily angered; another, trusting and therefore endlessly patient. One may be extremely sensitive to any hint of disrespect; another may have the confidence needed for a "thicker skin." Indeed, this aspect of the problem is even harder than it appears. A character-based reaction may seem realistic to the individual player but in fact be displaced from another situation, perhaps a family quarrel or insult. The characteristic may be temporary and not typical. It may also be feigned for tactical reasons—in what Irving Goffman called the "presentation of self."

Is This a Matter of Principle or Precedent?

A final reason for different players having different USOs in the same situation is so common and so important as to warrant separate treatment. Often a player can consider an action or an occasion either as a relatively insignificant event or as a highly significant matter of principle or precedent or symbolism. Which perspective is adopted will determine much of the party's understanding of the significance of the occasion. And feigning one perspective or the other may be an important tactical move.

If all the relevant parties agree, at least tacitly, to forego finding a general category into which the occasion falls or can be placed and to address it only on its particular facts, those facts and their implications will be all that is significant about the occasion. If all the parties see the occasion as presenting differing challenges to principle or as creating new precedents of different sorts, or embracing one or another lasting symbol, those expressive characteristics will alter or magnify each of their understandings of the significance of the occasion. If one player adopts the latter perspective and demands correspondingly great deference to the weight of his concerns, the others may be able to deny that they see any matter of principle or precedent on this occasion and insist that this decision will not form part of any argument they make in the future.

Let me illustrate with two examples. The first is from the period that led up to the presidential election in 1980, when I headed the Criminal Division of the U.S. Department of Justice. A subcommittee of the Senate Judiciary Committee was scheduled to hold oversight hearings on the occasion of the annual bill authorizing the budget of the Department of Justice. Several reporters wanted to write about their criticisms of the actions of the Public Integrity Section of the Criminal Division—in particular, its decisions not to prosecute various government employees on a dozen or so occasions. They raised their interest with Republican Senator Orrin Hatch, who requested that the department send the head of the Public Integrity Section, Tom Henderson, to the hearings to be questioned about these decisions. Those oversight hearings had the political advantage to Republicans that, in an election year, the Carter administration might be made to look indifferent to corruption.

As head of the Criminal Division, I could have agreed to Henderson being questioned, for there was no strong tradition of refusing to allow oversight questioning of attorneys at the level of section chiefs. I would not be seen to be abandoning a precedent. Alternatively, I could have refused, basing my refusal on the principle that any regular oversight of career section chiefs, particularly about politically sensitive decisions, would interfere with the non-partisan professionalism that we expect of prosecutors handling the most sensitive of cases. I would then be asserting a principle weightier for the Department of Justice than any individual oversight hearing. In fact, I did fear that prosecutors would be inclined, over time, to adopt positions that they believed would minimize embarrassment at oversight hearings. And it seemed unfair. I would not, after all, allow the White House staff or even the President to cross-examine federal prosecutors on their decisions not to prosecute particular cases. As an option, somewhere in the middle, I could have found some messy mixture of accommodation and resistance that would be difficult to interpret as a precedent one way or another. For example, I could have testified myself, with Tom Henderson at my side to answer questions to which he could best respond.

For a number of reasons, only some of which were high principle about the independence of prosecutors from political pressures, I flatly refused to send Henderson up to testify, offering instead to be the one to testify on the reasons the Criminal Division declined to prosecute on those occasions. I was aware that I was using a principle—protecting the professionalism and political neutrality of prosecutors—as an important justification for my refusal to produce Henderson. I was raising my stakes. I was not aware that, in making that argument, I was also sharply changing for many senators *their* understanding of the significance for them of what would otherwise be a trivial occasion well below the level of matters that merited their interest.

My principle could be and was portrayed as a broad challenge to the oversight authority and responsibilities of Senate committees. Any such general challenge could, unless carefully limited, shift the balance of powers between the President and the Congress in an important way. That I intended the challenge to reach only to prosecutors of politically sensitive cases, such as those in the Public Integrity Section, would be and was lost. Those who wanted Henderson to attend would portray the scope of my claim as very wide in order to broaden the range of senators for whom the occasion would trigger relatively serious concerns.

Soon I found myself in a battle, first with Senators Orrin Hatch and Dennis DeConcini, then with seven or eight senators from both parties on the Judiciary Committee, and finally with many more. My assertion that certain prosecutors should not testify elicited a responsive demand that not only should they testify, but also that they should produce records of closed cases so that they could be more closely questioned about their decisions. Making closed-case files public posed a far more significant concern to the Department of Justice than the testimony of Tom Henderson or other section chiefs. My claim for immunity from testimony at oversight hearings for lower-ranking officials within parts of the Justice Department appeared to many senators to be broad enough to require or justify, as a Senate response, an unprecedented claim of congressional rights to prosecutorial files at oversight hearings. Meanwhile, to senators not on the committee, who eventually voted overwhelmingly to demand that we produce the files sought by Senator Hatch and Senator DeConcini, the Department of Justice looked like it was questioning the propriety of any Senate oversight.

Eventually we reached a compromise that limited but did not preclude access to files and under which Henderson would join me in testifying before the Committee about the questioned declinations of prosecution. The resolution was muddied. The issues were soon fought again by the Reagan administration. But my having made its principles and its precedential importance—rather than Henderson's testimony—into the "real" issue had magnified the significance of the occasion.

Symbolism can as surely give weight to concerns on an occasion, as can precedent or principle. Consider, again, the case of proposals for needle exchange to reduce HIV spread among addicts. States can fund needle exchange programs for drug addicts (by 2007 they all did), so federal funding was not even necessary for such programs to exist. Funding of needle exchange was unlikely to affect drug use to any significant degree, so it had little relevance as a measure of President Clinton's determination in the "war on drugs." But, wielded as a weapon in the political battles to "own" the drug issue, a proposal of federal funding for needle exchange could be, and was, of great symbolic importance. Opponents of the policy characterized the issue as whether or not the federal government wanted to help addicts use drugs. This understanding of the significance of the occasion magnified the importance for many of an issue that could as easily have been treated—as Donna Shalala wanted—as a technical matter.

There are effective counters to tactical moves intended to inflate the significance of an occasion into a matter of principle, precedent, or symbolism. Symbolic concerns operate in a different, expressive world. Dealing with them—changing symbolism—may not require changing the purely instrumental parts of a proposal. Professor Mark Kleiman of UCLA suggested, at the time of the needle exchange debate, that the supporters would have been well advised to divide the proposal into two parts: (1) an offer to buy dirty needles for cash (whose symbolism is *reducing* the availability of the paraphernalia needed for drug use by addicts); and (2) relaxing—as many states have—the rules prohibiting sale of new hypodermic needles (a sale that would not involve the federal government).

Precedential consequences and acceptance of an applicable principle that others must accommodate are both social facts, depending on a shared understanding that they are at stake. If the precedential significance of an occasion or the "principles" involved are invoked by another player to display her greater stake in the outcome, the answer may be a simple statement that you regard this case as special and different for reasons that are unlikely to recur. Still, deflating the significance of the occasion does not always work. Even President Reagan, the great communicator, was unable to persuade others that ending a policy of denying certain tax benefits to private schools that discriminated against black Americans was a technical decision based on the language of the Internal Revenue Code and thus consistent with staunch adherence by his administration to a principle of non-discrimination. Similarly, the Reagan administration failed to deflate a contention that a principle ("no concessions to terrorists") was at stake despite its efforts to obscure the departure by arranging for Israel to sell TOW missiles (which we would then replace) to Iran in exchange for Iran exercising its influence with Hezbollah to release several U.S. prisoners.

A Final Example

Let me end with a relatively rich example of the variety of difficulties in seeing and appreciating a difference in USOs. At the time of the investigation into the cause of death of the Deputy White House Counsel Vince Foster in 1993, my friend Bernie Nussbaum was White House Counsel and I, as Deputy Attorney General, was representing the Department of Justice as well as the investigative agencies. I insisted upon the ability of the investigators to review at least enough of Vince Foster's files to be sure that what was involved was a suicide (which we all believed). I could see no danger of revelation of private materials of the President if we set up a process that gave only a brief and very partial look at each file to two very senior and highly respected Justice Department attorneys. Although I acknowledged that for several reasons the Department did not have a legal right to see these files, I thought there was immense importance to preserving the appearance of lawfulness in determining the cause of death. In terms of symbols, the American public was entitled to see, unmistakably, that the Department of Justice did not shy away from an investigation involving the White House. More practically, without a completely credible investigation there would be endless investigations of the possibility of a "cover-up"—a needless and costly distraction for the President and a source of suspicion of the Department of Justice.

Under the unwritten "rules," I thought the nature of the investigation was, in any event, a decision to be made by the Department of Justice, not by the White House or even the President. In the back of my mind and in the minds of the investigators was playing a "tape" of Watergate and the scandal of presidential control of an investigation that involved the White House. Many precedents since had assured the Department of Justice of its control of investigative decisions involving high-level administration officials. So precedent was also on my mind.

Besides wanting to protect the reputation of the Department of Justice for independence, my USO included a belief about the USOs of the investigative agencies—that they would automatically suspect a White House cover-up and would use this occasion to place the new leaders in the Department of Justice in the camp either of those willing to cover up for the powerful or of those unwilling to accept anything other than a full and fair investigation. Principle, too, was at issue; and, of course, I felt my reputation for integrity was at stake.

I would have been prepared to discuss some of these considerations with Nussbaum; other considerations, I would not. But the pace of the occasion hardly encouraged discussion. As the action played out, I concluded that Nussbaum was violating the process rules that required, at a bare minimum, my consent to any process for handling the investigation; he was making or precluding critical investigative decisions in a unilateral and secret way. I couldn't or wouldn't easily discuss an accommodation in that context.

The USO of Nussbaum and the White House staff would have been strikingly different from mine. Grief at the loss of a splendid man and a dear friend, Vince Foster, would have affected the USOs of many in the White House. So would a pervasive sense of unjustified attacks on the President by his right-wing enemies. Nussbaum's sense of his legal role as White House counsel would cause him to narrowly define his range of concerns—limiting them to zealously defending his clients' interests so far as the law permitted. Part of this was his acute concern over precedent—protection of the evidentiary rules of executive privilege. Nussbaum also thought that, given the absence of a legal right of access to Foster's files, the applicable rule of decision was that the Chief Executive or someone acting on his behalf, and not the Justice Department, should decide for the executive branch how the investigation in the White House would be run.

As the President's attorney, Nussbaum was privy to parts of the factual background hidden from me. He may have heard from his clients that they sharply disapproved of his initial agreement that would allow two senior Justice Department lawyers to see limited parts of the files of Vince Foster, who was also the President's personal attorney. Nussbaum had to be concerned about his reputation for tough loyalty with the President and Mrs. Clinton, a highly valued personal resource. Some of these concerns he would have been prepared to discuss openly; others, he would not.

When framed in this way, the prospect of anything like a coordinated approach to a common problem seems unlikely. Indeed, the situation quickly degenerated into one of suspicion and conflict that lasted for many months. Trouble arises when the differences in USOs are unseen or are as widely and deeply based as these, especially where suspicion precludes accommodation.

6

Agendas and Windows of Opportunity

In the preceding chapters I have discussed the types of matters or "concerns" that can motivate each player in a decision about a policy for which he or she shares responsibility; and I have noted how a fuller description of a player's reaction to a proposal by another player could be called "the individual's understanding of the significance of the occasion" (his USO). The latter was illustrated by the range of USOs facing Michael Pillsbury and Fred Iklé as they sought to change U.S. policy *from* a plausibly deniable covert operation furnishing Eastern European weapons to the Mujahideen *to* one that would furnish state-of-the-art U.S. surface-to-air missiles, thereby giving up plausible deniability. The Joint Chiefs of Staff would oppose the proposal for its reasons, the State Department for other reasons, and the CIA for still others.

Pillsbury, like any policy entrepreneur, had two ways to convince these other players who, because of the effect of the proposal on their jurisdictions, would be entitled both to be consulted and to have an opportunity to appeal to a higher level to express any strong opposition to the Stinger missile proposal. With their concerns a given, he must seek to bring skeptical parties to agree that the Stinger proposal was desirable by changing their understanding of the significance of the occasion. This could be done by changing either their assessment of the proposal itself (or modifying it to make it more attractive to them) or their assessment of the effects of cooperation in the current situation on their future working relationships. But before taking either type of measure, he will want to assess how far he has to move each of them—how committed each has to be for Pillsbury's policy-choice purpose on this occasion.

Levels of Support and Opposition

Take two different measures of "level of support" for a proposal. The player may be simply satisfied enough that she is unprepared to oppose the initiative openly in light of its importance to its sponsor. A far higher standard of commitment to the proposal would be for a player to be enthusiastic enough to propose to authorize it under her own delegated authority and assigned responsibility, or to spend energy and resources to try to influence others to embrace it. I will call the former level of commitment "weak commitment" and the latter "strong commitment." At best, the commitment of the CIA to Pillsbury's proposal was, in the end, weak; the commitment of Hatch and Abramowitz was strong.

Corresponding to these measures of support are two different standards of opposition to the proposal that a party like the Joint Chiefs of Staff might adopt. Weak opposition would consist in simply being prepared to deny consent to the proposal and, if the sponsor persisted, to require any dispute about its adoption to be resolved at a higher level of responsibility. That "weak opposition" can be contrasted with the "strong opposition" manifested by a willingness to join or form an alliance against the proposal or otherwise to work actively and to commit resources to defeat it.

What level of support or opposition by a particular player is necessary for the adoption or defeat of a proposal depends on the responsibilities and roles the players have been given. If a party, like the CIA, has been delegated authority to decide a particular class of matters, the general rules of shared decision making provide that it can proceed if it can win even weak support from all the other parties entitled to participate. If it can bring the other necessary players to the point at which they are unprepared to assert a demand that the matter be taken to a higher level, the CIA can go forward. So William Casey, the Director of the CIA, could act, after consulting the other necessary players, unless there was at least a weak objection by one of them (or unless he has reason to know that his superior, President Reagan, would want to consider this matter himself or at least have an opportunity to consider it before Casey proceeded).

The problem is far different for Pillsbury (or his boss, Iklé). With no delegated authority over the missile issue, he must first find a party who has the authority to order the delivery of the Stinger missiles to the Mujahideen; then he must convince that party to a high enough level of enthusiastic commitment to warrant the party's assumption of personal and institutional responsibility for this controversial matter. In short, an essential problem for Pillsbury is to get his proposal on the action agenda of someone with delegated authority to decide such matters. He needs the "strong" commitment of at least one player who has authority to deliver Stinger missiles. (Perhaps he can make do with the strong commitment of someone like Senator Hatch, who can bring significant pressure to bear on at least one player authorized to decide and some pressure on those whose acquiescence is needed. But the risk of a secret coalition to obstruct will be very great in that case.)

Even then, Pillsbury will have to assist his champion in seeing to it that every necessary party at least acquiesces in the proposal—that is, that none registers even weak opposition to the proposal; and even obtaining access to the others will be difficult. He must follow the rules requiring consultation with all other necessary parties, hopefully winning their acquiescence; for even weak opposition from another player can require a shift to a higher-level decision maker.

Even if he fails to win universal acquiescence, it makes a difference to Pillsbury whether the opposition that remains is weak or strong and whether it is opposition by many or only a few. True, any opposition will send the matter to a new decision maker at a higher level. But the reasons for that higher level player deciding to reject the proposal will be much stronger if the opposition is widespread and passionate. So is the case for not deciding at all.

The First Hurdle: Crowded Agendas

Moving forward for Pillsbury requires getting on some very busy player's agenda of matters that she will take the time and effort to address. Only certain players in a bureaucracy—by virtue of their delegated responsibility for dealing with concerns that a proposal would affect or by reason of their control of resources that the proposal would use—have the power to put an item on some other player's action agenda, forcing a decision for or against the proposal. That presents Pillsbury with his first hurdle. Neither Pillsbury nor Abramowitz nor Hatch has this responsibility, authority, or control of resources.

The problem of even getting a hearing from each of the necessary players is not trivial. After trying for some time to develop support for furnishing the Stinger missiles to the Mujahideen in Afghanistan, Pillsbury was told by his boss Iklé to forget it. The bureaucratic and political problem, Iklé thought, was hopeless. In light of the likely opposition, no one would take the proposal seriously enough to consider acting. In discussing concerns and understandings of the significance of an occasion, I made it sound as if action required only congruence of the predictable consequences of a proposal with the concerns of those who are defined as decision makers or who have been given the right to participate. But the problem really is harder and starts earlier. For a variety of reasons, busy players do not quickly put on their agendas even a proposal that looks desirable to them.

In two circumstances, getting on the agenda is especially difficult. If a proposal seems to significantly and adversely affect the activities or responsibilities of one party, that party (for example, the Joint Chiefs) will not only oppose the step when it is under discussion, but will purposely avoid placing the item on its agenda. Denying a matter the time needed to consider it is often far easier to justify than making a case against the proposal on its merits. Most players are too busy to consider everything that others would like them to consider. Deciding only that there is no time to address a proposal does not reveal a preference or alienate needed supporters. There is generally no need to explain why a player declines to place a new item on her crowded agenda.

A second circumstance in which getting a proposal on the agenda is particularly difficult arises when what is sought from a busy player is active support, in the form of energy and resources, rather than simply acquiescence. Actively supporting an initiative which has impact beyond the player's own jurisdiction (i.e., making a personal investment in the processes of persuasion that are described in the following chapters) costs time, energy, and resources of influence. For this reason, President Ford's Attorney General, Ed Levi, is reputed to have announced that he would concentrate on only three initiatives while he was in office. Six may be possible; sixteen rarely are.

The reason is simple: the demands on a player's time and influence generally greatly exceeds the supply. To get the results he wants, a player must, at a minimum, spend time and energy to build support for himself and for his proposals. If the proposals are not self-effectuating, to turn them into results he must address the culture, management information systems, and incentives of the subordinates expected to implement the program. If he wants to institutionalize a direction or an activity, he must spend time shaping the organizational culture and convincing its external supporters. These costs are already present for each of a set of attractive proposals. Because the demand for time and resources of influence is far greater than the supply, the price of buying into a new initiative is high. If its benefits, however real, are not obvious, or if its risks, however contained, appear excessive, the easy reaction is not to respond, for or against, a proposal. Nor is there any point in investing in something that is unlikely to be adopted in the political system.

For all of these reasons, it is often far harder to get a proposal on another player's agenda of items that will consume attention, time, and resources of influence than it would be to get the other player to acquiesce and express casual approval of the proposal. Pillsbury will not be able to get the Director of the CIA, William Casey, to place the transfer of Stinger missiles on his agenda for decision because the CIA opposes the proposal and Casey has no particular desire to have to explain the reasons for his opposition, which include such unshared concerns as loyalty to his subordinates and worry about the future of the CIA. Even if Pillsbury had a direct line to President Zia of Pakistan (which he did not), he could not get Zia to furnish active support for the proposal because other matters were more pressing on Zia's crowded agenda.

Like food products that must find their way onto crowded supermarket shelves before they can be bought, proposals must find their way onto crowded agendas before they can compete in a marketplace of ideas. Many will never find their way there, even though they could be quickly agreed upon if addressed. In June 2005, almost four years after September 11, 2001, President Bush accepted on a single occasion 71 out of 74 recommendations of the Presidential Commission on the Intelligence Capabilities of the United States regarding Weapons of Mass Destruction. In the 46 months since the attack on the World Trade Center, these 71 proposals had not made their way onto the President's agenda of decisions, although by June 2005 they all looked desirable or at least potentially desirable.

Windows of Opportunity

John Kingdon's much acclaimed book *Agendas, Alternatives, and Public Policies* (2003) focuses on the development and passage of major legislation, but its lessons also apply to executive decisions. It can explain the

Bush administration's sudden acceptance of 71 recommendations by the Commission on intelligence failures leading up to the invasion of Iraq—proposals that previously could not make their way onto the President's agenda. *Agendas, Alternatives, and Public Policies* describes the policy process in a wonderfully accurate, highly counterintuitive way. According to Kingdon, policy agendas in general are not set by political leaders, recognizing a problem or an opportunity and then carefully analyzing (or having subordinates analyze) the situation in order to devise relevant proposals or options to solve the problem. Instead, numerous minor players are constantly engaged in the process of developing proposals designed for other purposes; some of these minor players, operating as so-called "policy entrepreneurs," lie in wait for occasions when their "pet proposals" may be plausibly linked—as a purported solution—to a problem that has suddenly become salient (perhaps because of a focusing event such as an airplane crash). Other times, action addressing the problem or opportunity to which the proposal is attached has suddenly become feasible because of a change in politics caused by players newly put into positions of authority by election, appointment, or seniority. The Democratic Congressional takeover in January 2007 changed the opportunities for "liberal" proposals and their advocates, at least in the House of Representatives.

In both cases, a new problem or opportunity causes political figures to seek anxiously for answers or options. Advocates of policies that were designed at earlier times for other purposes become perfect partners at that point. They have their pet proposals fully developed and ready. By adjusting their arguments to the suddenly salient need, they can compete for attention and a place on an agenda that is, at other times, far too busy to accommodate more than a small fraction of an extremely large set of proposals being offered to it. Even if an advocate might engage the attention of one busy player at another, less promising time, that player's energetic involvement would have been likely to depend upon his seeing that other necessary players, who are also busy, would support the proposal. On certain opportune occasions, he can expect his colleagues to have an unusually similar understanding of the significance of the occasion and thus to be also likely to give time to the matter.

The occasion itself, not the proposal alone, must move numbers of elected officials to see that they must or can "do something." At that point, they choose among a number of proposals, which were generally developed to deal with other problems or to exploit other opportunities, and which have been reshaped by their sponsors to appear to respond to the attention-getting problem or opportunity. The same proposal or solution can be offered to any number of problems. In Kingdon's words:

> In the policy stream, proposals, alternatives, and solutions float about being discussed, revised, and discussed again. In contrast to a problem-solving model, in which people become aware of a problem and consider a solution, solutions float around in and near government, searching for problems to which to become attached or political events that increase their likelihood of adoption.[1]

A proposal will be most successful when it is responsive both to a perceived problem and to the valued political opportunities of elected officials. That requires immense persistence by advocates. Kingdon notes that the most important quality of successful policy entrepreneurs is persistence: "a willingness to invest large and sometimes remarkable quantities of one's resources."

Both factors are at work in the case of Stinger missiles. A policy planning operation, like that which Iklé headed, is in the business of developing proposals and then trying to attach them to problems the administration recognizes or to political themes of the President. Unable to move the Stinger missile proposal forward at first, Iklé declares the effort hopeless and tells Pillsbury to work on something else. Then a problem arises and forces itself onto the agenda of all the necessary players: the Soviets deploy new and better trained troops and new and better armored helicopters to Afghanistan—a combination that leads many of the American players to think that the Mujahideen may be defeated. A political window opens at the same time. A number of members of Congress from both houses and both parties come to see the Mujahideen as David fighting the Goliath Soviet Union, all much to our benefit, and demand that more support flow to the rebels to meet the new threat. Simultaneously, State Department official Mort Abramowitz becomes a convert to the Mujahideen cause.

In short, a pressing problem and a political opportunity have together opened a window of opportunity, of just the sort that Kingdon describes with regard to legislative policy decisions, for any proposal that can strengthen the hands of the Afghan Mujahideen. The Stinger missile proposal satisfies that description admirably. It serves as an answer to a new problem and to new political demands for options and alternatives. This is not to say that tactics and energy will not be required to sell the

Stinger proposal; they were, and Pillsbury and Iklé provided them. But they also exploited a window of opportunity that any official lacking decision-making authority would need in order to get a proposal on the executive agenda.

There is one major difference between executive and legislative decisions that directly bears on the manner and speed in which items find their way onto crowded agendas. Just as the President can define the situation in a way that requires all his subordinates to accept it as part of their understanding of the significance of an occasion, so too can the President put an item on the agenda of all his subordinates. Once Iklé had convinced President Reagan to redefine the mission in Afghanistan far more aggressively than it had been defined under Carter, and once President Reagan included in his State of the Union the message that "America will support with moral and material assistance, [freedom fighters'] right not just to fight and die for freedom, but to fight and win freedom," the President had created for his national security advisers a problem (to see to it the Mujahideen won) and an accompanying political demand as well (to keep the President's commitment). This type of presidential action amounts to a mandate, putting any promising solutions on the agendas of even his busiest subordinates.

A Final Example

A visa is a permission granted by an American consulate abroad, in the form of a stamp in a foreigner's passport, generally allowing multiple visits to the United States over a given period of time, often six months. On the basis of that permission, an individual would almost always be admitted to the United States at the U.S. border by the Immigration and Naturalization Service, which would set the duration of his or her stay.

When I was Acting Administrator of the Bureau of Security and Consular Affairs in the Department of State during the Vietnam War, I was responsible for the office issuing visas to people from other countries visiting the United States. In that position I adopted the somewhat ideological path of my predecessor, Abba Schwartz, who believed that America's traditions and interests lay in encouraging the freest possible exchange of ideas and experiences with citizens of other nations. This meant that American citizens should be free to travel abroad with as few constraints and as little investigation as possible, and that citizens of other nations should be encouraged to come to the United States by making their travel as unencumbered as reasonably possible. I was not particularly interested in the economic effects of this policy, but rather I hoped and believed that highly desirable cultural and political results would follow from international exchanges.

One big step toward that goal would be to substitute a lifetime visa for the four- or five-year multiple entry visas to enter the United States that were currently the longest duration permitted. The lifetime visa would be denied to anyone who was considered dangerous. Nor would it be issued to citizens of any but the friendliest of countries. It would only be issued to citizens of the many countries that admitted Americans without any visa requirement—simply on the showing of an American passport.

Unlike Pillsbury or Iklé, I had the delegated authority to change the regulations that set the durations of visas. Still, under well-understood rules, I had a duty to consult with my peers whose activities or responsibilities could be affected by the new visa proposal. Moreover, the matter was too big to be done without the consent of the Secretary of State, Dean Rusk. He would want to explore whether creating such a visa would revive heated liberal/conservative fights over the security of our borders at a time when we were at war with a Communist nation and its allies, and when he needed conservative support for that war. The relative unimportance of this politically risky matter, when no new problem was demanding an immediate decision, would clearly keep it off his very crowded agenda.

I could try to see Representative Michael A. Feighan, D-Ohio, the very conservative Chair of the Immigration Subcommittee of the House Judiciary Committee. His support would greatly reduce the political risks to the administration. But I would have little chance of winning a level of his support sufficient for him to put the matter on his agenda (much less that of his subcommittee) in competition with the other matters closer to his concerns. Even the head of the Immigration and Naturalization Service (INS) would be cool to my proposal. While creating as open a society as possible in terms of travel was high on my set of concerns, it would be quite low among the concerns of Secretary of State Rusk and Representative Feighan and those administering the present system. There was no reason for me to press hard for a lifetime visa in that unpromising context.

Then President Johnson announced that the administration and the nation had a problem that he was determined to address: a balance of payments "crisis" resulting from our massive expenditures in Vietnam. Not knowing what steps the United States might be able to take or, politically, what might "appear" to be an answer, the President appointed a committee within the administration to look for solutions to the balance of payments problem. He created, in other words, a window of opportunity for anyone who had proposals that might seem to be helpful to our balance of payments. I quickly understood the significance of this occasion. Representative Feighan would hesitate to oppose whatever might help President Johnson solve a national problem. Secretary Rusk would take some risks to help with the balance of payments crisis and its political cost to the administration. My proposal—designed for very different reasons—could plausibly encourage travel to the United States; and, to the extent that it did, the proposal would reduce our balance of payments deficits. At least all of this was plausible, if not very promising in terms of the actual problem.

Suddenly, my proposal could find its way easily onto the agenda of Representative Feighan and Secretary of State Rusk. Its priority had been raised immensely by the President's recognition of the seriousness of the balance of payments problem and the salience he had given it (just as the 74 proposals of President George W. Bush's Commission on the Intelligence Capabilities of the United States would appear as an answer to President Bush's embarrassment over flawed intelligence that led us into the Iraq war). It would also be viewed sympathetically throughout the administration and Congress by those whose even weak opposition might otherwise block it. The President himself had recognized a problem and made a commitment to work toward its solution. That created windows of opportunities for proposals, born of other purposes, at least to find their way onto the agendas of powerful actors and, likely, to find no opposition once they were there.

Within weeks, in response to the unrelated need for proposals to help with our balance-of-payments problem, all the parties whose strong or weak support the rules required if I were to extend the life of our visas were prepared to address an issue they had previously ignored. Soon we had agreed to extend the life of a visa so President Johnson could show one additional step he was taking to solve a balance-of-payments crisis.

7

Influencing Others

Although only one of the several possible decision makers will exercise ultimate decision-making authority over the Stinger matter, President Reagan's decision will be determined in large part by a set of influences purposely brought to bear on him. In a sense, then, the ultimate decision in the Stinger Missile Case is made not only by President Reagan but also by Michael Pillsbury, many layers below the President, and by a number of players in between.

Pillsbury has, and in fact uses, three broad avenues to influence the decisions of those sharing responsibility for the matter. He can, and does, change the proposal to make it less threatening and more promising in terms of the various concerns of the other players. Thus, we watch as he persuades CIA Director William Casey to offer assurances to the Joint Chiefs of Staff that the operation will be carefully designed to provide only a limited number of Stinger launchers to the Mujahideen at first, with additional missiles provided only in exchange for expended ones. Amended in this way, the proposal to furnish Stinger missiles greatly reduces the Joint Chiefs' concern that large numbers of missiles will find their way into the hands of potential terrorists.

Second, Pillsbury or others can affect the character and intensity of the concerns of other players through carefully choosing the timing of the proposal or by taking actions that change the situation in which the proposal's effects will be assessed by the players. Thus part of the CIA's opposition to furnishing the Stinger missile is based on its desire to maintain the plausible deniability of this long-lasting covert action. But that concern becomes irrelevant after someone makes public the nature of our involvement in the Soviet/Afghan struggle. Whoever disclosed that "secret" information about the hitherto covert CIA involvement in Afghanistan largely ended the element of the CIA's opposition that was motivated by the desire to keep the U.S. role secret (and thus keep the CIA in charge). Adoption of Pillsbury's proposal would no longer cost the CIA its plausible deniability, for that had already been lost anyway.

Finally, Pillsbury can use his own resources of influence, or bring other players to use their resources of influence, upon the ultimate decision maker and those to whom he turns. If his proposal is to be on the agenda for President Reagan to accept or reject, Pillsbury must seek to assure either that none of Reagan's trusted advisers and supporters are prepared to oppose it (making it unnecessary for the President to resolve a contested issue) or that the potential opponents are more than offset in numbers, strength of conviction, and potential influence with President Reagan by those who are prepared to support the proposal.

While "level of commitment" is critical if there is opposition, other factors will matter. Thus, we see that Pillsbury is interested both in the resources of influence that supporting and opposing parties enjoy *and* how committed players are in terms of their willingness to use those resources. Pillsbury understands, of course, that whatever the balance of resources and commitment, if the ultimate decision maker (President Reagan in this case) has a strong personal belief one way or the other, that may be more than enough to tilt the scales (though even a strong commitment is hard to hold if a substantial number of your advisers and supporters see the issue very differently and feel strongly about that difference).

How does one player exercise influence on another? What resources of influence do various players have? Although Pillsbury may ask and answer this question intuitively, there is also a systematic way of addressing it.

By an individual's "resources of influence," I mean whatever makes it possible for the individual to change the responses of another player to a specific proposal under consideration. Resources thus describe a relationship between specific parties. One player (X) may enjoy the influence that flows from another's (Y's) gratitude for a past favor, from Y's hope for a future benefit, or from Y's trust in X's judgment. Any of these might give X great influence with Y, but may still leave X powerless with regard to Z, who may occupy a position with far less prestige and authority than that of Y. A powerful committee chair may have great influence with the

Head of the Park Service but little with a Park policeman. The Secretary of Defense has many resources with regard to millions of individuals, organizations, and even states, but he may have little capacity to change the actions of a minor official at the Food and Drug Administration or in the Department of Justice.

Resources of Influence

The capacity to influence another player—one's fund of resources of influence—is best identified by beginning with the ways that one player can affect the actions of another. Setting aside the two broad situational strategies mentioned previously—redesigning the proposal and changing the setting—there are six forms of personal influence: (1) authority, (2) persuasion, (3) bargaining, (4) centrality or appeal to the need for coordinated leadership, (5) reciprocity and loyalty or friendship, and (6) what may be called moral authority. Each of these forms of influence depends on certain conditions existing in the relationship between players. The needed conditions describe certain characteristics or capacities which constitute "resources of influence." Let me illustrate.[1]

1. Authority

Any player can, within limits, take it for granted that another player will regard an authoritative decision or order of his superior as a directive from which he is not free to depart. The negotiators in Geneva seeking a peaceful settlement of the Soviet/Afghan conflict must obey the President. It is possible, however, to exaggerate the importance of authoritative directions. Very few orders are so specific that they do not allow discretion; ambiguity leaves room for choice. Especially when the directive is less than clear, much may depend on the attitude of the subordinate to the superior and to orderly process within a bureaucracy. If the subordinate questions the motivations and wisdom of the superior and doubts the importance of reliable action in this case, only the chance of detection and the prospect of sanctions will cause him to follow the directive. The military services, in a famous example, did not feel called upon to remove strategic missiles from their bases in Turkey at the direction of President Kennedy. Nonetheless, the authority of a superior position remains a powerful form of influence.

Other authoritative rules can be just as binding as the claims of hierarchy. The clearest examples involve legislative or constitutional mandates. Any player can invoke, even in discussion with a president, a constitutional rule or a statute that seems to require or forbid a particular action in a specific situation. Even President Bush would have hesitated to take the steps he did with regard to statutorily unauthorized electronic surveillance or apparently legislatively prohibited detention of Americans as part of the conflict with Al Qaeda without a certification by the Department of Justice that his actions were legal. In the Stinger missile case, Pillsbury advises President Zia that the law forbids an informal transfer of U.S. missiles from Pakistan to the Afghans. If the law is moderately clear on a given point, officials cannot afford to ignore it. Public and congressional attitudes toward clear violations of the law are so certain and so infused with the prospect of political sanctions that rarely can a legal duty be openly avoided.

The courts play a special role in the area of legal authority. A judicial decision forbidding or requiring some form of administrative action provides a powerful inducement even if there is no threat of enforcement by judicial sanctions. The risk of political sanctions for disobedience are just too great. Nixon delivered the Watergate tapes, although the courts had no armies. President Bush has not directly challenged Supreme Court decisions limiting his freedom in handling and trying detainees. As I have noted, the authorized executive branch interpreter of legal rules shares this influence, especially when matters are not subject to judicial review. Lawyers in government often claim expertness in, and enjoy the prerogative of, interpretation of judicial decisions, statutes, treaties, and the Constitution. Thus the general counsel of a department has authority over the head of the department when the lawyer can argue convincingly that an action is legally forbidden or required.

One final form of authority deserves mention. When a role in government decision-making is played by a group or individual too busy to decide for itself or himself what matters to attend to, consider, and act upon, someone else must be given the authority to set the agenda. A person authorized to determine what proposals others shall consider can obviously affect their decisions by denying them the opportunity to act on certain matters. In the Stinger case, someone must control the agenda of the Policy Review Group of the National Security Council and of the top-level National Security Planning Group, and with that control comes the power to prevent the consideration of some matters.

2. *Persuasion*

Even if he is clear about his concerns, a player is seldom certain how he should respond to a particular proposal. The relationship of the proposal to his views of the national interest is often obscure because he does not possess determinative facts and because understanding the relationship of any facts to his views may require more time, skill, or effort than he has available. The impact of the proposal on interested constituent groups or on his organization may be unclear. Even his personal stakes in acquiescence or refusal are frequently hard to decipher. Needing help with each of these questions, a player invites and relies upon the counsel of others whom he trusts and who can provide facts and analysis or simply conclusions. Persuasion is thus a second general way to influence the response of other players. It requires a number of resources.

To start with, persuasion requires access to the player to be persuaded. Access, in turn, can be based on organizational position, on friendship or the provision of past support, on the needs of cooperative interaction in this or other situations, on a recognized congruity of attitudes and beliefs, on reputation and surely on other bases as well. As a policy adviser to the Secretary of Defense, Fred Iklé's access to decision makers in agencies other than DOD depended in part on his membership in a powerful executive committee as policy planner for the Department of Defense. Pillsbury's access to Senator Orrin Hatch was based on personal history, friendship, shared beliefs, and the usefulness to each of an alliance. Access is a crucial resource that cannot be taken for granted and that can be broadened and deepened over time.

The importance of access as a resource is recognized in the rules that prohibit its use in certain circumstances. A subordinate (for example, someone working for Morton Abramowitz at State) cannot ask for direct access to a superior (Undersecretary of State Michael Armacost) of his immediate superior (Abramowitz) except in unusual circumstances. Similarly, a bureaucratic player is generally expected not to seek access to interested public groups or legislators in an effort to influence his superiors. While Pillsbury appears to violate this rule with some impunity (and is poorly regarded by some major players, no doubt partly for this reason), presidents have gone so far as to fire Cabinet members who violate this unwritten command. The phenomenon of subordinates in the executive branch "leaking" sensitive information (a phenomenon that has tormented every recent administration) is an attempt to secretly obtain this forbidden access.

Granting access is costly for a time-pressed player. High-level officials do not have the time to hear and resolve all matters that others would like them to act upon. Indeed, they generally lack even the time to decide what matters they should personally address. To deal with this last problem, they need and use staff resources to determine what matters they should and should not attend to and when. (As I have noted, this authority to decide who will enjoy what opportunity for persuasion, and when, is itself an important determinant of government action, and those who are given this authority by busy officials are given a major bargaining resource.)

Access is necessary but not sufficient for an exercise of influence through persuasion. Some measure of trust in the player's honesty is also necessary, and this often requires a reputation for trustworthiness built up over time. Trust also requires a conviction that the adviser has no undisclosed self-interest in the action he is urging. Pillsbury lacks trust with, for example, Armacost, who regards him as self-interested and manipulative; Abramowitz enjoys Armacost's absolute trust, built up over his long career in government.

Abramowitz's reputation for honesty is not sufficient for persuasion. Without a reputation for having a special knowledge of the relevant facts, a more general expertness in the area, or at least an unusual ability to analyze and clarify the issues in terms of the other person's beliefs and attitudes, a player has little to offer others in the way of help. Abramovitz's influence with a number of players who listen to his views on national security matters depends in part upon his knowledge and expertise in the areas of political/military relations and Soviet affairs. It depends even more on confidence in his capacity to analyze the relevant facts and choices. Each of these prerequisites of a power to persuade ("resources of persuasion") can be based in large part on having competent staff resources who can develop and analyze the facts more intelligently and completely than other players will.

Trust in Abramowitz's analytic capacity requires something more than raw intelligence: a demonstrated openness and responsiveness to evidence and argument. If such things as a player's personal concerns or his needs for admiration or reassurance or respect are thought likely to interfere with an open-minded response to the evidence and to arguments based upon that evidence, others will be reluctant to rely on him. This familiar reality has important implications for the force and effect of persuasive argument—for its capacity to change actions. Every player knows there is a real cost to holding stubbornly to a position that others consider indefensible or incomprehensible. When Pillsbury can show the Joint Chiefs of Staff that the Soviets already have the blueprints for the Stinger missile, even if they still oppose the proposal they can no longer rely publicly on their concern that theft of Stingers may empower the Soviets. When Casey proposes a system that is supposed to (but did not) limit the number of Stinger missiles in the hands of potential terrorists at any one time, the Joint Chiefs have to acknowledge that this concern is greatly diminished. When Pillsbury can assure the Chiefs that any Stingers given can rapidly be replaced in the production process, they no longer have a defensible concern about the availability of Stingers for their own use. Among the reasons for opposition to the Stinger proposal that are understandable and acceptable by the other players, including particularly the President, the Joint Chiefs have been left with practically nothing. The Joint Chiefs can stubbornly insist on their opposition to the proposal only at the expense of a resource every player treasures: a reputation for giving advice based on open-minded consideration of factors that the other players also take seriously.

The costs of stubbornly defending the indefensible can be avoided by superiors who are not always expected to account to their subordinates for decisions. The situation is in fact still more complicated. There is no loss of resources of influence if an actor is not pressed to account for his decisions or recommendations—if he need not give his reasons and arguments. Having to give such an account is one of the major constraints on the power of appellate judges in the United States and of trial judges in much of the rest of the world. Not having to explain and thus not having to bear the resource costs of an unpersuasive argument is itself one of the resources that superiors enjoy in dealings with subordinates (along with the authority to demand actions and define situations).

A great power of the FBI is the power to investigate without explaining why. A great power of a committee chair is to set the agenda of the committee without explaining why. Both are substantially the same as the power of the understanding that superiors can make decisions without accounting for them to subordinates. Indeed, if the subordinate presses too hard for an explanation, his conduct will be regarded (sensibly in terms of the superior's maintenance of power) as insubordination.

The persuading player may find his influence limited if he does not know, or is not able to show that he knows, the likely reactions of other players important to the person he is trying to influence, or if he does not know the personal, political, and organizational impact of his proposal on that person. There are many dimensions to the concerns of the people whom Pillsbury must influence. They are concerned with aspects of the ultimate outcome as diverse as maintaining their own resources to influence others, building their organizations, and getting elected. For example, Pillsbury can see and point out to the President and to the members of Congress the political benefits of support for the Afghans based on sympathy for their courage in fighting the mighty Soviet Goliath.

Finally, there is a part of trust that goes beyond a reputation for honesty and is based on either an unquestioned loyalty to the other player's self-interest or a substantial congruence of stakes with respect to a proposal; it is a powerful resource that can be sufficient to determine the response of the other player if he is busy with other matters. Abramowitz enjoys this resource in his relationship with Armacost. Pillsbury seems totally without the benefits of this form of trust. That, too, makes a difference.

3. *Bargaining*

Players can and do exercise influence upon each other's actions without reliance on authority or the capacity to persuade. One of the principal remaining devices is the implicit or explicit promise of future benefit or the threat of future harm that is often available to one or more players. President Zia's willingness to take the political risks at home and the military risks from the Soviets of delivering a transparently American weapon, the Stinger, for use against Soviet helicopters depended on the U.S. first furnishing Pakistan with that advanced weapon. But this example is obvious and familiar. Other types of bargaining assets are almost too varied for description, for they represent the control of any private or public resources that can meet or frustrate any of the needs of other political actors for accomplishing goals, building influence, or maintaining and improving their positions.

The President's staff, for example, controls access to the President that is needed for a persuasive effort to affect his use of authority. That control is a powerful resource for bargaining with those who need that access. A determined committee chairman can block or delay legislation wanted by the President; and the President can campaign in, and direct federal expenditures or campaign aid to or from, the legislator's state or district.

One executive branch official can assist another in difficult circumstances or he can refuse. A powerful Republican senator like Hatch can go out of his way to help or subtly harm CIA Director Casey in any number of ways, although he is restrained in part by the bargaining assets that Casey can use in response.

Not far beneath the surface of any discussion between political players lies a shared recognition of the capacity of each to affect directly or indirectly what is important to the other's views of his personal welfare or that of his organization, groups that are important to him, or to the nation. But a player's capacity alone does not shape the decisions of others. They must and will also consider the likelihood that the player will use the resources available to him to reciprocate, with benefits or interference, their helpful or harmful actions. A reputation for effectiveness with regard to a willingness and determination to reciprocate is a distinct resource that, combined with the capacity to help or harm, confers influence. Rarely are such considerations made explicit or related directly to a particular proposal, but they always influence the context of relationships over time, going far toward defining the deference that will be paid to the views and wishes of a player who will be involved in shared choices again and again.

4. Centrality

A fourth method of influence is closely related to authority and persuasion. Occupying a central position—a natural center for coordination—in any area in which governmental or organizational policy would obviously be harmfully fragmented in the absence of voluntary deference to the lead of a single responsible actor or organization is an important source of influence. It is like the influence spontaneously awarded to even a private citizen who undertakes to sort out a sudden gridlock of traffic. The sensed need for national unity and consistency in national defense creates a far heavier congressional presumption in favor of the President's views on major national security issues than on domestic issues. The need and the presumption are greatest in times of war but are barely less so on the occasion of great power negotiations. The need for a single voice in such negotiations requires even the President to give discretion to the centrally located negotiators. That is the power of the State Department team in Geneva, seeking some compromise between the Soviets and the Mujahideen. But, again, the concept is far more general than these dramatic examples.

The obligatory force that players attribute to directives of a bureaucratic superior is largely habitual, socially or organizationally reinforced, and unconsidered. In part, however, it is based on the legitimacy that flows from a recognition that only a coordinated effort can be truly effective in any policy area and that the superior is better situated to provide the necessary coordination by virtue of her broader view of relevant concerns and her clear accountability to elected, ultimately responsible superiors. That is, for example, much of the power of a dean over a tenured faculty. In many situations, players who are not hierarchic superiors of those they wish to influence can nonetheless invoke the same claims of legitimacy.

Thus the force of claims based on the centrality of a particular official's responsibilities with regard to a particular issue carries over with significant effects to relations among peers. Much of the influence, on the floor, of the House or Senate Intelligence Committees flows from the persuasive power of their claim to a deeper understanding of matters within their jurisdiction, such as covert assistance to the Mujahideen. But a committee often receives additional deference, even by those who are unpersuaded by the members' expertise, because others recognize the benefits of consistent and coordinated legislative actions and of centralized accountability in a specialized area, particularly if it involves national security. The same is true for executive branch officials with daily responsibilities for a program, like the CIA station chief in Pakistan. Moreover, a committee (or an official) can be expected to fight to maintain its reputation for competence and control with regard to matters central to its jurisdiction. The two effects are complementary to each other. The personal stakes warn that, in areas of his central responsibilities, a player will not easily give in to the views of others to avoid stalemate. At the same time, arguments based on the wisdom of deference to whichever organization or committee is best situated to provide badly needed coordination, consistency, and accountability suggest a sensible and face-saving basis for resolving such policy disputes.

Centrality as a source of influence comes into play in two different contexts: in terms of who speaks authoritatively regarding the impact of a proposal on particular concerns, and in terms of whose views carry the most weight when differing concerns suggest different government actions. The former is well illustrated in the Stinger missile case by the influence of the Joint Chiefs of Staff in assessing the risks of losing exclusive control of the Stingers. The skepticism of a clear majority of the

Joint Chiefs as to the desirability of exposing the United States to these particular risks carried the full weight of their central responsibility for fighting wars.

Equally important is the effect of centrality when differing concerns compete to control choice. No one short of the President is a common superior of the Assistant Secretary of Defense responsible for production of Stinger missiles and of the Assistant Secretary of State responsible for diplomacy in South Asia, as well as of the directorate of the CIA responsible for overseeing the provision of weapons to the Afghan Mujahideen. Yet important responsibilities of each overlap in this case, and their views differ. One player may look at arms sales in terms of defense needs; another in terms of relations with other nations; the third in terms of a capacity to conduct covert operations. A disagreement about most matters will not be worth the President's time, and it is likely to be beyond his technical competence. In this situation, one player or organization must defer to another or (like Barry McCaffrey in the needle exchange case) bear the costs of forcing a dispute on major Cabinet-level officers, often about a matter that should not occupy their time.

If both parties, though disagreeing on the merits, can see that each has a reasonable position, it is often natural to defer to the one whose jurisdiction includes formal responsibility for routinely deciding similar matters in the absence of any objection from the other—in this case the CIA. If that in turn is uncertain, the dispute is likely to be resolved by giving jurisdiction to the party whose regular operating responsibilities are more directly involved and more in danger of disruption. The assignment of jurisdiction over a matter to a particular committee by the party leadership in the House is crucial in determining the power of competing legislative committees, and this too is a decision often made in terms of the relationship of the matter to the central operating responsibilities of the various contenders. The committee that routinely processes similar matters can more credibly claim the right to handle the proposed legislation, with extremely important consequences for the ultimate outcome.

5. Reciprocity and Loyalty

Not every proposal is assessed in terms of its consequences for the player, his organization, or his view of societal needs; and few are assessed completely in such a calculating way. Government players, like everyone else, obtain much of their joy in life and work, their self-esteem, and their sense of community from cooperative relationships with others. Recognition of the claims of reciprocity and loyalty is the condition of being and feeling oneself a member of a team. When a valued coworker, friend, or ally approaches with a proposal, the valued relationship may provide not only access but also cooperation, at least in that high proportion of cases where not much else turns for the player approached on his choice of position with regard to the proposal. Thus, being in a relationship where one can assert claims of reciprocity and loyalty is itself an important resource of influence. Having done favors for or shown loyalty to another creates obligations that are resources.

The purely personal quickly becomes merged with long-term working relationships that dictate cooperative reactions for reasons that relate to the future as well as the past. Superiors, like Casey, often exchange trust for the personal loyalty of subordinates in a context of friendship. The resulting relationship creates felt obligations on the part of each to further the purposes of the other. Players with interlocking interests or with common views of the national interest become friends as they recognize the benefits of standing together on any proposal that one feels strongly about and the other does not. In effect, they have formed an alliance that creates influence for each with the other.

Much depends on whether the policy area has become a recognized battlefield of competing interests or is generally felt to be an area for sensibly working out differences among government colleagues who share very similar views and complementary interests. If the understanding is that competition is unrestrained and the stakes are high, the demands of loyalty to allies in any contest are great. This was the feeling among the camps of those supporting and opposing making the Stinger missile available to the Mujahideen. In a different context—if there is not unrestrained competition but rather anunderstanding that all are working together to find a sensible means to accomplish shared ends—friends and allies will be under far less pressure to accept particular policy positions, both because the policy skeptics are also owed consideration and because long-term alliances are far less important.

6. *Moral Authority*

Moral issues of a variety of sorts are one of the areas of concern that can affect almost any player. Victims of palpable injustice enjoy a moral authority that is likely to provide access to even busy players. Thus the representatives of the families killed in the terrorist attacks on September 11, 2001, could insist on meetings to press their reform proposals on powerful members of Congress and White House staff. Their moral authority—and not any other claim to influence—also made unacceptable presidential resistance to the formation of an investigatory commission and resistance to the creation of a new office they demanded: Director of National Intelligence.

In the case of the Stinger missiles, those speaking on behalf of the Afghans killed or maimed fighting our common Soviet enemy with inadequate equipment enjoyed the advantages of media and legislative resonance with that sacrifice, and concern that it not be in vain. Within the U.S. government, Mort Abramowitz and President Reagan shared this concern and were motivated to act accordingly. Finally, and importantly, the elevation of the Mujahideen cause to an issue of national morality tended to disempower technical or jurisdictional arguments cutting against the proposed transfer of the Stinger.

Changing the Setting That Another Player Faces by a Fait Accompli

A final way of influencing other players is simply to change the situation they face in order to change what they believe is an appropriate action. One way to accomplish that is a leak to the press, thereby precluding the possibility of the players taking, or failing to take, an action without facing public or congressional scrutiny and opposition. As soon as the proposal to send Stinger missiles to the Mujahideen becomes public—as soon as our previously secret pipeline of military aid is exposed—the costs in public disapproval for elected officials of withholding a critical weapon such as the Stinger missile escalate sharply. The revelation of escalatory moves involving Soviet troops and weapons has the same effect. In the case of the indefinite visa I discussed in Chapter 6, my decision to create a visa that was valid in most cases for ten years would, I knew, radically change the context of my later efforts to persuade others, including my powerful subordinate in the Passport Office, that Americans too should enjoy a document (a passport) valid for ten years. The spy who gave the design of the Stinger missile to the Soviet Union did not know he was thereby changing the situation for the Joint Chiefs of Staff and so winning their agreement to make it available against Soviet helicopters in Afghanistan. But he did.

Every player (X) decides her position with regard to a set of proposals by considering their consequences in the present situation for the nation, for the jurisdiction she represents, for her organization, and for her own concerns, including prominently her resources of influence. As a tactic, changing the situation X faces operates in much the same way as trying to persuade a player to understand the situation differently or threatening to change a relationship between players. Someone trying to influence X's attitude and actions can do this by changing the situation that brought her concerns into play. (The rules of the game may, of course, preclude a player from taking any action that sharply changes the situation for other players until after they have collectively arrived at a decision.)

Chains of Influence

The game of exercising influence personally—not through changing the proposal or changing the setting in which it is considered—would be relatively simple if it merely involved categorizing the resources that policy actors like Pillsbury have for exercising influence, in any of the above six ways, on ultimate decision makers like President Reagan. The complexity of the decisions that Pillsbury faces comes from the fact that he can and should seek to influence other players who are not themselves the decision maker, but who have resources of the sorts I just described with regard to the decision maker or with regard to still others who can influence the decision maker. In short, part of what Pillsbury must do is to seek to influence others to use their influence.

Indeed, the game is somewhat more complicated than even this suggests, for it is not limited to the necessary players—those who would have a claim that a unilateral decision could disrupt their decisions and responsibilities. Pillsbury can and does reach out to anyone who might have influence with that much smaller group of essential players. For example, he encourages a powerful senator, Orrin Hatch, to use his influence with the Director of the CIA, William Casey, in an effort to offset the influence on Casey being exercised by his subordinates in the Directorate of Operations. This is a quite short and direct chain of influence. Another path for using Hatch to reach Casey is far longer. It goes from Pillsbury to Hatch; from Hatch to the Chinese government; from the Chinese government to President Zia; and from Zia, by the way of a report from Pillsbury and Hatch, to CIA Director Casey. Zia's wishes can affect Casey, the Chinese can affect Zia, and Hatch can influence the Chinese to influence Zia—at least if Pillsbury can influence Hatch.

The chain in the State Department is not quite as long but is still notable for its complexity. Pillsbury influences Mort Abramowitz, who influences Armacost, who uses his resources to influence Shultz. Meanwhile, U.S. Senators are using their influence on Shultz. All of this is to offset the influence of those in the State Department who deal with the Soviet Union or Pakistan, and who are generally resistant to the Stinger proposal.

There is, theoretically, an optimal order in which Pillsbury should approach individuals to create a chain of influence. It depends on both the likelihood that he can persuade each of them and the influence that each, if persuaded, may have on others whose support Pillsbury needs. The sequence makes a difference. He should not necessarily approach first those who are most likely to be influenced by his resources. Imagine, for example, that to win President Reagan's support Pillsbury believes he must recruit both player X, who he is 70 percent likely to persuade, and player Y whose support he is only 50 percent likely to win. Because he needs both and because X and Y may be influenced by what the other does, he must consider how likely he is to get the second if he already has persuaded the other. If X cares a great deal about what Y does, the chance of getting X may grow to 90 percent if Y has already been persuaded—creating a probability of getting both that is .45 (.5 × .9) if Pillsbury approaches Y first. If Y, on the other hand, is totally indifferent to what X does, Pillsbury's chance of getting both is only .35 (.7 × .5) if he approaches X first.

Each new recruit brings not only his own influence on the final decision maker but also his influence on others whose resources in turn can affect the final decision maker. It is that combination of benefits which make it worthwhile, for example, for Pillsbury to recruit Director Casey at an early stage, for Casey's views will not only influence President Reagan, but will also be important to Secretary of Defense Weinberger, whose views are also important to Reagan.

So far we have looked at coalition formation as if it were the occupation of only one party on one side: Pillsbury pressing for the Stinger missile. If the Directorate of Operations in the CIA had been organizing opposition, it would have developed countermoves for each of these ways of exercising influence as well. But since Pillsbury faced no organized opposition, discussion of conflict among competing coalitions is best saved for a later chapter.

Part II
Loyalty and Respect

8

Trust and Loyalty, Leadership and Respect

I have now laid out the pieces that a policy entrepreneur needs to press her proposal effectively by shaping it, timing it, or using her resources of influence and those of others.

The understood rules, enforceable by a refusal to cooperate, if not by a reprimand, tell our entrepreneur who are the necessary parties and who are the optional parties that may (or may not) be called upon to influence them. How a party will react depends upon the concerns of the sort I have described and upon how the shape and timing of the proposal or the enthusiasm of its supporters and opponents affect those concerns. But to make the connection among the proposal, these forms of tactics, and the ultimate concerns, our entrepreneur has to understand how each player views the part of his world the proposal and its supporters will affect—*what that player understands is the significance of the occasion for him.*

Crucially, how much difference one player's views makes to another depends on the "resources" that each player has to influence the others (as well as his determination and skill in using them). Arising out of the fact that the players interact over time and about a variety of issues, resources are whatever it takes to use the six or seven ways one player can affect another's decisions. Preserving and building them is a major concern of every player.

I have so far been descriptive, not prescriptive, about policy choice in government. As we shall see, there are dangers as well as advantages for our government from the form of decision making I have described. The danger is that the parochial interests of the players or the distortions in their understandings of the situation that comes from their limited viewpoints and their narrow concerns may create agreement on a decision that a higher-level decision maker with a broader viewpoint would reject. The benefit of the process is the energy and imagination that it generates from many participants from many levels, subject to the at least partially adequate checks of a clearance system.

It would be easier and clearer for the reader if I now moved directly to the applicability of the factors I have described in the Stinger missile case to the domestic cases discussed in Part III (and the reader may choose to do this). But there are two powerful and almost invisible forces which interact in complicated ways with the pieces that I have just described: loyalty and respect. My job in Part II is to make them visible, in all their power, as they are to every political actor. In some ways, they overlap with the resources I have described. Both loyalty and respect, for example, can be conditions of persuasion. But they also play a less obvious and more pervasive role in government decision-making. So I will turn to them in the next two chapters.

There has been something missing in my description of a totally fragmented policy process where politics competes with hierarchy. In any real process, it is more often teams rather than individual players who play a particular role and work on a variety of problems over a period of time. Michael Pillsbury and Fred Iklé were such a team. Pillsbury could not have worked the system as he did without the constant backing of his boss, Iklé. *Together*, not individually, they were addressing a variety of problems stretching over time. Those in the State Department could be conceived of as another, larger team; so too could those working on Afghanistan in the CIA and the military.

Two changes occur if we address individual roles in these terms, recognizing that they are played in smaller or larger teams. First, any team, from baseball to policy making, demands loyalty to each other and to the organization they share. Second, the leadership within a team is only partially based on authority (like the subordinate/superior relationship of Pillsbury and Iklé) or on other discrete resources of influence. In large part leadership is based on levels of respect that create implicit understandings about who should do what. These understandings become a partial substitute for formal rules about who has the right to be consulted or to decide. Indeed, within ongoing teams what I shall call "respect" also determines how much weight should be given to different members in deciding what to do and how to do it. In other words, within teams a system parallel to that described in Part I is working simultaneously, using earned "respect."

The reasons that leadership tends to follow respect in a team are varied. In part it is because even if Y, who is most respected in dealing with a particular aspect of a team's decision, is a direct subordinate of X, maintaining the loyalty and cooperation of the team to which they both belong may require X to give even greater weight than he normally would to Y's recommendations. Beyond that, many teams are made up of members of a variety of organizations with no shared, central authority; so respect takes over in the gap. In the Stinger missile case, for some period the Joint Chiefs of Staff and the career members of the CIA were operating as such a team, with the CIA taking the leadership role. Finally, under pressures of high stakes, emergency, or confusion, there are increased costs of giving normal deference to hierarchical superiors if they are not particularly respected. In this situation, formal structures are likely to give way to more informal arrangements based on respect.

The reasons that loyalty becomes important need hardly be elaborated; they are obvious to everyone who has worked or played on a team. What we must examine in more detail are the conditions and boundaries of loyalty.

The Role and Problems of Loyalty

While respect is the almost invisible force behind the structure allocating trust in competence and judgment within a team, loyalty is the almost invisible force that binds a team together, despite differences in the members' individual concerns and in their perceptions of the situation. Recall the five types of concerns that motivate players. Several go to the sense of valued states of the world and of valued processes in conducting relationships and making decisions (morality). These are the only concerns that can generally be pressed with the public, the legislature, the press, or peers. Every subordinate is obligated to give great deference to these concerns of a superior, often stated as goals or rules.

Only a handful of players can be expected to respond to an individual's other categories of concerns: maintaining personal and organizational resources to influence others in joint decisions and concern about his own personal welfare, including comfort in playing his role. That handful of players who are responsive to all five categories of another's concerns, and not just to morality and goals, are often said to be "loyal." At a minimum, a player (X) loyal to another player (Y) must take seriously Y's concerns about his resources to influence future decisions and his personal well-being. In these categories, X cannot worry exclusively about his own personal and resource concerns. The more seriously X takes these concerns of Y, the more loyal X is. Although loyalty is often discussed as if it were an obligation of a subordinate to a superior, it can as easily run from a superior to a subordinate or among peers in a team effort. President Bush was loyal to Secretary of Defense Donald Rumsfeld and CIA Director George Tenet, just as they were loyal to him.

Perhaps for X it is almost always beneficial to show loyalty by making sure that he gives weight to Y's as well as his own personal and resource concerns. Claims of loyalty that require X to subordinate even his views of moral obligation and his deeply held social values to Y's personal and resource concerns may also win for X the reciprocal loyalty of Y. But taken this far, loyalty may not be good for the rest of us. If a CIA officer believed that the Director was lying about the evidence of weapons of mass destruction in Iraq, loyalty would not justify silence. If in the same context a Cabinet official were asked to state the facts falsely or to greatly exaggerate his conclusions from the available evidence, even more clearly he should say "no."

Indeed, loyalists can be divided between those who are simply willing to subordinate their own personal concerns to those of another and those who are also willing to subordinate their sense of what is socially desirable (even before a decision is made) or morally required. Of course, the lines are not always clear. Whether, in cases of genuine moral uncertainty, X should subordinate his belief that an action is immoral, even to Y's sincere conviction that the action is proper as well as wise, is as difficult an issue in governance as it is in religion.

A further difficulty in determining how much loyalty should be accorded arises when X is convinced that Y is making a decision that will damage the team effort to accomplish some specific objective or goal shared by all of them. Within a broad range of options, a subordinate and, in appropriate circumstances, peers or even a superior must recognize that the terms of a relationship of reciprocal loyalty must include significant leeway for Y to make decisions with which X disagrees. A loyal colleague will not pretend to agree with decisions he thinks are mistaken, although within some range of plausibility of the decision (or of uncertainty that it is foolish) X must defer. Problems of loyalty occur when the decision to be made by, for example, a superior, is important and, to the subordinate's eyes, plainly extremely foolish. Secretary of State George Shultz found himself in that position with regard to an exchange of missiles for hostages that President Ronald Reagan favored in the late 1980s—a case discussed in some detail in the next chapter.

The more firmly committed the superior is to an extremely unwise choice, the more forceful the dissent that is required of the subordinate and the more important it becomes for the subordinate to try to enlist others in persuading his superior of the error. Inevitably these steps strain other obligations of loyalty. If X is concerned about Y's personal welfare, he has to recognize that Y wants to make a decision and move on to something else—not to discuss a decision endlessly. If X is concerned about Y's resources of influence, he must see that Y wants the support of other subordinates in the decision and, by enlisting them, that X is undermining that support. X is also undermining Y's need for respect within the team. If the decision fails, Y wants the public and Congress to perceive the failure as a shared mistake, not a failure that was anticipated and predicted by X. So by putting his opposition in writing, X is undermining future support, in part to protect his own reputation.

Inevitably, a number of Y's concerns, relating to his well-being and resources, will be undermined as X tries to block a seriously mistaken policy. Indeed, in the case of subordinates, resignation is the most forceful argument, and it is plainly inconsistent with many of the concerns of the superior.

Louis Freeh, President Clinton, and Reciprocal Loyalty

In some relationships, loyalty is regarded by the public as undesirable. Here the risks to both parties are very great; for where all loyalty disappears between a superior and a subordinate, the result is likely to be disastrous.

President Bill Clinton may or may not have come to believe that FBI Director Louis Freeh intended to unseat him. The FBI investigations of the Monica Lewinsky matter came tolerably close to doing just that, leading to a trial for impeachment. Whether or not Clinton did suspect Freeh's good faith, Freeh came to question Clinton's.[1] The resulting relationship provides a reminder to both superiors and subordinates of the fragility and destructiveness that are sometimes latent in a relationship deprived of the glue of loyalty.

President Clinton and Freeh discussed, during the hiring stage, what the subordinate's role would be. Freeh emphasized the importance to him of independent decision making by the FBI. Only independence was fully consistent with his belief that the sole objective of an FBI agent or Director was to see that punishment was justly imposed on those who most deserved it. No less important, the confidence of the public and members of Congress in Freeh and the FBI as the custodians of dangerous enforcement powers depended upon their use being seen as free of partisan influence or even suspicions of such influence. Indeed, the Bureau's critical informal powers (to elicit voluntary cooperation) depended upon this confidence.

What Clinton and Freeh seem not to have discussed—quite understandably—was the potential difficulty in two areas. Sometimes the pursuit of justice would come into conflict with other perfectly legitimate obligations of the President. In the case of the investigation of the bombing of Khobar Towers by terrorists in Saudi Arabia, there could be a conflict between steps an investigator thought necessary and foreign policy needs. The bombing and the resulting deaths of American airmen represented, to Freeh, a powerful demand for the most motivating of all expressive values: the desire for punishment or retribution for a moral wrong done to one's people. The evidence pointed to Iranian intelligence. To President Clinton the investigation had to be managed in light of equally powerful concerns for developing working relations with a more recently elected, less hostile Iranian administration. Similarly, when allegations were made of improper administration fund-raising from Chinese donors, a conflict would arise about whether the information developed during the investigation should be made available to the Secretary of State, who was traveling to China and might find herself unknowingly dealing with some of the suspects.

The other problem was more foreseeable. Maintaining the credibility of the FBI and Freeh's own reputation for impartiality would require going at least a little, and perhaps significantly, further in investigating allegations against high-level members of the administration than in investigating other allegations. The public hardly understands how much discretion investigators have and use in deciding what not to investigate and how necessary it is to triage in light of the scarcity of investigative time. So normal exercises of the necessary discretion not to pursue a matter, when applied to high members of the administration, would be very likely to be taken, erroneously, as evidence of partisan influence.

A President's general understanding is that he can expect loyalty from every subordinate. That was plainly not consistent with Freeh's expectations as to the role of FBI Director when confronted with even implausible allegations of wrongdoing by high-level officials of the administration. Even without much else to fan the flames of distrust, this difference in the understanding of Freeh's role would disrupt a critically important relationship.

"Scenario" is what social scientists call the movie that is often playing in the head of an individual involved in social interaction. As an understanding of how certain relationships between individuals typically unfold, a scenario provides a template to alert the individual to the significance of what is happening and to help her determine the meaning and effects of her options. A police officer may have a "Dirty Harry" movie playing as he confronts a suspect. A law professor may have "Paper Chase" playing when she goes into class. The assumed scenario provides a rough idea of a story about what is likely to happen in an interaction. Freeh was watching the story of Watergate: President Nixon's cover-up compromising the independence and destroying the reputation of an overly loyal FBI and Department of Justice. President Clinton felt unfairly hounded by a self-righteous, ambitious, and hostile policeman—itself a familiar scenario.

Freeh's personal resources depended on his reputation for unflagging dedication to justice and deep commitment to non-partisanship. His capacity to produce results also depended upon the loyalty of his organization, which, in turn, depended upon his respect for the culture of the institution. That, too, was inconsistent with showing loyalty to President Clinton—something that every President regards as essential.

To make the relationship work the President had to recognize all this, plus the fact that there are pockets of independent power in the executive branch ("baronies") that are too costly to control by directive or sanctions. Because criminal justice is such an area, President Carter had allowed his Attorney General, Griffin Bell, to place the federal prosecutors off-limits for any direct contacts by the White House or Congress. Public and congressional fears of partisanship make the political costs of giving directives to the Director of the FBI very high indeed.

Still, even if Clinton had recognized all these reasons for giving independence and not expecting loyalty, he would occasionally have valid and important reasons for wanting to modify or qualify an investigative decision. In the case of Khobar Towers, President Clinton would have to consider the costs of pressing Saudi Arabia for evidence against Iran in terms of our hopes for better relations with each of these countries, particularly in light of some evidence of a democratic opening in Iran.

To make the relationship work, Freeh in turn would have to recognize the far broader responsibilities of the President without automatically suspecting improper motives. In the end, neither understood the role of the other.

In the absence of expected loyalty, Clinton thought that his FBI Director was a political opponent. Challenged in his independence, the confidence of Director Freeh that the President could be trusted to serve as the nation's chief law enforcement officer was utterly and totally lacking. He hardly disagreed with a senior subordinate who described Clinton as dishonest. Freeh's priority strategy for the FBI was to develop relationships with law enforcement overseas—something he could not do without the support of the President's national security establishment. The President's priorities for China and Iran could not be carried out, as he wished, without a minimal level of confidence from his FBI Director.

The reciprocal lack of trust was caused in part by totally different personalities and different notions of what virtues should be respected or rejected—not just by the absence of loyalty caused by differences in an understanding of personal and institutional roles. But this breakdown could not be resolved by the subordinate being asked to leave. A political leader can only fire someone investigating him or his administration at great political cost. So the two faced each other, displaying a mutual suspicion obvious to their peers, the Congress, and the public. Nor could they reconcile their differences by conversation. Indeed, the very idea of a private conversation would have been threatening to Freeh's sense of the importance of the reality and perception of independence to both the public's trust in federal law enforcement and the reputation and resources of the FBI.

Disloyalty mushroomed on both sides. Without support from the President, Freeh turned for support to powerful Republicans—former President Bush and Secretary of Defense Cohen. With or without Freeh's knowledge, the FBI made public its various suspicions of the President. The President responded by making known his doubts about the FBI Director, that is, his lack of confidence in Freeh's ability to do the job. Loyalty stopped flowing down and stopped flowing up, yet neither could terminate the relationship—the worst possible outcome of a superior/subordinate relationship.

The Role of Respect

Something else that is "team" related was also missing in my prior chapters. The unequal influence over decisions of different players is only partially explained in terms of specific capacities to influence particular other players and rules that locate ultimate authority to make a policy decision. Group processes are also organized and shaped by a less visible force: the more generalized respect that each participant enjoys from the others. A complete picture of the operating parts of a government choice would have to take account—would have to make visible—the way that respect shapes a group process. In many ways, in the Stinger missile case Pillsbury is surfing on the respect that Abramovitz enjoys in the Departments of State and Defense.

Respect has to enter into my description for another equally important reason. Obtaining and retaining it is a highly significant motivation or concern of most players. Professor Abraham Maslow became famous for describing a hierarchy of human needs that still enjoys major support. Until the lower-level needs are met, the higher-level needs are generally ignored. Immediately after physiological needs for air and food and safety come the needs to belong and to gain approval and recognition. They overlap, for the desire to belong to, and to enjoy the approval of, a task-based group requires not only loyalty to others on the team but also winning their respect for the role one plays in carrying out the task. Shaped by the context in which they operate, the needs for esteem and belonging are very prominent in governmental and other organizations. As we shall see in the cases in Chapter 9, in the context of government, these needs are powerful enough to lead to resignation or rebellion.

The *Oxford Dictionary* defines "respect" as "deferential esteem felt or shown toward a person, thing, or quality." That is too broad for the context of group or team decision making, including as it does such admired personal qualities as patience, humor, and consideration. For our purpose, the definition should be no broader than enjoying esteem and honor with regard to the set of characteristics that others recognize as needed or useful to play a critical role in their system of roles and goals. The characteristics that others perceive as needed for playing a valued role in a system composed of government decision-making officials are different from the set of characteristics and skills that win respect as a professor, a lawyer, a salesperson, an actor, an athlete, or a business executive.

For policy making, respect depends on one's contribution to the particular team's process of decision making being valued; and the respect must thus be given willingly and democratically—by subordinates and peers as well as by superiors.

Players who feel they are being denied respect correctly recognize that they are threatened in their entitlement to play the role they have been assigned and that they value. Denied respect, they are denied what Professor Maslow describes as an essential human need. In other contexts the human need for respect is enough to cause a group to riot, an individual to murder, or a youth to join in terrorism. We are, in short, considering a quality that is an extremely powerful motivator.

For a participant in policy advocacy, respect is shown by the willingness of others to defer to one's views either on an aspect of a decision or on the balancing of concerns necessary to reach the final decision. It differs subtly from my description of resources of influence. A may have immense capacity to influence B, although B may not respect A. B may show respect by willingly deferring to C on the ground that it is best for the group, whether or not C is in a central position or enjoys authority over the others or is even a recognized expert in an area.

Respect is different from status in that it is informal and situation dependent. It is based on one's experience in dealing with another in a particular context or on the reputation of the other with associates whose judgment one values. Respect is different from reputation because it involves a willing deference, while reputation may work by fear as easily as choice. Respect by one or two others is different from leadership in a group. But widespread respect within the group creates informal leadership, whether or not one enjoys a superior status or hierarchical authority or commanding personality.

It is important to examine both the organizing role of respect and its power to motivate. As to the first, contests for respect and the resulting deference to the winner of such contests are as much of an organizing principle of group decision making as any other process. At a faculty lunch table, professors vie for esteem and create invisible hierarchies of respect even when there is no decision to be made. In a governmental context, such contests constitute an invisible world operating in parallel and interacting with the world of rules, assigned responsibilities, valued processes and goals, and the uses of resources of influence that I've described in Part One. All of this can be made clearer by examples. But, unless you look carefully for the actions that political players are taking to receive deferential esteem from "teammates" in terms of the skills and characteristics necessary to carry out particular roles (including the role of leader) in the process of deciding and then executing a decision, you will be missing much of the action.

An Example to Make Visible the Organized Role of "Respect" in Group Choice

Sometimes a superior puts a team to work making a decision without allocating the role of leader. Considering such a case is revealing. The same operations that create structure and define leadership in such unstructured situations are at work, alongside authority, resources and sanctions, in all decision-making processes. Seeing how an unstructured group looks for natural bases for respect and leadership in the absence of hierarchy or resources of influence provides a window to something also of immense importance for familiar hierarchically structured organizations.

The fact is that a parallel world of competition for respect in the areas that justify leadership in the minds of others is always being played out at the same time as the processes I have described in Part I. The critical concepts for this parallel world are not the concerns and interests and are not the actual or implicit bargains that I have previously described ("world one"). The critical concept for this parallel world ("world two") is respect and the availability and use of that currency in continuing relationships. To illustrate, I will describe a televised "war game" as well as a real occasion that closely followed it; for it is almost impossible to obtain a sufficiently textured case study of how people interacted in a group, without delegated leadership—a team that is charged with handling an important and complex situation—particularly where facts are scarce, predictions are difficult, and results of any action thus quite uncertain.

In the mid-1980s, after several major hijackings of planes (e.g., TWA 827 taken to Lebanon) and one of a ship (the *Achille Lauro*), public television assembled a number of the best-known and most respected national security figures of the day to address what it called "A Terrorist Incident," a "game" designed to reveal decision-making processes regarding national security. The taped discussions provide a wonderful window on a major but unobserved part of the political world.

At the beginning of the "game" the participants are told that a U.S. commercial aircraft has been hijacked to Sicily and that the hijackers are threatening to blow it up. Before the group can act, the plane is blown up with explosives laced with radioactive material, a "dirty bomb." Since they assume that Italy will deal with the danger from radioactivity, the question for the U.S. group quickly changes from how to rescue hostages to how to punish those behind the explosion that has killed everyone on the plane. They are told that early intelligence indicates that Libya is a state sponsor of the attacks, and the debate focuses on a choice of military options, ranging from invasion through bombing to blockade or mining of Libya's Mediterranean outlets. If the event was not state sponsored, these responses will prove harmful, not useful. Yet, without knowing reliably of any state sponsorship, bombing of Libya is promptly ordered and the order executed. Delay for further investigation, it seems, would suggest a lack of determination or forcefulness.

Suddenly new information is introduced, linking the hijacking instead to Syria, then an ally of our superpower opponent, the Soviet Union. Now two decisions have to be made: whether to take military action against Syria and whether to stop bombing Libya. Throughout, the group assumes, apparently without any evidence, not only that the event (carried out by a handful of individuals from the Middle East) is state sponsored, but also that the Soviet Union is ultimately behind the event, supporting Libya or Syria. The Soviet Union, fearing that we will attack Syria, puts its intercontinental missiles on high alert. Although the U.S. President has already decided not to take the global risk of attacking Syria, he responds by putting our missiles on high alert, increasing the risk of an accidental nuclear exchange, so that the Soviets will not think that their actions caused us to back down.

The "game" was played two decades ago, but if we substituted Iran, Pakistan, and China for Libya, Syria, and the USSR respectively, perhaps nothing else would change or seem implausible well into the twenty-first century. At the end, the people who designed the game and the television commentator describe how remarkable it is that the group has not taken us to nuclear war with the Soviet Union over what, so far as we can tell, may have been the actions of a handful of terrorists unaffiliated with any state.

From the above account alone, it is obvious that something generally invisible is shaping the action as we watch such prestigious former national leaders as Jim Woolsey, Dick Helms, Les Aspen, Robert McFarlane, Brent Scowcroft, Eugene Rostow, and Admiral Thomas Moorer wrestling with a dangerous and highly uncertain situation from the roles they have agreed to play.

First, consider the nature of the arguments being made. The matters they discuss have little or nothing to do with affecting the behavior of Libya, Syria, or the Soviet Union. At one point Brent Scowcroft, acting as the National Security Adviser, recommends that we bomb the Bacca Valley in Lebanon to punish the Syrians without inviting Soviet intervention. Eugene Rostow, playing the role of Secretary of State, replies that we already know this will have no effect because the Israelis have been doing this repeatedly with no effect. Scowcroft responds sharply that that is an unconvincing argument because we have also been bombing Libya without results but we keep doing that. The absence of effect on the source of the danger is, surprisingly, not an argument that disqualifies an option from consideration.

Second, consider the lack of concern about factual reliability. The evidence on which the group acts is extremely thin. There was never strong evidence that Libya was behind the incident. There is no evidence at all that, as everyone in the group assumes, we are really dealing with the Soviet Union. But none of that changes the nature of the factual premises for the "argument." Several group members are happy to argue—to fool themselves, or the American public, or the world so that the strength of our commitment is not doubted—that the powerful evidence that emerges indicating that Syria and not Libya was behind the attack is actually uncertain and that Libya is still behind it.

What makes sense of the discussion is that it is really about presenting the United States as powerful and effective in a situation that we do not know how to affect—about maintaining respect. The critical concern of policy is how to dispel the appearance that we are a "paper tiger" at the hands of whoever the terrorists may be. That is why a number in the group believe that this consideration, plus preserving the President's own reputation for strength and competence, require us to continue to bomb Libya, even after new evidence shows that it was Syria and not Libya that was behind the attack.

Third, more is going on than maintaining the conditions of national prestige. To understand the behavior in the war game, one must also understand that a major concern of the players is the respect the President will enjoy. There is a constant worry that the President will lose respect by taking hours to get advice and then to decide what to do in this dangerous, complicated situation that, realistically, nobody could possibly sort out in less time. Brent Scowcroft as the National Security Advisor firmly admonishes the others that, "Nobody is to know that the President dilly-dallied." But it takes time to decide on one's position.

The decision maker in this case cannot have considered all the arguments for and against each of a number of courses of action. Feeling how comfortable he is with the values and the principles that underlie various arguments and considerations—how good the fit is with his set of values—takes at least as much time as it takes a judge to decide after hearing an oral argument. Assessing the basis for factual assertions and the plausibility of the predictions based on those assertions also takes time. And finally, each of these steps must be taken with regard to possible impacts in quite different domains of concern.

Carrying out these time-consuming tasks is generally critical to wise decisions. But the cost of taking the time to deliberate carefully may, in cases of near panic, be a loss of the respect on which leadership depends. Personality as well as wisdom affects respect.

Consider this description of Prime Minister Golda Meir of Israel, deciding to sacrifice perhaps thousands of Israeli lives rather than to engage in a preemptive attack on the massing Arab forces at the time of the Yom Kippur War in 1973. She took an hour and a half to make the decision, as Abraham Rabinovitz describes in *The Yom Kippur War*:

> When the presentations were done the Prime Minister hemmed uncertainly for a few moments, but then came to a clear decision. There would be no preemptive strike. Israel might be needing American assistance soon and it was imperative that Israel not be blamed for starting the war.[2]

There are two reasons the players worry about the predictable effect of any appearance of even temporary uncertainty on continuing respect for the President. Of course, one reason is politics. Les Aspen, as President Woolsey's Chief of Staff, notes that we need something dramatic for domestic political reasons. Daniel Schoor, as the Press Secretary, says, "You can't afford to admit to having goofed" in attributing the attack to Libya.

But there is more to this concern than elected politics. An important aspect of the situation they are dealing with, and the only aspect they can actually affect, is that the President's appearance of being comfortably in control is important to the respect that underlies the continuing capacity of the President to lead the United States and its allies. Only if he "looks" like a real leader in this dangerous situation will that respect and that capacity remain. Scowcroft warns the group that it must make the President look decisive.

There is a final invisible dimension that explains the peculiar detachment of the players from the causes of the danger and the effects of different national security steps on our possible opponents. They are all themselves involved in a game of seeking individual respect that is taking place parallel to the war game in which they are deciding crucial governmental issues almost exclusively in terms of creating appearances they think necessary if they are to preserve respect for the President and the nation. The President has left the group with a national security problem but without an obvious leader. That problem can only be resolved if the group acts in a somewhat unified way, and that requires leadership in organizing its work. Who will lead depends on respect and that will be affected, they see, by who acts with the appearance of most confidence.

That will not be former National Security Adviser, Robert McFarlane, who is playing the role of the Secretary of Defense. He is modest and diffident as he makes suggestions, prefacing one with the line, "I assert, but I invite criticism...." On the other hand, the person playing the role of National Security Adviser in the game, Brent Scowcroft, is certain and commanding. He says, "The Libyans are officially behind it," intending by his pronouncement of an official position on a wholly unresolved factual matter to end all questions and move the group on. He assumes the power to direct the group that "nobody is to know the President dilly-dallied," conveying the importance of an appearance of decisiveness. He announces what our international image is to be: "This was a great example of NATO allies working together," although there was no real cooperation at all with Italy or any other NATO ally.

Scowcroft is in the business of creating a social reality within which feasible action will garner respect for the country and its President. He is leading by first specifying and then responding to that reality. If the group takes certain matters as established, it is not because the evidence is in fact overwhelming. It is because of (1) a felt need to define what happened in an actionable way; and (2) the powerful tendency—whenever prompt action is required in a time of confusion or uncertainty—to follow an individual who is more certain rather than more deliberative. Together these create the social reality that shapes the way the game is being played.

Let me be more precise about what is going on here before we move back to actual cases and situations in which an individual with delegated authority is attempting to add the subtle powers of willingly accepted

leadership to her formally delegated powers. As the group decides what
to do in the face of "a terrorist incident," the members recognize that they
have to work together, combining their knowledge, to reach something
like a shared conclusion. Working together without a previously defined
set of roles requires leadership. Choosing, even implicitly, a leader can
help immensely by enabling the members of the team to impose some
organization on the work.

Although the members could, like a jury, begin their deliberations by
voting for a foreperson, in reality members are more likely to compete
for leadership by trying to show through their behavior that they are the
most likely, the most competent, to take the group where it has to go.
The group in "A Terrorist Incident" needs a leader and, feeling the pragmatic pressure of time and the emotional pressure of being without a
direction, a number will gravitate to whoever looks promising. Scowcroft
establishes his leadership by winning the respect of others through his
commanding participation; they do not, after all, have the time, perhaps
months or years, to become familiar enough with one another to evaluate
his special capacities and skills and compare them to others. In this way,
he wins their confidence early in the process and, in the absence of any
rule authorizing a particular mechanism for choosing a leader, his views
and questions become the single focal point of discussion.

The process is not irreversible. The confidence that Scowcroft can lead
the group can be lost by a clear showing of thoughtlessness or bewilder-
ment. This happened to President Bush in 2006 over the war in Iraq.
It can be challenged by a rival showing disrespect, but only at the cost
of incurring the resentment that comes with setting back the effort to
promptly meet the group's organizational needs. Scowcroft will have to
watch for any sign of disrespect and find a way to sanction or disempower the challenge of the disrespectful. In the long run, one or another
in the group could demonstrate that he deserves respect as a possible
leader, but the game, like a real crisis, is a quick one, and there is no time
to compare the capabilities of the members of the group. What happens,
in short, is that one or more player will invite respect by the way he presents himself to the others as, not only technically competent, but also
certain, decisive, and commanding.

Most broadly, importantly involved in the group process are the assertions of various members that they are entitled to enjoy the respect of
others for their special abilities relative to the task the group faces. For
the leader, it is the capacity to organize and inspire the necessary work

that is in fact directed to their common ends. That contest for the confidence of others underlies the "game" I have described.

Before turning to the role that respect and loyalty play in one particular relationship—between a superior and a subordinate—it is important to note a last point: that the attributes through which the members are competing for respect involve only a special category—a relatively small subcategory of the wide range of characteristics that can generate admiration. Machiavelli taught us that leaders must distinguish among the virtues that bring admiration to a reigning prince, arguing that some generally despised characteristics (including cruelty and deception) are more useful in controlling or influencing followers than others that are generally praised (inappropriate liberality, mercifulness, or honesty). We don't have to agree that the specifics of his argument still apply to see the continuing relevance of its framework—that the requirements for earning deference in any context of group work depend on what it takes in that context to play a role that others recognize as useful in the system of roles they share. Shortstops get respect for different characteristics than missionaries or even wide receivers.

In its most general form, Machiavelli's point is illustrated in my discussion of "A Terrorist Incident." Behavior that does not and should not generate respect in other circumstances may reveal a competence to "take charge" that underlies a claim to leadership or influence in an emergency in which roles are not well-defined. Brent Scowcroft takes a commanding role by displays of unusual confidence in the relationship of his experience and skills to the decision they face. Overconfidence may be useful in the battle for leadership. Oversimplifying the situation so that one's point can be quickly absorbed was useful in moving the group. So are such self-celebratory actions as requiring ceremonial shows of respect, for example when the President enters the room. The players in the war game demonstrate a willingness to lie that may appear useful in some situations, in particular to deny responsibility for mistakes. Displaying ruthlessness in punishing Libya, even without strong evidence, was valued by the group. In any occasion involving hierarchical authority, behavior that flatters the superior may be instrumentally useful.

9

A Structure Held Together by Respect

The two cases that follow illustrate that Professor Maslow was right in attaching great motivating power to the desire for belonging and for respect or esteem. But instead of describing how respect is acquired and used—how it provides structure for team decisions—these two cases examine the disruptive effects on a decision-making team of respect that is withheld or is simply absent. More than that, the cases allow us to observe the operation of the power of respect in one type of team that is pervasive and unusually important: teams made up of a superior and his immediate subordinates.

Every player except the President has a superior, and many players have immediate subordinates. The superior can purposely or negligently use the giving or withholding of respect as a powerful reward or punishment for a subordinate. Subordinates can use the giving or withholding of respect, even while providing support for the superior's decisions, as a way of affirming or questioning the legitimacy of the superior's leadership role. The force of even subtle exercises of these powers is remarkable.

There is also an immediate practical impact from the subordinate's point of view. The subordinate's ability to influence decisions made by the superior of course depends on the respect that he enjoys from the superior. Less obviously, his influence with peers and subordinates depends importantly on their sense of the respect that he receives from his superior.

Telling the Boss He's Wrong: George Shultz and Iran-Contra
A Case History by Kirsten Lundberg

In the summer of 1985, President Reagan's national security advisor came to him with a bold proposal.[1] Robert McFarlane advocated using Israel as a go-between in selling arms to the hostile Islamic nation of Iran, on the understanding that the Iranians would use their influence to secure the release of U.S. hostages taken prisoner in Lebanon by Iranian-directed terrorists. Reagan was enthusiastic. He had long been frustrated and disheartened by U.S. inability to do anything concrete about the hostages. Other administration leaders also responded warmly to the idea, from CIA director William Casey to chief of staff Donald Regan.

But within the inner circle there was a naysayer. Secretary of State George Shultz, an experienced bureaucrat with a long and honorable history in both the public and private sectors, thought the proposal outrageous.[2] In his view, the exchange was simply a ransom for the hostages and ran contrary to the declared U.S. policy of rejecting deals with terrorists. He predicted that it would only encourage more hostage taking. He worried the arrangement would become public and embarrass the United States, which would have violated its own embargo on arms shipments to Iran. Moreover, as Secretary of State, Shultz felt control over U.S.-Iran policy belonged in the State Department, not the National Security Council.

Though Shultz saw himself as essentially a team player, he nonetheless, by his own account, repeatedly expressed his opposition to the venture—to Reagan, to other members of the Cabinet, and to White House aides. For his pains, he was either ignored or treated with open hostility. Yet, when what became known as the "Iran-Contra affair" came under the scrutiny of special commissions and congressional hearings, Shultz was sharply criticized for not doing more to squelch the arms-for-hostages deal. "I cannot believe," said Representative Henry Hyde, R-Ill., "if you had been that forceful and that committed to opposing this flawed initiative, as much as [National Security Advisor Admiral John] Poindexter and [National Security Council aide Lieutenant Colonel Oliver] North were committed to advancing it, you couldn't have stopped it dead in its tracks." Similarly, the report of the Tower Commission[3] found fault with both Shultz and Defense Secretary Weinberger for their failure to speak out strongly in conversations with Reagan on the operation. "They protected their record as to their own positions on this issue," the report asserted. "They were not energetic in attempting to protect the President from the consequences of his personal commitment to freeing the hostages."

Shultz defended his actions to his critics, congressional and otherwise, pointing out in his later account of events that he had "argued vigorously and passionately on a number of occasions with the president...." But at the same time he acknowledged having his own doubts about the strength of his efforts to oppose the arms sale to Iran. Writing in his memoirs of the Iran-Contra affair, he recalled that at one point, "I felt I should have asked more, demanded more, done more, but I did not see *how*."[4]

George Shultz and His State Department

Trained as an economist, Shultz first joined the top ranks of government in 1969, when he accepted President Nixon's offer to become Secretary of Labor. Shultz left his position as dean at the University of Chicago's Business School for Washington and for several years did not look back. In 1970 he moved to become budget director; from 1972 to 1974, he served as Secretary of the Treasury. While at that post, he gained a reputation as a man of integrity after his highly publicized refusal to direct the IRS to provide confidential tax records of individuals on Nixon's "enemies list."[5] After leaving the Treasury Department, Shultz returned to private industry.

At the time Reagan sought him out as Secretary of State in 1982, Shultz was president of Bechtel, Inc., an engineering firm headquartered in San Francisco. He also taught part-time at Stanford University. Back in Washington to replace outgoing Secretary of State Alexander Haig, Shultz's reputation for integrity preceded him. On a personal level, Reagan seemed relaxed and at ease with Shultz.

Shultz, no doubt, welcomed the opportunity to work for a President who, as part of his campaign, had pledged to return control over foreign policy to the Secretary of State and the State Department. This implicitly downgraded the importance of the National Security Advisor, the Secretary of State's chief rival in the domain of foreign affairs. The National Security Advisor, a position created by President Eisenhower, is the staff director for the National Security Council (NSC)[6]; besides having an expert staff at his disposal, he has, by virtue of being located in the White House, ready access to the ear of the President. Over the decades, a spirited competition developed between the National Security Advisor and the Secretary of State over who should control foreign policy. The ascendancy of either was heavily driven by personality, particularly that of the President and his relationship with his Cabinet officers. The State Department is charged with coordinating the range of U.S. activities overseas, and the Secretary of State, who must be confirmed by Congress, is in principle the President's chief foreign policy advisor. However, powerful National Security Advisors have often turned the NSC into a forum for promoting their own agendas.

As Secretary of State, Shultz by early 1985 had sailed a fairly smooth course. While he could not claim any spectacular breakthroughs in foreign policy, neither had he made any major blunders. His lowest moment was the deadly bombing by terrorists of U.S. Marines in Lebanon in 1983. That attack had not inhibited his involvement in Middle Eastern diplomacy, however. Shultz was also increasingly intrigued by the possibilities for a new Soviet-U.S. relationship inherent in the rise to power of General Secretary Mikhail Gorbachev. U.S. relations with Iran, although clearly of concern, were not one of Shultz's priorities. Other administration officials, however, pushed Iran to center stage in mid-1985.

The Iran-Contra Affair: A Brief Overview

The arrangement to provide U.S. weapons to Iran in exchange for the promised release of U.S. hostages in Lebanon began with a draft National Security Decision Document (NSDD), which National Security Advisor Robert McFarlane circulated to Shultz, Secretary of Defense Caspar Weinberger, and Director of Central Intelligence William Casey.[7] The NSDD proposed to improve relations with the hostile Islamic nation by, among other things, providing "selected military equipment as determined on a case-by-case basis." This would contravene U.S. policy because Iran was in the midst of a protracted war with Iraq, and the United States had declared an embargo on arms shipments to both nations in an effort to force the two sides into a truce. It also appeared to contradict the administration's oft-repeated declaration that it would not make deals with terrorists. Not only had the Reagan administration rejected negotiation, but it had threatened military force in the case of hostage taking. "Let terrorists be aware," said Reagan one week after his inauguration in 1981, at a White House reception for the 52 American embassy hostages recently released by Tehran, "that when the rules of international behavior are violated, our policy will be one of swift and effective retribution."

Nonetheless, in July, McFarlane presented to Reagan the suggestion of a senior Israeli Foreign Ministry official, who proposed opening a U.S. dialogue with an allegedly moderate group in Iran in order to promote the release of seven U.S. hostages held in Lebanon by Iranian-controlled terrorists. In return, the Iranians would most likely expect a shipment of arms. Reagan liked the idea and encouraged McFarlane.

The arms shipments to Iran began that August. In the months that followed, the United States sent, with the help of Israel and other intermediaries, some eight separate shipments of weapons to Iran. One load was personally delivered by a delegation of U.S. officials, including McFarlane and Oliver North (McFarlane's assistant on the NSC), who arrived in Tehran for talks in May 1986 bearing, along with a partial shipment of spare parts, a cake decorated with a chocolate key and a Bible inscribed by President Reagan.

From August 1985 to November 1986, when the operation was abruptly suspended in the wake of revelations in the press, the arms-for-hostages initiative led to the sale of over 2,000 TOW antitank missiles and 18 HAWK missiles, plus spare parts, to Iran.[8] The numbers on the hostage side of the equation were disappointingly low. Although on a number of occasions the administration had expectations that all or most of the hostages would be let go, a total of three were released during the roughly fifteen months that the arms shipments were being made. This modest success, moreover, was offset by the capture of three new hostages in Beirut in September and October 1986.

All of the transactions in the operation—arms shipments and numerous related negotiations with Iranians and intermediaries—were kept under close wraps. Congress was explicitly excluded from knowledge of the affair. When the CIA became directly involved in a shipment in November 1985, Reagan was required to sign a presidential "finding" justifying the covert action on the grounds of U.S. national security interests. Such findings, as Shultz notes in his memoir, "were usually notified to the Senate and House committees dealing with intelligence."[9] Such was not the case with this finding, however. The document, which sought to authorize the action retroactively, specifically directed that Congress not be notified. Later, in January 1986, Attorney General Edwin Meese III approved direct U.S. sales of arms to Iran (instead of through Israel)[10] under the Economy Act and the National Security Act; again, Congress was not notified. Nor did Congress know of the most blatantly illegal act associated with the arms shipments: the diversion of millions of dollars in profits from the sales to fund a resupply operation for Nicaraguan insurgents, known as Contras, who were battling the Sandinista government. The diversion, spearheaded by Oliver North, was in violation of an act of Congress—the Boland Amendment—which barred the administration (specifically the CIA) from spending any money aimed at "overthrowing the government of Nicaragua."

But while the sale of arms to Iran remained a close secret where the public and Congress were concerned, within the top levels of the Reagan administration it remained a matter of ongoing debate.[11] Time and again, over the course of the arms initiative, Shultz, who remained unwavering in his opposition to it, was forced to confront the fact of its continuing existence and to consider what he might do to eradicate it once and for all.

Shultz and Arms-for-Hostages: Opening Salvos

From the time McFarlane drafted his June 1985 NSDD suggesting arms sales to Iran, Shultz found the idea "perverse." When freeing hostages was added to the mixture, Shultz dismissed the concoction as contrary to U.S. policy and interests.[12] "To reverse our present policy and permit or encourage a flow of Western arms to Iran is contrary to our interest, both in containing [Islamic radicalism] and in ending the excesses of this regime. It would seem particularly perverse to alter this aspect of our policy when groups with ties to Iran are holding U.S. hostages in Lebanon."[13]

Shultz was joined in this sentiment by Secretary of Defense Weinberger, who noted "almost too absurd to comment on" in the margin of the document. In July, Shultz did endorse McFarlane's suggestion that the U.S. take advantage of the opportunity through Israel to open a dialogue with the Iranians, but with no arms sale involved. Shultz emphasized that the U.S. posture should be "positive but passive. I do not think we could justify turning our backs on the prospect of gaining the release of the other seven hostages." But, noted Shultz, "[t]his situation is loaded with 'imponderables' that call for great caution on our part."

By early August, 1985 Shultz seemingly turned against even a tentative arrangement with the Iranians. In a regularly scheduled meeting on August 6 with Reagan, Shultz says he "argued strongly to the president and McFarlane that arms sales to Iran would be a grave mistake and that discussion of the possibility should be stopped. I thought that the president agreed, though reluctantly."[14] On September 3, however, he found out otherwise. McFarlane told him the Iranians wanted more arms than they first thought, and wanted them before any hostage release. "No, no arms," responded Shultz, adding he wanted the hostages out *first*. He had the impression McFarlane agreed.

Shultz was, he writes, unaware of the first two arms shipments that went to Iran in late August and early September. When, on September 14, Benjamin Weir—the first of the three hostages to be released—was freed, Shultz again remained in the dark. He learned of the release only two days later and then accepted the explanation given by the U.S. ambassador to Lebanon—that Weir's deliverance was meant to bring pressure for the liberation of Shiite terrorists being held in Kuwait. The Weir release seemed to Shultz to be separate from what he knew to be ongoing efforts by North to accomplish the release of all seven hostages—for which North required a false, State Department–issued passport.

Later that week, Shultz discussed the complexity of the situation with his deputies Michael Armacost and John Whitehead. They expressed concern that the U.S. government was denying publicly what it was actually doing in private—bargaining for hostages. Said Shultz, according to contemporaneous notes, "I'm not comfortable [but I] don't know what to do about it....The White House has taken control. When they want us to do something, they will tell us."[15]

As for Reagan, said Shultz, he was informed, "but he doesn't appreciate the problems with arms sales to Iran." Reagan had firmly adopted the idea that the arms sales were supporting a moderate faction in Iran, and were somehow entirely separate from hostage releases. Shultz, for his part, wanted to believe that the operation was suspended but, as he said in his memoirs, "I was left very uncomfortable and unsettled, fearing that I had not heard the last of the arms-for-hostages scheme."

The November 1985 Shipment

Shultz was right. On November 19, while in Geneva for the first summit between Reagan and Gorbachev, Shultz heard from McFarlane that four hostages would be released shortly. Then Iran would take delivery of 100 HAWK missiles. Shultz writes that he protested to McFarlane "with stony anger…that I had been informed so late in the operation that I had no conceivable way to stop it. I hoped the hostages would be released, but I dreaded what I feared would be an unfolding nightmare."[16]

When no hostages were released, Shultz says he assumed no arms had been sent.[17] He did hear that the HAWKs planned for the deal were worth some $30 million. "It was appalling to me," he notes. His distress must have deepened when McFarlane informed him that Reagan had cleared the plan. Thus, Shultz welcomed the opportunity on December 7, 1985 to make his views clear during a top-level White House meeting arranged by Admiral John Poindexter, who had just succeeded McFarlane as National Security Advisor. As he puts it, "I was ready to express once again to the president my opposition both to the project and to dealings with the operators who were allegedly representing Iran."

In advance of the meeting, Shultz complained to Poindexter that it was increasingly apparent the State Department was being cut out of cable traffic on the Iranian arrangements. Shultz also repeated his view that "[w]e are signaling to Iran that they can kidnap people for profit.…This thing has got to be stopped." Shultz marshaled once again for Poindexter his arguments against the entire undertaking. "I warned Poindexter that if this operation leaked—and I felt it inevitably would leak—the fact that we had violated our principles would be clear, and our effort to block arms transfers from other countries to Iran would be seen to be perfidious."

At the December 7 meeting, Shultz remained implacable. He opposed "vigorously" a plan that Poindexter put forward: asking third countries to sell arms to Israel to replace the ones transferred to Iran. Says Shultz: "Such an effort was still trading U.S. arms for hostages…and it would be a more complicated deal that would make us even more vulnerable: arms for hostages and arms to Iran were both terrible ideas! I argued that this was a betrayal of our policies and would only encourage more hostage taking."[18]

Secretary of Defense Weinberger supported these arguments, and Shultz left the December 7 meeting satisfied that "the point of view Cap [Weinberger] and I had argued had won the day." It must have been sobering for Shultz to learn from Poindexter that, after problems arose over the November shipment, Reagan himself had resisted a recommendation that the United States pull out of the arrangement. But within days, the Secretary of State took heart when his staff told him that during a December 10 White House meeting the operation was "completely turned off." Shultz professed himself "relieved, but still wary." He felt he had been able to persuade the President without resorting to any drastic measures, such as resignation. Ironically, he was already offering to resign on an entirely separate issue.

Polygraphs and Principles

In December 1985, President Reagan had signed an NSDD authorizing random lie detector tests for all government employees with access to classified information. This would have meant most of the State Department. On December 19, 1985, Shultz told reporters in a press conference that he was prepared to resign rather than submit himself or his staff to such testing. "The minute in this government I am told that I'm not trusted is the day that I leave," he asserted. Shultz said polygraphs had proven notoriously unreliable, more likely to trip up the innocent than finger the trained professional.

On December 20, Shultz made his arguments to the President, who agreed to modify the directive. Since the President had already signed the NSDD, it could not be undone without considerable embarrassment. Instead, after consultations with the NSC and the CIA, Reagan put out a statement that he approved of polygraphs in espionage cases. No mention was made of using it for all government employees. As Shultz noted with satisfaction, "I resisted, spoke out and the NSC staff and intelligence agencies backed away or were forced to do so by President Reagan."[19]

Shultz was not to enjoy the same satisfaction in his dealings with Reagan over Iran. Instead, he perceived a growing mistrust of both himself and the State Department on the part of the CIA and NSC. The polygraph ruling, said Shultz, "meant that the CIA would not work with or provide information in many instances to State Department officials because they were not subject to regular lie detector testing." This "screening out"—particularly regarding Iran—was only augmented in the new year, January 1986.

Further Debate

Any illusions Shultz might have had that the Iran operation was off were laid to rest during a January 7, 1986, meeting in the Oval Office on further developments in the scheme. Placed yet again in the role of protester, Shultz recalled arguing "fiercely and with passion against any arms sales to Iran, especially arms sales connected to the release of hostages."[20] In his testimony before the Tower Commission, Shultz recalled that he was "well aware of the President's preferred course, and his strong desire to establish better relations with Iran and to save the hostages." According to his account, Shultz "stated all of the reasons why I felt it was a bad idea and nobody, in retrospect, has thought of a reason that I didn't think of. I mean, I think this is all very predictable, including the argument against those who said, well, this is going to be secret or it is all going to be deniable; that that is nonsense. So, all of that was said." Moreover, Shultz added, "I expressed myself as forcefully as I could. That is, I didn't just sort of rattle these arguments off. I was intense. The President knew that. The President was well aware of my views. I wasn't just saying, oh, Mr. President, this is terrible, don't do it. There were reasons given that were spelled out....I took the initiative as the person in the room who was opposed to what was being proposed."

Despite his efforts, Shultz was left with the impression that President Reagan and Vice President Bush, along with Casey, Meese, Regan, and Poindexter, "all had one opinion and I had a different one and Cap shared it." Neither Shultz nor Weinberger, apparently, knew that Reagan had already signed a retroactive finding in December 1985 and a draft finding on January 6, and would sign an expanded finding on January 17, all three seeking to confer legal status on the Iran operation.

Not everyone, however, remembered the arguments made in the January 7 meeting in the same light that Shultz recalled. Chief of Staff Donald Regan recalled that the president "was told, but by no means was it really teed up for him of what the downside risk would be here as far as American public opinion was concerned....I don't believe the State Department in its presentation arguing against this really brought out the sensitivity of this."

If either Casey or Poindexter had had any inclination at that point to inform Shultz, the naysayer, more fully about the Iran project, it was probably checked by a Shultz-Poindexter conversation on January 17. During a lunch meeting that featured some heated conversation, Poindexter expressed concern to Shultz about leaks—implicitly fingering the State Department. In exasperation, Shultz replied "that in view of his concern about leaks, I didn't need to know in advance about every operational move."[21]

Later, in an appearance before the House Foreign Affairs Committee, Shultz characterized his knowledge of the ongoing arms sale operation.

"I learned," he said, "not as a result of being involved in the development of the plan, but, so to speak, as a plan was about to be implemented—as is always the case, you have bits and pieces of evidence float in and so I weighed in on the basis of that, restating my views. What I heard was conflicting: at times that there was some sort of deal or signal in the works, and at other times that the operation was closed down. So, again, there was this ambiguity from my standpoint...whenever I would be called upon to do something to carry out...policies, I needed to know, but I didn't need to know things that were not in my sphere to do something about."[22]

The Unstoppable Initiative

In this "bits and pieces" manner, Shultz heard periodically of the progress of the arms sale initiative. On February 11, for example, Casey and Poindexter again informed Shultz that all the hostages would be out on February 22 or 23. Shultz said he felt "frozen: I could not, at the last second, try to stop this effort, but I dreaded its consequences." At that meeting (a luncheon), the participants discussed at length the arms-for-hostages arrangements, including a proposed timeline for arms deliveries and a subsequent hostage release. Shultz says he has no recollection of discussing any timeline and may have left the meeting early.[23] On the eve of the anticipated release, Shultz—according to notes by his assistant—"pleaded with Poindexter that if [the hostages were] not [released] please shut it down." Shultz agreed with Weinberger, Casey, and Poindexter that there would be "no comment on any questions [about Iran]. But we will get crucified."[24] Then, once again, no hostages were freed.

But the project accelerated at the end of February when the Iranians asked for a meeting in Frankfurt to discuss issues other than the hostages. Shultz says he was shown a copy of the talking points that McFarlane, the designated U.S. representative, would take with him to the meeting with Iranian intermediary Manucher Ghorbanifar. The document shown to Shultz contained no reference to arms. The hostages were to be released during the meeting in Frankfurt. But by March, again there were no developments. Poindexter told Shultz that McFarlane had objected to some aspect of the arrangement.

Instead, the administration began plans to send a U.S. delegation, headed by McFarlane, to Iran. Shultz's assistant's notes, according to the

Final Report of the Independent Counsel for Iran/Contra Matters, "reflect discussion about the trip in advance, knowledge that weapons parts were transferred to Iran during the trip and, subsequently, the mission's failure to obtain the release of the hostages." Shultz was dragged into the affair on May 4 when word of it leaked to the U.S. ambassador in London. The Secretary of State, who was attending an economic summit in Tokyo, was alerted to this by his deputy, Michael Armacost, who cabled him that the ambassador had been told by an informant that: "The scheme is okay with the Americans. It has been cleared with the White House. Poindexter allegedly is the point man. Only four people in the U.S. Government are knowledgeable about the plan. The State Department has been cut out."

Shultz immediately sought out the President but could find only Donald Regan, Reagan's chief of staff. Says Shultz: "I expressed strong opposition across the board: on policy, legal and moral grounds, as well as my concern for exposing the president to a seamy and explosive situation. 'Stop!' I said. 'This is crazy.' I told Regan to go to the president: 'Get him to end this matter once and for all.' "[25]

Regan, Shultz recalls, "seemed to share my concern" and promised to speak to the President. But instead of ending the operation, Poindexter, on May 22, told Shultz once again that the hostages would be out immediately in return for a shipment of TOWs. McFarlane's delegation spent May 25–28 in Tehran. But there were no hostage releases, and McFarlane came home empty-handed. As the Shultz notes put it: *"Polecat died.* M.O. [McFarlane] to Tehran. Talks broke down + on way back."[26] In June, Casey and Poindexter assured Shultz that the operation was over.

Offer to Resign

In July, Shultz tried to bring Iran policy back under the control of the State Department by nominating a trusted Pakistani government minister as an intermediary with the Iranians. But he was aware that the NSC-CIA channels were very much alive. On July 2, in an "eyes-only" memorandum, Michael Armacost wrote Shultz that the NSC was in the midst of a "sub rosa provision of arms" to Iran and that a source was "upbeat" about an imminent hostage release. Armacost told Shultz he found the policy wrong, and warned it would inevitably become public. Shultz, discussing the business with aide Charles Hill, commented, according to notes, that: "Iran business [is] very uncomfortable. No one mentions it to me—my own fault. I sd [said] if I didn't need to know don't tell me. Casey said it was dead. It's not."[27]

Then suddenly, at the end of the month, a hostage—Father Lawrence Jenco—was released. Shultz's memoirs say he was told the liberation was "for reasons of health." In fact, it was in exchange for the latest arms shipment, worth $24 million. Whatever the reasons, Shultz was starting to smolder at the degree to which his department's responsibilities had been usurped by the NSC and CIA. On August 5, 1986, Shultz handed Reagan a letter of resignation. Shultz recalls the reasons: "[M]y sense of difference with the president on the Philippines, my disagreement with him the previous January on arms sales to Iran, the unease I felt in the national security community over my refusal to go along with lie detector tests applied as a routine tool of management, and the constant sniping I felt from low-level White House operatives."[28]

In testimony before the Senate Select Committee on Intelligence in 1987, Shultz provided an example of that sniping. Traditionally, he explained, the White House permitted the Secretary of State to use one of its fleet of airplanes maintained by the Air Force for state travel—a necessity, Shultz said, in times of tight State Department budgets. "But," he continued, "I started having trouble because some people on the White House staff decided that they were going to make my life unhappy and they stopped approving these airplane things. And we fought about it and so on....And so I told the president, 'I'd like to leave and here's my letter.' And he stuck it in his drawer and said, 'You're tired. It's about time to go on vacation and let's talk about it after you get back from vacation.' "[29]

Shultz stayed on, and the Iran operation continued, even though three more hostages were taken in September and October. Then, on November 2, David Jacobsen, the last of the three hostages to be released under the arms-for-hostages deal, was freed. Two days later the affair became public.

The Aftermath

Shultz's most determined battles began only after the first details of the arms-for-hostages exchanges were made public. While Shultz called for full disclosure of the facts, Weinberger and Poindexter advocated saying as little as possible. At a November 10 meeting of Shultz, Reagan, Bush, Weinberger, Meese, Regan, Casey, Poindexter, and an aide, the rift became open. Shultz pressed for assurances that no more arms would be sent to Iran; Reagan in response insisted that all present support his Iran policy and refrain from making public statements.[30]

Over the next month, Shultz met repeatedly with Reagan and attempted to demonstrate to him why the policy was publicly perceived as an arms-for-hostages deal. In a particularly blunt conversation, Shultz reminded Reagan of the November 1985 shipment of arms described by McFarlane even at the time as arms-for-hostages, but the President replied that while he knew of the shipment, it was not an arms-for-hostages deal. On November 19, Shultz said in an explosive television interview that, while he was opposed to any further arms transactions, he could not speak for the administration. Rumors of Shultz's impending resignation gathered steam in the media and the corridors of the White House. Yet Shultz stayed on, forcing changes in Casey's testimony on November 21 to the intelligence committees. Shultz's pressure resulted in the removal from the text of at least one outright lie—that the administration learned what was in the November 1985 shipment only in 1986.

Shultz Put the Blame Squarely on the President's Staff

Only after the public revelation on November 24 that North had diverted funds to support the Contras did the White House give up the fight and Reagan return responsibility for Iran policy to the State Department. Shultz recalls in his memoirs how he perceived the situation in November 1986. "The U.S. government had violated its own policies on antiterrorism and against arms sales to Iran, was buying our own citizens' freedom in a manner that could only *encourage* the taking of others, was working through disreputable international go-betweens, was circumventing our constitutional system of governance, and was misleading the American people—all in the guise of furthering some purported regional political transformation, or to obtain in actuality a hostage release[31]....They told the president what they wanted him to know and what they saw he wanted to hear, and they dressed it up in "geostrategic" costume. And they kept me as well as others who had constitutional responsibilities to advise the president in the dark. A responsible staff should have kept the president fully informed and should have continuously warned him of the legal and constitutional problems created by the actions taken or not taken. They should have called his attention repeatedly to the violations of his own policies and warned him that the intelligence about Iran was fragile at best and obtained from parties with strong interests and biases of their own."[32]

But as the Iran-Contra affair became the target of investigations, others lodged the same kind of charges against Shultz himself. The Tower Commission—after being told that Shultz, in January 1986, had asked to be kept informed on a "need-to-know" basis—judged him harshly for shrugging off his responsibility as chief foreign policy adviser. Shultz and Weinberger "in particular," the report asserted, "distanced themselves from the march of events. Secretary Shultz specifically requested to be informed only as necessary to perform his job.…Their obligation was to give the President their full support and continued advice with respect to the program or, if they could not in conscience do that, to so inform the President. Instead, they simply distanced themselves from the program." In a similar vein, Rep. Michael DeWine, R-Ohio, told Shultz during a June 1987 hearing on the matter: "You gave Admiral Poindexter complete authority to decide what you needed to know. You took the risk, and it was a risk, that he would give you enough information about the Iran initiative for you to do your job. In essence, you left the fox to guard the chicken coop."[33]

Like DeWine, Rep. Henry Hyde wondered why Shultz had not used the threat of resignation to bring an end to the arms sale. "I can't escape the notion that had you opposed this flawed policy and were willing to resign over this policy difference…you could have stopped it dead in its tracks."[34]

In reply, Shultz noted that in the early period of the initiative, "I opposed it; I thought I had taken part in killing it on more than one occasion.…It was clear as it went on that the President had a desire to do it, and I didn't just say, well, you seem to be leaning against me, I'm going to resign." Later on, as the operation continued, Shultz said, "I certainly did have the sense that Secretary Weinberger and I were on one side of the issue and everybody else, including the President, was on the other side, and that somehow or other this was going to move ahead. So again, I didn't say agree with me or goodbye.…There is a lot more going on around the world than this particular set of events.…Always in the question of whether you'll resign or not is the question of the chance to help the President accomplish some positive things.…Nothing ever gets settled in this town, and you can say, I'll give up and leave, or I'll stay and fight."

"I have never hesitated," Shultz added, "in my time in the Cabinet to speak up to Presidents, or to resign, if I felt the situation warranted it."

As to whether he should have spoken up to the President on more occasions than he did, Shultz told the independent counsel on February 13, 1992 that he could not account for the missed opportunities. "I...recognize that there were times when apparently from the things that you showed me...I knew about some planned events and I didn't renew my protest to the President. I don't know why that is."[35]

Such puzzlement apart, Shultz must have been gratified when, during his weekly radio address on March 14, 1987, President Reagan conceded that he should have listened to Shultz and Weinberger when they opposed the Iran initiative. Said Reagan: "As we now know, it turned out they were right, and I was wrong."

Reagan, Ransom, and Respect

The Iran-Contra example can drive home the reality of a second world—parallel to that described in Part I—where competition is as often for respect as for particular policies. With her few immediate and direct subordinates, a bureaucratic superior has a continuing relationship of a very special sort. She enjoys the legitimacy of hierarchical position. She can hire or fire or use shows of indifference to discipline—imposing costs that the subordinate can only reciprocate surreptitiously, if at all. The superior/subordinate relationship is thus unequal in terms of much of the capacity of each to command attention (or obedience). Still, the success or failure of their plans and reputations is also very closely intertwined. And the fact that superior needs the subordinate also gives the latter power in the relationship.

All of this is uncomplicated and familiar. So it would seem, logically but erroneously, that the nature of a particular relationship should be easily understood and differences easily accommodated. The primary needs of the superior are relatively clear, and she appears to have the authority and power to demand that the subordinate meet them. She wants specialized advice on the decisions she makes that will affect the subordinate's area. She wants the subordinate to make decisions that are not worth her time, but to make them consistently with her values and priorities. She wants the subordinate to manage the making of what may be a multitude of lesser decisions by those working for him, decisions that the subordinate will not make himself, and to bring his organization to follow in good faith the broad directions that are important to her, and to execute the decisions she has made herself. Like Ikle and Pillsbury, she wants the subordinate to work with others, not in her chain of command, to shape decisions and programs that cut across jurisdictional lines and that go beyond the area of her sole responsibility. Although all this seems straightforward enough, in fact it hides deep issues of organizational psychology and sociology.

Junior officers were, by 2007, questioning the conduct of the senior generals who too loyally allowed the flawed plans of Secretary of Defense Donald Rumsfeld for invading Iraq to go forward.[36] Only Chief of Staff General Erik Shinseki spoke out in public. Similarly, at the end of the Iran-Contra Affair, Secretary of State George Shultz was criticized sharply for not doing more to protect the President by blocking that disastrous policy—criticized by both prominent members of Congress and by the Tower Commission that was appointed by President Reagan in the aftermath of the scandal. Shultz had wisely and consistently opposed furnishing arms to Iran; he had no role in using the proceeds of such sales to arm the Contras in Nicaragua. As a loyal subordinate, his options were limited.

In order of ascending challenge to the President, he could have hammered away endlessly at his objection to the plan, but only at the cost of showing a willingness to strain President Reagan's patience and impose, perhaps unnecessarily, on the President's energies. He might have rallied resources of others by forming a coalition against a plan that the President plainly favored, but that would amount to weakening the President's influence or at least raising the price of the President's decision. He could have called for a formal decision process, but that would involve the risk of suggesting that the decision was not the President's alone to make.

What more could Shultz have done? In an escalating order, he could have put his views in writing, thus making clear that he would want his opposition known at a later date if something went wrong. The President would have known that that guaranteed Shultz's inability to loyally consider the President's reputation, respect, and resources if the plan turned out badly. He could have leaked the plan and his opposition to the Congress or the media. Each of these would involve some measure of disloyalty. Although Shultz would argue that he was thinking about the President's resources and personal concerns and not his own, in fact his primary motivation was to prevent the President from making a decision that would be harmful to the country as well as to his role, reputation, and department—a motivation not wholly consistent with loyalty.

Finally, he might have directly threatened to resign. Instead, he had distanced himself from the decision-making process after his views were rejected by the President, even suggesting to the National Security Advisor, John Poindexter, that he not be kept fully informed about matters that did not require State Department action. There is a great deal to be learned about invisible but powerful organizational forces by asking why the Secretary of State distanced himself from a matter so important to our foreign policy and did not threaten to resign.

To get at the full answer, we must first look at several obvious arguments against resignation. Ultimately the President, as his superior, had the right to decide whether we would, directly or indirectly, send arms to Iran in the hope of improving relations and of obtaining the release of American hostages. A subordinate cannot expect to press his disagreement forever. Once a subordinate has made his case clearly and, perhaps, passionately, the superior's right to decide must be accepted. Orderly decision making requires that someone be able to declare an end to the debate and direct a shifting of government into an action mode; the elected President (or whatever appointed official is nearer to levels of electoral accountability) should be that person. Moreover, elected leaders are likely to have a broader view of how diverse policy areas relate to each other. They also are better placed to see how politics and the need of electoral support link policy to public demands—and recognizing the wishes of interested publics is critical to democratic responsiveness between elections.

Still, these process-based arguments for a subordinate limiting his opposition are less than 100 percent convincing when the superior is about to make a decision as clearly wrong as this one was. The President had himself announced a clear policy of not making concessions for hostages, a practice that would only lead to further hostage taking (as it did in this case). The United States was a leader of an international embargo of arms to Iran and Iraq—which we were demanding that other nations follow—forbidding sales of arms to both states while they were in a very bloody war. The appropriate intelligence committees had not been informed, as a federal statute required, if sales were to be made in secret. The use of the proceeds of the sales to Iran to arm the Contras (a matter about which Shultz seems not to have been aware) violated a federal statute, led to an extensive criminal investigation, and did grave damage to President Reagan's final years in office. The prospects for changing our relations with Iran were small and the hopes ill informed. Perhaps most important, sending a cake to Ayatollah Khomeini, someone the American public and its allies had learned to regard as an extremely hostile enemy, made the President look like a suppliant, threatening the respect he would need in dealing with other problems.

Another reason for Shultz limiting his opposition was present but seems less persuasive. As he reminds us, Shultz had other battles still to fight—frequently a valid reason for not resigning. But Iran-Contra was a more important battle than almost any others. Moreover, this explanation is hardly consistent with the fact that he was not always so reluctant to leave. In fact, he had considered resigning twice during the short period of these events—first for being asked to install a system of periodic polygraphing of senior State Department officials to discourage leaks; and second, when his needed use of airplanes, which were at the disposal of the President, was purposely made difficult by small-minded White House staff.

There is a related justification: that resignation would be pointless. The Secretary of State could believe that a resignation without explaining his reasons would have little positive effect on the decisions he was opposing and that to explain his reasons publicly would be to violate the secrecy that he regarded as an overriding necessity in national security matters. Making public his reasons for resigning would require engaging in an open disclosure of material that he would have condemned anyone else for "leaking." Still, he repeatedly expressed his belief that the matter would become public. He knew that, when it did leak, he would either have to reveal his opposition to it or share in the blame for a decision he had always considered extremely unwise and had long opposed.

Thus each of these explanations for not taking bolder steps to block a clear mistake seems unconvincing in its own right. More revealing, each also leaves unexplained what Shultz in fact did—his willingness to separate himself from, and fail to engage with, the small group of decision makers who were involved, even suggesting that he not be kept fully informed. The pragmatic explanations of actions in the terms used in Part I of this book—the furtherance of present and anticipated policy and other concerns by building and using resources, by creating alliances of influence, and by careful design and timing of proposals—do not explain the Secretary's inaction. To understand the inaction, one has to enter a parallel, often ignored, second world organized around somewhat different factors—a world where the contest takes place in terms of relationships of respect and confidence. Shultz seems to have distanced himself from the processes that led to a very bad decision because he felt he was not being shown the respect he deserved from the President and, more pointedly, from other senior foreign policy officials.

There is a bridge between the worlds of Part I ("world one") and that of this Part II ("world two"). The capacity of a subordinate to affect policy depends largely upon both (1) the range of decisions over which he is delegated authority by his superior; and also (2) the extent to which his advice is sought and valued when his superior personally makes the largest decisions within their shared field of responsibility. These two determinants of a subordinate's powers within a particular field of government activity also determine how responsive those working under him will be, and the extent to which the superior is likely to support him in contests with peers. All this greatly affects the views of other players as to the powers the subordinate will be able to invoke to get his way in matters that have not yet arisen.

The superior can—at some risk and expense to herself in terms of weakening the subordinate's sense of responsibility and losing the advantage of his more current knowledge and greater accumulated expertise—disempower the subordinate by making decisions, unilaterally and without consultation, in the areas she has previously committed to the authority of the subordinate. The superior can punish the subordinate by leaving him out of decisions she makes, thereby also reducing his influence with peers. Even if these steps suggesting a lack of respect are not considered by the superior as a form of punishment—that is, even if they are simply taken as a matter of the superior's convenience—the effects on the powers of the subordinate are severe. His loyalty to the superior is likely to diminish as resentment takes over.

All this is another way of saying that Secretary of State Shultz, like any subordinate, depended upon the manifest confidence of his superior, President Reagan, to retain his influence in terms of his relations with others. Like every Secretary of State, Shultz found himself in some competition with the President's National Security Advisor in terms of where the President placed his confidence, and the stakes were very high. For these reasons, Secretary of State Shultz had threatened to resign when he felt his loyalty was questioned by the proposal of a polygraph and when he thought that the White House staff doubted his importance enough to insultingly deny him the needed use of a presidential plane. When he considered resigning over Iran-Contra, it was also because his views and those of his department were being ignored or given next-to-no weight in the discussions—at least as much as it was intended to force the President to change this particular decision. The sole effective action that Shultz could take—a public resignation that would sever his relationship with the administration—was only considered on the set of occasions when he felt in danger of losing the power that depends on the President's respect for his stature and judgment.

For Shultz there are two decisions being made by President Reagan: what to do with regard to American hostages and Iran; and who is the President's leading foreign policy advisor? The latter is the more important question to Shultz. His influence within and outside the State Department—his influence on decisions not made by the President as well as his influence on decisions made by the President—depends on that. Indeed, there is even more in "world number two": because of the psychological and social effects of a superior-subordinate relationship, Shultz doubtless cares independently and emotionally about the President's views of him as Secretary of State. A subordinate is generally hurt when he feels his superior is denying him respect. This is especially true if he was hired because he had a long and admired record in government, as Shultz did.

The emotional part of the demand for respect is reciprocal. The fact that Shultz's superior, President Reagan in this case, also wants the respect and confidence—not just the fear and obedience—of the subordinates whom he chooses is the bonding, emotional part of what superiors regard as "loyalty." Recognizing that need of the President for respect may be one of the main reasons that Secretaries Shultz and Weinberger fail to emphasize far more dramatically the folly of the plan being put forth, in turn, by National Security Advisors McFarlane and Poindexter. And the superior's need for respect becomes particularly acute when the subordinate, like Shultz, comes to the appointment with a reputation for competence in a particular area that exceeds the superior's. In this situation, the pragmatic wisdom of the superior taking seriously the advice of the subordinate she chose is sometimes overwhelmed by her felt need to demand the respect and confidence of the subordinate for a decision already largely made. That President Reagan could be as gracious as he was to Secretary Shultz even after the project had become a disaster and even knowing that Shultz had correctly foretold that result tells us more about the unusual self-confidence of the President than about the general reaction of a superior to a subordinate's greater wisdom.

There is no hint of a lack of respect for his superior, the President, in Shultz's behavior or later account of the Iran-Contra affair. The focus of his criticism is the White House national security staff, whom he believes misled the President. Indeed, even when he felt that the President was not showing the necessary confidence in his judgment, Shultz's respect for and loyalty to Reagan continued. This is not always so.

President George W. Bush and Paul O'Neill: Respect and Revenue

In long-term relationships, superiors need the type of confidence Shultz continued to have in Reagan as much as subordinates need respect from their superiors and from the others interacting with them on a very regular basis.[37] This can be summarized in terms of self-respect. Each of us is powerfully motivated by the need to maintain respect and self-respect; both are threatened in that need by any lack of respect shown by a credible and admired source. If respect and self-respect are threatened, there are only three familiar reactions: to be angry and fight back, to adjust one's views of the credible source, or to reduce the sense of self-respect that we value so much. Different people will act in different ways, but the choice becomes inevitable when respect between a superior and a subordinate disappears.

Sporadic interactions are different from these ongoing relationships. It was not necessary for Pillsbury to believe that George Shultz was doing a good job as Secretary of State or Bill Casey as Director of the CIA for the three of them to engage together in the process of considering a changed policy with regard to Stinger missiles in Afghanistan. Occasional and precisely limited, that decision was not part of a continuing team effort. But confidence that the other is holding up her end of the shared responsibilities is the essential prerequisite to the successful operations of a small policy team. Thus, it was necessary for Secretary of State Shultz to enjoy the confidence of Secretary of Defense Weinberger and National Security Advisor Poindexter as well as of the President (and for each of them, including the President, to enjoy the confidence of Shultz and the others) if the foreign policy team of the Reagan administration was to work. Thus I will argue that President George W. Bush asked Vice President Cheney to remove Paul O'Neill as Secretary of Treasury, after only two years in that role, as much because he felt that O'Neill lacked confidence in him, as because he lacked confidence in O'Neill's capacities as Secretary of the Treasury. Ron Suskind entitles his description of O'Neill's tenure "The Price of Loyalty." But O'Neill was not disloyal to the President. Loyalty means maintaining support for the superior against all opponents, not only when the superior is wrongfully attacked, but even when the superior has made a mistake, at least when the issue is a matter of legitimate disagreement. It does not mean an unwillingness to criticize within the team when the superior is wrong. Leaders, like the players of any other policy roles, need emotional support from team members; they also need direct criticism from team members, as the Iran-Contra case illustrates. But the same person cannot generally provide both at the same time.

All of this starts at the hiring stage. President Bush, like any superior, could choose a Secretary of the Treasury for any one or more of four reasons:

1. The superior may want the political or other private support that the choice can bring in any of a number of forms. The Secretary of the Treasury, for example, has to be chosen with the confidence of the markets in mind.

2. The superior may choose a candidate either because of the person's knowledge of the field or to obtain more general skills in areas of policy and management. The two are different. A President may pick a Secretary of Defense because of his knowledge of national security matters. Clinton picked Les Aspin and Bush picked Donald Rumsfeld on this basis. Kennedy picked Robert McNamara and Eisenhower picked Charles Wilson (not to be confused with Rep. Charlie Wilson) because of their record of successful management of very large private companies.

3. The superior may also pick a subordinate because she believes that he agrees with her views on important issues in the area where he will operate. President George W. Bush knew that he wanted a mammoth tax cut and might have wanted a Secretary of the Treasury who regarded that as a desirable step.

4. Finally, a superior may pick her subordinate for absolute loyalty—that is, because of the emotional and social support that the subordinate provides the superior and because of the subordinate's willingness to subordinate his policy preferences to hers, even at the stage of internal discussion of what should be done. President George W. Bush may have picked Attorney General Gonzales on that basis.

President Bush picked Paul O'Neill to be Secretary of Treasury on the recommendation of Vice President Cheney, and O'Neill seems to have taken the job because of his confidence in Cheney. What recommended O'Neill was his reputation as CEO of two immense and successful

American corporations and his many years of experience in policy roles in the federal government, particularly in dealing with the federal budget. These would bring support from the markets. O'Neill was not picked because of his views, which seem to have been unknown, or his political ideology, which was somewhat out of line with the President's, or for any exceptional willingness to subordinate his views to the interests of the President. In each of those categories he was not a promising choice.

O'Neill took the job because he felt strongly about certain aspects of federal policy, including a view of fiscal responsibility that was inconsistent with the mammoth tax cut that President Bush had made a pillar of his campaign. O'Neill also took the job because he regarded the position of the Secretary of the Treasury as one of immense importance and one that a relative novice in the fields of Treasury concern, like President Bush, would draw upon for advice on a number of critical issues. President Bush offered the job in the hope of getting valuable political support for the policies on which he had run for President. In retrospect, it is clear that someone was going to be disappointed in the appointment.

The evolution of the relationship, as O'Neill describes it, reflected a fundamental disagreement about roles and, perhaps also, a substantial difference in personalities. But, above all, the relationship was doomed by the lack of confidence flowing in either direction, particularly upward. Given the rare privilege of regular meetings with the President, O'Neill still found that the President was hardly listening to O'Neill's discussions of what he felt the economy needed. On this, and on the issue of global warming—of intense interest to O'Neill, although well outside the core area of his responsibilities—O'Neill came to conclude that a small circle of White House advisors—including prominently the Vice President and the Senior Economic Advisor to the White House, Lawrence B. Lindsey—were using the access and confidence that they enjoyed with the President (much like the National Security team in the Iran-Contra case) to obtain the President's agreement to policies, often acting secretly and manipulatively. O'Neill felt excluded and concluded that the President intended O'Neill's role to be simply providing an image of fiscal responsibility. Having taken the job to influence policy, O'Neill was not getting what he expected. Having a Secretary of the Treasury who spoke out in ways that were not always reassuring to the markets, and whose views were often misaligned with the President's, Bush was not getting what he expected.

The superior always has an option in this situation of turning increasingly to others for advice and to be given delegated responsibility. The subordinate's first option in response—taken by O'Neill as it was by Shultz—is to focus increasingly on the areas where his own delegated powers, or the confidence he enjoys as an individual, can provide the influence over policy that motivated his taking the job. What he has lost is that large part of influence over policy that comes from having, and from the recognition by others that he has, the support of a more powerful common superior—in this case President Bush. O'Neill turned his attention to such matters as the problem of HIV infection in Africa, earning some sharp, non-private sarcasm from a President unwilling or unable to discuss their disagreements openly. Indeed, it was Vice President Cheney who was asked to end the relationship.

A basic difference in the concept of the job was, as is frequently true, supplemented by the disrespect that follows some differences in personality that reflect what each of the participants in the relationship considers important characteristics for the job. Paul O'Neill was hard-working, dedicated to seeing and dealing as rigorously and transparently as possible with complexity, and a believer in a significant role for government, although he was fiscally conservative. President Bush had firmly held views based on premises that did not require detailed factual analysis of particular issues, believed in staying with positions already taken, did not value long discussions or detailed analysis, and enjoyed a far more political and ideological approach to governing.

Perhaps these differences could have been reconciled, as they were in the case of Reagan and Shultz, by a willingness to recognize that each had a different role to play and by a mutual valuing of the other's way of playing his different role. This does not seem to have occurred to either, and the basis for a compromise acceptable to both was probably not there anyway. Often the only real option in such a situation is to try and talk through the difference, but an irony lies in the way of that option. If the subordinate asks the superior to talk through the difficulties, he is implicitly placing the two on an equal basis, and telling the superior how he should be doing his job. He is thereby further challenging the entitlement to confidence of a superior who feels distrusted or disrespected. O'Neill could not expect President Bush to sit still for a discussion of how they were failing one another. When a superior and subordinate disagree about a relationship, it is easier for the superior to end the relationship, or to find substitutes around it, than to undertake difficult changes in his own behavior.

What seems to have doomed the relationship between President Bush and Treasury Secretary O'Neill was not the differences in understanding of roles and in understanding the ways the other played his role. It was a lack of reciprocal confidence and respect. President Bush could not have felt respected by O'Neill, and he was not. O'Neill could not have felt that he enjoyed the confidence of President Bush in the most important areas in which the Treasury Department dealt, and he plainly did not. For a while the President was prepared to work his way around the Secretary of the Treasury, but that produces resentment and evasion, not the respect, confidence, and loyalty that the superior feels he needs. These attitudes have to flow upward in the relationship as well as downward.

Part III
Nicotine for Teens

10

Similarities and Differences

It is hardly surprising that the way I shall urge the reader to think about the two cases that follow is very closely related to how I discussed the case of Pillsbury and the Stinger missile. After all, my primary building blocks of rules, concerns, and resources are the same in both areas. The previously described array of types of action a policy advocate can take is also very comprehensive: designing the proposal in light of the relevant players' concerns and their understandings of the significance of the occasion; timing the proposal in light of the salience of particular concerns at particular times; forming coalitions to maximize the usefulness of the resources of influence possessed by those supportive of the proposal; and taking steps to prevent the formation of rival coalitions with rival proposals.

These similarities persist, although the two cases that follow involve domestic, not foreign, policy; accordingly, Congress plays a far larger role. The cases describe two sequential stages in an effort to prevent the many harms of smoking—a subject to which a new Surgeon General would return in 2006. In the first, Dr. David Kessler, Administrator of the Food and Drug Administration (FDA), proceeds to promulgate an administrative rule that he hopes will protect teens from the dangers of nicotine. In the second, culminating shortly before a Supreme Court decision struck down the Kessler rule by a narrow 5–4 decision margin, consumer advocate Matt Myers tries to bring a coalition of nongovernmental organizations opposed to smoking to reach an agreement with the cigarette companies on legislation that would accomplish goals much like those of Kessler.

In the end, neither policy entrepreneur succeeded directly, although in the years after these two efforts the United States experienced a substantial reduction in the use of tobacco by teenagers and a substantial change in the behavior of Philip Morris, the most formidable opponent of Kessler and Myers. From 1996 to 2004, current smoking by twelfth graders declined from over 22 percent to 16 percent. The decline in smoking among eighth and tenth graders was far greater. The number of young people who had even tried cigarettes also declined radically. In the meantime, Philip Morris adopted a corporate strategy designed to gain moral legitimacy in the United States by developing a well-publicized campaign to prevent kids from smoking.

The tobacco cases are important because they raise several new aspects of policy advocacy. Let me start at the end with the Matthew Myers case, "Dealing with the Devil." It brings in a whole new set of rules—those applicable to legislative action. It involves a somewhat different cast of characters: nongovernmental players, who represent public and private interest groups; and the media, which stimulates and expresses the views of a far broader public but through the lens of its own interests and biases. Both are important because of their resources to influence elected officials, which are different from the resources we have examined earlier. Some of the tactics are also new. Matt Myers faces a far more complicated form of coalition building than Michael Pillsbury faced. Myers must build a coalition among interest groups that are themselves coalitions and, at the same time, deal with competitive efforts at building a rival coalition that are also unlike anything Pillsbury faced.

Congress and interest groups are important but remain in the background of the David Kessler case, "Taking on Big Tobacco: David Kessler and the Food and Drug Administration." The media are at center stage. Playing to a far broader audience than Pillsbury's audience of national security insiders, much of Kessler's task is to define his proposal in a way that will appeal to many in the executive branch and Congress and, simultaneously, to generate so much public support that opposing his proposal would be a risky option for any elected official. Finally, moving backward to the place we will begin, Kessler has to choose between using executive and legislative authority—a very fundamental and important choice among action paths.

The Situation Facing David Kessler
A Case History by Esther Scott

In 1994, David Kessler, commissioner of the Food and Drug Administration, took the first step on a path that would lead him and his agency into unexplored regulatory territory.[1] In a letter to an anti-smoking organization, he announced his intention to investigate whether the FDA could exercise control over cigarettes. It was a move that the agency—whose basic mandate was protecting the integrity of the food and drugs Americans consume—had shunned under past commissioners, who had argued that the FDA could not properly claim jurisdiction over tobacco products. Kessler—who was regarded as a champion of the American consumer by some and a regulatory "zealot" by others—believed, however, that new evidence of cigarette manufacturers' intentions and practices justified a second look at the issue. While many praised Kessler's decision as a long overdue effort to curb an industry whose products resulted in hundreds of thousands of deaths each year, others attacked it as a case of regulatory overreach and a distraction from the agency's basic mission.

FDA: Duties and Powers

David Kessler was named by President George H. W. Bush to head an agency that had long been a regulatory fixture in the United States, but which had, in the years immediately before his appointment, found itself enmeshed in controversy. The FDA's earliest roots stretched back to the mid-nineteenth century and a laboratory set up in the U.S. patent office to conduct chemical analyses of food products, but its modern era could be said to begin in 1938. In that year, Congress passed the landmark Food, Drug, and Cosmetic Act, which expanded the FDA's regulatory reach and gave it responsibilities beyond simple policing. For one thing, the law added cosmetics, as well as therapeutic "devices," to the FDA's existing bailiwick of food and drugs. More important, in the case of drugs, the 1938 act established a provision for "premarket approval," which required drug manufacturers to demonstrate that a new drug was safe before it could be marketed. In addition, reflecting the agency's concern that the existing definition of a drug—that is, a product "intended for use in the diagnosis, cure, mitigation, treatment or prevention of disease"—was too narrow (precluding, for example, drugs that were used to ease the side effects of pregnancy or to treat obesity), the 1938 bill expanded the statutory meaning of the term. A drug could now also be a product "intended to affect the structure or any function of the body." This proved to be a fateful change: when the issue of FDA regulation of tobacco arose, the additional language would be cited by both sides to bolster their position in the debate over jurisdiction.

In the decades following passage of the Food, Drug, and Cosmetic Act, Congress periodically added to the FDA's mandate, often in response to tragedies or scandals. In 1962, for example, legislative action followed closely on the revelation that thalidomide, a sedative often prescribed to pregnant women, had caused major birth defects in thousands of babies in Europe; although the drug had not been available in the United States, the tragedy led to calls for more rigorous regulation. As a result, the 1962 amendments raised the bar on market entry for new drugs: in addition to demonstrating that their products were safe, drug manufacturers would have to show that they were effective as well.[2] In 1976, another scandal— this time involving the Dalkon Shield, an intrauterine device blamed for eighteen deaths and thousands of miscarriages—led to further amendments mandating stricter regulation of medical devices as well, including, for some products, a requirement of premarket approval.[3]

By the early 1990s, the FDA had amassed an impressive array of regulatory duties. It was, among other things, responsible for ensuring the safety and wholesomeness of all foods, except for meat, poultry, and some dairy products (the province of the Department of Agriculture), as well as the safety and, in some cases, the effectiveness of all drugs, medical devices, cosmetics, devices that emitted radiation (including televisions and microwave appliances), animal feed and drugs, and the nation's blood supply. The sheer range of items that fell under the agency's purview was breathtaking: it encompassed, for example, devices as simple as tongue depressors and as sophisticated as artificial hearts, and medicines as familiar as aspirin and as experimental as chemotherapy drugs. In all, as the FDA's *Almanac* proudly declared, the agency regulated over $1 trillion worth of products, accounting for 25 cents of every dollar spent annually by consumers, or one-quarter of the nation's gross national product.

To perform its many tasks, the FDA employed roughly 9,300 people by 1994, the largest single contingent (3,400) in the Office of Regulatory Affairs, which was responsible for enforcement. Its budget for that year amounted to about $856 million, including user fees levied on pharmaceutical companies for new drug approvals. The agency was housed in the Public Health Service within the Department of Health and Human Services (HHS); the FDA commissioner—a presidential appointee—reported to the Assistant Secretary for Health, who headed up the Public Health Service division.[4] By virtue of the span of its authority, the FDA was considered, according to one account, "the most influential regulatory agency on earth...."[5] It was also, for many years, generally a highly regarded one, both at home and abroad, for the watchful care it brought to its duties. In perhaps the most famous instance of this, the conscientious work of a medical officer at the FDA had held up the application to market thalidomide in the United States, thus sparing the nation the anguish experienced by thousands of families in Europe, where the drug had been sold in twenty countries. It was such incidents, as one account noted, that "made FDA approval the worldwide 'gold standard' for medical products." The numbers appeared to bear out the agency's reputation: according to one study, from 1970 to 1992, there had been 31 drug recalls in France, 30 in Germany, 23 in Britain; but in the United States, there had been only nine.[6]

But in the 1980s, the agency had begun to fall on hard times. Under the Reagan administration, it had suffered a series of budget cuts and resulting reductions in its staffing, even while Congress continued to add to its regulatory duties. The consequences of these cuts were felt most acutely in the enforcement side of FDA. According to the findings of an advisory panel appointed in 1990 by HHS Secretary Louis Sullivan, the number of inspections had dropped by 40 percent over the preceding decade, and the number of enforcement actions—seizures, injunctions, and prosecutions—had "declined sharply since the 1970s."[7]

Even in areas where the FDA had previously won high marks—for example, the evaluation of new drugs—it had begun to come under sharp attack. The thalidomide scare notwithstanding, critics argued that the agency was taking too long to approve new drugs. According to one study, the length of time it took to bring new medicines to the market had almost doubled since the early 1960s—from eight to fifteen years. Pharmaceutical companies were not the only ones complaining about the FDA's ponderous approach to new drug approvals. As the AIDS epidemic spread throughout the United States in the 1980s, the agency found itself the target of blistering attacks from activists who decried its insistence on completing formal clinical trails while patients suffered debilitating symptoms that could be mitigated by new drugs and therapies.[8] As it struggled to stay abreast of a wave of increasingly sophisticated, and sometimes risky, new medicines and medical technologies, the understaffed FDA found itself faced with a burgeoning backlog of applications for new drugs and medical devices. The agency was, in the words of one account, in a state of "near-collapse." After the Sullivan-appointed advisory panel had completed its study of the FDA, the chairman of the group, former FDA Commissioner Dr. Charles Edwards, described it as an organization "in disarray, to put it in the mildest term."[9] It was during this low ebb in its fortunes that David Kessler was appointed commissioner of the FDA by President Bush in November 1990.

Kessler Takes Over

David Kessler came to the FDA with the reputation of being something of a "wunderkind," in the words of a *New York Times* report. For one thing, at the age of thirty-nine, he was the youngest person to head the agency since 1912. For another, his education and career made him, in the opinion of many, uniquely qualified for the post of FDA commissioner. He had earned a degree in law from the University of Chicago in 1978, and one in medicine—he was a pediatrician by training—from Harvard Medical School the following year. In 1984, Kessler was appointed director of medicine at Albert Einstein College of Medicine in the Bronx; he also taught food and drug law at Columbia University, positions he held until he was tapped by HHS Secretary Louis Sullivan to head the FDA. Kessler did not, however, spend his entire pre-FDA career in academia. While completing his pediatric training at Johns Hopkins School of Medicine, he worked part-time for Senator Orrin Hatch, R-Utah, helping to draft food and health legislation for the Labor and Human Resources Committee. Looking back, Kessler felt his experience in Congress had been a key part of his education. "As a doctor," he told one reporter, "I'm supposed to say that my most important training was my medical internship, but frankly, my years on Capitol Hill were the most important. That's what taught me how this town works."[10]

The First Years: A Brief Overview

Soon after arriving at the FDA in late 1990, Kessler set out his two chief priorities for the agency. He intended, the *New York Times* reported, to "beef up the agency's power of enforcement, and at the same time streamline the many-layered procedures that can delay approval of drugs and medical devices by months or years in some cases." In his first few years in office, he would meet with success on both counts, although his critics increasingly questioned both his choices and his aims.

Kessler moved quickly on enforcement, hiring a team of 100 criminal investigators in his first months as commissioner and signaling his determination to revitalize what one observer called "a moribund enforcement process" at the FDA.[11] "Nearly every other week since [his appointment]," the *Times* reported in June, "he has announced enforcement actions against food and drug manufacturers intended to regain the agency's credibility...." Perhaps the most notable of these came in April 1991 when, after a dispute with Procter and Gamble over what the FDA contended was misleading labeling—using the world "fresh" on cartons of Citrus Hill orange juice, which was made from concentrate—Kessler ordered agency officials to seize 2,000 cases of the juice from a warehouse. The episode, which received widespread coverage in the press, was the opening salvo in a major agency campaign to "clean up" misrepresentations by food manufacturers and expand the content labeling of food products; the action won a mix of criticism from those who characterized it as publicity-driven, and praise from those who applauded it as an effort to bolster the agency's effectiveness. Kessler, meanwhile, continued to speak out strongly against questionable labeling practices, singling out, for example, products that made misleading claims about cholesterol. While his stand on the issue earned the support of consumer groups and some press commentators, others expressed uneasiness about the new commissioner's priorities. "It is now my hope," said Kessler's former mentor, Senator Hatch, in June 1991, "that he will put as much emphasis on expediting approvals of new therapies for life-threatening diseases and assuring the public of this commitment."[12]

Hatch's comment foreshadowed what would be an increasingly strong tide of criticism from those who were clamoring to bring new drugs and medical devices to the market at an accelerated pace. For Kessler, the issue was complicated by competing demands on the agency: advocates were calling for speedier drug approvals, while "the public is saying, be vigilant." Nonetheless, he did succeed in significantly cutting down the length of time it took the FDA to review a completed application—from an average of 33 months in 1987 to 19 months in 1992. In addition, as a result of agency negotiations with the pharmaceutical industry, Congress passed legislation permitting the FDA to levy user fees on drug manufacturers; the income from the fees allowed the agency to hire over 600 additional staff to meet tighter deadlines for drug approvals. Still, some critics were not appeased. They argued that the clinical testing requirements before the final application could be submitted had actually lengthened the application process in Kessler's tenure—a contention Kessler strongly denies—and that Kessler's efforts to limit dissemination of "off-label" drug information had further squelched the development of new treatments.[13]

Kessler became further embroiled in controversy as a result of one of the most difficult issues to face an FDA commissioner in recent times—the question of what to do about silicone gel breast implants. A trickle of news about possibly serious side effects associated with silicone leaking from the implants, beginning in 1991, had turned into a torrent by early 1992, creating a climate of fear for many women and uncertainty for implant manufacturers. In the absence of definitive data about either the safety or the risks of implants, Kessler was under heavy pressure from two sides in the debate: consumer groups, such as Dr. Sidney Wolfe's Public Citizen Health Research Group, which argued for a blanket moratorium on the sale of implants; and professional groups, such as the American Society of Plastic and Reconstructive Surgeons, which insisted that women who wanted the implants should have access to them. Based on the information submitted by manufacturers, Kessler and an expert panel concluded that the available evidence was insufficient to meet the statutory standards of safety or effectiveness. Kessler first declared a moratorium for several months, and then, after the expert panel had issued its report, placed sharp restrictions on the use of implants, in particular for cosmetic purposes, until further studies were completed. His actions sparked the kind of division that would characterize reaction to a number of his initiatives and rulings over the years. The FDA decision in this case was hailed by consumer advocates and their allies in Congress, such as Rep. Ted Weiss, D-N.Y., who called Kessler's action "a reasonable compromise."[14] And it was excoriated by the medical industry and their allies, who said Kessler's actions were, in the words of one physician-critic, based "largely on the exaggerated claims of consumer advocacy groups and on poorly documented assertions."[15]

After a few years at the helm of the FDA, Kessler had become, as one account later put it, "Washington's most admired—and reviled—regulator."[16] His admirers praised him for "reviving a demoralized agency"[17] and for taking an activist approach to the FDA's mandate in such areas as food labeling, while his detractors characterized him as "confrontational" in style[18] and anti-business in orientation. In the course of his tenure at the FDA, he had met with some rebuffs: when he attempted to rein in the health benefit claims made by the makers of herbal medicines and vitamin supplements, for example, Congress—responding to a letter-writing campaign—passed legislation expressly restricting the scope of the FDA's regulation of dietary supplements. But at the same time, he had won wide recognition for beefing up the enforcement side of the FDA.

Kessler, said a former FDA associate chief counsel, had taken "an agency that was viewed as a paper tiger in the '80s and turned it into a tough enforcement agency in the '90s."[19] Kessler's strengths as commissioner were sufficient to recommend him to Bill Clinton after he beat George Bush in the presidential election of November 1992. When Clinton took office in January 1993, Kessler was one of only two top Bush appointees kept on by the new administration.[20]

A little over a year later, Kessler was back in the news. This time, the issue did not concern what to do with a product the FDA regulated, but what to do with one that the agency had heretofore studiously avoided bringing into its regulatory fold. In taking up the question of controls over tobacco, Kessler was choosing to walk into a lion's den of political and legal entanglements from which few had emerged victorious.

The Regulation of Tobacco

In terms of federal control, tobacco could be said to lead a charmed life. Although it had been identified as "the leading cause of preventable death in the U.S.,"[21] tobacco had managed to elude both classification as a drug or hazardous substance and, to a significant degree, the regulatory embrace of the federal government. Tobacco had, for example, been exempted from the provisions of the Hazardous Substances Act, the Toxic Substances Control Act, and the Controlled Substances Act, among others.[22] And while various pieces of the tobacco industry did fall under the purview of several federal entities—the Federal Trade Commission, for example, regulated cigarette advertising, and the Bureau of Alcohol, Tobacco and Firearms collected federal excise taxes on tobacco—no single agency had overall responsibility for the sale, distribution, or marketing of tobacco products.

Most observers attributed this state of affairs to tobacco's unique place in the U.S. economy and to the enormous political and financial clout wielded by the industry. Tobacco had been, the *New York Times* noted, "a bedrock cash crop since Colonial times—a legacy commemorated in the carved stone tobacco leaves adorning the columns of the Capitol itself." In the early 1990s it accounted for hundreds of thousands of jobs and poured some $12 billion in taxes into the coffers of federal, state, and local governments.[23] Moreover, with $54 billion in annual revenues, tobacco companies had ample resources to spread around—to a wide variety of cultural and sporting events (everything from ballet to auto racing) and, more significantly, to the election campaigns of numerous politicians. In the latter area, they had given generously, in the form of both "soft" money to political parties and political action committee (PAC) contributions to individual candidates. Over a ten-year period, from 1986 to 1995, according to a *Common Cause* report, tobacco "interests" (i.e., companies, lobbying groups, and their executives) would spend $20.6 million in political donations; in 1992 alone, according to another study, cigarette companies contributed almost $2 million in soft money, the bulk of it—$1.34 million—to Republicans.[24]

In view of the industry's power—and the fact that an estimated 45–50 million Americans were smokers—Congress had shown little appetite to place sharp curbs on tobacco products. Lawmakers had taken aim at tobacco several times. In 1965, for example, they passed the Federal Cigarette Labeling and Advertising Act, which required warning labels on all cigarette packages and advertisements, and in 1970 voted to ban cigarette advertising on radio and television. In both instances, Congress acted in response to the prospect of action by an administrative agency—in the first case, the Federal Trade Commission, and in the second, the Federal Communications Commission. Years later, in 1990, Congress voted to prohibit smoking on airplane flights. But it had stopped well short of passing legislation that would either restrict the sale of tobacco or explicitly confer comprehensive regulatory control on a federal agency, including the FDA. For its part, the FDA was content with this arrangement. Where tobacco was concerned, the agency was, as the *Washington Post* put it, "more than willing to keep its hands off."

The FDA and Tobacco

The agency's hands-off approach to tobacco rested primarily on its long-held conviction that it did not legally have jurisdiction over tobacco. Over the years, FDA officials offered a number of arguments in support of this position.

First, the FDA maintained that, under the language of its authorizing statute, it could not claim jurisdiction over tobacco. The 1938 Food, Drug, and Cosmetic Act had defined a drug in part as a substance "intended to affect the structure of any function of the body." The key term in this definition, at least in regard to tobacco, was what was meant by "intended." Historically, the FDA had accepted the tobacco companies' assertions that their intent in selling tobacco products was to provide "smoking pleasure"—not drug effects—to their customers. Only in the few instances when a tobacco firm had made therapeutic claims—as in the case of "Trim" cigarettes, which were marketed as a weight loss aid—did the FDA step in and claim jurisdiction.[25] Otherwise, the FDA pointedly stayed out.

In addition to the issue of intent, the constraints of the FDA's congressional mandate, the agency had argued, would make any FDA action on tobacco necessarily severe. If the FDA were to assert jurisdiction over tobacco on the ground that it was a drug, agency officials pointed out, it would effectively lead to a total ban on tobacco products—a logical consequence of the agency's obligation to ensure the safety and effectiveness of the drugs that came under its purview. In 1972 congressional hearings, Commissioner Charles Edwards drove home this point, warning that "if cigarettes would be classified as drugs, they would have to be removed from the market because it would be impossible to prove they were safe for their intended use." Such a move, Edwards continued, "would be inconsistent with the clear congressional intent." Congress had "decided in 1970 [in amendments to the cigarette labeling act]," the FDA's chief counsel testified in 1972, "that cigarettes should not be banned, that they should be allowed to remain in commerce with the warnings decided on by Congress, and we therefore feel that we have no basis for making any kind of determination literally contrary to the congressional determination."

Finally, some in the FDA argued, the record of congressional intent on FDA jurisdiction was clear. As the tobacco companies would themselves later point out in comments to the FDA, Congress had on a number of occasions declined to pass measures that would grant the FDA explicit regulatory authority over tobacco. Moreover, in the few pieces of legislation that Congress did enact with regard to cigarettes, the FDA was given no role in their implementation.

The combined arguments of manufactures' intent, statutory obligations, and congressional intent had kept the FDA and tobacco at arm's length for decades, despite the ongoing efforts of anti-smoking organizations to engage the agency in a regulatory relationship with tobacco products. In 1977 the FDA had rejected a "citizen petition" from Action on Smoking and Health (ASH) that had asked the agency to regulate cigarettes. In 1988 another group, the Coalition on Smoking OR Health, submitted a citizen petition seeking FDA regulation of tobacco, this time arguing that the marketing of low-tar cigarettes as a healthier alternative to full-strength brands constituted a health claim, and as such met the statutory definition of a drug.[26] The coalition's request, along with a number of similar petitions, was still before the FDA when Kessler assumed his post in November 1990. After he had been in office for about six months, he asked for a briefing to discuss what to do about them.

At the briefing, Kessler heard a full range of views from the assembled FDA staff. Some urged the commissioner to grant the petitioners' request on the ground that smoking represented an "enormous public health problem," while others stressed the "enormity of the task" of regulating tobacco. Some "old hands," the *Washington Post* reported, labeled a venture into tobacco control "a fool's mission."[27] After hearing out the staff members, Kessler came to a number of conclusions. First, he told them, he did not feel ready yet to grapple with the issue directly. "I remember saying that I would get to it," Kessler later recalled, "but I would need some time."[28] He was particularly concerned about making progress on the objectives—in food labeling, enforcement, and expedited drug approvals—that he had placed on the agenda at the beginning of his tenure. In addition, he did not think that the petitioners' proposed regulation of low-tar cigarettes for health claims, while leaving regular cigarettes untouched, made sense. Kessler did, however, direct a small group of "very bright" FDA officials—lawyers and policy analysts—to work together to "think about what might be the right approach."

A Fresh Look at Tobacco

Over a period of about a year, the group worked on the issue, occasionally meeting with Kessler to discuss their findings. In the course of these conversations, the group began to make what one member characterized as a "tectonic" shift[29] in their regulatory focus, from cigarettes to one of their key ingredients—nicotine—and to a view of cigarettes, as had been argued by ASH in its citizen petition, essentially as devices engineered to deliver a dose of nicotine to the smoker. In recent years, nicotine had come under scrutiny in a number of scientific studies that sought to examine its pharmacological and other effects on the body. A 1988 report by Surgeon General C. Everett Koop summed up the conclusions of many of these studies in what amounted to the first official declaration of the addictiveness of nicotine. "An extensive body of research," he wrote, "has shown that nicotine is the drug in tobacco that causes addiction. Moreover, the processes that determine tobacco addiction are similar to those that determine addiction to drugs such as heroin and cocaine." For Kessler and the FDA staff studying the issue of tobacco regulation, the question now became: Could nicotine be considered a drug under the specific terms of the Food, Drug, and Cosmetic Act? In other words, could the standard of "intent" be met? While past commissioners had answered "no," some of the new information being turned up by FDA staff increasingly inclined Kessler to answer "perhaps."

The key factors influencing this change came chiefly from evidence that staff members had discovered in the public record. They had, for example, found data on industry patents, which they believed provided important clues to cigarette manufacturing practices. Over the years, according to later congressional testimony by Kessler, the tobacco industry had taken out a number of patents for devices and processes that would variously allow cigarette manufacturers to increase, extract, enhance, or manipulate the nicotine in cigarettes. While none of these patents was necessarily in current use, they left "little doubt," Kessler would later testify, "that the cigarette industry has developed enormously sophisticated methods for manipulating nicotine levels in cigarettes." The questions raised by these discoveries, Kessler says, went to the heart of the statutory definition of a drug. "The issue of control [of nicotine]," he maintains, "goes to the question of intent." It was an assertion that the tobacco companies would strongly dispute.

Information from other sources also made its way to the FDA, providing what staff members considered telling glimpses into the way the industry viewed its controversial product. A 1972 internal memorandum by a Philip Morris executive, which had been introduced as evidence in a civil lawsuit brought by the family of a deceased smoker, offered the following vivid imagery: "Think of the cigarette pack as a storage container for a day's supply of nicotine," the author of the memorandum wrote; "think of the cigarette as a dispenser for a dose unit of nicotine.…Think of a puff of smoke as the vehicle for nicotine." Such statements could be taken to show, Kessler would later testify, that manufacturers regarded cigarettes as "high technology nicotine delivery systems that deliver nicotine in precisely calculated quantities."

Taken together, the studies on nicotine's addictive properties, the data on industry patents and practices, and the material filtering in from lawsuits could be said to represent, at least potentially, a new body of evidence that had previously been unavailable to the FDA and would therefore justify revisiting the agency's earlier finding on its jurisdiction over tobacco. In 1992, about a year after the FDA first began looking into tobacco regulation, Kessler and his staff were ready to take a first public step. They began by drafting a response to the Coalition on Smoking OR Health's citizen petition. It was, Kessler would later say, "probably the most important letter [the FDA] has ever sent."

The agency, by Kessler's recollection, worked for months on the letter. Once it was completed, some time in 1993, the letter was approved, according to a later account, by HHS Secretary Donna Shalala and "cleared by White House officials."[30] It was officially released on February 25, 1994, and received wide coverage in the press, where it was seen to signal, in the words of the *Washington Post*, "a momentous policy shift."

Kessler's Letter

The letter, addressed to Scott Ballin, executive director of the Coalition on Smoking OR Health, outlined the case the agency had begun to build on the issue of tobacco regulation. In it, Kessler noted the FDA's traditional stance in regard to the question of intent. "Although it has been well-known for many years that some people smoke for the drug effects of nicotine," he wrote, "cigarette vendors have in the past been given the benefit of the doubt as to whether they intend cigarettes to be used for this purpose...." However, he continued, "[e]vidence brought to our attention is accumulating that suggests that cigarette manufacturers may intend that their products contain nicotine to satisfy an addiction on the part of some of their customers." As examples, Kessler pointed to evidence that "manufacturers commonly add nicotine to cigarettes to deliver specific amounts of nicotine," and that "some individuals involved in the manufacture of cigarettes in the 1970s regarded their products as nicotine-delivery systems." Such data, Kessler concluded, "suggests that cigarette vendors intend the obvious—that many people buy cigarettes to satisfy their nicotine addiction." If the agency were to "make this finding based on an appropriate record or be able to prove these facts in court," he concluded, "it would have a legal basis on which to regulate these products under the drug provision of the [Food, Drug, and Cosmetic] Act."

At the same time, however, Kessler was mindful that the consequences of a "strict application" of the provisions of the law could lead to "the removal from the market of tobacco products." In view of the "widespread use of cigarettes and the prevalence of nicotine," he acknowledged that a ban on tobacco products could have negative health effects and possibly lead to a black market for cigarettes. Therefore, Kessler declared it was "vital in this context that Congress provide clear direction to the agency. We intend therefore to work with Congress to resolve, once and for all, the regulatory status of cigarettes under the Food, Drug, and Cosmetic Act." Looking back, Kessler observed, "I think we [were] saying two things in this letter. One, the agency can act if it has a sufficient basis, and we are starting to look at the evidence. Two, there is certainly a large societal question, and we need to tee it up for others if they want to start looking at this, too."

The Social Context

Kessler's letter came at a time when the nation as a whole seemed ripe for grappling with the societal questions involved in smoking. To an unprecedented degree, tobacco interests were on the defensive, legally as well as politically, a trend that would intensify over the course of 1994. On the legal front, the impregnable armor—underwritten by the industry's vast cash resources—which had thus far shielded tobacco companies from paying "even a nickel in damages," as *Time* magazine put it, to litigants suing them for the costs of smoking-related illnesses, had shown a tiny chink. In 1988 a jury awarded damages for the first time in a smoking case, to the family of Rose Cipollone, a smoker who had died just as the case was going to court.[31] The award was eventually overturned in the Supreme Court (essentially on the ground that the industry had provided health warnings on its cigarette packages as mandated by Congress), but the lawsuit had brought with it other costs to tobacco companies: it was the Cipollone case that had turned up the Philip Morris memorandum that was used by Kessler and others to bolster their arguments about the industry's intentions with regard to nicotine. Meanwhile, a so-called "third wave" of lawsuits was beginning, in which groups, instead of individuals, pitted their collective resources against those of the tobacco companies. These would include a number of class action suits—one of them filed on behalf of all smokers in America—as well as suits brought by the attorneys general of several states to recover the public tax dollars spent by Medicaid programs on smoking-related illnesses.

While the tobacco industry was facing a growing challenge on the legal front, it was also being squeezed by a series of anti-smoking actions at the local level, spurred on largely by reports on the risks of secondhand smoke.

More than 500 communities—including Los Angeles, San Francisco, and the state of Vermont—had restricted smoking in malls, restaurants, and other public places.[32] At the national level, there was some action as well. In March 1994 the Occupational Safety and Health Administration proposed a sweeping regulation that would ban smoking in the workplace nationwide. The Department of Defense has already prohibited smoking in its workplaces throughout the world.

In the media, tobacco was coming under close scrutiny in newspaper articles and television programs that cast the tobacco industry in a strongly negative light. Perhaps the most notorious example of this was the broadcast of a report on ABC-TV's newsmagazine show, *Day One*, which accused tobacco companies of "spiking" cigarettes with nicotine. Philip Morris promptly announced it would file a $10 billion lawsuit, largely over *Day One*'s somewhat loose usage of terms such as "spiking"; ultimately, ABC apologized and agreed to pay the company $15 million in legal fees. Nonetheless, the program generated considerable publicity, most of it adverse from the industry's standpoint.

Finally, the political climate in the nation's capitol seemed more favorable for a consideration of tobacco regulation than at any time in the recent past. For one thing, the new occupant of the Oval Office was viewed, in the words of one account, as "a friendly face in the White House for anti-smoking forces,"[33] and early signs seemed to confirm that view. Although Bill Clinton smoked cigars on occasion, the Clintons nonetheless banned smoking from the White House; and the President had begun to float the idea of a massive hike in the federal cigarette tax to help pay for his then-evolving health care reform plan. Meanwhile, in the Democrat-controlled Congress, observers perceived a shift in power. Anti-smoking forces, according to a report in *Time*, for the first time outnumbered the pro-tobacco members. "The tobacco industry, while still a powerful force," the head of ASH declared, "has lost its virtual stranglehold on Congress."

Still, most observers agreed that tobacco interests remained a formidable presence on Capitol Hill, capable of thwarting anti-smoking initiatives. A 1993 bill introduced by Rep. Henry Waxman, D-Calif., chairman of the Energy and Commerce Subcommittee on Health and the Environment and a prominent tobacco foe, had twice been forced to cancel votes on a measure that would ban smoking in almost all buildings except private homes, after it became apparent it would not pass. But congressional opponents of tobacco were increasingly optimistic about the prospects of future legislation against smoking. "I personally think what [tobacco interests are] faced with is a tidal wave," said Rep. Ron Wyden, D-Ore., "and when you talk to tobacco-state legislators, they know that."[34]

In the spring of 1994, Rep. Waxman gave smoking issues a new prominence in a series of high-profile hearings before his subcommittee. Kessler himself was the star witness in the first hearing on tobacco, on March 25, 1994, during which he expanded on the preliminary findings and issues that he had touched upon in his letter four weeks earlier to the coalition. Several weeks later Waxman summoned top executives of the nation's seven largest tobacco companies for a grilling before a packed hearing room and network TV cameras. A highlight of that hearing, which was often acrimonious in tone, came when each executive was asked if he personally believed—as the tobacco industry had insisted—that nicotine was not addictive; each in turn affirmed that belief.[35] A couple of months later, on June 21, Kessler was back to testify before the subcommittee, this time with more evidence on industry practices. He related, first, the story of a genetically engineered high-nicotine tobacco plant, code-named Y-1, that the Brown and Williamson Company had developed and then grown under contract with farms in Brazil, and second, information on the use of ammonia—one of 599 ingredients that cigarette companies added to tobacco—to enhance the delivery of nicotine to the smoker. After reviewing this and other data, Kessler said in conclusion: "These findings lay to rest any notion that there is no manipulation and control of nicotine undertaken in the tobacco industry." His statement presaged a shift within the FDA's internal deliberations, as the emphasis moved away from an inquiry into whether nicotine could be classified as a drug, to a consideration of how it would best be regulated.

Choosing between Regulation and Legislation

Let's step outside of the case account for a moment. Two decades earlier, David Kessler's friend, Michael Pertschuk, had been chair of another administrative agency with power to make quasi-legislative rules that would bind private parties: the Federal Trade Commission (FTC). At a time of conservative resurgence, and while the FTC was already considering an unusual array of such regulations, Pertschuk had tried to promulgate a regulation banning advertisements addressed to very young children on Saturday morning television programs—many for sugar-coated cereals.

An alliance of cereal makers, advertisers, and media—each of which was powerful and profited handsomely from advertising to young children—joined his other business opponents and the ideological conservatives in Congress in attacking the proposal as wildly paternalistic, usurping the normal role and responsibilities of parents. The coalition had been strengthened significantly by enlisting members of Congress who were outraged by Pertschuk's stretch of his claimed powers to regulate matters that they believed were more appropriate for congressional consideration. The result was the prompt legislative reversal of the regulation in the form of an appropriations "rider," forbidding the use of any funds to enforce the new rules, followed by a number of other devastating attacks on the FTC.

In retrospect, Pertschuk said he would have been wiser to present his proposal to the appropriate committees in the Democratic-controlled Congress. The chairs, at least, of these committees were sympathetic to his proposal. Even if there was no prospect of legislation, they would have been willing to hold hearings designed to show dramatically the moral and health-based case against selling sugar to very young children. At a minimum, each chair could bring the committee to encourage the FTC to explore both legislative and regulatory options, protecting the FTC against charges of usurping legislative authority. Pertschuk's case for new regulations would, in the meantime, have been made persuasively for the public at congressional hearings, rather than being developed far less publicly in the Federal Trade Commission.

Kessler had the same choice in 1994. For example, he could take a legislative route relying on the support of Subcommittee Chair Henry Waxman in the House. Or he could act on his own, using authority long ago delegated to the FDA by Congress. Using the FDA's own regulatory powers was more promising in terms of avoiding stalemate or rejection in the Congress. Legislation was more promising in terms of avoiding the risk of judicial reversal of his actions as not legislatively authorized.

Another advantage of the legislative route was that he would not be giving his opponents the rallying cry of regulatory overreaching, and he would be reducing the risks to his own resources of being defeated and rebuked after a bold and highly public regulatory effort. That had been Michael Pertschuk's fate. And, of course, legislation authorizing his actions would automatically end the threat that the courts might find them unauthorized. But the disadvantage of going the legislative route was also great. Congress would be very unlikely to pass legislation of the sort Kessler thought was needed.

The advantages of adopting an alternative to legislation, exercising the regulatory authority of the FDA, are obvious. Having the authority to promulgate a policy that is binding unless both Houses of Congress and the President reject it by legislation is a great source of power because it does not require congressional support. The policy simply requires congressional inaction, and legislative action can be blocked in many ways. Because Congress seemed sharply divided on the issue of regulating tobacco, it might well not be able to act to overrule a regulation. And even if both Houses of Congress passed a statute forbidding the regulation of tobacco products—an unlikely event in a Congress with a Democratic majority—President Clinton could still veto that statute.

All this is a mere first cut at one of the most significant decisions that Kessler had to make in light of his judgments regarding the attitudes of Congress, the courts, the President, and influential private sectors of the public. To complicate the problem, his prediction of the actions of any crucial party might differ depending on the actions of the others. For example, the response of Congress would depend in part on the response of the courts.

Five Concerns That Enter into Kessler's Understanding of the Significance of the Occasion

How should Kessler address this first choice? To decide, he must review his own concerns in light of his understanding of the situation he faces, that is, in terms of his assessment of the attitudes and likely reactions of others. Consider his concerns one at a time.

1. A good place to start is the importance of the occasion to that aspect of the social welfare for which the individual player feels responsible. Stated broadly, the core responsibility of the FDA was to assure the safety and efficacy of drugs and many other products. Whether the statute granting the FDA power could be read to authorize the regulation of the use by teenagers of cigarettes and chewing tobacco was far from clear. What was clear is the closeness and power of the relationship between any broad and vague statement of the agency's core responsibilities for the safety of products Americans ingest and the fact that close to 400,000 Americans die each year as a result of the addictive effects of a drug, nicotine, which they began smoking when they were teenagers or younger. Every day 3,000 new youth would begin smoking, and 1,000 of them would eventually die because of it. These figures dwarfed the impact of

any health issue facing the FDA, even including efforts to speed up the process of approving new prescription drugs.

2. Kessler's second concern—the effects of launching a high-profile proceeding against tobacco on his resources of future influence—was hard to assess. It would increase his prestige—indeed make him a hero—among those concerned with issues of public health and consumer protection. He could anticipate becoming a more powerful spokesman for public health interests because of the salience of this issue and the boldness of his actions. That would win him support among public interest groups and some segments of the press, and those in turn could influence members of Congress or the President. Exercising his powers to their very limits would also increase his stature among those who wanted a vigorous regulatory agency in charge of protecting American health against the presumed avarice of American and foreign businesses.

On the other hand, undertaking a regulation of cigarette sales would make Kessler a symbol of big government and dangerously uncontrolled regulatory powers in the eyes of supporters of business and conservative Republicans (who would in fact take over both Houses of Congress after the 1994 election). Congressional conservatives might conduct time-consuming and embarrassing oversight hearings, reverse his initiative by legislative measures, and reduce his agency's appropriations. In the future, he could anticipate hostile negotiations with Congress on even the most routine issues facing the FDA. Perhaps in light of all this, Kessler decided to resign his position at the FDA soon after playing out the very bold regulatory steps we shall examine.

3. As to a closely related category of concerns—personal effects—the attacks that would come from the opponents of big government would be personal, fierce, and painful. He would become the target of a great deal of highly public hostility and would have to spend a good bit of time defending his own reputation. If he valued privacy—many do not—or relative anonymity, those would be sacrificed. Still, attempting to regulate tobacco could and did build for Kessler, even long after he left the FDA, an extremely powerful and prominent stature in the field of public health, right next to a former Surgeon General, Dr. C. Everett Koop.

4. A fourth possible concern—though one he may have discounted—was a separate and important question of morality. How certain did Kessler have to be that the courts would sustain his claim of authority to regulate tobacco before he could subject the tobacco companies, growers, and users to a prolonged period of uncertainty and, for the companies, the immense expenses and disruption of litigation?

Kessler himself thought that the very process of developing and revealing the facts needed to justify a regulation would powerfully change the politics and the public understanding of the issue, whether or not the courts ultimately sustained any regulation. Still, he had a moral obligation not to make claims of authority that he was very unlikely to be able to sustain. For example, the Reagan administration had purposely subjected thousands of disability claimants, who were winning close to 100 percent of their appeals on the contested issues, to the cost of litigating every claim before they could obtain the disability payments to which the courts had repeatedly ruled they were entitled. Whatever the administration's internal judgment on the correctness of the courts' decisions, this was wholly unjustified harassment and an abusive use of government resources.

Kessler in fact would send his proposed arguments supporting FDA authority to the Department of Justice, whose attorneys advised that he had a case that the courts might well sustain. In that situation there was nothing morally questionable about proceeding, even if he felt certain that a number in Congress would disagree. If, on the other hand, the Department of Justice had thought the odds were very much against a regulation being sustained in court, it would be questionable to use the FDA's hearing, publicity, rule-making, and litigating powers simply as a political force. The wealth of the FDA's opponent, of course, makes a difference in this calculation, but Kessler could not properly use his agency's rule-making powers unless his real purpose and expectation were to promulgate a legally sustainable administrative rule.

5. Finally, Kessler would have to analyze carefully the effect on the resources of his organization, the FDA, of attempts, even limited to youth, to regulate and reduce smoking. If the FDA looked, to a majority of each House of Congress, like an agency whose priorities were badly distorted—preferring adventures in regulation at or beyond the border of agency power to the more solid work of speeding the process of approving new drugs—the committees would use legislation, oversight, and reductions in appropriations to signal their displeasure, as they had with Pertschuk's FTC two decades earlier. By legislatively overruling a regulation that was promulgated by the FDA, Congress could impose sharp new limits on agency power and signal future vulnerability of the FDA to legislative attacks by the private parties it tried to regulate. Certainly, Congress would not grant requested new powers or new funds. Committees could make any appointments in the agency more difficult, any reorganization less likely.

The logic of this fifth and last area of concern is very simple. Kessler's concerns about his agency's resources would, as we have noted, be very real. He would need the agency's powers and resources to pursue the values and objectives that led him to take the job. To maintain and enhance them, the head of any executive agency must choose public goals—priority activities and expressive themes—that are feasible and that will generate the support the agency needs from Congress and the President. This notion can be captured in a simple diagram (Figure 10.1).

The requirement that the goals be within the internal capacity of the organization, or at least within the capacity that its leader could imagine creating within a reasonable period of time, reflects not only common sense, but also a political reality: promising an achievement that the agency cannot accomplish either legally or administratively will soon prove costly for the agency.

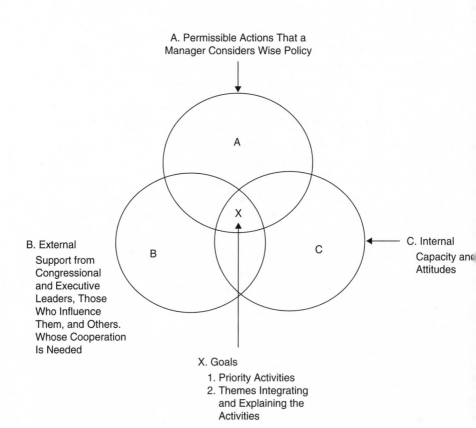

A. Permissible Actions That a Manager Considers Wise Policy

A

X

B. External Support from Congressional and Executive Leaders, Those Who Influence Them, and Others. Whose Cooperation Is Needed

B

C

C. Internal Capacity and Attitudes

X. Goals
1. Priority Activities
2. Themes Integrating and Explaining the Activities

Figure 10.1.

As to the external support his agency would need, Kessler would have to expect serious opposition from conservative members of Congress on committees that would be needed to provide that money and those powers. The present opposition would become vastly more hostile, widespread, active, and coordinated if the FDA tried to regulate tobacco. As we have noted, Kessler could anticipate the nature of the attacks. When the Republicans came into power after the 1994 elections, legislative opponents might well obtain a statute forbidding regulation of tobacco products, reduce the appropriations or the powers of the FDA, or engage in oversight hearings designed to undermine the legitimacy or reputation for competence for the FDA. (After all, Kessler's ally, Rep. Henry Waxman, had used oversight hearings to great effect, prior to the 1994 election, to undermine the legitimacy and the reputation for trustworthiness of the CEOs of the cigarette companies by bringing them to swear that they believe that smoking was not addictive.) A presidential veto could partially protect his agency from some of the worst consequences, but not forever and not if, for example, a reduction in appropriations—or a "rider" forbidding expenditures to regulate tobacco—was buried in a massive bill, the overall benefits of which made a veto undesirable to the President.

Applying the Concerns in the Context of a Prediction of Consequences

At this early stage, in order to decide whether to go the regulatory or legislative path, Kessler would have to know more than his own concerns. The consequences for his concerns would differ depending on whether he could obtain legislation—with the support prior to the 1994 election of Rep. Waxman and others—and on whether a regulation would be popular with the public, adopted by the President, tolerated by Congress, and affirmed by the courts.

Congress

To develop even a crude guess of probabilities as to the possible outcomes in Congress, Kessler would need to look carefully at the positions that carry with them unusual influence in each House of Congress and to assess the attitudes toward his proposal of those occupying those positions. As we shall see, the power of committee chairs and party leadership is just part of even a rough cut at prediction.

Another part involves looking at the influence of his private opponents. Philip Morris and its allies had many resources of influence with members of Congress: the effects of very large and regular campaign contributions; the persuasiveness of highly paid and highly skilled lobbyists; the electoral impact of large supportive constituencies made up of farmers, other workers, and smokers; and, not least important, an ideological agreement with many of the Republican majority on the dangers of "excessive" regulation.

It would also be important to judge whether the issue would be partisan or nonpartisan—not in the sense that more Republicans than Democrats will favor an attack on any new regulation (which they will), but whether party leaders are likely to make it costly for a legislator of their party not to follow a carefully chosen party line.

Finally, he could see that, especially if he could rely on a veto, it would be far easier to prevent Congress from overturning a regulation than to persuade Congress to pass a statute.

The Attentive Public

Much of the reactions of elected officials would turn on how the issue played out with the press and public. If the regulation turned out to be a popular proposal with voters and, especially, if the tobacco companies could be made to look like greedy drug-dealers, attacking it would be an unpromising alternative for Republicans, and a veto of any effort would be more attractive to the President. If, on the other hand, Kessler's actions could be made to look like overreaching and interference with American liberties, then targeting Kessler and the FDA would be popular. Public opinion on these issues would be shaped by what the courts had to say about the extent of FDA powers; so he must consider his prospects in court. It could be shaped by Waxman's friendly hearings; so he must assess the prospect of those continuing. These relationships are captured in Figure 10.2.

Not many matters resonate with significant portions of the public in the "D" circle, but those that do will enjoy the "megaphone" effect of having interest groups and the press increase their volume and duration considerably for those in the inner circles. This in turn inevitably influences elected officials, at least when they have reason to fear that significant numbers of constituents will, with the help of those in circle "C," be attentive to the position they take on the

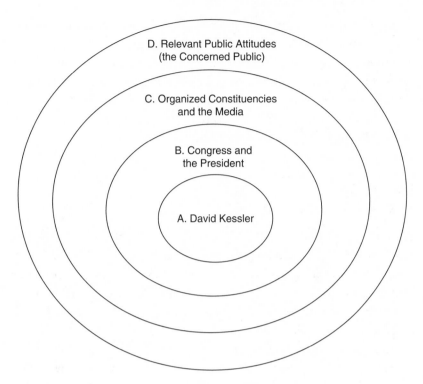

Figure 10.2.

matter. Predictions as to the reaction of elected officials are, for reasons I have described, central to the decisions of an unelected official such as Kessler.

The President and the Courts

As I have noted, to assess the impact of his possible actions on his concerns, Kessler would also have to predict the chance of the President and the courts supporting such a regulation. To determine the former, he would have to know not only the views of President Clinton "on the merits," but also the likely advice that Clinton would receive in light of the responses of various segments of the public. As to the courts, Kessler can foresee that any challenge to the regulation would be brought initially by his opponents, hoping for regional bias, in the courts of a tobacco-producing state, but eventually would be resolved by the Court of Appeals or the Supreme Court on the basis of what his regulation required and the legal arguments he and his opponents would make. His lawyers could advise him on his prospects in court.

All of these predictions of the impact of the situation in terms of Kessler's concerns—his understanding of the significance of the occasion—would be crude. Unsure of which way to proceed, Kessler directed his staff to get ready for a regulatory as well as legislative attack on tobacco, and so the story continued.

Inside the FDA
A Case History by Esther Scott

During the period between the release of Kessler's letter to the Coalition on Smoking OR Health and his June appearance before the Henry Waxman subcommittee, the agency had been engaged in a full-scale investigation into the issue of cigarette manufacturers' intent.[36] At the time the letter was written, Kessler says, "I don't think that anyone believed...that the evidence we had on hand was sufficient to make that finding." It was conceivable, he reflects, that the agency could have legally made a case simply on the basis of scientific findings on nicotine. "The surgeon general," Kessler explains, "issue[d] a report that the scientific community says, 'This is an addictive product.' The world now knows it's addictive. Can you say, 'I don't intend it to be addictive,' even though the whole world knows it's addictive? That may be all that's necessary under intent." But, Kessler says, "we did not stop just at [such] foreseeability evidence."[37]

As it proceeded, the FDA investigation uncovered, both through documentary research and field visits, what it considered to be hard evidence of the industry's ability to control nicotine levels and, hence, its intent to create and maintain addiction. In addition to its own research—which had turned up, among other things, the information on Y-1 and the use of ammonia in cigarettes—the FDA inquiry had the benefit of revelations contained in a cache of documents stolen from the Brown and Williamson Tobacco Company by a paralegal and first reported on the front page of the *New York Times* in May 1994. Included in these was a 1963 memorandum written by Addison Yeaman, then the company's general counsel, in which he predicted that smoking would eventually be linked to such ailments as lung cancer and emphysema. In urging the company to research and develop safer products, Yeaman mentioned cigarette filters, which would reduce the smoker's exposure to hazardous substances, he noted, "while delivering the full flavor—and incidentally—a nice jolt of nicotine." More striking still, Yeaman wrote, "We are, then, in the business of selling nicotine, an addictive drug effective in the release of stress mechanisms." For the FDA, such statements marked, in Kessler's words, "a major moment, beyond which all went in one direction."[38] Looking back, he says, "No one, when we issued that [February] letter, would ever have thought there would be documents that [state] in the company's own words that 'we are in the business of selling nicotine, an addictive drug,' and not from some low level [staff member], but from a general counsel."

Formulating a Regulatory Strategy: Focus on Youth

By the summer of 1994, Kessler and his staff had begun to turn their attention to the regulatory tools available to the agency, were it to assert its authority over tobacco products. In their deliberations, they were, Kessler says, "essentially [asking], what is the right public health response? And also, what is the right statutory response?" The option of imposing an outright ban—which the FDA might be compelled to do under the statutory provisions governing drugs—was considered infeasible. Kessler maintains, "It's not a practical response, and we rejected [it] immediately." Instead, they proposed, cigarettes could be regulated as nicotine-delivery devices. Unlike the drug provisions of the law, the statutes governing such medical devices offered regulators more flexibility and a variety of tools—including the option to impose restrictions on the sale, distribution, and use of devices—to apply to the particular circumstances at hand.

At the same time, the FDA was also engaged, in Kessler's words, in "trying to figure out what the right approach [to regulation] was." Eventually, the agency concluded that what "made sense from a public health point of view" was a strategy designed to "intercede before somebody has become addicted"—that is, one that concentrated on children. There were a number of reasons to justify a focus on youth. For one thing, studies had indicated that people who had not smoked by late adolescence were unlikely to begin; for another, there was evidence that the earlier a person began to smoke, the greater the likelihood that the person would become a heavy smoker. In addition, in their investigations, FDA staff members had turned up documents indicating that tobacco companies had developed marketing strategies aimed specifically at attracting young smokers.

With the basic answers to their question concerning the right public health and statutory responses in hand, the FDA staff members broke up into two teams. One team would put together a "jurisdictional analysis," laying out the agency's basis for determining that nicotine in cigarettes was a drug under the Food, Drug, and Cosmetic Act. The other would draft a proposed rule that would set out the FDA's plan for regulating cigarettes as devices and the statutory basis for it. The process of writing the two documents, Kessler notes, would help the agency see "whether the case was there."

But while the FDA was still at work on the documents, events were taking place that would dramatically alter the political landscape in Washington. As a result of the November 1994 elections, both chambers of Congress would be controlled by Republicans, many of whom were strongly interested in retaining the regulatory hand of the federal government. As the political balance of power shifted, Kessler would find his tobacco initiative—and his leadership of the FDA—under sharp attack.

Under Siege

The changes wrought by the election, in terms of the FDA's fortunes, were almost immediately felt. The agency, in the words of one account, became "a lightning rod for the anti-government sentiments that changed the face of American politics...."[39] Long-simmering dissatisfaction with the pace of drug and device approvals now erupted into sometimes vitriolic criticism in the press and elsewhere. One anti-regulatory organization, the Washington Legal Foundation, ran a series of print ads that read: "If a murderer kills you, it's homicide. If a drunk driver kills you, it's manslaughter. If the FDA kills you, it's just being cautious."[40] Meanwhile, on Capitol Hill, the new Congress sought a general rollback on federal government controls—beginning with a moratorium on most new government regulations—but it seemed to train its sights particularly on the FDA. The agency, declared newly anointed Speaker of the House Newt Gingrich, was "the leading job-killer in America." Even before the Republicans formally took charge of Congress, proposals to reform the agency—some of them the handiwork of conservative think tanks—had begun circulating on Capitol Hill. One, for example, would "semi-privatize" the FDA by farming out reviews of new medical devices to government-certified bodies; another would allow companies to bring drugs and devices to market—with a warning label attached—that had not been approved by the FDA.[41] By August 1995, at least a dozen schemes for overhauling the FDA had been aired, and Democrats as well as Republicans were calling for a comprehensive reform of the agency. In addition, Congress had shown its displeasure with the FDA by deleting budget funds earmarked for a new headquarters, which would have enabled the agency to unite its scattered organization onto one campus.

Kessler himself became the target of sometimes harsh criticism, both for his "zeal" as a regulator and for what critics considered to be his failure to address chronic problems in the agency's product approval process. Gingrich characterized the FDA chief as "a thug and a bully," while conservative commentators called for his ouster. "First Step to an FDA Cure," declared a December 1994 op-ed piece in the *Wall Street Journal*, "Dump Kessler."[42] Using more moderate language, Rep. Thomas Bliley, R-Va., asserted that "Dr. Kessler has led the agency away from its core mission into areas that are either peripheral to the public health or for which other agencies hold the statutory mandate." Bliley himself was now in a position to have some effect on one major component on Kessler's agenda: the tobacco initiative. As a result of the November elections, the Virginia Republican had ascended to the chairmanship of the Commerce Committee—whose Subcommittee on Health and the Environment had been a key forum for airing smoking-related issues under former Chairman Henry Waxman—and made it clear early on that the hearings on tobacco were a thing of the past. "I don't think we need any more legislation regulating tobacco," he told reporters shortly after the election.[43] Henry Waxman held one last sparsely attended lame-duck session on tobacco in late November and, with that, the *Washington Post* wrote, "the curtain came down...on a dramatic series of congressional hearings about tobacco industry practices." The FDA's dialogue with Congress on smoking seemed at an end and, for the moment, the prospect of FDA regulation of tobacco seemed to disappear, at least from public view.

The first major choice that Kessler faced was among: promulgating regulation; seeking legislation; and or avoiding the issue of nicotine addiction, as all his predecessors had done. That choice depended importantly on the political setting. After January 1995 there would be a radical change in the consequences that he would predict for his concerns. He was forced to reconsider his options as the holders of positions of power changed dramatically.

11

Creating Change in the Setting for Policy Choice

With the Republican sweep of both houses of Congress in 1994, the critical choice for Kessler was no longer between seeking legislation and promulgating an administrative regulation that the courts might find exceeded the statutory powers of the FDA. After the new Congress took office, there would be no real prospect of legislation. The relevant question for Kessler became whether or not to proceed against tobacco sales to youth by a regulation. That was by no means a clear decision for anyone heading the FDA in the late fall of 1994.

Why was legislation no longer an option? Previously, a legislative proposal by Kessler would have gone to the Subcommittee of the Commerce Committee on Health and Environment, whose Chairman, Rep. Henry Waxman of California, would share Kessler's beliefs and attitudes about smoking. Waxman would have set the agenda for the Subcommittee for both hearings and mark-up. His considerable resources of influence with other Democratic members of his Subcommittee would help him to shape the Democratic majority position. His influence with the Democratic leadership, also likely to be sympathetic to the proposal, could have brought a committee bill to the floor.

On the floor, the majority would have been Democratic, although not all would have been supportive of legislative proposals like Kessler's. But the Committee would have had advantages with other members that derive from its expertise as well as their desire to enjoy a certain amount of reciprocal deference from members of the Commerce Committee. Rep. Waxman and the Commerce Committee Chair, Rep. John Dingell, D-Mich., would both have had additional influence from the brokerage

that comes with occupying a position that the President needs for legislation that he cares about. Both would also enjoy the support that comes
with a reputation for success in passing legislation that discourages others
from incurring the costs of organizing opposition.

With the partisan shift in Congress, all these previous advantages have
now turned into disadvantages. Support has turned into hostility. Hostility could now be expressed from positions that carry with them very
significant resources of influence.

The new Chair of the relevant Subcommittee of the Commerce Committee, Rep. Thomas Bliley, would not hold hearings on Kessler's proposal. The Chair of the full Committee would not make it part of the
legislative agenda of any of the Commerce Committee's subcommittees.
Even if it made its way to the agenda of the full Committee, it would be
rejected by the new Committee majority. The new Republican leadership would not bring it to the floor, whatever the Committee had done.
A majority would vote against it if it ever came to the floor.

If the prospect of legislation enacting something like Kessler's proposal was not already absolutely dead, it would soon be, as the Republican leadership radically increased centralized party control in the House.
By a series of major moves, Republican Representatives Newt Gingrich
and Tom DeLay had radically changed the setting for any policy decision.
As we have seen, the 1994 election had succeeded in placing in positions
of great influence within the legislature a new group of players with
very different sets of concerns and a very different set of beliefs from
those of the Democrats that preceded them. The possible tactics of any
policy advocate—designing a proposal in light of the relevant players'
understandings of how their concerns would be affected by the proposal
in the situation as they saw it; timing the proposal to take advantage of
particular concerns especially salient at particular times; forming coalitions to maximize the usefulness of the resources of influence possessed
by those supporting the proposal, and taking steps to prevent the formation of rival coalitions with rival proposals—are all designed to take
advantage of the "play" or indeterminacy within the setting of players
with resources of influence who are proceeding according to rules. But
the set of possibilities has now been reduced by a very advanced form of
policy advocacy that we have not discussed before.

Very sophisticated players can seek to change the very nature of the
political environment. Elections are intended to allow the public to place
new people, with different concerns and beliefs and subject to new party

pressures, into established positions with substantial resources of influence. That is what democracy is about. In the election of 1994, minority leader Newt Gingrich of Georgia had accomplished this in exceptionally dramatic fashion.

His success would be followed by a number of other steps designed to maximize control by the party leadership and to make that control as nearly permanent as possible. The political world would, for more than a decade, be very different for David Kessler and for Matt Myers, the protagonist of the next case. The major architect of making the changes semi-permanent was Rep. Tom DeLay, who became majority whip in 1994.

These developments would cut sharply across Kessler's assaults on smoking. For DeLay and his many allies, opposition to new regulation was almost as much a core belief as opposition to new taxation. DeLay, who was rated 95 out of 100 by the anti-tax Americans for Tax Reform and by the United States Chamber of Commerce, also received a rating of 0 out of 100 from the Sierra Club and the League of Conservation Voters. By changing rules, the occupants of positions of power, and the resources of influence that sympathetic players enjoyed, DeLay intended to permanently and totally change the setting for dramatic regulatory efforts like Kessler's.

It is worth watching how a keen observer of power works to make it far more supportive of his views. DeLay sped the end of a tradition of reliance on seniority in choosing committee chairs and committee members. In discussing Representative Waxman's prior role, I have noted the resources of influence that accompany committee positions and make them very powerful. DeLay wanted these resources wholly in the hands of those supportive of his views and loyal to his leadership. Moreover, using the prospect of future committee chairmanships as a way to demand support even from Republicans far more moderate than he was provided a powerful new incentive.

Members want to be reelected. DeLay set out to raise millions of dollars for members running for reelection—at the same time making clear that their policy support was a condition of the funds being made available. He used the stick of threatening to finance rivals in primaries for those Republicans who regularly opposed a set of policies that he and other Republican leaders were pressing. Rep. Barney Frank, D-Mass., called the results "the same kind of discipline [as is enjoyed] by the British Conservative or Labor party."

Interest groups that provide funding could also be a source of power. DeLay altered the rules for access to his office and that of other members, requiring the lobbyists to meet standards of loyalty to the Republican Party. He also used their services to expand the "whip" system, developing a new pattern of requiring lobbyists to seek support for bills from other members.

The matter for which he was indicted in 2005 illustrates most dramatically the sophistication of DeLay's effort to make more permanent his control of the setting in which political initiatives of concern to him would be resolved. If the Republicans could draw the district lines for the next Congressional elections in Texas, DeLay's home state, they could pick up as many as seven Congressional seats. This would make far more secure the narrow Republican majority of the House of Representatives, and that in turn would guarantee DeLay's capacity to use the tools just described to create a political environment sympathetic to his views.

Districting in Texas was initially in the hands of the Texas legislature, where the Democrats controlled at least one House and had thus been able to block a partisan Republican redistricting. If the Republicans could get control of the Texas legislature, they could use a clause of the state Constitution that allowed a Republican dominated committee, the Legislative Redistricting Board, to draw the districts.

To accomplish the series of steps that would lead to greater assurance of a lasting supportive environment for his views in the House, DeLay raised large amounts of money for the Texas legislative elections, including corporate money, the legality of which became the focus of his indictment. The Republicans won both Texas Houses and, again in a change of rules, set up a mid-decade redrawing of districts. The result of the new gerrymander was a near Republican sweep of seats in Congress that had been previously held by Democratic representatives.

The result of that sweep was to provide some assurance of a continuing Republican majority in the House and therefore leadership of the House of Representatives by DeLay and a few colleagues. It would be a House of Representatives whose actions would reflect DeLay's priorities and reject those of people like Kessler. The total plan, occupying several years while DeLay was also involved in daily policy battles in the House and in building his power with the present majority membership, required the capacity to plan an intricate and interrelated set of moves. The outcome—in terms of the resources available to those with the priorities, themes, and alliances that were important to DeLay—was a setting extremely sympathetic to a large number of his proposals and unsympathetic to those of his opponents.

Very sophisticated policy advocates work to change the setting and thus to expand the set of possibilities open to them for the proposals they favor and to contract the risks they see of adverse policies being adopted. By changing the set of opportunities facing various proposals, the most skilled policy advocates can make very sweeping changes, reducing the cost of getting a number of their favorite proposals adopted and raising the difficulties their opponents face. Moreover, by focusing on these wholesale change—matters that are often ignored by rivals—they may be able to get sweeping changes without raising the attention and resistance of potential opposition as they would for far narrower changes.

Dramatic changes in the setting take place along the set of dimensions that describe a political situation. A sophisticated policy advocate can seek to change the rules; to change the players who occupy the positions that the rules make powerful; to alter the interests or beliefs of whatever players have positions of influence; and to increase or reduce the power of particular positions that the rules make relevant. DeLay was a great expert at all this and a passionate opponent of any expansion of federal regulatory power, let alone as bold an effort as Kessler's.

In this new setting, Kessler had to decide whether to proceed with a dramatic regulation of smoking (legislation being clearly unavailable) and, if so, in what form and with what tactics. Predictions as well as his own preferences had to go into these decisions. With a particular set of actions by him (Set X) in support of the promulgation of a regulation with certain characteristics (Characteristics Y), there would be a particular probability that a majority of the Congress would overrule the regulation and a corresponding probability that it would not. For every variant of X and every variant of Y the probability of Congress acting is a little different. So too is the probability of the President vetoing the action of both Houses if the regulation were reversed in Congress. (We can ignore as trivial the likelihood of a veto being overridden.) Kessler recognized that, even if his regulation was overruled by a statute, there might be real benefits in terms of public health just from the publicity associated with making an effort to regulate teenage smoking. But he also could see that for each likely set of actions and each likely configuration of the proposal there was, beside the risk of being overruled, a certain probability of other painful forms of congressional retaliation against the FDA and against himself as its chief.

Shaping Public Attitudes to Broadly Affect Political Outcomes

There is another way to make major changes in the receptivity of a political setting to a particular proposal or a particular class of proposals. Returning to the simple diagram in Figure 10.2 of Chapter 10, a sharp change in public attitudes toward a policy proposal, at least if the change has certain characteristics that I will describe, is likely to change the concerns and even the beliefs of players with authority to make a decision about the policy. The mechanisms for changing attitudes in this way are obvious. If a matter is important enough to constituents to cause them to hold an official's support of, or opposition to, a particular policy against him at election time, the official would be wise to change his position. Moreover, what comes to seem obvious or accepted wisdom about the desireability of adopting a proposal or rejecting it also affects the beliefs of elected officials. As to their opinions and beliefs, humans live largely in a socially constructed reality.

The limit of the effectiveness of changing public attitudes toward a proposal is also important. If the new attitude or, more likely, its intensity is likely to be temporary, political actors who would prefer to reject the public's view have available a rich array of delaying tactics with which they can "wait out" the public demands. They also have devices to hide their position on the policy from their constituents. They can speak and vote in its favor on one occasion and later kill the proposal in a way too complex or too obscure for constituents to understand.

As we've already seen in describing his testimony before Congress and his public speeches, much of Kessler's strategy depends upon bringing about this particular type of broad change by influencing public attitudes toward smoking. Even if Speaker Gingrich and Majority Leader DeLay are personally firmly opposed to further regulation of smoking, and even if they have cornered now and control immense amounts of the power and discretion available in the House of Representatives, it will not be in their interest to use their power to pass a statute overruling Kessler's regulation if that would be plainly costly to the Republican Party in terms of public support.

Still, the question remains: How should Kessler analyze his situation and how should he proceed? One matter is clear. Much depends on how the proposal is expressed, for very few members of the general public will find it worth their while to spend more than a very few minutes reacting to any but a very few government proposals. Consider the following example. Soon after President Reagan was elected, appointed officials in the Department of Justice and the Department of the Treasury decided to end a ten-year practice of denying various federal tax benefits to schools that discriminated on the basis of race. They had entirely plausible arguments that the Treasury regulation, perhaps like Kessler's proposed regulation, went beyond the authority given the Commissioner of Internal Revenue by the Congress. They noted that, under applicable legal precedent, granting tax benefits did not trigger the same Constitutional and statutory prohibitions of governmental support of racial discrimination that other forms of federal support did. They said that if the Commissioner of Internal Revenue, as a simple policy matter, could decide when to deny tax benefits, he could become the dictator of the nonprofit world. But these arguments are hard to understand and evaluate. If the issue were to become salient, as it predictably and very quickly did, it would be because of—and it would play out as—a question of whether the nation was going to change its policy of hostility to all forms of racial discrimination.

The argument that what was really involved was a highly technical construction of the powers of the Commissioner of Internal Revenue and of the limits of the obligations of the federal government to avoid supporting discrimination simply could not carry the day in a debate that was also about fundamental values of great concern to very, very large numbers of Americans. To the average constituent who would not spend some hours studying the law or the underlying political philosophy put forth by the Reagan administration, the issue was simply whether the United States was for or against racial segregation. In fact, President Reagan had to beat a quick and embarrassing retreat from his administration's technically defensible but publicly indefensible proposal.

It is in such very simplified terms that Kessler must assess the way in which people will react to his proposal. Kessler will speak of smokers addicted and dying. The companies will argue that Kessler is proposing a form of governmental, paternalistic control inconsistent with American traditions valuing personal liberty. But "everyone" knows that letting children decide what risks to take is not part of that tradition. Nor is it a free choice to be a drug addict. He can see that his opponents will accuse him of trying to exercise powers he was not granted in order to regulate the free choices of liberty-loving Americans, all at a time when he and his agency should be focusing on speedy delivery of lifesaving drugs such as those to combat AIDS. But these arguments will pale in comparison to Kessler's arguments that 3,000 adolescents each day start an addiction from which 1,000 will eventually die. His points can be understood much more quickly and will be felt much more intensely by a very broad public.

What is less obvious is that a contest for public opinion has not only a dimension of policy but also a dimension of attitude toward the advocate of a policy. How influential a position will be with the public depends on the messenger almost as much as on the message. A party, and thus its message, can be discredited by being effectively portrayed as unworthy of trust, or too self-interested to be believed, too uninformed on the subject, too arrogant, or even simply too unlike, in style or associates, the audience to which he is appealing.

Kessler will be portrayed as a wild-eyed, radical regulator who is indifferent to individual freedoms. But the cigarette companies have been systematically exposed by Rep. Waxman and by Kessler to a barrage of revelations dramatically inconsistent with the public image they have tried to portray. Long after the scientific facts were established, Waxman had the CEOs of each of the company stand and swear that they did not believe nicotine to be addictive. Papers found during discovery by civil plaintiffs or pushed over the transom by whistle-blowers revealed internal documents describing cigarettes as a vehicle for nicotine, nicotine as addictive, and the future of sales as dependent on reaching a youth market. Other documents revealed secret efforts by the companies to adjust the amount of addictive nicotine in a cigarette.

One of the less attractive qualities of national politics in the twenty-first century—pervasively present in the Bush administration's defense of its national security policies—is to delegitimize the party making an argument instead of rebutting the argument itself. The *ad hominem* arguments we were taught to reject in logic classes work. Developing the facts that will show that cigarette companies' executives knew that nicotine was addictive and exploited that knowledge lethally to target minors will be a powerful argument for Kessler with both the public and President Clinton. Senator Bob Dole looked foolish and crass in defending the cigarette companies during the presidential campaign of 1996.

Of course, Kessler as a protagonist is also vulnerable to accusations—in his case, of power grabbing and paternalism. It may be far easier for opponents to attack the player for personal failings than for positions that the opponents reject, but that the public regards as highly persuasive. A player anticipating such attacks will want to diffuse them. In fact, Kessler goes to some pains to present himself as an unbiased fact-finder trying to apply the words of the statute as any fair-minded lawyer would. He does not present himself as a leader, let alone as a crusader. He may be both, but he presents himself as an honest government employee doing his best to discharge the legal terms of his employment. Archibald Cox took much the same position in explaining why he could not compromise on the issue of subpoenaing President Nixon's tapes dealing with Watergate.

Kessler's Choice: What to Propose
A Case History by Esther Scott

The two FDA documents Kessler had requested produced a jurisdictional analysis and a proposed rule comprising roughly 600 pages of legal analysis and rule making, later supplemented with another 200,000 pages of supporting material.[1] Taken together, they presented a comprehensive rationale for FDA regulation of tobacco products. While some maintained that the agency's arguments were built solidly on its statutory mandate, others contended that, in some points, it had plunged into uncharted legal and regulatory waters, which would open it to challenges in court.

The Legal Analysis

The analysis presented the agency's case for claiming regulatory jurisdiction over nicotine on the ground that it was indeed a drug under the provisions of the Food, Drug, and Cosmetic Act. The heart of the document could be said to lie in the arguments it advanced on the key issue of intent. In what some would view as a departure from its previously narrow conception of intent in regard to tobacco, the agency took the position that an expansive definition of intent—known as "objective intent"—was the "appropriate standard" to apply in the case of nicotine. Under the argument, the agency did not have to restrict itself, as the tobacco industry had asserted, to a consideration of the express representations and claims of cigarette manufacturers and vendors; it could take into account, among other things, "the totality of the relevant evidence showing the seller's awareness of how its product is actually used and affects the structure or function of the body, regardless of how the product is labeled or advertised." This standard allowed the FDA to make far greater use of such things as internal memoranda and manufacturing practices as evidence of intent to affect the structure or function of the body, and, therefore, justify the agency's assertion of regulatory jurisdiction.

Having made the basic finding of jurisdiction, the analysis—in conjunction with a section on "legal authority" in the proposed rule—proceeded to lay out the FDA's strategy for regulating tobacco products.[2] As with the issue of intent, the agency's solution to a long-standing regulatory conundrum—how to regulate tobacco products without banning them outright, as the drug provisions of the law would require it to do—was viewed by some as a legally questionable tactic. Essentially, the agency determined that it would regulate cigarettes and smokeless tobacco not as drugs, but as "combination products"— that is, products that were considered both drug and device—which it contended it was permitted to do under 1990 amendments to the food and drug statute. The FDA determined that (1) the nicotine in both products was a drug, "achieving its effect through chemical action within the body"; and (2) cigarettes and smokeless tobacco were "drug delivery systems whose purpose is to deliver nicotine in a manner in which it can be most readily absorbed by the consumer, and are, therefore, devices...." The analysis likened a cigarette to a "metered-dose inhaler," which delivered a measured amount of an aerosolized drug through inhalation, and smokeless tobacco to "infusion devices or transdermal patches," such as the nicotine patch (in each case, products that the FDA already regulated).

Under the terms of the amendments governing combination products, the agency was required to determine a product's "primary mode of action," for the purposes of assigning it to one of its regulatory arms. In the case of cigarettes and smokeless tobacco, the FDA concluded, the primary mode was "that of a drug, due to the nicotine." Nonetheless, the analysis maintained that this designation was "not determinative...of which provisions of the act apply"—that is, the drug provisions were not automatically invoked by the conclusion that cigarettes and smokeless tobacco acted primarily as a drug. Instead, the agency had the discretion "to use drug provisions, device provisions, or a combination of drug and device provisions in regulating these products." Noting the draconian consequences likely to issue from an application of the drug provisions, the agency sought a regulatory approach that would "provide flexible tools that allow FDA to establish and move towards the public health protection goals that are most practicable for cigarettes and smokeless tobacco products." Therefore, the agency would use its device authority, which, it noted, included "provisions designed to permit a staged, multi-tiered approach to assuring the safety and effectiveness of long-marketed products."[3]

The Regulation

The basic elements of the FDA's regulation closely followed those that Kessler had outlined in his March 1995 speech at Columbia Law School. The proposed rule was intended, the agency wrote, to "reduce children's and adolescents' easy access to cigarettes and smokeless tobacco as well as significantly decrease the amount of positive imagery that makes these products so appealing to them." The rule would not, however, "restrict the use of tobacco products by adults." In presenting its rationale for a youth-oriented regulation, the agency, repeating Kessler's earlier phrase, labeled smoking a "pediatric disease" whose addictiveness turned youthful smokers into long-term users of tobacco products. More than three million American adolescents currently smoked, according to the FDA, and another one million used smokeless tobacco; moreover, recent studies indicated that, after years of decline, the "prevalence" of smoking among youth had begun to rise. Between 1900 and 1994, for example, the prevalence of smoking by eighth graders rose 30 percent, from 14.3 to 18.6 percent; among twelfth graders, it increased from 28.3 to 31.2 percent. Young smokers, the agency pointed out, generally had easy access to cigarettes and smokeless tobacco; although all fifty states prohibited the sale of tobacco to anyone under eighteen, the document noted, the state laws were "rarely enforced." Meanwhile the tobacco companies pumped huge sums into advertising and promotion campaigns—an estimated $6.2 billion in 1993—creating "ubiquitous images and messages [which] convey to young people that tobacco use is desirable, socially acceptable, safe, healthy, and prevalent in society."

In consequence, the FDA's proposed rule focused closely on issues of access and appeal. It would, among other things, ban cigarette vending machines and other "impersonal" methods of sale that did not readily require age verification, and prohibit the distribution of free samples of cigarettes. In addition, the rule placed restrictions on the advertising of tobacco products. Advertising in any publication "that reaches children" would be limited to black-and-white, "text-only format"[4]; and outdoor advertising within 1,000 feet of schools and playgrounds would be banned. Other promotional activities would face restriction as well. The rule banned, for example, the sale or distribution of non-tobacco items—such as hats or tee-shirts—that bore the brand name of a tobacco product or "other identifying characteristic," as well as the use of a brand name in the sponsorship of athletic, artistic, cultural, and other similar events. Finally, the rule would require manufacturers to "establish and maintain a national educational campaign in order to counter the pervasive imagery and reduce the appeal created by decades of pro-tobacco messages...." The FDA estimated the cost of the educational program would amount to $150 million annually. If these measures did not result in the agency's goal of reducing "by roughly one half the percentage of young people using tobacco products" in seven years' time, the proposed regulation stated, the FDA would "take additional measures to help achieve" its objective.

A Step Back from the Case History for Perspective. Both the likelihood of congressional action to overrule any regulation Kessler proposed and the willingness of President Clinton to make clear that he would veto any such effort depended significantly on how the interested public would view the proposal. By now Kessler had, with the important assistance of Rep. Waxman, already made the case that the cigarette manufacturers must have known that cigarettes were addictive as well as lethal, and that they were prepared to deceive the public about both these underlying facts and their knowledge of the facts. He would, of course, emphasize the very dramatic consequences of youth smoking: 3,000 beginning the practice every day and 1,000 destined to die of a smoking-related disease.

Kessler could easily anticipate the arguments his opponents would make. Americans believe in free choice, even the choice to take severe risks. They resent paternalism. They believe in elected government; and his proposal would be a major form of law-making by an appointed official at a time when the nation had made clear its suspicion of increasing regulation and taxes. He would be portrayed as a wildly overreaching and ambitious appointee. Indeed, his opponents would argue that the law clearly forbade the FDA from approving the use of any drug the dangers of which greatly exceeded its benefits, leaving Kessler—on his theory that nicotine and smoking were within the powers of the FDA—no legitimate option other than to ban a drug on which almost 50 million Americans were heavily dependent.

For the proponent of a new policy, arguments can be met not only with counterarguments but also by designing the proposal in such a way as to eliminate most of the objection. To the claim that regulation of tobacco was paternalism and contrary to American's love of liberty, Kessler could respond that minors had never been left free to make whatever choices they desire, but only if he limited his proposal to youth. And so he did. This design of the proposal amounted to a supplement to the argument that addicts cannot make free choices. A technical legal argument—one well beyond the ability of non-experts—could be incorporated in the proposal to meet the claim that the FDA had no options other than completely forbidding the use of a drug such as nicotine. Because neither of two competing highly technical arguments are likely to have any impact on an uncertain public opinion, he would not have to deal publicly with this "got you" attack. He could thus *publicly* offset an argument, which ultimately persuaded the Supreme Court, by a technical argument of his own that he could use his wider power over medical "devices" (than over "drugs") and treat a cigarette as a device for delivering a drug.

The public responds to the messenger as well as the message. Kessler and Rep. Waxman had already gone far in delegitimizing the cigarette companies and thereby undermining their persuasiveness with the public and members of Congress. Knowing that the attacks on him would be for ambition, arrogance, and lack of a decent sense of restraint, Kessler strove to appear modest, driven by the law, and neither self-motivated nor willing to assume unconstrained responsibility for the health of the American public.

Kessler's Choices: Winning President Clinton's Support

Whatever made more persuasive Kessler's proposals, the arguments that support them and the legitimacy of their proponent would affect the public context of any partisan debate. So would whatever made less persuasive the arguments of the cigarette manufacturers for the right of individuals to choose to engage in even extremely dangerous conduct, and the credibility of those endorsing this position. Congress would be affected directly, as well as indirectly through public reaction, by these factors. Whatever made the Republican majority in Congress less likely to unite in an attack on the FDA or on Kessler's specific proposals made it easier for President Clinton to support them.

Thus the steps that Kessler was already taking would help to persuade the President. But there was also much more that he could do, and did, to persuade the President. For the President's support would make a great deal of difference with some members of the Congress and with the public at large, and the prospect of the President's veto would, in all likelihood, make a Congressional reversal of the proposed regulations impossible. Beyond that, Kessler owed loyalty to President Clinton for his appointment and knew that the FDA proposal could affect the President's prospects in the coming 1996 election.

The starting point for Kessler's effort to win the support of the President was to recognize the President's options in dealing with the proposals, his concerns, and finally, how each of the options, when applied to the situation as the President would see it, would appear to affect his concerns. Let us consider each of these in turn.

The President's Options

1. If Kessler had asked President Clinton two years earlier whether to proceed with a regulation of smoking that would be bound to create major public and legislative controversy, Clinton almost certainly would have said "no," on the difficult-to-question ground that he already had too many other items on his agenda—items that he had raised during his campaign and wanted to pursue first. But after the FDA had spent years investigating the matter and appearing at congressional hearings on the issue, keeping the matter off of his agenda would be far more difficult for the President. Asking Kessler not to go forward would be a public, embarrassing, value-revealing decision—not just an indication of how busy the President was. So keeping the entire issue away from his administration was no longer a live possibility. By proceeding very publicly before approaching Clinton, Kessler assured a place on the President's agenda.

2. Clinton could have left the decision to the delegated responsibility of Kessler or Kessler's boss, Secretary of Health and Human Services Donna Shalala. But when a decision within an administration has such great public impact that the President is as likely to incur criticism for not taking responsibility as he is for taking one side or another, there is not much to be gained, other than time saved, in leaving the choice to subordinates.

3. The President might reject the proposal, a step that Kessler would probably have to accept, whether or not Kessler believed that, technically, the FDA had independent authority to act. But with as much well-publicized investment as Kessler had made, rejecting the proposal could well have led to Kessler's resignation on a matter of principle that would resonate with many of Clinton's core supporters.

4. The President could, alternatively, hedge as some of his aides urged, giving the tobacco companies an opportunity to negotiate an informal agreement with his administration in lieu of facing an FDA regulation. Again, he would have to fear the public effects of Kessler's reaction.

5. Finally, President Clinton could embrace Kessler's proposal, making it part of his coming campaign. This would discourage congressional opposition by promising or hinting at a veto. It would put the President eyeball-to-eyeball with the new highly conservative Republican Congress, but that would have some real advantages for him. This might be an effective issue in running against Republicans like Senator Bob Dole (who in fact became far too closely identified with the increasingly notorious cigarette manufacturers). And, with the presidential election less than two years away, President Clinton could foresee that all of his legislative initiatives would be extremely difficult if not impossible to achieve in the new Republican Congress. If he wanted to appear forceful and in control of events, a dramatic regulatory step could be the best measure available to him.

The President's Concerns

How should Kessler think about approaching the President on this issue? In some ways, the President is very, very different from almost every other executive or legislative player. His responsibilities are far broader. He is far busier and therefore needs a far larger staff. His resources of influence are vastly greater. His wide-ranging policy concerns are dependent on continuing supportive relations with a very broad audience, including the public at large. The last—the broad public's crucial role as the source of his position and his personal influence—makes policy and politics a richer mixture than for any other executive official. Still, with all these differences, at least the categories of concern remain the same: policy outcomes, personal resources of influence, organizational resources, issues of morality, and more personal matters. Kessler must try to relate to those as they operate in the vastly more complicated situation of the President.

Dick Morris, President Clinton's political advisor during this period, has written of the concerns that were most salient to President Clinton in considering Kessler's proposal. On the one hand, the President worried about reducing his influence with Congress by alienating members strongly opposed to the proposal. His influence had already been greatly weakened by the loss of the House and the Senate in 1994. His aides also warned him about the loss in 1996 of two out of the four tobacco states that he still had a chance to win. Powerful Democrats from these states subjected him to lobbying efforts. On the other side, he recognized and cared about the dangers of smoking, and Dick Morris' polls showed that a proposal focusing on youth would be popular even in the tobacco states.

Clinton knew that the cigarette companies were his political enemies, and he was personally angered by the evidence of the falsity of their public denials of knowing that cigarettes were addictive. He wanted to appear forceful to the public at a time when legislation seemed out of the question. Appearances of power are a large part of having and exercising the powers of the presidency. Finally, he worried that Kessler had taken the tobacco proposal so far along the road that he might resign (resulting in a loss of base support for Clinton) if the President pursued a more conciliatory path of seeking voluntary concessions by the cigarette companies.

A Coalition to the President

The prospect of a presidential veto was Kessler's insurance policy against Congressional action to legislate a reversal of his efforts. Whether the President promised or exercised the veto depended on his understanding of the significance of the occasion to him, but that understanding itself would also depend on the use of persuasive resources by those he trusted, and their use of resources would depend in turn on the efforts of Kessler to influence them. In short, the path to President Clinton would be shaped in significant part by coalition formation of the same sort as we saw in the Stinger missile case. It is not necessary to describe again the logic of coalition formation; but it is useful to illustrate its generality by following Kessler's efforts as he later described them in his book *A Question of Intent* (2001).

Kessler described his effort to "surround" the President. By the time Kessler was through he would have the following people on his side, pressing the President to support his proposals: Secretary of Health and Human Services Donna Shalala; Vice President Al Gore; White House

Counsel Abner Mikva; former Representative and good friend of the President, Mike Synar; and perhaps Hillary Clinton. There is no need to review again what resources people can have to influence a decision maker or precisely what resources each of those mentioned above had to influence the President. We can stay at the level of coalition building to see Kessler at work trying to supplement the persuasiveness of the case he could make by himself for his proposal in terms of the President's own concerns by adding to that the influence of others with Clinton.

Kessler started by making his case to Secretary Shalala, who responded sympathetically but urged him to meet with other representatives of her Department, many of whom were still absorbing the political costs of having failed to obtain legislation on the President's health care plan and who worried about a further weakening of the resources of the Department to influence members of Congress.

Fearing he might be blocked at this level, Kessler decided to seek support in the White House. Kessler asked an associate, Bill Schultz, to contact Abner Mikva, the White House Counsel. His argument to Mikva may have won an ally, but a cautious one. Kessler's focus on children eliminated many of the concerns that had made Mikva cautious. Still, Mikva wanted to explore the possible alternative of negotiations with the tobacco industry for voluntary steps to protect children.

Kessler then found a contact to approach Vice President Gore. He contacted Dick Morris who, favoring the proposal, argued persuasively that the President was wrong to think that his position on tobacco, along with his position on gun control, had cost him control of the House in the 1994 election. Finally, Kessler called on Clinton's good friend, former Congressman Mike Synar, to make a pitch to the political people at the White House that Kessler's regulation would be helpful, not harmful, politically.

When Kessler finally met with the President himself in July 1995, Clinton was deciding between supporting the FDA regulation now and, alternatively, threatening regulatory action sometime in the future, if the cigarette companies did not "voluntarily" provide new protections against sales to children. Most of those present—Secretary Shalala, Vice President Gore, and Abner Mikva—were reliable supporters of Kessler's proposal. Only Leon Panetta retained doubts about how the choice should be made.

Of course, persuasive argument and not just the influence of the others would determine the President's decision. Kessler showed Clinton the most shocking documents that had emerged during civil suits or Kessler's investigation. The documents acknowledged that the cigarette companies were "in the business of selling nicotine, an addictive drug." The scandal the documents would cause promised strong public support for the regulation but they also motivated the President morally. According to Morris, Clinton's reaction to being shown that the cigarette companies knew very well about the addictive effects of nicotine was: "I want to kill them; I just read all those documents, and I want to kill them."

Assuming the stance of a "mere" executor of what the law plainly required, Kessler argued that, in light of the admissions by company officials, "it would not be credible for us not to move forward." Implicit in that statement of moral obligation was a warning of the risk the President would face if, choosing a course that was "not credible," Kessler was to resign as a matter of principle. But conscience was also a target. In all, Kessler invoked the President's conscience, politics, sense of legal obligation, and anger at the cigarette companies. And all of this was done personally by Kessler only after he had surrounded the President with supporters of his position.

Completing the Story
A Case History by Esther Scott

With work on the two documents completed, word that the proposed rule had been sent to the White House for review began to filter out into the press.[5] There was some astonishment that Kessler would take such a step at a time of regulatory retrenchment. "After the Republican takeover of Congress last November," *Business Week* reported in late July 1995, "the brash commissioner of the Food and Drug Administration lowered his profile as Washington's most zealous regulation czar. But behind the scenes, he was plotting one of his most audacious moves yet: In mid-July, Kessler sought White House authority to regulate Big Tobacco." Others offered more pithy views of Kessler's initiative. "The FDA," said Speaker Gingrich, "has lost its mind."

At the White House

In theory at least, the FDA, having concluded that it had jurisdiction over cigarettes and smokeless tobacco, had the authority to press forward with its regulation. But, as the *New York Times* noted, "in a sign of the delicacy of the issue—and of the opposition in the Republican Congress to new restraints on smoking—the agency is not using the authority to act on its own. Instead, it has thrown the issue to the President...."[6] For the Clinton administration, the FDA's proposed rule was a mixed bag, politically speaking. On the one hand, there appeared to be popular support for the kind of restraints that the FDA regulation would place on the sale and distribution of cigarettes to children. A national survey by the Robert Wood Johnson Foundation in 1994, for example, indicated that Americans strongly backed bans on vending machines and restrictions on sales and advertising aimed at minors.[7] On the other hand, the electoral calculus, just one year from the start of a presidential campaign, was a complicated business. It would be a risky proposition to take a step that was bound to alienate the tobacco states. Clinton's support in the South was shaky at best; he had won only two southern states in the 1992 election—Kentucky and Tennessee—and a move to regulate tobacco could ruin whatever chance he had to improve his position there. At the same time, as *Newsweek* pointed out, "bashing tobacco will play well in health-conscious, vote-rich California."[8]

Discussions among senior officials in the White House on what to do about the FDA rule began in mid-July. As they pondered the issues, aides to the president, including Chief of Staff Leon Panetta, were visited by Democratic allies from key states—Senator Wendell Ford of Kentucky and Governor Jim Hunt of North Carolina—who sought to dissuade the administration from giving the green light to the FDA.[9] By late July, the White House was reported to be debating "two different government strategies" on the issue of tobacco: okaying the FDA regulation or using "the threat of such regulation to extract concessions from the tobacco industry." In the latter category, the administration was considering a number of "voluntary" options, such as having the tobacco industry take action to limit minors' access to cigarettes or to fund an educational campaign aimed at children.[10] "For weeks," wrote journalist Philip Hilts in *Smokescreen* (1996), "the struggle for the heart of the White House went on, and at different points each side seemed to have the edge." Finally, with the outcome still up in the air, "the decision was left in the hands of Clinton himself."[11] At that point, Kessler and HHS Secretary Donna Shalala were summoned to the White House to discuss the issue with the president.

Clinton was by this time familiar with the FDA's proposals, and with smoking issues in general. He had, *Newsweek* reported, read a July issue of the *Journal of the American Medical Association*—which strongly supported tobacco regulation—devoted to the health implications of smoking. "It's hard to argue with this," he reportedly told his aides. Nevertheless, at their meeting, according to Hilts' account, the president asked Kessler to present the findings of the agency's investigation; the FDA chief then handed him pages from the jurisdictional analysis, which contained statements about nicotine drawn from internal tobacco company documents. As Clinton read the statements, Kessler made his final pitch. "Mr. President," he said, "it would not be credible for us not to proceed."[12] Soon thereafter, on August 10, 1995, Clinton held a press conference to announce, in the *Washington Post's* words, "a historic crackdown on underage smoking...."

The President Speaks Out

On the day of the news conference, the *Washington Post* reported, the White House "rolled out the full public relations regalia" for the event, including "a parade of medical, sports, and political authorities to praise the decision and a concerted effort to describe the action as a sign of presidential courage fraught with political peril." Speaking from the Oval Office, "surrounded by children and leaders of tobacco-control interests,"[13] the president declared: "Today I am announcing broad executive action to protect the young people of the United States from the awful dangers of tobacco." Citing grim statistics on smoking among the young—3,000 young people began smoking every day, 1,000 of them ultimately doomed to die from smoking-related illness—Clinton concluded, "The evidence is overwhelming, and the threat is immediate. Our children face a health crisis that is getting worse." After outlining the steps that he was "authorizing the Food and Drug Administration to take," Clinton made a nod in the direction of Congress. No one, he said, "much likes government regulation, and I would prefer it if we could have done this in some other way. The only other way I can think of is if Congress were to write these restrictions into law." But absent such action, and in the face of the tobacco industry's "massive marketing and lobbying campaign," the president concluded, "clearly I have no alternative but to do everything I can to bring this assault to a halt."

Reaction

The immediate response to the president's announcement of the FDA's proposed rule, which along with the jurisdictional analysis was released for public comment that day, was predictably mixed. The action was warmly received by anti-smoking activists and medical officials, such as the president of the American Heart Association, who called the regulation "probably the most important public health move by the government in the last 30 years." Kessler himself received a share of the praise. The FDA commissioner, said Matthew Myers of the Coalition of Smoking OR Health, had "resisted the easy temptation of a shotgun approach that would affect both adults and children" in favor of a regulatory program focused on youth. "He has given up a spectacular short-term gain," Myers continued, "for a far more substantial long-term progress."[14] Positive responses to the FDA action crossed political line in some cases. Writing several months before the rule was made public, conservative columnist William F. Buckley, Jr., applauded the conception of smoking as a pediatric disease ("Three Cheers for Dr. David Kessler," he wrote), and the steps proposed to curb it among the nation's young. "Fifteen-year-olds would undoubtedly resist such acts of paternalism," he wrote. "Thirteen-year-olds at the deathbed of one or another parent would weep with frustration that the pressures hadn't been brought to bear early enough to affect the habits of their mother or father."[15]

For its part, the tobacco industry and its allies vociferously attacked both Kessler and the regulation. The FDA chief was "an unelected bureaucrat" who was "on a power grab" and "trying to make this his own personal issue," declared Steve Parrish, a senior vice president at Philip Morris.[16] Parrish darkly hinted at more drastic measures to come. "Make no mistake," he said, "the real hidden agenda here is prohibition." The tobacco companies did not limit their response to angry comments. The same day the FDA regulation was issued, the nation's five largest tobacco companies were in federal district court in Greensboro, North Carolina, seeking to block the agency from asserting regulatory authority over cigarettes. Later, two more suits would be filed—one by a consortium of advertising and publishing associations, and another by two smokeless tobacco companies—disputing the FDA's authority to regulate tobacco products.

In Congress, meanwhile, the regulation was criticized by members from tobacco states and by conservatives like Sen. Don Nickles, R-Okla., who labeled the proposed rule "heavy-handed, big government," and argued that it was up to Congress to decide whether action on tobacco control was needed. Even some Democrats—who, Philip Hilts pointed out, also benefited from the tobacco companies' political largesse, albeit more modestly of late than the Republicans—voiced reservations about FDA regulation. Senate Minority Leader Tom Daschle of South Dakota, for example, suggested that a voluntary approach would be "a much more plausible and viable option."[17] Some members of Congress with strong anti-smoking records also worried about the efficacy of the FDA's action in light of the protracted legal battles that almost certainly lay ahead. "I don't suggest that the federal government shy away from a fight because of the tobacco industry's firepower," wrote Rep. Ron Wyden, D-Ore., who had earlier proposed in Congress a plan to require tobacco companies to finance enforcement of state tobacco laws. "But faced with years of delay and uncertain prospects in implementing FDA regulation, other options for saving this generation of kids should be examined."[18]

Beyond immediate expressions of support or outrage, however, lay questions about the appropriateness of the FDA's decision to regulate tobacco products and the effect that such a move would have on the agency. Some critics argued that a regulatory rationale which allowed products whose "primary mode of action" was that of a drug to be regulated as devices was legally shaky at best. The text of the agency's proposed rule, one observer maintained, "revealed just how much Kessler had to twist around the Food, Drug, and Cosmetic Act to justify his proposal."[19] Others asked how an agency already pressed to meet its existing regulatory obligations and short on inspectional staff could shoulder the enormous task of policing its tobacco regulations. "I can't comprehend how Dr. Kessler will find resources to enforce any tobacco restrictions," wrote former FDA investigator James Phillips in a letter to the House Commerce Committee, "when he doesn't have enough field investigators...to properly inspect foreign drug products entering this country." The FDA, Phillips asserted, was ignoring other "pressing needs" because of its "preoccupation with tobacco."[20] Even Kessler's friends, *Business Week* reported, "wonder if [he] might not do better to spend his time expediting approval for new drugs and medical devices, and fixing other FDA shortcomings."

Finally, critics, and even some supporters, questioned the fit between the regulation of tobacco products and the FDA's basic mission. Kessler, the *Washington Monthly* maintained, in a generally laudatory profile of the agency, "is a hero for facing up to the tobacco companies. But is his agency the most sensible place for such regulation? It seems more appropriate for agencies responsible for fighting drug abuse—who now deal almost exclusively with illegal drugs—to spend some of their $14 billion annual appropriation curbing the abuse and youth-oriented marketing of cigarettes and alcohol." Regulating a product like cigarettes seemed to clash, moreover, with the FDA's historic mandate to ensure the safety and effectiveness of the products under its purview. "Ordinarily," wrote Philip Hilts in the *New York Times*, "when a drug is brought under the FDA's jurisdiction, the agency requires rigorous animal and human tests to determine its safety and effectiveness." In the case of cigarettes, he continued, the tests had long ago been carried out, and "they showed that tobacco is not fit for human consumption." If the FDA were ultimately to take on the regulation of cigarettes, Hilts observed, it would find itself "thrust into a rather odd role: monitoring the marketing of a substance whose chief side effect is death for about one in three of the people who use it."

Kessler, too, seemed thrust into an odd position by the controversy over tobacco regulation, alternately hailed for being "gutsy" or lambasted for being "on an ego trip."[21] Perhaps the paradox of his position as head of an agency charged with safeguarding the public health was best summed up in the critical remarks of one commentator, who wrote: "Although there is strong agreement that reducing smoking, especially among young people, probably would do more to improve the public health than anything short of discovering a cure for cancer, Kessler's willingness to disrupt the important work of FDA and undermine its statutory authority raises questions about the quality of his leadership."[22]

Making It Final

When it issued its proposed rule, the FDA had set a deadline of January 2, 1996 for all comments. On the last day of the public comment period, the tobacco industry delivered 47,000 pages of documents—2,000 pages on its statement of position and the remainder in supporting documents.[23] In all, the FDA received 710,000 comments, or as Kessler puts it, "51 gigabytes of information"—the most it had ever received in response to a ruling. The industry's massive response systematically disputed every point in the FDA's jurisdictional analysis and proposed regulation, beginning with its assertion of jurisdiction over tobacco, which it labeled as "unlawful." The tobacco companies also took issue with the agency's expansive view of "objective intent," arguing that, on the basis of congressional language, the FDA's own regulations, and "well-settled case law," objective intent "is to be determined from a product's label, labeling, promotional material, advertising, and any other representations in conjunction with the distribution of the product." The "internal memoranda, published research, patents and other materials whose contents have never been communicated in marketing claims for a product," they continued, "are irrelevant in determining 'objective intent.'" The industry further disputed the FDA's assertion that it had the discretion to decide which regulatory authority to apply to tobacco products—a claim it characterized as "truly a breathtaking, and wholly unprecedented, assertion of Agency authority to override the will of Congress." These and many other contentious points between the agency and the tobacco industry were not expected to be resolved any time soon. Prospects for legislative action were dim at best: Rep. Bliley had made it clear that he would leave it to the courts to decide the issue of jurisdiction.[24] The legal battles over the FDA's ruling were expected to end up in the Supreme Court, and to last well beyond the 1996 elections. They did.

In the meantime, however, the issue of tobacco regulation emerged as a political issue in the early months of the presidential campaign. The Republican nominee, Senator Bob Dole, had been "an important ally of the tobacco industry" during his tenure in the Senate, the *Washington Post* reported, and a beneficiary of its financial contributions.[25] Dole underscored his opposition to the regulation of tobacco in a number of campaign appearances. During a June 1996 visit to Kentucky, for example, Dole spoke out explicitly against the FDA's actions against tobacco, telling reporters, "I wish the FDA would spend a little more time on medical devices and approving new drugs to help people."[26] He also raised some eyebrows by arguing that cigarettes were not necessarily addictive. And while agreeing with the goal of preventing children from smoking, Dole remarked, "We know it's [smoking] not good for kids. But a lot of other things aren't good. Some would say milk's not good." President Clinton quickly pounced on such remarks in his weekly radio address. Asserting that he had spent months campaigning for rules to prohibit cigarette sales and advertising aimed at children, the president maintained that when political leaders "say cigarettes are not necessarily addictive and oppose our efforts to keep tobacco away from our children, they continue to cater to powerful interests, but they're not standing up for parents and children. In fact, they're making the job of being a parent even harder."[27]

A couple of months later, on August 23, 1996, the president himself made public the last step in the tobacco rulemaking process. In another widely covered news conference—this one held in the Rose Garden and attended by Vice President Al Gore—Clinton announced the FDA's final rule on tobacco restrictions. The final version, which was to take effect in one year, differed slightly from the proposed regulation unveiled a year earlier at the White House—it somewhat softened the restrictions on vending machines, for example, banning them only in locations where children would have access—but in most respects, it adhered closely to the original. Flanked by a group of children wearing "Tobacco-Free Kids" tee-shirts, the president declared: "With this historic action we are taking today, Joe Camel and the Marlboro Man will be out of our children's reach forever."[28]

Most observers, however, took a more cautious view of the final outcome of the FDA's tobacco initiative. The regulation faced court challenges not just on jurisdictional grounds, but on free speech principles as well, and the likely judicial disposition of the case was by no means clear. Still, Kessler believed that the agency's long process of investigation and rule making had marked an irrevocable step on the road to tobacco controls. At the beginning of that process, he reflects, "who would have ever thought the president of the United States would have stood up at a press conference and said, 'It's time to take steps [on tobacco].' Once the president…takes a stand like that, you can never reverse that." While, he acknowledged, "the outcome of this is still up in the air, there are certain things there's no going back on." Whatever happened ultimately in the courts or in Congress, Kessler concluded, "I think it's fair to say that it's a very different debate."

In November 1996, David Kessler announced his resignation as Administrator of the FDA. He took with him some of the Congressional anger that would otherwise have threatened any agency he headed.

12

Rival Coalitions and Congress as the Decision Maker

Congress did not act to overrule Kessler's regulation of tobacco. But, the appellate courts were skeptical of his exercise of FDA powers, albeit ruling against the regulation by very narrow margins. On April 25, 1997, Judge William Osteen of the Federal District Court in Greensboro, North Carolina, ruled that the FDA had jurisdiction under the Federal Food, Drug, and Cosmetic Act to regulate nicotine-containing cigarettes and smokeless tobacco.[1] The Court held that "tobacco fits within the FDCA's definition of 'drug' and 'device,'" and that the FDA can regulate cigarettes and smokeless tobacco products as drug delivery devices under the combination of the "product" and the "restricted device" provisions of the Act.

On August 14, 1998, the Fourth Circuit Court of Appeals reversed this decision by a 2–1 vote.[2] The judges in the majority rejected the proposal on the grounds that Congress did not intend to delegate jurisdiction over tobacco products to the FDA.

On March 21, 2000, the Supreme Court affirmed the decision of the appeals court by a 5–4 margin, with Justices Rehnquist, O'Connor, Kennedy, Scalia, and Thomas in the majority.[3] In the opinion of the majority, written by Justice O'Connor, no matter how "important, conspicuous, and controversial" the issue, and regardless of how likely the public is to hold the Executive Branch politically accountable, an administrative agency's power to regulate in the public interest must always be grounded in a valid grant of authority from Congress. To the majority, the FDCA as a whole—and in conjunction with Congress's subsequent tobacco-specific legislation—clearly showed that Congress had not given the FDA the authority that it sought to exercise in this instance. Justice Breyer, joined by Justices Stevens, Souter, and Ginsburg, wrote the dissent. In his view, the Court was holding that a regulatory statute aimed at unsafe drugs and devices does not authorize regulation of a drug (nicotine) and a device (a cigarette) that the Court agrees are unsafe. And far more than most, this particular drug and device risked the life-threatening harms that administrative regulation was intended to rectify.

The Action Shifts to Congress

In the meantime, and prior to the Supreme Court decision in 2000, with the uncertainty about the regulation hanging over the battle-fields where manufacturers of tobacco products fought anti-smoking advocates, the action moved to the legislature. Without legislation, the tobacco companies still worried that they might find themselves subject to the regulatory power of the Food and Drug Administration. They still faced very dangerous lawsuits by the states and by class action plaintiffs focusing on claimed deception about the addictive qualities of nicotine. They faced anti-smoking ordinances and a bar-rage of very public revelations that they had behaved scandalously over recent decades in hiding evidence of the addictive effects of nic-otine and of the targeting of youth in sales campaigns. For all these reasons, their stock prices were deeply depressed.

On the other hand, the passionate opponents of smoking also faced risks. It was by no means clear that Kessler's regulation would survive judicial review. (It did not.) The history of litigation that sought to impose large judgments on the companies had never succeeded in the past and, as we shall see, did not succeed in the future (with the sole exception of the cases brought by state attorneys general). Children were still learning to smoke at the rate of 3,000 per day, and one-third of them would still die from smoking-related causes.

With both warring factions facing grave uncertainties and the distinct possibility of results far worse than those they might be able to negoti-ate with the other side, both could see that the time might be right for compromise. Some important aspects of any settlement—such as limits on liability, clearly establishing the jurisdiction of the Food and Drug Administration to regulate tobacco, and a tax to reduce sales to youth—would require legislation. Normally the legislation would result from the stimulation, by one of these parties, of the introduction of a bill either in the House of Representatives or the Senate. Then the proposal would be assigned to a committee in that House. Depending on the views of the chair and the other members of the majority party, it would or would not receive hearings and serious attention. If it did, the competing private groups would have an opportunity to testify, to lobby members separately, and to generate favorable attention to their views and hostile publicity for its opponents. The committee would then "mark up" its own version of the bill and send it to the party leaders in that house (including the Rules Committee, if it was in the House of Representatives) to be scheduled for floor debate under such terms and conditions as custom or the majority leadership specified.

A similar process would have to go on in the Senate. Differences in the bills that resulted from the process in each House would be reconciled in a conference committee whose membership, from both Houses, would be determined by the leaders in each house. Then a unified bill would be sent to both Houses for passage. Finally, the President must sign it to make it legislation. His position would be influential with his party in the Congress throughout the process. The likelihood that he might veto the measure would be important to the opposing political party even if it controlled one or both Houses of Congress.

That is the formal setting for the effort by the diverse anti-smoking interests (and, simultaneously, the somewhat varied tobacco interests) to develop a negotiated compromise between the warring parties. Each group saw that it must first form a coalition with its chosen allies. Then the two coalitions would seek an agreement before going to Congress. That this effort would proceed in a private context and without the leadership of either side's supporters in Congress could mean that even its success would not guarantee legislation. For example, Rep. Waxman, a long-time leader in the anti-smoking camp in the House of Representatives, was angered by the departure from familiar committee-centered procedure.

There is a non-obvious relationship among the three steps involved in this strategy: (1) forming a coalition among friendly private parties; (2) then negotiating with a rival coalition; and (3) finally, using the political influence of those in the now-united grand coalitions to persuade a majority of each House of Congress to accept the negotiated compromise. The more inclusive the "friendly" coalition at stage one, the greater its influence with Congress and the weaker the influence of those "friendly" groups left out of this stage. But the price of broadening the coalition on each side at stage one would inevitably be the inclusion of those less willing to compromise at stage two. So those seeking a negotiated solution must choose between the important political benefits at stage three of having accommodated the demands of their natural allies and the costs of this accommodation when negotiation is attempted with their opponents at stage two.

With the value of their stock discounted greatly by the risk of liability, the cigarette companies were prepared to give up much of their freedom of action, particularly with regard to young smokers or potential smokers, in exchange for some reasonable ceilings on their potential liability for harm or death to individuals from smoking. They had diversified into other fields and the attacks on the sale of cigarettes might affect their other businesses. They did not want the illegitimacy of smoking to infect their new businesses. They had a huge market abroad for cigarettes; and they anticipated being able to continue to sell cigarettes to adults within the United States. In a sense, what Kessler had tried and failed to take from them, they were now willing to give up in the form of clearly valid congressional legislation, in exchange for a reduced risk of hundreds of billions of dollars in jury awards.

For those in the world of public health, whose aim it is to protect the next generation from the extremely serious risks of smoking, the prospect of legislation that would do just that looked extremely attractive, compared to the costs of giving up an uncertain chance of compensation for those whose health it was too late to protect.

It therefore looked like a coalition of major companies manufacturing cigarettes (and chewing tobacco) and a coalition of major organizations concerned about reducing the harms of smoking to future generations could agree after what would certainly be some difficult negotiations. But even if they agreed, would they together have enough influence on the congressional players whom the rules empowered—the 435 members of the House and the 100 Senators—to win a majority in each house or, if there were a filibuster, a majority in the House and 60 percent of the votes in the Senate? The answer to that question would depend upon whether each of the two parties to the final, grand negotiation could hold together its own coalition under the strains of negotiation with "the enemy," and even then whether players unrepresented in either coalition could block the formation of a sufficient coalition of legislators. The contest would be both within coalitions and between coalitions. We shall look at these processes from one side—that of the anti-smoking forces focused on a negotiated solution.

"Dealing with the Devil": The Tobacco Control Negotiations of 1997-1998
A Case History by Esther Scott, based on Smoke In Their Eyes: Lessons in Movement Leadership from the Tobacco Wars, *by Michael Pertschuk*

In the early spring of 1997, Matthew Myers, executive vice president of the National Center for Tobacco-Free Kids, received a highly unusual request: he was invited to sit down with representatives of the major U.S. tobacco companies, and other parties, to help hammer out what might be called a peace treaty.[4] The tobacco industry, besieged by lawsuits from states seeking to recover Medicaid costs for smoking-related diseases and by a series of class action lawsuits, and under fire from the Food and Drug Administration, the press, and even Congress for its manufacturing and marketing practices, had proposed what heretofore seemed unimaginable: that it would pay billions in damages to settle the suits and would accede to comprehensive federal regulation of its products. In exchange, however, it asked for what heretofore seemed unacceptable: some form of protection from further legal liability.

The attorneys general from a number of states that had brought Medicaid suits, as well as some private attorneys, had agreed to begin negotiations with the industry for a "global settlement," which would eventually need to be enacted into law by Congress. Myers was asked to join the talks as the sole representative of the "tobacco control movement"—a loose coalition of national public health organizations, advocacy groups, and community activists who had fought for decades to reduce smoking in the United States.

For Myers, a veteran of the anti-smoking cause, it was an unprecedented moment—one that afforded the first glimmerings of hope that the single greatest scourge to the nation's health would be brought under control. But it carried risks as well—that the attorneys general would agree to terms that were too soft, and that the tobacco control movement would be too fragmented, and too militant, to seize what he believed was a once-in-a-lifetime opportunity. And for him personally, it brought the risk that by sitting down with a long-demonized adversary, he would undermine the credibility that he had built up over long years on the frontlines of the tobacco wars.

Background: The "Tobacco Wars"

From the viewpoint of the anti-smoking movement, the decades following the 1964 Surgeon General's report linking smoking to lung cancer and other diseases had been marked by painfully slow progress in the campaign to bring tobacco—its manufacturing, marketing, and advertising—under comprehensive regulatory control. Congress had passed some tobacco control legislation—first requiring warning labels on cigarette packs, then banning cigarette ads on television and, later, banning smoking on airplanes—but many regarded these measures as neither adequate to the urgent task of reducing the harms caused by smoking, nor punitive enough to curb the well-heeled tobacco industry's aggressive marketing tactics, especially those aimed at young people. The ban on TV ads, for example, was not without its benefits to the industry, since it also put an end to the anti-smoking counter-ads required by the Federal Communications Commission; and even when the warning language on cigarette packs was strengthened in the mid-1980s, it still fell short of advocates' goal of labels that bore the term "addictive."[5]

Anti-smoking crusaders attributed the federal government's reluctance to bring its regulatory powers to bear on tobacco, despite mounting evidence of its hazards to health, to the $54 billion industry's famously deep pockets. The five major tobacco companies—Philip Morris, R. J. Reynolds, Brown and Williamson, Lorillard, and Liggett—spent liberally on Democrats and Republicans alike, although by the mid-1990s they had begun to direct significantly more of their contributions to Republicans. In 1996, according to one account, the companies were "the largest corporate contributors" to both parties, dispensing almost $11 million "during the election cycle."[6] Millions more were spent on lobbyists in Washington. This political largesse, along with the powerful bloc of members who hailed from tobacco-growing districts, had made the industry seem virtually unassailable in Congress, where strong tobacco control measures commonly met a quiet end in committee. The tobacco companies had appeared equally unassailable in the courts, where for decades, thanks to their vast financial resources, they had managed to escape being found liable for a single dollar in damages in the hundreds of personal injury lawsuits brought by dying smokers or their families.

New Developments

By the early 1990s, however, some chinks in the tobacco industry's seemingly impregnable armor had begun to appear. The first sign of vulnerability came in 1988, when, for the first time, a jury awarded damages to the family of a deceased smoker, Rose Cipollone. As it turned out, after years of exhaustive appeals by the tobacco companies, the Cipollone family never collected a penny from the industry,[7] but the case inflicted damages of another sort on the tobacco companies. During the discovery process, lawyers for the plaintiffs subpoenaed thousands of pages of documents, some of which appeared to confirm what many had long suspected, and the industry had long denied: that tobacco companies knew of the addictive properties of the key ingredient in cigarettes—nicotine—and had manipulated the levels of it in their products to ensure addiction. Further revelations of the industry's practices followed after a whistle-blower at Brown and Williamson leaked secret documents to the press in 1994, indicating the company's awareness not only of the addictiveness of cigarettes but of their potentially deadly health effects.

The year 1994 would prove to be a rough one for the tobacco companies. In February, Dr. David Kessler, head of the Food and Drug Administration, announced that his agency would investigate whether it could regulate tobacco products—an unprecedented step by the FDA, which had historically steered clear of any claim of jurisdiction over tobacco. Over a year later, in August 1995, Kessler followed up his announcement with a proposed rule that would classify cigarettes as a "drug delivery device" and, as such, bring them under the FDA's regulatory umbrella. In keeping with Kessler's campaign to frame smoking as a "pediatric disease," which addicted most smokers in their teens, the rule focused on advertising and marketing restrictions designed to reduce the appeal of cigarettes to young people, as well as access to them; adult smokers would face no restrictions. The rule faced a long test in the courts, with the outcome far from certain, but Kessler's bold move represented the most aggressive attack to date on the industry by the federal government. Moreover, Kessler appeared to have the backing of President Bill Clinton, who had already put his stamp on the smoking issue by banning tobacco use in the White House. The President had himself unveiled the FDA's proposed rule and, urged on by Vice President Al Gore and First Lady Hillary Clinton, would become increasingly forceful in speaking out against smoking, particularly among the nation's youth.

At the same time, there were ominous developments for the industry on the legal front in the form of a new round of lawsuits, commonly referred to as the "third wave." Unlike the earlier personal injury suits, which sought damages for individual smokers and their families, the third wave took a different tack. In May 1994, Mike Moore, the attorney general of Mississippi, filed suit against cigarette makers, seeking to recover $940 million in Medicaid expenditures on smoking-related illnesses. "It's time these billionaire tobacco companies," Moore declared, "start paying for what they rightfully owe to Mississippi."[8] Moore's broader focus on the cost of smoking to taxpayers, instead of to smokers themselves, attracted the notice of other attorneys general in the United States. Before long, several states—Minnesota, West Virginia, and Florida—followed suit. How these long-shot lawsuits ("Hail Mary" efforts, as one observer called them) would fare in the courts was uncertain, but the movement steadily gained momentum, as more states joined the legal bandwagon and filed Medicaid lawsuits of their own.

In addition, the companies were hit by a series of class action lawsuits brought by private trial lawyers on behalf of groups of smokers. The largest of these was the *Castano* suit, filed by a group of sixty-five law firms, which for the first time accused cigarette makers of intentionally addicting smokers by manipulating levels of nicotine.[9] Like the Medicaid suits, the fate of *Castano* and other private class action suits was uncertain at best, but the sheer number and size of the third wave legal actions posed an unprecedented challenge to the embattled tobacco industry.

Meanwhile, tobacco manufacturers took an unwelcome turn in the public limelight when Rep. Henry Waxman, D-Calif., a longtime foe of tobacco interests and chair of the Energy and Commerce Subcommittee on Health and the Environment in the Democrat-controlled House, held a series of high-profile hearings on smoking issues. The hearings were perhaps most memorable for the moment when the top executives of the nation's seven largest tobacco companies were asked to state under oath whether they personally believed that nicotine was not addictive—which each in his turn did, while photographers and TV cameras captured the spectacle on film.

Not all the news was bad for the industry in 1994. In the November elections that year, Republicans regained control of both chambers of Congress. In general, many Republicans, philosophically opposed to governmental regulation of business, did not favor federal tobacco control legislation; and in particular, some of its key leaders, such as Rep. Bliley— the Chairman of the House Commerce Committee—were longtime supporters of the industry.

Still, despite a friendlier atmosphere for industry in Congress—under Bliley's chairmanship, hearings on smoking-related issues came to a halt— the challenges to the tobacco companies continued otherwise unabated in the mid-1990s. State attorneys general pressed their cases in court in ever greater numbers—by late 1996, some seventeen states had launched suits against the industry[10]—and various private class action suits were proceeding as well. The industry's legal expenses by now amounted to $600 million a year[11] and, while many doubted that the wealthiest firms could be bankrupted by the court cases, Wall Street investors had begun casting a wary eye on tobacco manufacturers; tobacco companies' stock prices began to tumble. The "significantly undervalued" stock in turn threatened to affect "many of [the] nontobacco and nondomestic business assets" of the tobacco manufacturers' parent companies.[12] Perhaps the most telling sign of trouble came in February 1996, when the Liggett Tobacco Company, the smallest of the five major firms in terms of profits, broke ranks with the industry and made separate agreements with five states and with the lawyers in the *Castano* case. In its settlement with the states, Liggett agreed not only to pay damages, but to withdraw its opposition to the FDA's proposed rule to regulate cigarettes as drug delivery devices. In return, it would be absolved of further liability for damages.[13]

It was against this backdrop of mounting legal woes and cracks in its previously solid front that the tobacco industry made its first covert overtures for peace, quietly signaling an interest in a "global settlement" that would encompass not only the ongoing lawsuits, but the issue of federal regulation as well.

Peace Overtures

By 1996 the leadership of the top two tobacco companies had changed hands—a matter of some significance. Neither Geoffrey Bible, who took the reins of Philip Morris in 1994, nor Steven Goldstone, who became CEO of R. J. Reynolds (RJR) in 1995, had sworn before Waxman's subcommittee that nicotine was not addictive. There were other differences as well. Goldstone, unusually, was not a veteran "tobacco man";

he had been a lawyer with a Wall Street firm and longtime counsel to
RJR before assuming the top post there. He did not share the company's
"always fight" philosophy; in fact, as one company executive reported,
Goldstone "always tried to settle cases before going to court."[14] While
Bible did have a background in cigarette sales, and had been an unapologetic smoker and a tough combatant in the tobacco wars, he was also "a
pragmatist," as one account put it, ready to try, in his own words, "a new
route."[15]

And, increasingly, it seemed to these two industry leaders that a global
settlement offered the best way out of the box that tobacco manufacturers found themselves in. "We could not continue to be seen as a ren-
egade industry," Goldstone would later say. "We had to come into the
process for our long-term well-being." The industry's victories in court
were "Pyrrhic," he maintained, "because nobody is putting a value on our
earnings....The likelihood of a long-term healthy future for this industry,
or even for a manageable decline, became more and more unlikely."[16]
The tobacco industry's leaders hoped that a settlement, in which they
would, for the first time, agree to make major concessions—both in paying damages to states and in accepting federal regulation—in return for
some sort of immunity from future litigation, would allow them to shake
their pariah status and, perhaps most important, to quantify their liability costs and "regain investor confidence."[17]

First Efforts

In June 1996, Mississippi Attorney General Mike Moore and Richard
Scruggs, a trial lawyer who would handle the litigation for the state, were
approached by two intermediaries—lobbyists John Sears and Tommy
Anderson—who indicated that the tobacco industry was interested in
reaching a comprehensive settlement.[18] There was, in fact, an interest
on both sides. The Medicaid lawsuits represented considerable risks for
Moore and his fellow attorneys general, who had set off into unknown
legal terrain with their Medicaid lawsuits, not always with the blessing of
their governors or legislatures. Strategically, moreover, Scruggs believed
that a settlement represented the best resolution for high-stakes legal
battles. "[U]sually a good settlement," he maintained, "is far superior to
trench warfare, trial-by-trial litigation."

Secret talks began that summer, chiefly between Moore and Scruggs
on one side, and Anderson and Sears on the other. In a matter of weeks,

however, the talks broke down, their end hastened by a leak to the *Wall Street Journal*, which published a story on the clandestine negotiations. But despite the early setback, the interest in a global settlement continued. In late 1996, while playing golf with North Carolina's governor, Democrat Jim Hunt, Steve Goldstone discussed his wish to reach some kind of agreement that would put the industry's problems behind it. Through Hunt, Goldstone retained Phil Carlton, a former North Carolina Supreme Court judge, to meet with White House advisor Bruce Lindsey in November 1996 and enlist his aid in bringing about settlement negotiations.[19] Hunt himself—the head of a major tobacco-growing state—met with President Clinton in December to urge him to take a more active role in facilitating talks between the litigating states and the industry. Clinton agreed and set Lindsey the task of helping to bring the parties together.

Even before the White House became actively involved, however, Matt Myers had been anticipating the resumption of global settlement talks, mulling over what position the "public health community"—broadly speaking, the organizations and individuals who advocated for tobacco control—should take regarding a comprehensive agreement.

Matt Myers and the Tobacco Control Movement

A lawyer by training, Myers had earned his credentials in the anti-smoking movement as executive director of the Coalition on Smoking OR Health, a Washington-based organization created by the American Cancer Society, the American Heart Association, and the American Lung Association. It was from that post that he led a lobbying campaign in 1984 to persuade Congress to improve the contents of the warning labels on cigarette packs. While the campaign failed in its efforts to insert the term "addictive" onto the labels, it did succeed in getting stronger language, larger print, and rotating warnings on all cigarette packs, despite the determined resistance of the tobacco industry. In the mid-1990s, after fifteen years with the Coalition, he was recruited as the chief legislative strategist and lobbyist for a new advocacy organization—the National Center for Tobacco-Free Kids, and its companion coalition, the Campaign for Tobacco-Free Kids. The new coalition was funded chiefly by the Robert Wood Johnson Foundation, as well as by the American Cancer Society, the American Heart Association, and the American Medical Association, and was headed by Bill Novelli, a former advertising executive.

Myers had been electrified by Kessler's bold effort to bring cigarettes under FDA control. After years of chipping away at the tobacco industry through legislative initiatives both federal and local, Myers felt the anti-smoking movement had stalled. "We had made real progress since 1964," he noted, "but by the mid-1990s, the tobacco control movement had been dancing around the periphery of accomplishing anything meaningful for years. As if health warnings that are an inch bigger are going to change the world." In Kessler's action, Myers discerned the possibility of far more comprehensive regulation of tobacco than the incremental gains in Congress had thus far afforded—and more than even the FDA was contemplating at the time—if the courts ultimately upheld the agency's assertion of regulatory authority. "Suddenly," Myers said, "you had an agency that had the potential to try things that no one had ever tried with this industry, to bring about a fundamental change in the product itself," by controlling the contents of cigarettes, in particular, nicotine. He believed the public health community should rally in defense of Kessler's initiative and work to extend the FDA's reach beyond the limited authority it sought in its proposed rule.

At the same time, while Myers applauded the efforts of the states in their Medicaid lawsuits, he worried that they would ultimately fall far short of the public health protections that he envisioned. He feared that the state attorneys general, concerned about the risks of going to trial, would be eager to reach an agreement and, inexperienced in dealing with the wily tobacco industry, would settle for too little or give up too much. Myers was equally concerned about the fate of a settlement once it reached Congress, which would have to enact legislation implementing key parts of any deal, including immunity from liability and—although this was less clear—an extension of FDA authority to encompass tobacco products.[20] He believed that congressional action could open the way, as it had in the past, for "Trojan-horse compromises," engineered by allies of the tobacco industry, which would undercut the FDA's authority or provide unacceptable liability protection.

On the recommendation of Mitch Zeller, then a deputy to David Kessler at the FDA, Myers had been involved in discussions with Moore and Scruggs during their secret negotiations with tobacco companies in the summer of 1996. Zeller noted that Moore and Scruggs had "no connections with the public health community" as the settlement talks commenced, "and I said to Scruggs, 'The one person they should involve, above all others, if he would be willing, is Matt Myers.'" Myers was skeptical of the industry's intentions, and in any event, the talks soon collapsed; but he believed that the negotiations would resume before long. The White House was interested, as were the state attorneys general and the leaders of the tobacco industry, who had indicated an openness to discussing more significant concessions than they had ever been willing to put on the table. The tobacco control movement, Myers felt, had to be prepared to play a role other than that of naysayer. If, for example, Congress produced a bill that "has surface appeal but actually does little, and public health's answer is just, 'No, we will accept no compromise,'" Myers argued, "no one's going to take that as credible. We're going to have to know what it is we really want—and what we're willing to give up to get it."

This would be, Myers acknowledged, unfamiliar ground for many anti-smoking advocates. "We were a public health community—really a bunch of individuals—who never had to cope with hard, hard choices and competing values," he observed. "We had all been able to operate at the level of broad rhetoric, because we had never before come close to achieving any of our most ambitious objectives. We could all recite the laundry list of desired policies, but it was very hard to get people to go below the surface rhetoric."

Myers sought an opportunity for participants in the tobacco control movement to air their views on a possible global settlement. He chose a mid-November 1996 annual meeting of the American Public Health Association in New York City as the occasion to invite a diverse group of anti-smoking advocates to a meeting to explore together what priorities they held in common and what concessions they might be willing to make to achieve them. Those invited included the "health voluntaries"—large national organizations that were an established presence in the public health community and the tobacco control movement: the American Cancer Society, the American Lung Association, and the American Heart Association. Also invited were representatives from key medical societies that had taken an interest in smoking issues—the American Academy of Pediatrics and the American Medical Association; the Robert Wood Johnson Foundation, the only major U.S. foundation actively sponsoring anti-smoking advocacy; and Ralph Nader's Public Citizen Litigation Group, which supported tobacco control litigation. In attendance as well were two veterans of the tobacco wars—Stanton Glantz and Julia Carol—whose views would carry great weight among some segments of the movement, and who would likely prove reluctant or unwilling to accept trade-offs in service of public health goals.

The Grassroots Activists

Unlike the major health voluntaries, Glantz and Carol did not represent large national constituencies or command armies of volunteers, but they wielded considerable influence in the tobacco control movement by virtue of the success of their grassroots campaigns and their very different, but equally effective, roles in organizing popular support for anti-smoking initiatives.

Glantz, a member of the faculty at the University of California Medical School in San Francisco, had founded a small grassroots organization, Californians for Nonsmokers' Rights, which focused its efforts on pushing for smoke-free public places in cities and towns. The author of a leading text on medical statistics, Glantz was adept at transforming dry facts and figures on secondhand smoke into powerful political rhetoric. He attracted the attention of the tobacco control movement after he and his organization successfully fended off a well-funded campaign by the tobacco industry to repeal San Francisco's landmark nonsmoking ordinance. With Julia Carol, whose gifts lay in community organizing, he attacked the tobacco companies at the local level, where their political clout was weakest, beginning in San Francisco and moving to towns and counties across California, which one by one adopted nonsmoking ordinances. Later, with their organization renamed Americans for Nonsmokers' Rights (ANR), Glantz and Carol spread the gospel of local ordinances in towns and cities across the country.

Julia Carol stayed on to become co-director of ANR; Glantz left the organization, but remained a strong, though unaffiliated, presence in the tobacco control movement, using his command of complex scientific data to produce potent anti-smoking messages that the public could easily grasp. He was a fearless warrior, outspoken and aggressive, willing to confront the tobacco companies and their defenders in debate, and impatient with his more timorous and sedate colleagues in the health voluntaries. Glantz was quick to perceive the potential of the Internet, and by the late 1990s he had developed an e-mail network of over a thousand of the movement's most ardent activists, whom he exhorted to action with daily broadsides against the tobacco industry.

Both Glantz and Carol were convinced that the path to victory against the tobacco companies lay in local action. While city and town councils were generally unfriendly to tobacco interests, state governments were, in their view, easy prey for industry lobbyists seeking to undermine local initiatives. Glantz and Carol were constantly on the lookout for "Trojan-horse" state laws that would purportedly mandate smoke-free indoor environments statewide, but that invariably included preemption language that overrode stronger local ordinances.

At the federal level, it was worse. In Glantz and Carol's eyes, Washington was putty in the hands of special interests, none more so than the well-heeled tobacco lobbyists. As proof of Congress's willingness to do the industry's bidding, they could point to the preemptive language in the 1965 Cigarette Labeling Law, which prevented state and local governments from regulating the advertising and marketing of tobacco products. In contrast, grassroots activism had led to a host of tough local anti-smoking ordinances, and to a citizens' initiative in which California voters directly approved a 25-cent excise tax on every pack of cigarettes. Actions like these had helped drive down smoking rates in California significantly and, they believed, could do the same elsewhere in the nation. "We need a national strategy," Carol would say, "not a federal strategy."

Carol saw other virtues in campaigning for tobacco control at the local level. An ardent community organizer, she believed that the determination to end tobacco use had to come "from the bottom up," and as such was best served by community activism. In her view, local initiatives such as clean-indoor-air laws represented more than good policy; they also helped mobilize communities to embrace the reduction of smoking as a shared goal.

Although Glantz and Carol were supportive of Kessler's proposed rule, they put little faith in the FDA's long-term power to regulate tobacco. Kessler was an anomaly in Washington, they believed, and would eventually move on; they did not expect his successor to bring the same initiative to the issue of smoking. But if any future FDA head did try to take more aggressive action against smoking, they considered it likely that Congress would act quickly to weaken the agency's authority. Consequently, they saw little reason to make compromises with the tobacco industry in exchange for FDA regulatory authority that would, in the end, prove temporary.

Myers viewed things differently. While admiring Glantz and Carol's victories in local tobacco control advocacy, he saw more reason to put faith in Washington. He believed there were times and circumstances when the federal government could, and did, act more effectively than local governments, as it had during the civil rights movement. Over the many years he had spent in Washington, he had grown familiar with the workings of the political process, and had developed allies in Congress, the executive branch, and the press. His experience in campaigning for stronger warning labels on cigarette packs, while only a qualified success, had taught him that the tobacco lobbyists could be bested in Congress.

Moreover, Myers noted, there were signs that local initiatives might have reached the limits of their effectiveness. "We had seen a decade of intense antismoking activity in states like California," he said, "but the smoking rates—even in California—bottomed out at roughly 20 percent of the population, with teenage smoking actually beginning to increase. Unless we were willing to accept a society with 15–20 percent of the population smoking, we had to think about something dramatically different." That dramatically different approach was, to him, comprehensive FDA regulation of the safety and addictive properties of cigarettes, as well as their marketing and advertising; for such a goal, Myers, at least, was willing to consider making concessions as part of a global settlement with the tobacco industry.

A Gathering of the Movement

On November 18, 1996, tobacco control advocates gathered to discuss a possible global settlement. Myers approached the meeting with modest expectations. "I had no faith that the public health community was prepared to make choices or that they had thought through their priorities," he recalled. "But I believed, perhaps naïvely, that if we could cut through the rhetoric, we could develop—not a full consensus, because there's no such thing in our community—but a pretty broad consensus." That hope, it was soon clear, would not be realized. As Myers remembered it, "Stan [Glantz] skillfully took the floor and drew very harsh rhetorical lines as an advocate: you were for good (no compromise) or you were for evil (compromise)—as opposed to a substantive debate about the issues. Stan almost single-handedly cowed the others."

But for some, Glantz's, as well as Carol's, position resonated deeply, particularly for those concerned with the issue of civil justice and with liability protections for the tobacco companies, which many of them strongly opposed. The representative from the Public Citizen Litigation Group argued that, with Congress and even the presidency in the industry's pocket, the courts and the tort liability system were the sole remaining bastion against the power of tobacco interests. More worrisome to Myers was the emotional response of the volunteer president of the American Lung Association, who maintained that on moral grounds tobacco manufacturers should be held accountable for their misdeeds and their victims should not be deprived of their day in court. While it was perhaps to be expected that a Public Citizen litigator would take a stand against granting the industry any immunity from lawsuits, the impassioned opposition of a representative of one of the major health voluntaries was, to Myers, a sign that many in the tobacco control movement were not yet prepared to weigh public health priorities against civil justice goals.

Toward the end of the meeting, Myers put forth a hypothetical proposal in which the industry would agree to every major public health aim of the tobacco control movement in return for a large cash settlement of *all* the litigation against them, and asked the group if such an arrangement would be acceptable. Carol was the first to respond. "I can't think of anything wrong with your hypothetical," she acknowledged. "But I'd be against it."

Glantz was more emphatic in his opposition. "The fundamental reality of tobacco," he would later say, "is that the way to beat them is to beat them, not to make a deal with them. I have never found a single instance anywhere, anywhere, where a compromise with the industry served the public health. Never." Glantz believed that a global settlement would prematurely cut off a far more effective route to tobacco control. He was convinced, as he later wrote in an op-ed piece in the *Los Angeles Times*, that the state attorneys general would eventually win enough Medicaid lawsuits to bring the tobacco industry "to its knees," paving the way for the federal government to strip companies of their tobacco business—leaving them with their "cookies, cheese, and beer"—and take over the production of "plain cigarettes"—with no additives, "fancy brands," or advertising campaigns—"for smokers that can't quit."[21]

Others at the meeting were more ambivalent about striking a deal with the tobacco industry. Nancy Kaufman, the senior program officer for substance abuse at The Robert Wood Johnson Foundation, recalled her mixed feelings. "There was a lot of conflict at that meeting," she said later, "and as I look back, I was very conflicted. I did not speak out with a strong position, one way or the other, because one part of me was saying, 'Yeah! The benefits would be terrific.' And the other part of me was saying, 'Why would you ever dance with the devil?'"

In the end, two accounts of the meeting emerged. Myers sent out to participants a summary of the "shared consensus" of the gathering.

Citing a laundry list of concerns, he wrote, "All of these issues were reflected in a strong group sentiment that it is premature to be pushing a global legislative solution." But Myers concluded his memo on a carefully worded cautionary note. "The strong sentiment against a rush to a legislative solution," he wrote, "was tempered but not altered by the risks that accompany the current threats to the tobacco industry....It was agreed that these concerns bear close watching to be certain that the public health community does not misjudge the opportunities/risks, but that we should also avoid the traditional inclination to compromise for too little too quickly." His notes to participants, Myers later explained, had been "crafted to strongly reflect the general sentiment and yet reflect what I knew were the understated views of a large number of people at that meeting. If you read the notes carefully, you will see that they leave openings for compromise."

Glantz's own brief summary of the meeting was far more sweeping, and different in its conclusions. Five months after the meeting, in an electronic message to activists, he wrote: "Remember October [he meant November]: Last October, there was a meeting at which *everyone* felt that *any* kind of Congressional global deal would end up being bad for public health."

A Different Tack. Not surprisingly, Myers did not agree with Glantz's summary of the November 18 meeting. "I walked away believing that there was a significant segment in Stan and Julia's camp," he recalled. "But there was another significant segment who were struggling with the issues; who, but for Stan and Julia's presence, might or might not have come down in the same place, but would at least have engaged in a different dialogue getting there." The meeting, which Myers called a "failed effort," was to him an example of "the power of the strongest voices to frighten everybody else [in]to silence." Myers had left the gathering "incredibly frustrated," he said, feeling that "we're going to have a very hard time having the open, constructive dialogue that we, as a movement, have to have. I walked away realizing that, in our larger community, we were not going to be able to do that."

Myers discussed his concerns with his boss, Bill Novelli, president of the National Center for Tobacco-Free Kids. Novelli was dismissive of Glantz and Carol, whom he regarded as zealots; he considered Myers's attempt to engage them in an "open, constructive dialogue" a waste of time that conferred more legitimacy on them than their status in the

tobacco control movement warranted. Both he and Myers did agree, however, on the urgent need to continue the search for a consensus on the
terms of a possible global settlement with the tobacco industry. "I knew
we were going to have important choices to make—core questions, such
as the balance between righting the wrongs of the past, and preserving
lives in the future," Myers said, "and I felt strongly that it was an abdication of responsibility to take the easy path and do nothing but oppose.
I wasn't prepared to do that."

To Novelli, such questions were best taken to those he considered to
be the real leaders of the tobacco control movement: the heads of the
major public health voluntary associations, especially the CEO of the
American Cancer Society, John Seffrin, and the CEO of the American
Heart Association, Dudley Hafner, both of whom sat on the board of the
Tobacco-Free Kids Center. Once dismissed by activists as conservative
organizations bent more on not offending corporate donors than on taking strong stands on public health issues, the American Cancer Society
and the American Heart Association had undergone significant changes
under the stewardship of Seffrin and Hafner. Previously, both health organizations had conceived their mission as raising money to fund research
and uncontroversial public education programs; by the mid-1990s, however, both CEOs had given new prominence to advocacy and, in part
through organizations such as the Coalition on Smoking OR Health and
the National Center for Tobacco-Free Kids, had invested heavily in the
fight to curb tobacco use.

Beginning in December 1996 and continuing into the following month,
Novelli and Myers held a series of conversations, both one-on-one and
conference calls, with Seffrin and Hafner, as well as with the heads of the
American Lung Association, the American Medical Association, and the
Academy of Pediatrics. Myers's aim was to push these senior decision
makers to take responsibility and make choices in the event of global
settlement talks. "I wouldn't have gone off on a crusade of my own," he
explained. "I absolutely wouldn't have done that….The goal was to say,
okay, I had tried one mechanism to get people to talk and think, and I had
failed. I'm still not going to make a decision for people, but I'm going to
do whatever I can to make people think through these choices."

To help the CEO group think about the options, Myers offered roughly
the same hypothetical settlement that he had presented in the November 18 meeting: a broad mandate from Congress that would include FDA
regulatory authority over tobacco and other public health goals in return

for some form of liability protection for the industry. Their responses, Myers recalled, were "extraordinarily favorable." "It was clear from those discussions," he said, "that at least the CEOs of those major organizations came at this from an entirely different approach than the sentiment that had dominated in that November meeting. John Seffrin wasn't alone or out of the mainstream at all in advancing the notion that if there really was an opportunity to bring about major change in these core areas, that had to be explored....To a person, the reaction at the time was euphoric on their part."[22] Moreover, he noted, "the liability issue"—the source of greatest contention at the November discussion—"wasn't a lightning rod at all."

On the basis of these conversations, Myers began to craft and circulate a series of "core principles" for the CEOs to mull over. But by early April 1997, abstract considerations of principles and bargaining positions would become concrete, as the tobacco industry began pressing for the resumption of settlement talks. Industry leaders were perhaps spurred on by news that, on March 21, Liggett had reached a second, more comprehensive settlement, this time with twenty-two states. Among other things, the company agreed to turn over sensitive documents detailing its discussions on legal matters with other tobacco companies, and to admit to what were referred to by some as the "three lies": that cigarettes caused health problems, that nicotine was addictive, and that the industry marketed its products to youth. In exchange for these and other concessions, Liggett was granted protection from further smoking-related litigation.[23] Soon after that, attorney Richard Scruggs called Myers to say that White House advisor Bruce Lindsey wanted Myers, Scruggs, and Mississippi Attorney General Mike Moore to get together with Phil Carlton, the tobacco industry's intermediary. At the meeting, on April 1, 1997, Carlton did not mince words: "Let me put it plainly," he said. "Tobacco wants to negotiate. We want peace."

Myers's Decision

The following day, Carlton called to invite Scruggs and Moore to another meeting, this time with the two industry leaders, Bible and Goldstone, in attendance as well. Scruggs, in turn, asked Myers to sit in. The talks, it was stressed, would be secret.

The meeting, held on April 3, was much larger than the earlier session with Carlton. It included Bible and Goldstone, as well as a phalanx of other industry officials, attorneys, and lobbyists (including former Senate Majority Leader George Mitchell); Moore and Scruggs and four other attorneys general; and trial lawyers representing the *Castano* class action group. At the meeting, as Myers recalled it, Bible and Goldstone made their pitch: that this was "a different era" and they were "different people" from their predecessors, prepared "to make fundamental changes in the manner in which we do business." The price tag for those changes would be steep: the tobacco companies sought full immunity from all present and future litigation—something many anti-smoking advocates would fiercely oppose.[24] But what they were willing to concede in terms of government control—in addition to hefty payments to the states—was unprecedented in the annals of the tobacco wars. "What they want is peace," one industry attorney told the group, "and what they are prepared to do in return is to become 'an entirely regulated industry.' "

At the end of the talks that day, there was enough interest on the part of both the attorneys general and the industry to agree to continue discussion—still in secret—starting the very next day. The question for Myers was whether to participate, as the only representative of the public health community invited to the table. Myers remained skeptical of the industry's sincerity, and wary of possible "Trojan-horse compromises" that would weaken their apparent concessions, but at the same time he was struck by what he had heard from tobacco officials that day. "It was clear from the beginning that it would take hard negotiations," he reflected, "but what they appeared willing to give up on public health was light years beyond what anybody ever thought about getting from these guys." The more he thought about it, he said, the more "comfortable I became with the non-emotional answer that these negotiations—even with the devil—could hold the key to our public health goals." In short, he believed, it was "the opportunity of a lifetime for the tobacco control movement."

Still, it was uncomfortable—and personally risky—to be the sole representative of the tobacco control/public health community engaged in secret talks. Myers asked Moore and Scruggs to approach David Kessler, who had left the FDA to be dean of Yale Medical School, about participating in the negotiations. Kessler declined, for two reasons. First, he noted, the settlement would mean "big legislation" that would take more than one Congress to accomplish. "This is just way too big. And I probably said," Kessler recalled, "you've got to involve Bliley and Waxman [now the ranking Democrat on the Health and Environment Subcommittee].

My sense was, if you get these two guys and this was theirs, even if it was big, that was the way to do it." In addition, Kessler noted, "I didn't want to be co-opted. Perhaps co-opted is the wrong word, but when you are at the table as part of a negotiation, you are a party of that negotiation. I made a deliberate decision to stay out."

Bill Novelli came up with an alternative. "I said," he recalled, "'Okay, let's do it; but let's not do it alone.' ...The deal was that we had to do this [negotiating] in full confidentiality. We said, 'We'll abide by that, but we can't really abide by full confidentiality. We have got to keep a few people abreast.'" Accordingly, he and Myers chose a handful of officials in the public health community whom they would keep informed of the negotiations: Seffrin of the American Cancer Society and Hafner of the American Heart Association, as well as the past president of the American Medical Association and the president of the American Academy of Pediatrics. Seffrin and Hafner responded enthusiastically. "We were very positive," Hafner recalled. "This was something very, very significant and we owed it to the public to see it through."

The Settlement Negotiations

The settlement talks began in earnest on April 8, 1997, and continued, with some breaks, into June. There were many tough issues on the table, but the most contentious concerned the extent of the FDA's regulatory powers, the size of the industry's payments to states for damages, and—most challenging of all—the kind and degree of industry "immunity" from legal liability. On this last point, Myers was, unlike many in the tobacco control movement, willing to consider some modest form of protection from litigation. In the draft of "core principles" he had drawn up in February 1997 for the CEOs of the health voluntaries to consider, he had written that the "rights of victims of the tobacco industry to be justly compensated for the injuries they have suffered should not be abridged and the tobacco industry should not be immunized from accountability for its own wrongdoing." But the principles left the door open for imposing restrictions on civil actions if some form of "just" compensation—for example, an industry-funded compensation plan—could be set up for people with smoking-related diseases or their families. And while Myers had written in uncompromising opposition to any immunity for future wrongdoings, he was silent on how compensation for past misdeeds might be handled.

The industry, however, was seeking much stronger protections. Over a series of negotiations, in which the tobacco companies agreed to FDA regulation of their products,[25] and to pay hundreds of billions of dollars in damages to states, they refined the immunity concessions they sought to two: no punitive damages could be awarded for past or future wrongdoing,[26] and no new class action suits could be brought. For Myers, both provisions were unacceptable. But some of the state attorneys general involved in the negotiations took a softer line, reasoning that immunity was the price of an agreement, however unpalatable. "Mike Moore was concerned and sympathetic" when he voiced his objections, Myers recalled, "but absolutely convinced that the liability concessions were necessary and that they were a price he was willing to pay for the public health concessions." In the end, after Bruce Lindsey intervened with a compromise proposal—the industry would pitch in an additional lump-sum payment in lieu of possible future jury awards of punitive damages—the attorneys general agreed, to Myers's great dismay, to bar future class actions and punitive damages.

On June 20, 1997, the negotiators wrapped up their talks and held a press conference to make public the terms of the settlement. Moore struck a triumphant note. "We are here today to announce what we think is—we know is, we believe is—the most historic public health agreement in history," he declared. On the face of it, the terms of the settlement were impressive: the tobacco industry had agreed, among other things, to pay the states that were parties to the agreement a whopping $368.5 billion over 25 years, with an additional $15 billion a year thereafter in perpetuity; to pay hefty "lookback" penalties if targets for reducing youth smoking were not met; and to submit to FDA regulation of the manufacture, marketing, and distribution of tobacco products. In return, they would be protected from punitive damage awards and from class action suits, but not from individual suits seeking compensatory damages.[27] The settlement, Moore proclaimed, represented "the beginning of the end for the way the tobacco industry had treated the American public." Another attorney general, invoking two icons of cigarette advertising, put it more colorfully. "The Marlboro man," he said, "is riding off into the sunset on Joe Camel."

Myers was not on the podium to share the triumphant moment. He had not disavowed the settlement, unhappy as he was with the immunity provisions, but, persuaded by some of his colleagues at the Center for Tobacco-Free Kids, who advised him to distance himself from the agreement, he did not stand at the microphones with the state attorneys general. However, both he and Novelli spoke immediately after the settlement was announced. Both their statements fell short of an endorsement, but were nonetheless supportive. "This agreement isn't perfect," Myers said. "You only make perfect agreements when you don't have to face reality." While there were "things in this agreement that I would prefer to see changed," he continued, "and there are things in this agreement that anyone can find to criticize, if you look at the overall, comprehensive scope of this agreement, it represents the single most fundamental change in the history of tobacco control in any nation in the world."

But Myers and Novelli would be almost alone among anti-smoking advocates in their qualified praise for the settlement. It quickly became the target of sharp criticism from many segments of the tobacco control movement, who saw little to like in the landmark settlement.

Outcry

Even before the agreement was announced, it had generated considerable ill will in the public health/tobacco control community, much of it aimed at Myers himself. On April 16, in the early days of the settlement talks, the wall of secrecy surrounding them was breached, once again by the *Wall Street Journal*, which provided some details—not all of them accurate—of the emerging terms of the negotiations. The news that Myers was participating in the clandestine talks outraged hard-liners like Glantz, who charged that Myers had "chose[n] to ignore a consensus among public health groups not to enter a deal with the industry," and, in one heated moment, labeled him a "fool" who had been "misled" in negotiating with tobacco interests.[28]

Perhaps more wounding than Glantz's blasts were the attacks leveled at Myers by respected leaders in the public health community, with whom Myers had worked for years. Chief among these was Dr. C. Everett Koop, the former Surgeon General and a hero of the tobacco control movement for his strong stand on such issues as the addictiveness of nicotine and the dangers of secondhand smoke. Shortly after news of the talks broke in the *Journal*, Koop spoke out on PBS, taking aim at the liability issue. "Why should those people have immunity," he asked. "I just don't believe they should." Myers later apologized to Koop for not keeping him "fully informed" of the talks, and thereafter tried, along with other negotiators, to update him on their progress. In their private conversations, according to Myers, Koop seemed amenable to the terms of the negotiations, including those dealing with liability protection, but publicly he remained critical of the settlement.

Rep. Henry Waxman, a longtime ally of the tobacco control movement, was equally vociferous, although he directed his anger more at Myers for presuming to negotiate legislation than at the terms of the negotiations themselves. "I was critical of Matt Myers and whoever else was in there [negotiating]," Waxman said. "They didn't coordinate with their colleagues in the advocacy world; they didn't coordinate with their allies on the Hill....It's arrogance that you think you can go out and make the deal, and you also think you know all the answers. You don't have the benefit of information that you should have. Certainly the tobacco industry consulted with each other." Another important figure in tobacco control—David Kessler—was more muted in his response, though he did participate in a press conference Waxman had called to denounce the settlement talks. Later, on PBS's *Frontline*, Kessler explained again why he had demurred when invited to join the talks. "I didn't want to be captured," he said. "I wanted to be able to evaluate it for what it was. I wanted to have some distance to be able to look at it and see whether I thought it would be in the public interest."

Kessler would have that opportunity in his capacity as co-chair, with Koop, of an advisory committee set up by Waxman to scrutinize whatever settlement emerged from the talks and report their judgment of it to Congress. Even before the committee began its formal deliberations, however, it was clear that the agreement would have trouble getting the panel's stamp of approval. On June 23, Kessler told the *New York Times* that he had gotten "really angry" at "all those loopholes, at the lawyering" he found in the settlement—in particular, language that appeared to compromise the FDA's ability to order the removal of nicotine from cigarettes.[29] When the Koop-Kessler committee met on June 25, even members who had supported the negotiations objected to the FDA language, which Dudley Hafner of the American Heart Association called "a deal killer." John Seffrin of the American Cancer Society was one of the few who urged the group to try to salvage the settlement, despite its flaws. Bill Novelli, who along with Myers also sat on the advisory committee, cautioned members against seeking a "utopian" agreement that would only alienate the tobacco industry and its allies in Congress. "It will not serve the public health," he warned, "if we all go back to trench warfare." In the end, however, the committee adopted a statement that included no words of support for the settlement, or an amended version of it, issuing instead a laundry list of its faults.

With this less-than-ringing endorsement from the public health community, the settlement now moved from the negotiating table to the halls of Congress, where its terms would be hammered into legislative language and then put to a vote.

On to Washington

In the months between the announcement of the agreement, in June 1997, and the commencement of legislative action on it, in March 1998, proponents and opponents of the settlement busied themselves jockeying for support for their positions, testifying before Congress, and gauging the mood of the White House, which had so far maintained a wary neutrality on the issue. Within the Clinton administration, opinion on the settlement had been divided between those forces, led by domestic policy advisor Bruce Reed, who were interested in fixing the flaws in the agreement and those, led by Health and Human Services Secretary Donna Shalala, who appeared hostile to the agreement and disposed to take a hard line against the tobacco industry. The overriding concern at the White House, according to some observers, was retaining the goodwill of the public health community, which regarded Clinton as a champion of its causes. It was perhaps for this reason that it was especially solicitous of the views of Drs. Koop and Kessler, arguably the most prominent figures in public health. The White House, said Jeff Nesbit, an aide to Kessler, "was always working for what it would take to get Dr. Koop and Dr. Kessler's blessings."

And, increasingly, both doctors seemed inclined to withhold their blessings from the agreement. In testimony before the Senate Commerce Committee in July, they spoke out strongly against the settlement, urging members to set it aside. "The settlement," Koop declared, "gives the tobacco industry everything it wants, but shortchanges the public health." Kessler, who had applauded some "elements" of the agreement in June, seemed to have hardened his position in the intervening weeks. "You don't need the industry's money," he told the Commerce Committee. "You don't need the industry's permission. You can accept the settlement, tinker with it. That will make some difference but keep the industry booming and profitable. Or you can do right without ceding an inch to those forces that have lied and killed for years."

Myers, too, testified before Congress, urging members to view the agreement as an imperfect document that could be improved. In an appearance before the Senate Judiciary Committee, he noted that while the settlement's flaws "need to be carefully reviewed and debated," it nevertheless "has the potential to significantly reduce the number of our children who become hooked on tobacco over the next decade." Myers followed up his testimony with an op-ed piece in the *Washington Post*, in which he cited the American Cancer Society's estimate that one million children "alive today will be saved from a tobacco-caused death" if the goals of the settlement were achieved. "Do we need any other reason," Myers asked, "for concluding that this agreement represents an opportunity that we cannot pass up?"

But opponents within the tobacco control community were unmoved by Myers's arguments and continued to press their case for rejecting the agreement. A group of them formed a new organization, "SAVE LIVES, NOT TOBACCO, the Coalition for Accountability" (or, more succinctly, the SAVE LIVES coalition). The members and supporters of the coalition were a mixed group, with different motives for banding together. Some, like Julia Carol of Americans for Nonsmokers' Rights, feared that Congress—and the White House—would make a deal that would preempt the clean-indoor-air ordinances and other local actions they had been championing. Others, like members of Nader's organization, adamantly opposed any form of liability relief for the tobacco industry. One group of supporters—the American Trial Lawyers Association—was concerned about the precedent that would be set in an agreement that limited future litigation. The costs of the SAVE LIVES coalition were underwritten by the law firm that was representing the state of Minnesota—which had not joined in the settlement—in its Medicaid suit against the tobacco companies.

More broadly, the SAVE LIVES coalition had organized in opposition to yet another group spawned by the settlement, this one composed of a number of mainstream health voluntaries—the American Cancer Society, the American Heart Association, and the American Medical Association—as well as the Center for Tobacco-Free Kids. The group, called Effective National Action to Control Tobacco (ENACT), had been formed at the instigation of Kessler, who had seen it as an opportunity to join forces with Myers; almost immediately, however, the group was riven by dissension, and Kessler soon disassociated himself from it. There were disagreements over a number of issues, but at the heart of the division

lay serious differences over how tough a line to take on liability. While
Myers, who became spokesman for the coalition, believed that ENACT
members should "at least be willing to talk about variations on liability,"
Kessler and Koop had together come to view liability protection as a
last-ditch concession, to be taken only when their backs were to the wall.
"One of the things that separated the public health community," Koop
maintained, "was that, come hell or high water, we would never acquiesce to immunity for the tobacco industry, unless we came to the end
and it was all over. And that's where I parted company with Matt." Both
Kessler and Koop were united on this point, he added. "David and I said
to each other," Koop recalled, "we will compromise where it gets to the
point where we cannot survive without compromising."

Meanwhile, Glantz kept up his own attack, through his e-mail network, on the members of ENACT, labeling them as "pro-immunity"
and even "pro-preemption." These labels proved particularly effective
in dividing the volunteers and staff in the state offices of some public
health voluntaries from their national leaders, like John Seffrin and Dudley Hafner, who supported a negotiated settlement. Glantz, said Hafner,
"stirred up our California folks.... [W]e would be flooded with faxes and
phone calls from three, four, or five volunteers in California that Stan had
convinced that we were getting ready to support the worst thing in the
world." In the AMA, activists tried to force its leadership to resign from
ENACT and join the SAVE LIVES coalition; though unsuccessful, their
effort did serve to strengthen the AMA's opposition to any concessions
to the tobacco industry.

It was during this time of roiling controversy within the anti-smoking
community that Congress prepared to take up what promised to be the
most important piece of tobacco control legislation in decades.

In Congress

Normally, any settlement with real teeth in it could be expected to
face an uphill fight in a Congress led by Republicans, who for reasons
both philosophical and pragmatic were generally considered allies of
the tobacco industry on the issue of regulation. But in early 1998, few
Republicans seemed eager to take on the role of defender of tobacco
interests. No less a person than Newt Gingrich, speaker of the House,
declared that the "more we have learned about tobacco's deliberate
campaign about addicting children and the more we have learned about

their lying, the weaker their negotiating position has become." A number of reasons were offered for this apparent turnabout—among others, political embarrassment over a Republican-led effort to grant tobacco companies a $50 billion tax credit to offset the $368 billion settlement payment; further revelations from company documents of the industry's focus on youthful smokers; and the general sense that Republicans' ties to tobacco could be politically costly. Whatever the precise cause, the effect was hardly a promising one for the industry. "Some party strategists are arguing that [its ties to "Big Tobacco"] could leave GOP candidates in a vulnerable position going into the 1998 elections," the *Wall Street Journal* reported in mid-January. The *Journal* quoted a former Gingrich aide, who said, "I think Republicans should throw the industry overboard."

Nevertheless, there were worrisome signs for Myers and others in the tobacco control movement who hoped to see the terms of the settlement strengthened and drafted into a viable bill. For one thing, the Clinton administration had not come out with a strong position on tobacco control legislation. Back in September, the president had unveiled five "principles" to guide settlement legislation, but to some these were so broad and general that, as Myers put it, they "papered over, but did not resolve any of the differences." In particular, they made no mention at all of the thorny issue of immunity (see Figure 12.1 for the five principles). As it came time to work on the bill, the White House had yet to throw its support behind any concrete legislative proposals.

---

(1) A comprehensive plan to reduce youth smoking, including tough penalties if targets are not met
- Tough penalties and price increases to reduce youth smoking
- A public education and counter-advertising campaign
- Expanded efforts to restrict access and limit appeal

(2) Full authority for FDA to regulate tobacco products

(3) The tobacco industry must change the way it does business

(4) Progress toward other public health goals
- Reduction of second-hand tobacco smoke, expansion of smoking cessation programs, strengthening of international efforts to control tobacco, provision of funds for health research

(5) Protection for tobacco farmers and their communities

Figure 12.1. President Clinton's "Five Principles"

Equally troubling was the decision by Senate Majority Leader Trent
Lott to assign the legislation to the Senate Commerce Committee, one
of five panels claiming jurisdiction over tobacco-related issues. Lott was
hostile to strong tobacco control legislation, and to its proponents—in
a meeting with Seffrin in March, he referred to Koop and Kessler as
"Dr. Kook and Dr. Crazy"—and had given the bill to the committee that
he judged would be least zealous in imposing regulatory controls on the
industry. The committee was chaired by John McCain of Arizona, a conservative; its two senior Democrats, Ernest Hollings of South Carolina
and Wendell Ford of Kentucky, were from tobacco-growing states.

But Senator McCain surprised Myers by being open-minded and
even supportive of the aims of the tobacco control community—or at
least that segment of it interested in a legislated settlement. In a private
meeting with McCain and his staff on March 6, Myers found the senator "engaged fully; he had a task; he wanted to get this done....But he
warned us, 'Before I venture down this road, I want to know if you're still
willing to make some of the basic compromises that would be necessary
to get this legislation out.'" The Commerce Committee, he reminded
Myers, was "fundamentally conservative," and without some concessions,
"it's not going to happen." In response, Myers told him that "we're prepared to work with you. We're not out there on the fringe. For us this
isn't rhetoric....We want a bill." McCain also asked about "where Koop
and Kessler would stand," Myers recalled. "And I replied that I would be
the last one in the world to be able to predict."

Perhaps most heartening to tobacco control proponents was McCain's
decision to bar tobacco industry attorneys and lobbyists from negotiations over the legislation. "McCain was adamant that the industry would
not be represented," Myers said. "He wanted to be able to say with honesty and sincerity that this bill represented the best he could do and that
he had not fashioned it to satisfy the tobacco industry."

Hammering Out the Terms

McCain had put those working on the settlement legislation on something of a forced march. His ambitious timetable called for a bill to be
crafted and brought before the full committee for a vote in three weeks'
time. What followed—for Myers, the state attorneys general, and others involved in the negotiations—was a series of intense, late-night bargaining sessions over the key points of the settlement. Some, like the

particulars of FDA regulation, took considerable time to iron out, but were eventually resolved to most—though not all—parties' satisfaction.[30] But once again, the question of immunity threatened to sink the public health community's support for the settlement.

As it evolved, the McCain bill provided two concessions on liability. One, which Myers considered acceptable, would have set an annual cap of $6.5 billion on the amount of additional damages the industry would have to pay to smokers. This cap did not set an overall limit on damages, and it did not include the billions that the industry was required to pay out in their settlement with the state attorneys general. Essentially, it would enable the tobacco companies to spread out their additional payments over a period of time if jury awards in any one year exceeded the cap. But what Myers considered unacceptable were provisions that would have freed the companies from liability for punitive damages based on past misdeeds as well as from class action suits based on past wrongdoing.

Myers's unyielding opposition to these last concessions angered some of his fellow negotiators and cost him his seat at the negotiating table; but the prospect of alienating Koop and Kessler, who would certainly oppose the liability concessions, along with some prodding from the White House, eventually persuaded McCain to change his mind. On March 30, he agreed to drop all of the liability provisions except for the cap, if Kessler and Koop would endorse the bill. McCain did not, however, wait to hear either doctor's response to his compromise. He scheduled a press conference later that day to announce the bill he would shortly present to the full committee for a vote.

By most standards, the legislation that McCain unveiled on March 30 represented a significant strengthening of the original settlement. It raised the price increase on cigarettes—which Kessler had strongly urged—from 63 cents to $1.10 a pack; it gave the FDA full authority over tobacco; and it removed the protections from class action suits and punitive damages. There were still flaws—the environmental tobacco smoke provisions could be interpreted to preempt stronger state and local regulations, for example—but, as the New York Times would note a couple of days later, "[n]o other measure before Congress this year could lead to such fundamental changes in society."

On April 1, 1998, the Commerce Committee met to vote on the settlement bill: it sailed through, 19–1, on a wave of bipartisan support. It should have been a triumphant occasion for Myers, but in fact, he later reflected, it was for him "a horribly low moment."

Storm Clouds

Myers's gloom stemmed from the knowledge that he would not be able to build a strong consensus within the public health community in support of McCain's bill. In a conversation with Myers on March 30, Koop had expressed dissatisfaction with the price increase on cigarettes—he wanted it to be at least $1.50 per pack—and with the cap on liability. Although their discussion was inconclusive, Koop's unhappiness with the bill led Myers to decide that he should not attend McCain's press conference that day to showcase the legislation. It was a decision Myers made reluctantly, but as spokesman for ENACT, he did not feel free to follow his own wish to stand with McCain; he knew ENACT members would be uneasy about backing the legislation unless Kessler and Koop gave it their seal of approval, which he felt was by no means certain. McCain was understanding and gracious, but Myers came to regret his—and ENACT's—decision to withhold their endorsement. "I felt strongly that I should have been there," he said, "that we should have been there, standing with McCain....We acted out of a desire to maintain unity, but John McCain did everything we asked for and he deserved our support."

The ENACT coalition did manage to issue a mild statement of support on April 1, commending the senator and his staff for their "tremendous work," but also expressing reservations about the bill's provisions. This faint praise nonetheless contrasted starkly with Koop's strong condemnation, which the Associated Press reported on March 31. The McCain legislation was "a sellout," he declared, singling out the price increase on cigarette packs for particular opprobrium. "They're teaching kids just how to manage to spend a few cents a year to get their fix....That just won't do it. It must be more than a kid's allowance can afford." Kessler's response was more temperate; in an interview with the *Wall Street Journal*, he mentioned "problems that must be fixed," but also noted that the bill included "lots of good provisions," and applauded McCain for his courage in shepherding the measure through the committee. But Myers feared that Kessler, and therefore ENACT, would be unwilling to break with Koop and support the bill. It was this bleak assessment that muted his celebration of McCain's achievement. "We had this unbelievably good bill, despite its flaws—a 19–1 vote," he said, "and there wasn't a single representative from the public health community who was enthused."

As others in the tobacco control movement weighed in on the bill, it quickly became clear that more than a lack of enthusiasm was at work.

Ralph Nader attacked the inclusion of any "liability limits" in the legislation, arguing that "they create a sense in which tobacco seems a 'fin-
ished' issue and remove the litigation spur to media, public, legislative
and regulatory focus on tobacco. The result will be to foreclose, or at least
slow, future public policy health innovations." Others charged that the
legislation was essentially tailored to the tobacco companies' specifications. "The McCain bill," Glantz declared, "is indeed the 'briar patch' that
the industry wants to be tossed into!"

Some observers believed that the denunciations by the activist bloc of
the tobacco control movement reinforced Koop's own growing militancy.
In any event, when he addressed the Senate Democratic caucus on April
20, he lit into the legislation with his strongest language to date, calling
the liability sections of the bill "the most egregious to the public health
community. Indeed if there were one segment which I think might have
been written by the tobacco industry, it is this one. In short, [the McCain
bill] is a windfall for the tobacco industry." And, lest anyone imagine that
Kessler thought differently, Koop added, "Let nothing that is said today
nor anything that has been quoted in the press—sometimes out of context—as said separately by Dr. Kessler or me indicate that Dr. Kessler and
I are not of one solid mind on the issue of tobacco control."

In counterpoint, Myers and Novelli wrote an op-ed piece in the
Washington Post on April 24—under their own names, as officials with
the Center for Tobacco-Free Kids, not on behalf of ENACT—praising
McCain and the Commerce Committee for throwing off "decades of
influence by the tobacco industry" and for crafting legislation that provided "the best opportunity yet to reduce tobacco use by young people."
At the same time, they urged the Senate to make improvements in the
bill. Meanwhile, the press had begun to mirror the critical tone used
by the tobacco control movement, publishing editorials that depicted
the McCain bill as flawed and in need of strengthening. Eventually, the
combination of outcry from activists in the tobacco control community, critiques in the press, and Myers's lobbying efforts did force some
toughening of the bill. On May 16, shortly before the measure reached
the Senate floor, the White House and McCain announced an agreement
on amendments to the bill. These included an increase in the annual
liability cap, from $6.5 billion to $8 billion, and higher penalties if the
industry failed to meet targets for reducing youth smoking. With these
and other modifications, the President pledged to give the bill his full
endorsement and sign it into law.

Others, however, were not willing to jump on the bandwagon yet. Kessler, the *Washington Post* reported, "was cautious, [saying], 'There's still a substantial way to go.' Former Surgeon General C. Everett Koop called the changes 'an improvement, but let's go further.'" But in the meantime, the other major party to the settlement had begun to balk as well.

The Industry Speaks Out

Their critics' assertions notwithstanding, the tobacco manufacturers did not appear to be happy with the McCain bill, which one industry official labeled an "act of vengeance." The tobacco companies' response had been relatively muted until April 8, when R. J. Reynolds CEO, Steven Goldstone, speaking at the National Press Club, delivered the industry's angry judgment: "The extraordinary settlement reached on June 20 last year that could have set the nation on a dramatically new and constructive direction," he declared, "is dead, and there is no process which is even remotely likely to lead to an acceptable comprehensive solution this year." Washington, he continued, "has rushed to collect more tobacco revenues while playing the politics of punishment." Goldstone faulted the administration for its failure to exert "bold political leadership" and for subjecting the agreement to "partisan positioning." He also pointed his finger at "some leading public health advocates who, seeing the realization of all the programs they had ever fought for, for years, to obtain—and some others they had never even dreamed of asking for—added a new cry: a demand for retribution." Finally, Goldstone signaled the start of an industry counteroffensive. "We are going to speak out and engage in a public policy debate on the issues that affect our industries and our customers.…The primary issue is taxation. Is it fair to increase the taxes on cigarettes by huge amounts to pay for new federal spending programs or to provide tax cuts for wealthy Americans?"

With that, the industry rolled out an ambitious television and print ad campaign—with a price tag estimated by some at $40 million—aimed at arousing the public's dislike of the entity called "Washington." "Big Taxes. Big Government. There they go again," declared one print ad, invoking a famous line from Ronald Reagan's first presidential campaign. One TV ad featured a weary-looking waitress who said plaintively, "I'm no millionaire. I work hard. Why single me out?" The industry also employed standard grassroots tactics, such as displaying petitions to Congress at truck stops, convenience stores, and others places where "confirmed smokers" gathered. The campaign, the *New York Times* reported in mid-May, "has been remarkably successful in turning what tobacco opponents view as a bill that would discourage teen-age smoking into a tax issue and an assault on working stiffs who cannot afford to pay more for cigarettes."

While it was difficult to gauge precisely the effects of the campaign, there was some evidence that public support for tobacco control legislation was weak. On April 23, the *Wall Street Journal* reported the findings of a poll showing respondents evenly divided on the McCain bill, with 47 percent in favor of passing it, and 46 percent opposed. More respondents called the bill "too tough" than "too lenient," and most seemed skeptical of the motives behind it: 70 percent believed the chief interest of the bill's sponsors was not reducing teenage smoking but raising tax revenues.

Perhaps most troubling to those who sought passage of the bill was the finding that only two in ten respondents indicated that they would be less likely to vote for a member of Congress who opposed the bill; 63 percent, the *Journal* wrote, "say it would make little difference."

Endgame

In the weeks following the Commerce Committee's nearly unanimous vote on the measure, prospects for the McCain bill's passage began to grow dim. With polls showing that tobacco would not be a major issue in the November elections, Republican leaders had begun to show less appetite for tobacco control legislation. Whereas earlier in the year Newt Gingrich had reportedly told Koop, "Just give me a bill and we'll pass it," by late April, he was using language reminiscent of the tobacco industry campaign, calling the McCain legislation "a very liberal, big government, big bureaucracy bill." Trent Lott, never a friend of the settlement in the first place, dismissed the administration's support for the bill as wholly self-interested. "All they have seen in the tobacco settlement," he remarked, "is a cookie jar for them to get money."

It fell to Lott to find a way to dispose of the bill quietly, without opening himself or his colleagues to accusations of being a tool of tobacco interests. He took a number of steps to make the legislation unpalatable to members. For one, he replaced the tobacco farm provisions in the McCain bill with ones authored by the Agriculture Committee, which were less favorable to tobacco farmers, thereby losing the support of a few key senators from tobacco-growing states. For another, he opened the bill to all amendments, regardless of how much time they took to debate, thus delaying the final vote on the bill—which gave the industry's campaign additional time to influence public opinion—and weighing it down with provisions that were likely to alienate would-be supporters. So, for example, Senator Phil Gramm of Texas proposed an amendment that would end the income tax "marriage penalty" (whereby married people with two incomes paid more taxes than they would if single), and that would use a large portion of the tobacco companies' payments under the agreement to recover lost revenues—a move that infuriated the states, which would otherwise get half the payments as their share for settling their cases. The amendment passed, as did one that capped fees for the private attorneys who had handled the state Medicaid cases—a blow aimed at a financial mainstay of the Democratic Party, trial lawyers.

Possibly the most complex amendment, in terms of motive and impact, was the Gregg amendment, which proposed to strike the annual cap on liability payments, the only liability concession left in the bill. The amendment—co-sponsored by conservative Republican Judd Gregg of New Hampshire and liberal Democrat Patrick Leahy of Vermont—had the support of the SAVE LIVES coalition and even Dr. Koop, who lobbied enthusiastically for its passage. It was also attractive to some senators who could protect themselves from charges of being in the industry's pocket by casting a "no immunity" vote, but then vote against the entire bill. Opposing the amendment were McCain, John Kerry—his Democratic ally in the Commerce Committee—and the White House; they feared that its presence would, in Myers's words, "in the long run cost us the swing votes the bill would need for final passage." Their pleas fell on deaf ears; after a vote to table the Gregg Amendment failed, 61–37, it passed by a voice vote. Koop proudly called it "one of my greatest political triumphs because the president and I were on the opposite sides of the fence and he was calling the same people [soliciting their votes on the amendment], and we won...." But a lobbyist for the American Heart Association reached a different conclusion. "That was a dead bill," he said, "once that liability language came out."

Ironically, with the elimination of the liability cap, the public health community was at last united behind the bill—even Glantz took a turn lobbying for it. But Myers watched the proceedings on the Senate floor with growing foreboding. Although he and the Center for Tobacco-Free Kids had "reluctantly supported the Gregg amendment to maintain unity," he had serious misgivings about the wisdom of such a move. "I don't know what would have happened if we joined with President

Clinton in opposing the Gregg amendment," he mused. "The criticism we would have received could have destroyed the public health coalition completely. On the other hand, passage of the amendment doomed the bill, I think. It was an excruciating choice."

Debate on the McCain bill had begun on May 18, 1998. By the time Lott decided to invoke cloture—a vote on whether to close off debate on amendments and allow the Senate to vote on final passage of the bill itself—almost a month had passed. The bill was by this point top-heavy with wide-ranging amendments that blurred the original focus on youth and tobacco use. "With each new amendment," Myers observed, "the bill looked less like a disciplined effort to reduce the harm of tobacco and gained more opponents." On June 17, in a closed-door meeting of the Senate Republican caucus, Lott urged his colleagues to vote against cutting off debate—which would effectively kill the McCain bill, without requiring members to go on record against it. Sixty votes were needed to invoke cloture. When, later that day, the Senate convened, the cloture vote came up three votes short, 57–42. The McCain bill was dead and, with it, the global settlement forged almost exactly a year earlier.

The following day, an editorial in the *New York Times* excoriated Republicans, and Lott in particular, for "chicanery" in engineering the bill's defeat without bringing it to a vote. "Their craven performance," the *Times* thundered, "will not be forgotten by voters in the election season." But when November rolled around, not a single congressional race proved to be affected by the vote on the McCain bill, or by the issue of tobacco regulation in general. Looking back, Koop reflected on his "disappointment" over the demise of tobacco control legislation. "I just figured," he said, "that if someone with my credibility and my access to the Senate and to the White House, which was unlimited, couldn't pull it off, with the kind of record I had and the support of the people I had around me like David Kessler, you probably couldn't do it. We were up against insurmountable odds...."

As for Myers, the long and ultimately fruitless battle for a global settlement left him frustrated over a "missed opportunity" and bruised from the battering he had taken from his colleagues in the public health community. While he had expected "a firestorm among some advocates" over his participation in the settlement talks, he later noted, he was unprepared for "the ferocity, the nastiness, the viciousness" of their criticism. Even more painful was the failure of "key allies"—including Kessler and the leaders of some of the large health voluntaries—to spring to his defense publicly against the harsh and sometimes *ad hominem* attacks aimed at him. "It was not our opponents who surprised me," he reflected, "it was the people and organizations whom I assumed were allies." The lack of support—and the attendant sense of abandonment—took its toll. At one point during the heated debate over the settlement talks, a friend encountered Myers looking "almost devastated," she recalled, "like all the joy had gone out of his life. At one point, he said, 'I never thought I'd say this before, but when this is over, I don't want to have anything more to do with the tobacco movement.'" She urged him to wait until the settlement process had run its course. "I will," he replied, "but the hurts are just too great."

On the other hand, the passionate opponents of smoking also faced risks. It was by no means clear that the Food and Drug Regulation would survive judicial review (and it did not). The litigation that sought to impose large judgments on the tobacco companies had never succeeded in the past and, as we shall see, did not succeed in the future (with the sole exception of the cases brought by state attorneys general). Children were still learning to smoke at the rate of 3,000 per day, and one-third of them would die from smoking-related causes.

13

The Politics of Coalition Formation to Influence Legislation

The critical concepts I have been using in dealing with the Stinger missile case and the David Kessler case should by now be familiar. There is a set of rules that say who can make the decisions, what processes and participants are required leading up to the decision, and what processes and participants are permissible. This gives us a list of possible decision makers, a list of necessary players, and a list of optional players. Each of these players, whether executive or legislative, has a small set of types of concerns that may motivate her actions: the good of society, her continuing resources of personal influence for future occasions, her organization's resources, her moral constraints, and her personal interests.

These will provide the bases for reacting to any new proposal, but that reaction also depends upon the way in which they are shaped and integrated by her beliefs about how the proposal relates to those concerns—her understanding of the significance of the occasion (USO). This means that an important mediating category is her set of factual beliefs about: the likely USOs of the people with whom she is dealing; understandings shaping the processes of decision making; what happens at the meeting point between governmental action and the decisions of private individuals, organizations, or groups; and so on. Some of these factual ingredients of her understanding of the significance of the occasion are officially prescribed (for example, the rules of decision making). Some are dictated by her organization. Others are personal and have emerged from her experience. All may change as either unexpected events in the world or changes in control of resources of influence make some times more or less auspicious for various proposals.

The decision maker herself, as well as the players whose views will affect the decision maker, will be influenced not only by the likely impact of the proposal on each of their concerns but also by the influences that one or another of them can bring to bear through persuasion, authority, bargaining, moral authority, loyalty, and reciprocity. The capacity that a player has available to affect the other players on this occasion—her power in this situation—depends on the extent to which she has whatever resources are required to exercise influence in one of those ways. For example, persuasion requires a belief in one's honesty, loyalty (or at least support for the general views of the person being persuaded), knowledge of the pertinent facts, and thoroughness of analysis.

The advocacy tasks of the supporter of the proposal are to: design the proposal; time its introduction; mobilize sequences of exercises of influence by supportive parties on others who are uncertain or even opposed; and discourage the organization of opponents. Sometimes, from some players, what is needed is a strong form of support; from others, acquiescence would be enough; from still others, it will do if their opposition is restrained and tentative.

In short, what Michael Pillsbury and David Kessler had to do—and the challenge for Matt Myers in this third case—was to follow a handful of steps that define a political strategy for a particular policy. First, identify the rules of the game. Second, use those rules to identify the critical players. Third, develop an adequate understanding of how each of them will understand the significance of the occasion. Fourth, define and time a proposal to win as much support as possible (at this stage negotiation about the proposal may be critical, for it will reveal exactly what form of the proposal will elicit needed support). Fifth and finally, decide how to use—and to discourage opponents from using—the capacity to influence others so as to magnify the influence of the forces in support of his proposal.

Analyzing a Legislative Contest

The thought process is much the same for Matt Myers and the other leaders of interest groups seeking legislation during the tobacco control negotiations of 1997 and 1998. But in a legislative context, several factors are different quantitatively or qualitatively from those in the previous executive cases.

First, although many resources of influence are always distributed by the rules of process, legislative rules are very different from executive rules. The legislative process described in the last chapter gives certain positions great resources in the form of bargaining powers, authority to decide who has a special opportunity to be heard by a committee, ability to control the decision agenda, control of production of pertinent information, and much more.

The occupants of the positions of party leadership and the committee chairs enjoy disproportionate resources of influence because they run the complex legislative process. As majority leader, Senator Trent Lott can decide, within bounds, to what committee he will refer the tobacco proposals; and he can decide what process will be used when the committee's proposals return to the floor. If the House has passed a different bill and there must be a conference, Lott will select the conferees from the Senate. As Chair of the Commerce Committee, Senator John McCain can shape the proposal, decide what hearings are to be held, and allocate differing amounts of access to the process to various parties (he excludes the tobacco lobbyists from the early stages). He will also enjoy the deference that many members will give to Committee recommendations on the floor, where he will also lead the debate.

A second difference is that each of the many elected players taking part in the decision can be influenced both by the financial or other support of those he needs for reelection and by the views of his constituents and the organizations that represent them on a particular matter (at least if that reaction is likely to be unified and strong enough to affect votes months later). In the meantime, the supporters of a proposal will use the press in a way that will attempt to give shape to public opinion about smoking. Success in such efforts allowed Speaker Gingrich of the House of Representatives to seriously consider support for tobacco regulation only a few years after he labeled Kessler as "mad" for asserting that regulatory authority. The times have simply changed. Cigarette companies now look illegitimate; their opponents have generated moral authority; the Republican Party does not want to continue to be seen as closely allied with tobacco interests.

A third major difference in a legislative context flows from the multiplicity of those with decision-making authority. This requires a quite different approach on the part of the policy advocate. The rules for legislative choice are, as we have seen, straightforward. Passage of a negotiated compromise dealing with the four major issues—federal regulatory authority, restrictions on company liability, taxes to discourage youth from smoking, and some economic protection for tobacco farmers—will require half of the Senators to support the measure and, if there is a filibuster, the rules will require the support of 60 percent of the members of the Senate. But how can Matt Myers (or his opponents) begin to think of forming a coalition of 50 or 60 individuals? Except on rare occasions, the advocate does not have the time, energy, and resources to plan 60 campaigns like the one Pillsbury success-fully mounted to influence President Reagan. What can influence *groups* of Senators, not individuals, becomes the central question.

The members of either House of Congress (henceforth I will focus on the Senate because that is where the events took place) can decide how they want to vote on a particular bill in any of several ways. First, there may be partisan demands from the elected official's party to support or oppose a proposal, particularly if the President has taken a stand. The party leaders have available a variety of benefits and threats to put weight behind such demands if loyalty to friends and party alone is insufficient. Using partisanship is one path to reach groups of Senators.

Second, matters of relatively broad ideology or political philosophy not only go far toward explaining party affiliation; they may also deter-mine the vote of a sizable number of members. Steering into or out of these currents is another critical step. For example, Matt Myers and the other parties to the negotiation might initially divide the members of Congress into five ideological groups:

- Those adamantly opposed to almost any expansion in the regulatory or taxing powers of the federal government.
- Those generally inclined to support business interests.
- Those open to persuasion on the merits, considering the matter too important to decide on one of the other bases.
- Those seriously concerned about the dangers to the youth of America of a smoking addiction.
- Those adamantly anti-tobacco and extremely hostile to the tobacco companies.

In terms of such very broad initial presumptions, there are two pos-sible broad coalitions of members that might support new legislation. One possible coalition, combining those who are pro-business, those who are open to persuasion on the merits, and those who are pro-health, later formed and took the name ENACT. The other possible coalition would try to combine the last three categories. That coalition also formed, calling itself SAVE LIVES. The opponents of any new legislation on tobacco would also try to ride ideological currents. In these terms, it would be easy for them to form a coalition to fight SAVE LIVES. It would be far more difficult to organize a broad coalition to compete against ENACT, for a rival coalition's members would then have to contain parties from the opposite extremes of ideological commitment.

Third, a legislative coalition need not consist entirely of members who have a policy or ideological position about an issue. It may combine members affected in the particular case by any of the legislative resources that influence votes. In this case, such factors may be at least as important as party or ideology in determining votes. Members may defer to the committee that reports the bill, either because of respect for the work and thought that the committee has put into the process or out of a desire to enjoy reciprocal deference for the work of the committees to which they are assigned. That is a focus of Myers's efforts. Here the Commerce Committee vote was overwhelming for legislation and non-partisan.

Fourth, the vote may, alternatively, be determined by whether or not the bill has a favorable or unfavorable effect in the Senator's state or the Representative's district. The prospect of voters' reactions and a sense of moral obligation to constituents are both important to their representative. That will be true of Senators from North Carolina and Tennessee. On the other side in the contest, it will also be true of senators from states expecting to profit handsomely from damage awards.

Fifth, the Senator may instead respond to the claims of interest groups on behalf of, or against, particular proposals because of the support the interest groups have given him and may give him or simply out of a strong sense of loyalty to the group's beliefs and out of long-term partnership with the group's members. Here powerful interest groups are trying to reach an agreement that they would then take to the Senators who may be influenced by their views.

What coalition of interest groups would be best, from his point of view, is far from clear to Matt Myers. The bases of influence he finds most promising to combine are eclectic. He has been invited to help bring together a new coalition including the national health organizations (to win liberal votes), the tobacco companies (for pro-business Senators), and state attorneys general for the local effects (damage awards paid to the state) on the Senators from their states. The hope is to use their combined resources to bring pro-business Senators into a novel voting alliance with pro-health liberals and Senators from the states likely to gain from the settlement of their liability suits. Such an alliance would have to cut across and override what would be the more traditional ideo-logical and partisan divides. A requisite for bringing the companies into that coalition (to get pro-business votes) is to set ceilings on their future liability. The "prices" of the other two partners are real health benefits and very substantial payments to the states.

There is a second possibility for Myers. He could seek to unite: those organizations broadly concerned about health; those individuals and organizations that have dedicated themselves to fighting cigarette companies as forces of evil; and those states, victims, and attorneys most interested in the continued liability of cigarette manufacturers. This coalition would not win conservative, pro-business support, but might be able to override its opponents at a time of deep public skep-ticism about tobacco companies (which Waxman, Kessler, Clinton, and others by now had engendered). The "price" of keeping the last two groups in that coalition is *not* to set limits on vast, possible future liability payments. In short, the conditions for forming each of the two possible coalitions are inconsistent.

So Myers is going to have to choose which coalition to try to form. The ENACT group of organizations has a much better chance of passing the legislation he seeks, but can only be formed around a proposal Myers finds far from ideal. His customary ideological alliance is to the SAVE LIVES coalition (which includes many of his friends and ideological col-leagues, who will not soon forgive his deserting them), but that grouping would have much less chance of commanding a majority, or even of get-ting on the agenda, of a Republican-controlled Senate.

The USOs of the Individuals and Groups Opposed to Smoking

Knowing what sort of proposal it would take to form a coalition among all those who have long been opposed to smoking requires considering their various understandings of the significance of the occasion—not just their differing concerns. A number of players would have to be satisfied both as to ends and as to means if no one were to be left out. If some are to be left out, Myers's remaining coalition will be weaker in its own influence with Senators, and it will be faced with the active opposition in the Senate of those left out.

First, there are the national health organizations dealing with cancer, heart disease, and lung disease, plus the American Medical Association

(AMA). Their primary concern will be the future health benefits of any compromise. Based in Washington, D.C., or New York and relatively conservative politically, they are comfortable with decisions being made by the Congress at a national level.

At the opposite extreme are the Californians, Glantz and Carol, whose focus, for tactical or moral reasons, is on the effects of smoking on third parties. They are intensely suspicious of Congress and even of state legislatures, fearing that one or the other will pass a weak protection of third parties from smoking—an action that the courts will then hold preempts and forecloses the far stronger city anti-smoking ordinances which Glantz and Carol have been very successful in obtaining. Carol also believes deeply in the need for a grassroots movement far from the "suits" in Washington. Both worried that the industry would trade measures designed to reduce the sale of cigarettes to youth for preemption of the protection of third parties.

Then, third, there were the state attorneys general whose states have huge financial stakes in the settlement of their uncertain lawsuits against the cigarette companies to recover amounts paid in Medicaid. Mike Moore of Mississippi is their leader. They are also concerned about future, health-based regulation. They look to Congress as the most promising path to their goals.

The interest in compensation for past injuries is naturally central for the trial lawyers whose hopes to gain immense wealth depend upon the cigarette companies not obtaining some protection against liability as part of a compromise in exchange for health benefits for youth. The lawyers who represent Ralph Nader also believe deeply in the political importance of maintaining liability of the cigarette companies. They believe that the economic and political power of the cigarette companies in the executive and legislative branch is only checked by the judiciary and then only in liability suits.

There may be as much ego as medical or financial stakes in the positions of the next two. Any Senator who supports a compromise bill rejected by both former Surgeon General Koop and former Food and Drug Administrator Kessler has to fear the reaction of constituents most concerned about health and those most hostile to the cigarette industry. These two men are the great heroes of the anti-smoking drive. Their credibility, largely unimpaired, will tell large numbers of voters how to sort through otherwise confusing and contested claims.

Finally, although the action is in the Senate, Rep. Waxman, who has long taken the legislative lead in attacks on smoking, feels left out from the prolonged negotiations taking place among private parties. He will be in no hurry to sign on to their agreement, and his absence can influence others.

With all their differences, this set of parties has only one set of shared beliefs. They all agree that the tobacco companies are fundamentally evil. They all suspect the motives of the tobacco companies in compromise and fear being outsmarted by the tobacco companies as they feel they have been on previous occasions. They fear the companies' power in Congress. There is no necessary inconsistency among their objectives; but that inconsistency would quickly appear if the price of obtaining a negotiated agreement with the "smoking" coalition requires compromises in either the primary aims or the deepest beliefs about means of one or more of these groups.

The understandings of the significance of the occasion for those who might oppose any bill in Congress, unless it was also in the interest of the cigarette companies, are also diverse, though hardly revealed in our account of the events. The old leaders of the tobacco companies believed in giving no ground on these issues and in fighting through campaign contributions, advertising campaigns, mobilization of workers and farmers, and other measures. Because the price of this strategy had gone up substantially with the Clinton presidency, the pending FDA regulation, the Medicaid lawsuits brought by the state attorney generals, and the release of many embarrassing documents, new leaders were looking for a way out. They noted their severely depressed stock prices and wanted to manage the risk of liability and to become acceptable, legitimate, and admired members of the business community. To accomplish this, they were willing to take real steps to protect youth against smoking. They could make up for lost sales through diversification and foreign sales. With political peace, the price of their stock could again reflect only earnings and the growth of earnings. (Within a decade, they will in fact have accomplished that.)

Members of Congress from the tobacco states and powerful Democrats from that area would worry about the effect on tobacco farmers who were not represented in the pro-smoking coalition. Other Senators would maintain their opposition to any increase in government regulation or taxation.

Alternative Coalitions of Groups to Bring About Tobacco Legislation

In terms of interested groups and individuals, the starting coalition that bargained over the proposal (ENACT) was not carefully formed to represent all the interests that would be required to influence Congress in the final stage. Rather, it arose out of lawsuits and consisted largely of the new leaders of cigarette companies and the state attorneys general who were suing them. With the future congressional stage in mind, they asked for the participation of the prestigious national health organizations that Matt Myers represented. (The alternative majority coalition for the health leaders seeking some form of new anti-smoking legislation would have been very different, excluding the tobacco industry and including instead Ralph Nader, the class action lawyers, the Californians favoring ordinances prohibiting public smoking, and Kessler or Koop. With the help of the national pro-health groups like the cancer and heart associations, this alternative coalition (SAVE LIVES) would try to use its collective influence in Congress to run over the opposition of an already weakened tobacco industry.)

Either ENACT or SAVE LIVES *might* be able to enlist a legislative majority, or the 60 votes necessary if there were a filibuster, although the power of the Republican leadership to use its leaders' control of procedures and use of partisan loyalty to assist the industry would make it particularly difficult for the hard-line, anti-tobacco coalition, SAVE LIVES, to assemble the necessary Senate votes.

Who would eventually join what anti-smoking coalition was partially a result of the initial moves (i.e., was in part path-dependent), but depended even more on around what provisions that coalition was formed. The position taken by Matt Myers and his initial allies on the three crucial aspects of the proposal—regulatory powers, immunity from damages, and taxation of cigarette sales—would define who would be willing to join him. The opposite is also true: deciding what coalition he hopes will support him in the Senate will determine what positions he must take on the nature of the proposal.

But there are political laws of motion that exclude some alternatives. Almost impossible to imagine is a single grand coalition that has, in the same alliance supporting anti-smoking legislation, both those who were too adamantly anti-tobacco to support *any* company immunity from future liability and those who were pro-business, including the tobacco companies. If such a coalition were possible despite the radically inconsistent interests of its members, it would be influential with a very broad range of Senators. But no such coalition was possible. Yet that is exactly what Matt Myers attempted to create.

Consider the ways in which Matt Myers could have perceived the situation. He could have looked at the understandings of the significance of this legislative occasion of the parties he was proposing to join in a single coalition. Having done this, he would have found little enthusiasm for any compromise on the part of those most hostile to the tobacco companies (who in fact want to destroy that business), at least unless the terms of the proposal were such that they would be unacceptable to the hard-pressed tobacco companies. In fact, what happened is that the effort to add provisions adequate to win the support of those most hostile to the industry caused the companies to abandon the negotiation and carry with them the members of Congress who were generally pro-business. (Alternatively, he could have looked at the tactical advantages in terms of disruptive capacity enjoyed by those in any subgroup deeply opposed in principle to the direction negotiation was leading a larger group with which they had temporarily allied themselves.)

We have already seen the reasons why the cigarette companies, seeing that their stock was severely undervalued because of the risks of liability and regulation, might want a negotiated resolution that provided protection from massive future liability, regulatory stability, and increased moral legitimacy. These objectives might well prove consistent with the aims of the establishment health organizations for cancer, lung, and heart disease, who care little about liability and far more about regulation and perhaps taxation of the sale of cigarettes to deter young smokers and thus protect health. Not only were the most valued ends consistent; so were the means. These parties, on both sides, were used to working on a national stage and were relatively comfortable with Congress as the decision maker. Nor would the goals of the state attorneys general be inconsistent. They have been involved in lawsuits, and their client states will be paid handsomely out of the proceeds of any negotiated settlement; so they are less concerned about sacrificing future prospects of litigation awards to private parties. They do care, as do the health organizations, about health-based regulation.

This coalition might itself be able to win a majority of Senators to its side. But it could not hold together if the most valued objectives of any its members were rejected. Bringing in other opponents of the cigarette companies (hoping to produce more influence with the Senate) would require just such a fatal split in the coalition. The importance attached to litigation by Ralph Nader and the trial lawyers; the suspicion of a historic alliance between the cigarette industry and the members, particularly Republican, of Congress, by the Californians; and the historic enmity toward big tobacco of the warriors Kessler and Koop were incompatible with the initial ENACT coalition, however much Myers would have wanted their company.

The trial lawyers and Ralph Nader's litigating arm are determined not to see immunity from liability. The lawyers themselves have huge financial stakes. The Nader group, and its allies, do not, but they see the lobbying power and wealth of the industry as overwhelming in Congress and with the President. They therefore want nothing to reduce the effectiveness of litigation, the only really sure weapon they believe consumers have. These groups qualify as determined, hostile opponents of the cigarette industry.

They are joined in this by grassroots and locally based anti-smoking activists from the West Coast: Glantz and Carol. These Californians have a totally different understanding of the significance of the legislative occasion than Matt Myers and his allies have. They have been focused on the effects of smoking on third parties and, as to preferred means, have worked at the local level, believing passionately that the deep pockets and battle-wise tactics of the tobacco companies give the industry an insuperable advantage in Congress and in the state legislatures (forums in which, not incidentally, Glantz and Carol are not themselves repre- sented). Glantz is a guerrilla fighter with a highly confrontational style. Both have impassioned grassroots constituencies. Both fear that the result of any Congressional action may be to pass a federal statute, noticeably weaker than the local ordinances banning public smoking, but which will, by the technical operations of the law, cleverly preempt and replace their victories with a new, much weaker federal alternative.

The Familiar Structure of Rival Coalitions

Note that on the more radical side of the anti-smoking forces, the very process of negotiations leading to action in Congress looks dangerous and undesirable. Matt Myers believes, perhaps reluctantly, in the good faith of both sides. He thinks that they are indeed working toward common interests. But the Californians do not.

The structure of these negotiations is a familiar one that favors obstruc- tionists. In Figure 13.1, assume that "Red" is the natural and historic alli- ance of the anti-smoking forces (or the Prime Minister of Israel). Imagine that "Blue" is the natural and historic alliance of the tobacco industry (or a leader of the Palestinians).

Myers and the change-oriented part of the tobacco leadership are try- ing to form a new coalition between the B and C groups. But the A and D groups need only generate enough hatred or suspicion among either the

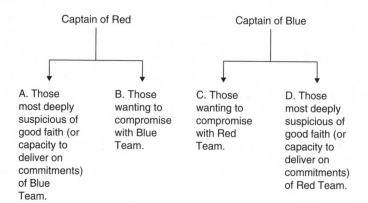

Figure 13.1.

Red or the Blue—their natural allies—to prevent this. And that is often a surprisingly manageable task because of the importance groups that feel threatened attach to loyalty to historic alliances. Matt Myers is unwilling to choose either the new coalition or the old alliance. He understands, intellectually, that only a coalition that includes the cigarette manufacturers can win in a Republican-controlled Congress; and he believes that this coalition can be formed around a proposal that will be immensely desirable as a public health matter. But his historic loyalties are with the groups that have together fought the cigarette companies for a long period of time, including the Nader groups and those created by Glantz and Carol in California. The more vicious the contest, the stronger the demands for loyalty to a traditional alliance among those on each side.

The tobacco contest has long been a war, and Myers cannot free himself from his sense of obligation to his allies of decades in that war. So he never forcefully supports any of the compromises that would be necessary to accomplish the health benefits he wants. In the end, he campaigns vigorously in favor of a proposal that removes all liability protection from the cigarette companies, thus guaranteeing their opposition and the opposition of all their allies in the Congress. This SAVE LIVES coalition of the tobacco-hating parties, determined not to make concessions on liability, comes close but cannot quite win against the opposition that the companies and their supporters in a Republican-controlled Congress can mount.

The other possible coalition for Myers—a new and fragile alliance with the tobacco companies and the state AGs—could have won, but only at the expense of a sharp split within the anti-smoking group and, even then, perhaps, only if it could have enlisted either Koop or Kessler. The motivation of these national symbols of public health depended in important part on maintaining the conditions of their influence as trusted heroes of those determined to end the ravages brought about by smoking. So their interest was to hold out as long as possible for a total denial of immunity for the cigarette companies and then to concede when and if it became necessary to achieve health benefits. Although it was to the advantage of the health of American youth, it was not to their personal advantages to press a compromise that would split the community that they, at least symbolically, led. Reconciling those competing concerns could be accomplished by Kessler and Koop joining a negotiated settlement only at the last moment, after making every effort to support even the most extreme parts of the anti-smoking coalition.

Senator McCain, otherwise an inspiring figure, seems to have thrown away the keys to victory when he went forward with his final, most health-oriented, proposals without insisting that his support for them would be contingent on Kessler and/or Koop also supporting them. If either Kessler or Koop had gone along at that stage, as Koop suggests they might have, the ENACT coalition would have carried the day. The cigarette companies would have enjoyed the benefits of reduced liability and, in exchange for that, supported the bill.

Looking at the process with tactical lenses, we can see that the opponents of compromise—the anti-smoking side and the cigarette companies in the very final stages—have clear tactical advantages over those moderates on both sides who are seeking agreements. Those deeply opposed to agreement on either side can behave in a way that is so hostile to the other side that it strengthens the hand of the more radical group of their opponents. By supporting an elimination of all immunity provisions, Glantz can strengthen the hand of those on the industry side who, like him, do not want a compromise at all. Glantz can accomplish the same ends of defeating negotiation by attacking the loyalty, in a political war, of any of his historic allies who would make the concessions the cigarette companies need if they are to remain interested in compromise. Glantz does this effectively to Matt Myers.

The Choice of Coalitions

The benefits of including the tobacco companies in any coalition were obvious. They had great influence with the leadership and membership of the Republican Party, which controlled both houses of the Congress. But any coalition based, as it would have to be, on trading protection of the future health of youth for reduced liability for the past and thus ensuring the future financial health of the cigarette companies would be plainly unacceptable to the trial lawyers, the Nader forces, and the Californians. If it also proved to be unacceptable to Kessler and Koop—perhaps because any compromise with the hated enemy would undermine their extraordinary statures—liberal senators concerned about health would hesitate to desert historic allies to support the new cross-ideological coalition.

The cigarette companies would have to be left out of the SAVE LIVES coalition; those most passionate in their opposition to the cigarette companies would have to be left out of the ENACT coalition. Whenever a powerful subgroup is left out of a coalition that normally should, or historically does, include it, it is likely to try and break up the new coalition, and it is likely to have a substantial capacity to do so. That is true whether it is Mahmoud Abbas trying to negotiate an agreement while leaving out the settlers and Hamas or whether it is the health groups and the tobacco companies trying to negotiate a settlement while leaving out the most radical haters of the companies.

The party left out can threaten to abandon a historic alliance, as southern Democrats did in response to Democratic leadership support of the civil rights movement of the 1960s. They can encourage the more radical part of the opposite group, thereby frightening the other potential members of the new coalition. They can argue that attempting to negotiate a compromise is a fundamental mistake for any of several reasons: because, as Glantz seems to believe, better results could come from fighting to the end; or there is no trusting the other party to the agreement to deliver on what it promises; or simply out of the fear that the coalition will be tricked or out-negotiated as the anti-tobacco groups had been in the past.

All these risks, as well as the personal cost of deserting old friends and former allies from heated battles of the past, led Myers to try to maintain both coalitions simultaneously, although two facts seem obvious in retrospect. The prospects of legislative achievement of the health benefits that were of core importance to Myers were much greater if the cigarette companies would support this part of a legislative compromise. At the same time, no coalition that gave the legitimacy and liability protection that was fundamental to the cigarette companies while trusting Congress to enact an agreement in good faith could win the support of several members of the historic, anti-smoking team. Indeed, they would predictably fight, with considerable capacity, against the only coalition that could potentially deliver what Myers regarded as of fundamental importance.

So he had an excruciatingly difficult personal choice. But he adopted the worst alternative: not choosing which coalition he would side with and thereby losing both the health benefits he so desperately sought in the legislation and the personal trust and reputation he had enjoyed among the leaders of the anti-smoking side. His mistake of hoping for too much began early. Right at the start, Myers called a meeting of all the anti-smoking groups to arrive at a common position. He should have known that any position acceptable to every last anti-smoking advocate would depend on terms that would not be accepted by the cigarette companies. Had this been Pillsbury, he would have met with the people he thought he needed for his proposal one at a time, building a coalition by using his influence with those who could influence others. Myers did the opposite. At stage after stage, Myers felt unable to give his full support to those with whom he was negotiating a cross-ideological coalition, for fear of losing the support of his ideological colleagues. Yet the negotiation itself, beginning without the involvement of Koop and Kessler, was bound to generate suspicions.

The efforts to keep Carol, Glantz, Nader, Koop, and Kessler aboard required a constant reduction in the liability protection that very largely motivated the participation of the cigarette companies in the negotiation. As McCain tried to win more and more support from the anti-smoking side—and remarkably failed to condition his acceptance of reduced protection of the companies on the endorsement of his legislation by Koop and Kessler—the tobacco companies stood to get less and less, until they abandoned the compromise.

When they did, they had a variety of resources available to defeat the ideological and interest group coalition with which Myers was by then firmly allied. They could use advertising to portray the tax provisions of the bill as designed to raise more revenue for an unpopular Washington, rather than, as they were, to increase the price of a pack of cigarettes to the point where youth could not afford to smoke. The Republican leadership, having decided that they would not cut off debate, needed only 40 votes to prevent the McCain bill from coming to a vote. They could drive members of the Republican majority into the needed voting block by allowing amendments to make the bill more and more unacceptable to business (a tactic that had the double advantage of allowing conservatives to publicly display a hostility to—or, at least, independence of—the cigarette companies, which provided them embarrassing financial support, before voting to allow debate to continue endlessly). They could permit amendments that made the bill unattractive to the trial lawyers and to the attorneys general. In the end, McCain almost carried the day, but he did not.

Part IV

Conclusion: Interrogation and Foresight

14

The Dependence of Policy Outcomes on Processes of Choice

I have described the political processes of policy choice, but I have not discussed their costs and benefits. In the case that follows, defining torture in the "War on Terror," the political processes chosen, and the people chosen to carry them out, produce results that nobody wants while targeting outcomes that only a fraction of our citizens would find morally acceptable. How this comes about is the subject of my conclusion.

It is not inevitable that politics will create a process that leads to shortsighted decisions, with results that no one wants. In fact, the United States has had some remarkable successes. We have as a nation turned sworn enemies into powerful and democratic allies after the Second World War. We contained the Soviet Union until its collapse, without a war. We have spread democracy, although not necessarily the rule of law, throughout the Western Hemisphere. At home we reversed a dangerous, immoral, and demoralizing history of first slavery and then segregation. We have guaranteed medical care to the elderly and begun to do the same for poor children. These amazing triumphs were not the fruit of good luck or a single heroic genius. They resulted from wise political processes designed to consider a broad range of consequences and to create the legitimacy needed to win and hold the support of the nation's citizens.

Still, on many other occasions we have shown remarkable shortsightedness. Two of the cases we have studied are dramatic in that regard. It was surely madness for President Reagan to give surface-to-air missiles that could shoot down commercial airliners to the Afghan and Arab Mujahideen fighting the Soviet Union in Afghanistan, especially when they were so close to winning without having the missiles that could later threaten us. Yet no one seems to have thought about the possibility that, to the Mujahideen, the Soviet Union was only the first of two super-powers whom they would take on in a faith-based war of many battles. Again, in the Iran-Contra affair, President Reagan and most of his closest advisors seem to have missed the immense domestic and international political costs—as well as the unlikelihood of real benefits in terms of release of hostages—from furnishing missiles to Iran during its war with Iraq. Something went badly wrong in these cases.

The unavoidable politics of bureaucratic decision making among spirited and opinionated players has its benefits and its costs. It encourages creative accommodations among actors delegated discrete responsibilities and also trade-offs between their present and future concerns. It relieves high officials of the impossible task of making a multitude of decisions. Compliance with the rules guarantees against unexpected and unwanted results within the areas of responsibility assigned to any player, for every player will be defending her area.

But the costs are also obvious. The amount of investment in any single decision is likely to turn on its importance to various players and not on its importance to the nation, especially if no single player will be held accountable for the results. There is thus too little incentive to consider the future; the long term is likely to become a policy orphan.

Worst of all, one path to political success prescribed by Pillsbury—denying the opposition the knowledge necessary to develop an effective response—is intended to deny the decision maker needed information and advice and the pressure toward reasoned choice that comes with those forces. Sometimes, as in the case of "Defining Torture," the decision maker may even want such a "blinded" process for political reasons. If so, it is frequently within his capacities to bring it about.

We can no longer, as a nation, afford these costs. If there were ever times when there were no major issues on the political horizon, that is certainly not the case now. If terrorism is with us for decades, we will have to resolve questions of separation of powers and protection of civil liberties and human rights, which we were able to leave only half-resolved in the years immediately after September 11, 2001. We will also have to find a way to neutralize the aggressive imperialistic force of religious and ideological commitments if we are to manage coexistence between an economically thriving, socially diverse, democratic west and a Muslim world whose population is exploding along with its religious politics and its resentment of the United States and its allies. To deal with the possibilities of failure in that effort, we will have to find a way to substantially reduce our traditional dependence on fossil energy. The vast problem of global warming will require that as well. We will have to come to terms with the incredible speed with which technical capacities to gather and handle information are increasing. The impact of globalization on everything from wages to crime has not yet been addressed.

This list is merely illustrative. The United States needs wise and broadly accepted decisions, not simply the outcomes of contests among smart players of the games of bureaucratic and legislative politics. Wisdom is not so complicated. The process of making policy choices must address systematically what a broad range of tangible and intangible consequences are likely to be, stretched out as far as one can reasonably predict. Beyond that—and only when we have planned for as much as can be reasonably predicted—might presumptions based on broad ideology have sway. And finally, a wise decision for a democracy like ours must ultimately reflect a choice among the possible sets of consequences of different actions that is determined by the processes, and in terms of the values, the American people expect and hold (or will hold if and when leaders propose and support them). If even the best of decisions, let alone the worst, is to continue to command the support it needs for a long enough time to be effective, the process that produced the decision must create the force of legitimacy.

The final case describes the politics of a decision process designed from the top to produce a particular result by foreclosing dissenting argument and public opposition. Unlike earlier cases, where the leeways within the rules of process were exploited to achieve particular decisions, in the case of the torture memos, the very process was designed for that purpose. But unsurprisingly, it produced many consequences that none of the players wanted and, expressively, was based on values that, while temporarily held, would obviously not be accepted for long by the American people. We should consider what mistakes brought that about.

Defining Torture in the War on Terror: "Checking with the Professionals"
A Case History by Esther Scott

In the aftermath of the devastating attacks on the World Trade Center and the Pentagon on September 11, 2001, President George W. Bush launched a military offensive in Afghanistan aimed at hunting down the Al Qaeda terrorists responsible for the destruction and at ousting the Taliban regime that had harbored them.[1] But, as administration officials were quick to note, this would be a "different kind of war," fought against an unconventional and elusive enemy whose intentions toward the United States were nakedly malign. Although the Taliban proved no match for the might and sophistication of the U.S. military and its allies, Al Qaeda's terrorist network was diffuse and not easily disrupted. The group's leader, Osama bin Laden, had managed to evade capture, and no one could predict what further terrorist plots he or his lieutenants might be hatching, or when and where they would strike next.

In this atmosphere of uncertainty and dread, the "war on terror," as it was soon called, became more a quest for intelligence on Al Qaeda's activities and plans than a battle for military supremacy. As the first prominent Al Qaeda operatives from Afghanistan and elsewhere were captured and brought into American custody, the issue of how to extract crucial information from them became of paramount importance to top officials in the Bush administration. The Central Intelligence Agency (CIA), which held many of the highest-ranking captives in secret detention centers overseas, wanted to apply more aggressive methods of questioning—what it called "enhanced interrogation techniques"—including, among other things, sleep deprivation, "stress positions," and "waterboarding," or simulated drowning. Such "brass-knuckled" tactics, it was argued, were needed to convince tight-lipped detainees to reveal what they knew about Al Qaeda's operations. The times, some believed, demanded a tougher approach to America's adversaries. "There was a before 9/11, and there was an after 9/11," Cofer Black, then head of the CIA Counterterrorist Center, famously told members of Congress on September 26. "After 9/11, the gloves come off."[2]

But the CIA was concerned about the legal consequences of employing harsher forms of interrogation. There were international treaties, to which the United States was signatory, mandating the humane treatment of prisoners of war and detainees, and banning torture and "cruel, inhuman or degrading" acts against them. Moreover, there were federal laws implementing these treaties that imposed severe penalties on those who violated their terms. Worried that its agents would be vulnerable to prosecution, the CIA sought a clear statement from the administration as to how far it could legally go in its efforts to force detainees to talk. Alberto Gonzales, then the White House counsel, directed the CIA's request to the Office of Legal Counsel (OLC), a small but influential unit within the Justice Department that wrote legal opinions for the executive branch of government. "I felt I had an obligation as a prudent lawyer," Gonzales later explained, "to check with the professionals at the Department of Justice."[3]

It would thus fall to OLC, then under the leadership of Assistant Attorney General Jay Bybee, to determine which interrogation practices fell outside what was permissible under the law—in particular, what legally constituted torture or "cruel, inhuman or degrading" treatment. It was, by any measure, a challenging task. The language of anti-torture treaties and the laws implementing them were far from clear, and there were few legal signposts OLC could turn to for interpretation. Moreover, the issue was a morally charged one, in which the safety of a threatened nation would be weighed against the legality of acts that many would judge to be in violation of long-held international standards of humane treatment in times of war.

Once rendered, OLC's legal opinion would essentially have the force of law. With the administration anxious to be "forward-leaning" in its efforts to prevent more loss of American lives, OLC could expect its ruling on interrogation to have a direct impact on the treatment of detainees in CIA custody. Reflecting on the challenges and anxieties surrounding the deliberations on the issue, John Yoo, then deputy assistant attorney general at the Office of Legal Counsel, observed: "I don't think people understand how difficult was the work we did, how difficult the questions, how recent the 9/11 attacks were." "There was no book at the time you could open and say, 'under American law, this is what torture means.'"[4]

Background: The Office of Legal Counsel

An elite unit within the Department of Justice, OLC was, in the words of one account, "the most important government office you've never heard of."[5] It acted, as one observer put it, much like "an in-house law firm for the executive branch."[6] Among its duties, OLC assisted the attorney general "in his function as legal advisor to the president and all the executive branch agencies"; gave "legal advice to the executive branch on all constitutional questions"; and provided oral advice and written opinions in response to requests from the White House counsel and the agencies of the executive branch. These latter requests "typically deal with legal issues of particular complexity and importance or about which two or more agencies are in disagreement."[7] Its legal rulings on such matters carried weight. OLC's "carefully worded opinions," in the words of one account, "are regarded as binding precedent—[the] final say on what the president and all his agencies can and cannot legally do."[8]

OLC was a small office, comprising twenty-two lawyers, headed by an assistant attorney general—the fifth-ranking position in the Justice Department—and four deputies, all of whom were political appointees. The rest were staff lawyers—called "attorney-advisors" or, colloquially, "line attorneys." Most of them were non-career attorneys who were appointed by the OLC head and generally reflected the judicial and political philosophy of the administration in power; but four were, by tradition, permanent lawyers, career civil servants who were considered "non-political." For those who aspired to it, the leadership of OLC often provided a pathway to a prestigious seat in the judiciary. Heads of OLC, one commentator noted, were "judges in waiting to the highest courts in the land both during and after their tenure."[9] Among the most illustrious former OLC heads were Supreme Court Chief Justice William Rehnquist and Associate Justice Antonin Scalia.

Drafting Opinions. While many federal agencies turned to OLC to settle their disputes, the office's "biggest client," according to former OLC head Charles Cooper, was the president himself.[10] The process of resolving agency disagreements was a formal one, involving written statements from the disputants, but White House requests for legal advice were conveyed—directly to OLC—on a more informal basis, by phone or in conversation. Typically, explains Jack Goldsmith, who led OLC from October 2003 through July 2004, the White House counsel would say that "we need advice about X, we need a legal opinion about X before we go forward." Once the request was made, it was assigned to one of OLC's deputies, who would work on the opinion with the line attorneys; after it was completed, the draft opinion would be reviewed by the OLC head and then given to another deputy for "a critical read," in Goldsmith's words. The involvement of the Attorney General in reviewing opinions appeared to vary. Under John Mitchell, President Nixon's Attorney General, OLC rulings were, in the words of one legal expert, "sent to the White House without the Attorney General's input" unless they were "quite spectacular."[11] According to some press reports, OLC opinions were "typically...not screened by" John Ashcroft, the Attorney General during George W. Bush's first term in office, "or other top Justice officials."[12] But Goldsmith, who served under Ashcroft, recalls that it was his practice to run "non-trivial" opinions—"anything I thought was important enough for his consideration and input"—past the Attorney General before they were finalized.

It was also, according to Goldsmith, "normal procedure," as in any lawyer-client relationship, for OLC to send opinions in draft form to the White House for comment. "If you made mistakes or if there are wrong facts or something that the client doesn't like, you at least want to know about it," Goldsmith observes. A lawyer "doesn't necessarily listen to the client when he says don't do this or do that, but you always want to know what the client thinks." Whether to accede to the client's wishes was, he adds, "the lawyer's judgment role." Over the decades since the Office of Legal Counsel was first established in 1933, during the administration of Franklin Roosevelt, the delicate question of how to balance the wishes of the most powerful person in the United States, if not the world, with the imperatives of the law was one that every leader of OLC confronted. The "central dilemma" of the OLC head, wrote one commentator, was "how to provide his clients, particularly his key patrons, the White House counsel and the Attorney General, with advice and opinions they find generally congenial while at the same time upholding the reputation of the office as an elite institution whose legal advice is independent of the policy and political pressures associated with a particular question."[13]

How well OLC had managed its balancing act—or should manage it—was a matter of some debate. To some observers and former members of the office, OLC had traditionally been a source of "nuanced, almost scholarly legal analysis" and "disinterested advice."[14] Some veterans of OLC, such as Douglas Kmiec, who ran the office during the administrations of Ronald Reagan and George H. W. Bush, viewed it as "the conscience of the Justice Department," willing to stand up to the President on constitutional principles. "One of the least happy days in my life," Kmiec recalled, "was telling President Reagan that he could not exercise an inherent line-item veto"—because the Constitution did not warrant it—"even though he dearly wanted it."[15] But others dismissed this view of OLC as "sentimental" and "distorted." OLC's "jurisprudence," two University of Chicago Law School professors maintained, "has traditionally been highly pro-executive" in its opinions.[16] This was an assessment with which Goldsmith largely agreed. While it was OLC's "self-conception" that it provided the "most objective legal advice in government," he notes, "you can't look at OLC opinions from any administration and not detect that they're [influenced by] the fact that they're inside this political organization called the executive branch."

There was debate as well about whether the Office of Legal Counsel was obliged to address moral or policy issues in the opinions it rendered to the White House and the executive branch. Some strongly argued in the affirmative. "A good lawyer," said Stephen Gillers, a professor of legal ethics at New York University, "does not think of himself as merely a technician. A good lawyer advises on the wisdom of a particular course of conduct." But Charles Fried of Harvard Law School argued otherwise. "When a government is faced with a situation and is faced with options," he told the *New York Times*, "surely one of the questions it asks—but only one of them—is, what does the law require? Another is, is it effective? Another is, is it moral? Those are not the same questions." Fried maintained that the role of the lawyer was, as the *Times* put it, "to answer the first question."[17]

The ongoing debate over OLC's proper role as legal advisor to the executive branch would be thrown into sharp relief in the months following September 11, as the administration prepared its counter-offensive against Al Qaeda and its supporters.

The War on Terror

The September 11 attacks on their own soil shocked Americans into an awareness that the United States was the target of a violent and committed enemy. Since 1993, when a massive explosion from a truck bomb rocked the North Tower of the World Trade Center, Islamic extremists had assiduously sought to kill Americans at home and abroad—attacking U.S. servicemen in Saudi Arabia in 1996, two U.S. embassies in Africa in 1998, and a naval vessel in 2000. When, only a week after the destruction of the World Trade Center, letters containing anthrax were mailed to the offices of five news media outlets and two U.S. senators, the sense of vulnerability intensified, and a jittery nation wondered apprehensively where and how it would next be attacked.[18]

At the White House, there was determination to respond to the attacks forcefully. Describing the mood of the administration after September 11, a former State Department official recalled, "The Twin Towers were still smoldering. The atmosphere was intense. The tone at the top was aggressive—understandably so. The Commander-in-Chief had used the words 'dead or alive' [in reference to the capture of bin Laden] and vowed to bring the terrorists to justice or bring justice to them. There was a fury."[19] But the president was equally determined to prevent another attack on the United States and, according to one observer, had made it known to his aides that he wanted them to take, in the words of the *Washington Post*, "an aggressive approach" in their counterterrorism efforts. Bush, a former senior administration official told the *Post*, "felt very keenly that his primary responsibility was to do everything in his power to keep the country safe...."[20]

It was against this backdrop of uncertainty and urgency that a number of "high-value targets"—top lieutenants in the Al Qaeda terrorist network—were captured in late 2001 and early 2002. These included Mohammed al-Kahtani, thought to be the "twentieth hijacker," who was supposed to have participated in the September 11 attacks; Abu Zubaida (also spelled Zubaydah), believed to be Al Qaeda's operations chief; and Ibn Sheikh al-Libi, who had run an Al Qaeda training camp in Afghanistan. Over the coming year, other high-ranking terrorists would come into U.S. hands. The question was what to do with them.

A CIA/FBI Debate. At the time of the capture of the first "big trophy" from Al Qaeda—al-Libi—in November 2001, during the fighting in Afghanistan, the FBI, not the CIA, was in charge of questioning detainees. The two agencies immediately began sparring over the proper handling of al-Libi and other valuable suspects. The FBI, according to several accounts, favored a "carrot-and-stick" approach that doled out rewards for information, a technique its "bin Laden team" had considered effective in the past.[21] The CIA—which had not yet built up its own experienced corps of "interrogation specialists"—was pushing to take a harder line with al-Libi, including threatening his life and family. But the FBI, the *Post* reported, had "never authorized such methods," wanting to "preserve the purity of interrogations so they could be used as evidence in court cases."[22] The two agencies' disagreement made its way up to their respective heads and, ultimately, to the White House, with the result that al-Libi was handed over to the custody of the CIA. In turn, the CIA bundled him up and sent him to Egypt for questioning—a procedure known as rendition, in which a suspect was turned over to a foreign country, usually one with a reputation for extremely harsh interrogation practices.[23] Eventually, al-Libi provided the CIA with information on an alleged plan to blow up the U.S. embassy in Yemen and "pointed officials in the direction of" an even more valuable target: Abu Zubaida.[24]

Posing the Question. It was, according to a number of accounts, the capture of Abu Zubaida, one of bin Laden's top aides, that reignited the debate over interrogation techniques within the Bush administration.

Zubaida, wounded by gunshot, was seized in Pakistan in March 2002 and was brought to one of the secret detention centers for high-value captives that the CIA had established overseas, reportedly under authorization from President Bush.

By this time, the White House had concluded that terrorism should be treated as a "national security issue rather than a law enforcement matter," and had given the lead role in questioning detainees to the CIA.[25] The FBI chose to remain aloof from CIA-led interrogations, knowing, according to a report in the *Washington Post*, that they "could be harsh" and might "impeach" FBI agents' testimony.[26] Some FBI officials also questioned the efficacy of enhanced interrogation techniques. "Brutalization doesn't work," said one. A person subjected to coercive questioning "would tell you anything....There's no value in it."[27]

The FBI's misgivings notwithstanding, the CIA was eager to employ whatever means it could to persuade the "close-mouthed" Zubaida to talk. Zubaida had proved resistant to "standard methods," and the CIA stood ready to apply—or, according to some, already had applied—"stress and duress" tactics, such as sleep deprivation; hooding; forcing a subject to stand or hold painful positions for long periods; and, most notoriously, waterboarding, which induced a sense of drowning.[28] Proponents of such practices were unapologetic about their harshness. "If you don't violate someone's human rights," one official said, "you probably aren't doing your job. I don't think we want to be promoting a view of zero tolerance on this. That was the whole problem for a long time with the CIA."[29]

But, as the intelligence agency knew, there were treaties and laws governing the treatment of detainees and criminalizing breaches of anti-torture statutes. The penalties for violations of the law could be severe, and the CIA was anxious to protect its agents on the frontlines of the war on terror from prosecution. At the same time, with the administration intent on avoiding future attacks, there was pressure on the agency to extract timely information from recalcitrant detainees. Accordingly, the CIA turned to the "top lawyers in the Bush administration," *Newsweek* reported, with a question: "how far could the agency go in interrogating terror suspects?..."[30]

The Laws of War

Any answer to the CIA's question would have to begin with a consideration of existing treaties and statutes that set out the rules for interrogation in times of war and conflict. Chief among these were the four

Geneva Conventions for the Protection of Victims of War, approved by a "diplomatic conference" in 1949 and signed by more nations than any other treaty concerned with "the laws of war."[31] Each of the conventions, or treaties, focused on a particular segment of the population affected by war (for example, civilians, wounded soldiers and sailors); the Third Convention specifically dealt with the treatment of prisoners of war (POWs). Under the terms of that convention, those eligible for POW status were either members of the armed forces of a party to the conflict, or members of militias or "other volunteer corps," including "organized resistance movements," provided they fulfilled a number of conditions, including being commanded by "a person responsible for his subordinates," having a "fixed distinctive sign recognizable at a distance," "carrying arms openly," and "conducting their operations in accordance with the laws and customs of war." In the event of uncertainty as to whether combatants qualified as POWs, the Third Convention stipulated that they should be protected under its provisions until their status could be determined by a "competent tribunal."

For those who met the POW criteria, the Third Geneva Convention offered important protections. Prisoners of war, the treaty stated in Article 13, "must at all times be treated humanely," and shielded from "acts of violence or intimidation...." More specifically in regard to interrogation, Article 17 prohibited "physical or mental torture" or "any other form of coercion" to "secure from [POWs] information of any kind whatever. Prisoners of war who refuse to answer may not be threatened, insulted or exposed to any unpleasant or disadvantageous treatment of any kind."

The four Geneva Conventions were intended to apply to "all cases of declared war or of any other armed conflict which may arise between two or more of the High Contracting Parties" to the treaty. In addition, however, "Common Article 3"—so-called because it was common to all four conventions—offered protections in the case of an "armed conflict *not* of an international character occurring in the territory of one of the High Contracting Parties..." [emphasis added]. "[A]s a minimum," parties to such conflicts were expected to treat humanely all persons "taking no active part in the hostilities," a category that included non-POWs who were being held in detention. For those who fell under its protective umbrella, Article 3 prohibited, among other things, "violence to life and person," including torture, as well as "outrages upon personal dignity, in particular humiliating and degrading treatment." (See Figure 14.1 for full text of common Article 3.)

Convention (III) relative to the Treatment of Prisoners of War. Geneva, 12 August 1949.

Article
Part I: General provisions
Art. 3 – Conflicts not of an international character

Article 3
In the case of armed conflict not of an international character occurring in the territory of one of the High Contracting Parties, each Party to the conflict shall be bound to apply, as a minimum, the following provisions.

(1) Persons taking no active part in the hostilities, including members of armed forces who have laid down their arms and those placed 'hors de combat' by sickness, wounds, detention, or any other cause, shall in all circumstances be treated humanely, without any adverse distinction founded on race, colour, religion or faith, sex, birth or wealth, or any other similar criteria. To this end, the following acts are and shall remain prohibited at any time and in any place whatsoever with respect to the above-mentioned persons:

(a) violence to life and person, in particular murder of all kinds, mutilation, cruel treatment and torture;

(b) taking of hostages;

(c) outrages upon personal dignity, in particular humiliating and degrading treatment;

(d) the passing of sentences and the carrying out of executions without previous judgment pronounced by a regularly constituted court, affording all the judicial guarantees which are recognized as indispensable by civilized peoples.

(2) The wounded and sick shall be collected and cared for.

An impartial humanitarian body, such as the International Committee of the Red Cross, may offer its services to the Parties to the conflict.

The Parties to the conflict should further endeavour to bring into force, by means of special agreements, all or part of the other provisions of the present Convention.

The application of the preceding provisions shall not affect the legal status of the Parties to the conflict.

Figure 14.1-Exhibit 1

The United States ratified the four Geneva Conventions in 1955, but although each signatory nation was expected to enact legislation implementing penalties for "grave breaches" of the treaty's provisions, Congress did not do so, reasoning that existing laws offered "adequate means of prosecution."[32] But in 1996, Rep. Walter B. Jones, a conservative Republican from North Carolina, introduced a bill that would impose penalties—including life imprisonment or death—on anyone who committed a "war crime," defined as, among other things, a grave breach of the Geneva Conventions. According to an account in the *Washington Post*, Jones sponsored the 1996 War Crimes Act to protect American troops captured abroad, but "the Pentagon supported making its provisions applicable to US personnel because doing so set a high standard for others to follow." Moreover, the bill was amended a year later, without a hearing, specifically to include violations of Common Article 3 as a war crime.[33] (See Figure 14.2 for text of the War Crimes Act.)

The Convention against Torture. While the Geneva Conventions applied to victims of war, a more recent treaty—the Convention against Torture and Other Cruel, Inhuman or Degrading Treatment or Punishment (often shortened to the Convention against Torture, or CAT)—covered a broader set of circumstances, including "the custody, interrogation or treatment of any individual subjected to any form of arrest, detention or imprisonment." Adopted by the United Nations General Assembly in December 1984, the CAT, unlike the Geneva documents, provided a definition of torture. It was, according to the treaty, any act "by which severe pain or suffering, whether physical or mental, is intentionally inflicted on a person" for the purpose of obtaining information, punishing, or intimidating him, "when such pain or suffering is inflicted by or at the instigation of or with the consent or acquiescence of a public official or other person acting in an official capacity." The treaty did not provide a comparable definition of "cruel, inhuman or degrading treatment"—sometimes mockingly referred to as "torture lite"—but stated that each signatory nation must undertake to "prevent in any territory under its jurisdiction other acts of cruel, inhuman or degrading treatment or punishment which do not amount to torture as defined in [the treaty]." The CAT also required each party to the convention to enact laws criminalizing acts of torture and attaching penalties appropriate to "their grave nature."

Since its adoption by the UN General Assembly, over 140 nations had signed the Convention against Torture. The United States became a party

U.S. Code Collection

Title 18 > Part I > Chapter 118 > § 2441

§2441. War crimes

(a) **Offense.** Whoever, whether inside or outside the United States, commits a war crime, in any of the circumstances described in subsection (b), shall be fined under this title or imprisoned for life or any term of years, or both, and if death results to the victim, shall also be subject to the penalty of death.

(b) **Circumstances.** The circumstances referred to in subsection (a) are that the person committing such war crime or the victim of such war crime is a member of the Armed Forces of the United States or a national of the United States (as defined in section 101 of the Immigration and Nationality Act).

(c) **Definition.** As used in this section the term "war crime" means any conduct

(1) defined as a grave breach in any of the international conventions signed at Geneva 12 August 1949, or any protocol to such convention to which the United States is a party;

(2) prohibited by Article 23, 25, 27, or 28 of the Annex to the Hague Convention IC, Respecting the Laws and Customs of War on Land, signed 18 October 1907;

(3) which constitutes a violation of common Article 3 of the international conventions signed at Geneva, 12 August 1949, or any protocol to such convention to which the United States is a party and which deals with non-international armed conflict; or

(4) of a person who, in relation to an armed conflict and contrary to the provisions of the Protocol on Prohibitions or Restrictions on the Use of Mines, Booby-Traps and Other Devices as amended at Geneva on 3 May 1996 (Protocol II as amended on 3 May 1996), when the United States is a party to such Protocol, willfully kills or causes serious injury to civilians.

Figure 14.2-Exhibit 2

to the treaty in 1994, but with some "reservations" and "understandings." One of these concerned its reading of torture. "The United States," a Senate report stated, "understands that, in order to constitute torture, an act must be specifically intended to inflict severe physical or mental pain or suffering…." In the case of mental pain or suffering, the effects must be "prolonged" and caused by: the infliction of severe physical pain, or the threat of it; the use of mind-altering substances or procedures that would "disrupt profoundly the senses or the personality"; the threat of imminent death; or the threat of death or of other severe pain and suffering to a third party. The language of this understanding was incorporated into the 1994 law passed by Congress to penalize acts of torture. In addition, the United States noted in a reservation that it considered itself bound to prevent cruel, inhuman, or degrading treatment "only insofar as the term….means the cruel, unusual and inhumane treatment or punishment prohibited by the Fifth, Eight, and Fourteenth Amendments" to the Constitution (in particular, any form of treatment that "shocks the conscience"). Finally, the federal anti-torture statute was limited to acts committed outside the United States. Offenders could serve terms of up to twenty years for violations of the law; if, however, their actions resulted in death, they could face life imprisonment or even the death penalty.

Confronted with the constraints of the sometimes ambiguous language of these treaties and their implementing legislation, the Bush administration would have to hammer out a policy on the interrogation of Al Qaeda and other terrorist suspects being held abroad. The Office of Legal Counsel would play a key role in the development of the White House strategy. Even before the question of CIA interrogation practices arose, OLC found itself on the receiving end of "a barrage of questions" from the White House on whether and how anti-torture treaties and laws applied to the treatment of suspected terrorists captured on the battlefields of the war on terror.[34] Its initial opinions on these matters could be said to set the stage for the memorandum on torture.

Early Rulings

On September 25, 2001, just two weeks after the destruction of the Twin Towers, the Office of Legal Counsel issued its first major opinion related to the event—a memorandum on the President's "constitutional authority to conduct military operations against terrorists and nations supporting them." It was addressed to the deputy White House counsel—Timothy Flanigan—who had asked OLC for an opinion on the "scope" of the President's power to "take military action" in response to the terrorist attacks. In brief, OLC concluded that the Constitution vested the chief executive with "plenary"—essentially, absolute—authority to use military force abroad, especially in times of "grave national emergencies created by sudden, unforeseen attacks" on the United States. "The power of the President is at its zenith under the Constitution," the

---

U.S. Code Collection

Title 18 > Part I > Chapter 113C > § 2340

§2340. Definitions

As used in this chapter–

(1) "torture" means an act committed by a person acting under the color of law specifically intended to inflict severe physical or mental pain or suffering (other than pain or suffering incidental to lawful sanctions) upon another person within his custody or physical control;

(2) "severe mental pain or suffering" means the prolonged mental harm caused by or resulting from

    (a) the intentional infliction or threatened infliction of severe physical pain or suffering;

    (b) the administration or application, or threatened administration or application, of mind-altering substances or other procedures calculated to disrupt profoundly the senses or the personality;

    (c) the threat of imminent death; or

    (d) the threat of another person will imminently be subjected to death, severe physical pain or suffering, or the administration or application of mind-altering substances or other procedures calculated to disrupt profoundly the senses or personality; and

(3) "United States" means the several States of the United States, the District of Columbia, and the commonwealths, territories, and possessions of the United States.

Figure 14.3 -Exhibit 3. Source: http://www4.law.cornell.edu/uscode/html/uscode18/usc_sec_18_00002340-000-.html

U.S. Code Collection

Title 18 > Part I > Chapter 113C > § 2340A

§2340A. Torture

(a) **Offense.** Whoever outside the United States commits or attempts to commit torture shall be fined under this title or imprisoned not more than 20 years, or both, and if death results to any person from conduct prohibited by this subsection, shall be punished by death or imprisoned for any term of years or for life.

(b) **Jurisdiction.** There is jurisdiction over the activity prohibited in subsection (a) if

(1) the alleged offender is a national of the United States; or

(2) the alleged offender is present in the United States, irrespective of the nationality of the victim or alleged offender.

(c) **Conspiracy.** A person who conspires to commit an offense under this section shall be subject to the same penalties (other than the penalty of death) as the penalties prescribed for the offense, the commission of which was the object of the conspiracy.

Figure 14.3 (*Continued*). Source: http://www.law.cornell.edu/uscode/18/usc_sec_18_00002340-A000-.html

memorandum declared, "when the President is directing military operations of the armed forces, because the power of Commander in Chief is assigned solely to the President." While the Constitution gave Congress the power to declare war, it argued, that was not "tantamount to making war"—the sole province of the President.

The September 25 opinion was authored by John C. Yoo, a professor of law at the University of California at Berkeley who had been appointed Deputy Assistant Attorney General at OLC in July 2001. Yoo, who had clerked for Supreme Court Justice Clarence Thomas, was reported to be a "protégé" of David Addington, then general counsel for Vice President Richard Cheney and widely considered one of the most influential members of the Bush administration. Addington, an outspoken proponent of presidential power, had assembled a circle of like-minded lawyers—including Yoo; White House Counsel Alberto Gonzales and his deputy, Timothy Flanigan; and William Haynes, general counsel for the Department of Defense—who together, according to press accounts, had a strong hand in developing the legal underpinnings for the administration's conduct of the war on terror.[35]

Over the ensuing months, OLC issued a number of memoranda on the handling of terror suspects captured in Afghanistan in the early days of that war. On November 6, it ruled that it would be legal to try the suspects in military tribunals instead of civil courts; and on December 28, Yoo advised the Pentagon that detainees held at the U.S. Navy base on Guantanamo Bay in Cuba would be beyond the jurisdiction of U.S. federal courts—and, hence, unable to mount a legal challenge to their detention.[36]

Perhaps more consequentially, Yoo coauthored a draft memorandum to William Haynes, dated January 9, 2002, on the "application of treaties and laws to Al Qaeda and Taliban detainees" at Guantanamo. The ruling, forty-two pages long, took up the thorny question of whether the protections of the Geneva Conventions—and, in particular, the Third Convention, governing treatment of prisoners of war, and Common Article 3—should be extended to members of Al Qaeda and their Taliban supporters being held by the U.S. military. In their reading of both the relevant portions of the treaty and the implementing legislation, the War Crimes Act of 1996, Yoo and his coauthor—OLC Special Counsel Robert Delahunty—concluded that the answer in both cases was no. Al Qaeda, the ruling stated, was "merely a violent political movement or organization and not a nation-state," and as such could not be a party to the Geneva conventions. Further, Al Qaeda did not meet the "eligibility requirements" for POW status under the Third Convention; nor did the provisions of Common Article 3, which covered conflicts that were not international, apply to the terrorist group. Common Article 3, the January 9 memorandum argued, referred to civil wars, but the "current conflict" in Afghanistan was a hybrid event—a war that was international in character, but not between nation-states.

The situation was more complicated where the Taliban was concerned. Afghanistan was a "High Contracting Party" to all four of the Geneva Conventions, as the draft memorandum noted, and since the Taliban was the "de facto government of that nation," its militia should, in theory, be accorded all the safeguards provided for POWs under the treaties. But the opinion argued that, during the period of Taliban rule, Afghanistan was a "'failed State' whose territory has been largely overrun and held by violence by a militia or faction rather than by a government." As a result, members of the Taliban militia, like those of Al Qaeda, were "not entitled to the protections of the Geneva Conventions."

Finally, the draft memorandum maintained that, regardless of whether Afghanistan under the Taliban was considered a failed state or not, the president had the power, "[a]s a constitutional matter," to suspend some or all of the United States' obligations under the Geneva Conventions "during the current conflict." The power to suspend was discretionary, and could be based on the grounds that, for example, Afghanistan "lacked the capacity to fulfill its treaty obligations" or was in "material breach" of those obligations.

Controversy. The January 9 draft ruling sparked a vigorous debate between OLC and the State Department, which objected specifically to the findings that Afghanistan, as a failed state, had ceased to be a party to the Geneva Conventions, and that the President could suspend the nation's obligations under the Conventions, an assertion that William Taft IV, the legal adviser to the State Department, labeled "legally flawed and procedurally impossible at this stage." In a January 11, 2002, memo to Yoo, Taft wrote that the United States had "dealt with tens of thousands of detainees in past conflicts" without "repudiating its obligations under the Conventions." Only the "utmost confidence in our legal arguments"—which, Taft made clear, he did not have—could "justify deviating from the United States unbroken record of compliance with the Geneva Conventions over the past fifty years." In his response to Taft, Yoo politely but firmly rejected the State Department's arguments. Although the memorandum was revised, the final version, which was issued on January 22 with OLC head Jay Bybee's signature, was not altered in its major points.

Meanwhile, though, the State Department had taken its arguments to Gonzales, who discussed them in a draft memorandum to President Bush, dated January 25. In it, Gonzales summarized OLC's legal analysis of the treaties in regard to Al Qaeda and the Taliban, an interpretation that he termed "definitive." Although the President had already determined, on Gonzales's advice, that the Third Geneva Convention did not apply to Al Qaeda and the Taliban, Secretary of State Colin Powell "had requested," Gonzales wrote in his memo, "that you reconsider that decision." In his arguments, as presented by Gonzales, Powell asserted that, among other things, Bush's decision would mean that the United States could not invoke the protections of the Third Convention for its own forces if they fell into enemy hands in Afghanistan and, further, that it "would likely provoke widespread condemnation among our allies and in some domestic quarters...."

Gonzales, however, found these and other arguments marshaled by Powell "unpersuasive," and countered that the "new type of warfare" being waged in the war on terror had never been contemplated in 1949, when the Geneva Conventions were drawn up. The "nature of the new war," he wrote, placed a "high premium on...the ability to quickly obtain information from captured terrorists" and to try them for war crimes "such as wantonly killing civilians." This "new paradigm," Gonzales maintained, "renders obsolete Geneva's strict limitations on questioning of enemy prisoners...."

Bush's Decision. Secretary Powell tried one more time to advance his arguments in a January 26 memo to Gonzales, but it was a losing cause.[37] In the end, Bush accepted the legal conclusions of OLC, although he chose to act on them selectively. In a February 7 memorandum, the President agreed that he had the authority to "suspend Geneva as between the United States and Afghanistan," but declined to exercise it "at this time." Bush did, however, conclude that the provisions of Common Article 3 did not apply to either Al Qaeda or the Taliban and that, further, the Taliban detainees were "unlawful combatants" and, like the Al Qaeda captives, did not qualify as POWs under the Third Geneva Convention. But, he added, "our values as a Nation...call for us to treat detainees humanely, including those who are not legally entitled to such treatment." As a matter of policy, therefore, U.S. armed forces would be required to treat Al Qaeda and Taliban detainees humanely "and, to the extent appropriate and consistent with military necessity, in a manner consistent with the principles of Geneva."

The President's February 7 memo appeared to settle the issue of detainees in military custody at Guantanamo, although the ambiguous meaning of "to the extent appropriate and consistent with military necessity" could be said to leave the door open to a flexible interpretation of "humane" treatment. But the legal ground rules for interrogating the high-value captives—there were an estimated two to three dozen of them—being held by the CIA in secret detention centers overseas had yet to be spelled out. It was this matter that OLC took up, at Gonzales's request, in the summer of 2002. The resulting fifty-page document would later be known as the "torture memo."

The Torture Memo

The memorandum was at once a narrow interpretation of the meaning of torture under the law and a broad reading of presidential powers under the Constitution. Unlike previous memoranda on detainees, which focused on the Geneva Conventions, OLC's opinion on CIA-held captives addressed the issue of "standards of conduct" under the Convention against Torture and Other Cruel, Inhuman or Degrading Treatment or Punishment, as implemented in Sections 2340–2340A of Title 18 of the U.S. Code. That law specifically prohibited acts of torture "outside the United States" and attached severe penalties—including death—to violations of the statute. In its exegesis of the law, the OLC memorandum concluded that the "proscribed acts...must be of an extreme nature to rise to the level of torture within the meaning" of the law. It found, further, that "certain acts may be cruel, inhuman or degrading, but still not produce pain and suffering of the requisite intensity to fall within [the law's] proscription against torture."

Citing both dictionary definitions and statutory precedents,[38] the opinion found that "severe physical pain or suffering," as used in the implementing law, would have to reach the level associated with a "sufficiently serious physical condition or injury such as death, organ failure, or serious impairment of body functions" to meet the standard of torture. Similarly, the OLC opinion looked closely at the statutory language defining "severe mental pain or suffering" and concluded that it would mean "significant psychological harm of significant duration," lasting "for months or even years." The memorandum analyzed the four "predicate acts" causing "prolonged" mental pain, as listed in the law, to determine what would legally constitute torture. For example, in the case of "mind-altering substances," the memorandum argued that the law did not prohibit all use of drugs during interrogations; instead, it barred only those drugs that were, in the words of the statute, "calculated to disrupt profoundly the senses or the personality." To meet the standard implied by the word "profoundly," moreover, the drugs would, according to the OLC memorandum, have to "penetrate to the core of an individual's ability to perceive the world around him, substantially interfering with his cognitive abilities, or fundamentally alter his personality."

Furthermore, alluding to the use of the term "specifically intended" in the law, OLC determined that the infliction of both mental and physical pain would have to be done with "specific intent" to rise to the level of torture. This was distinct from "general intent"—that is, the knowledge that severe suffering "was reasonably likely to result" from an action. "As a theoretical matter," according to the memorandum, "knowledge alone that a particular result is certain to occur does not constitute specific intent." Even if a defendant knew that his actions would inflict severe mental or physical pain, "if causing such harm is not his objective, he lacks the requisite specific intent...." He would be "guilty of torture only if he acts with the express purpose of inflicting severe pain or suffering on a person within his custody or physical control."

The memorandum also returned to a theme that OLC had pursued in earlier post–September 11 opinions: the scope of presidential power in wartime. As before, it concluded that the President held sweeping constitutional powers in his role of commander-in-chief, which would take precedence over the mandates of the CAT implementing legislation. "Even if an interrogation method arguably were to violate Section 2340A," it asserted, "the statute would be unconstitutional if it impermissibly encroached on the President's constitutional power to conduct a military campaign."

To underscore the need for the untrammeled exercise of presidential authority in a time of war, the OLC opinion noted that the "situation in which these issues [addressed in the memorandum] arise is unprecedented in recent American history." After detailing the string of terrorist assaults on U.S. interests that culminated in the September 11 attacks, it observed that Al Qaeda "continues to plan further attacks" and that "the capture and interrogation of [terrorists] is clearly imperative to our national security and defense." As evidence, the opinion pointed to the case of José Padilla, a U.S. citizen who was alleged to have been involved in an Al Qaeda plot to detonate a "radioactive dispersal device"—popularly known as a "dirty bomb"—in the United States. It was, the memorandum said, the interrogation of Al Qaeda "operatives"—Abu Zubaida himself, according to the *New York Times*[39]—that "allegedly allowed US intelligence and law enforcement agencies" to track down and detain Padilla in May 2002.

But it was largely on constitutional grounds that OLC argued that presidential wartime powers essentially should trump the provisions of the anti-torture law. "In order to respect the President's inherent constitutional authority to manage a military campaign against al Qaeda and its allies," it declared, "Section 2340A must be construed as not applying to interrogations undertaken pursuant to his Commander-in-Chief authority." Congress, the memorandum continued, lacked "the authority under [the Constitution] to set the terms and conditions" under which the President wielded his powers "to control the conduct of operations during war." This applied as much to intelligence operations as it did to military ones. "Congress may no more regulate the President's ability to detain and interrogate enemy combatants than it may regulate his ability to direct troop movements on the battlefield." This authority, moreover, extended to those who did the chief executive's bidding in wartime. "These constitutional principles," the memorandum argued, "preclude an application of Section 2340A to punish officials for aiding the President in exercising his exclusive constitutional authorities.... [W]e conclude that the Department of Justice could not enforce Section 2340A against federal officials acting pursuant to the President's constitutional authority to wage a military campaign."[40]

Shaping the Opinion. According to his own account, John Yoo "helped draft the main memo defining torture," though he did not identify who else worked on it.[41] Later, when the torture memo was made public—like all OLC opinions relating to the war on terror, it was initially kept secret[42]—numerous accounts in the press, citing anonymous sources, gave Addington a major role in the development of the memorandum, maintaining that he had "helped shape" it or was even its "principal author."[43] Yoo strongly dismissed such depictions of the drafting process as "utterly without foundation in the truth." Although prohibited by the Justice Department, he wrote, from discussing the particulars of the torture memorandum, out of concern for "revealing confidential information," Yoo maintained that no one outside the department ever wrote "a single word" of any OLC opinion. Reports also surfaced that the State Department and the Department of Defense had not been shown the torture memo, but Yoo, without providing details, indicated that this would not be an unusual circumstance for opinions "involving intelligence matters." In such cases, the client intelligence agency, in conjunction with the White House counsel, normally decided who would review an OLC memo. "Sometimes," Yoo wrote obliquely, "neither State nor Defense lawyers would know about the opinion."[44]

Within the Justice Department, Yoo wrote, the memorandum on torture went through a "normal" review, though, in view of the sensitive nature of the issue, the draft opinion was shown only to a "restricted circle" within the department.[45] There were, however, contradictory reports in the press as to Attorney General John Ashcroft's involvement with the memorandum. According to a story in the *New York Times*, Justice Department officials said that the opinion had been sent "directly from the Legal Counsel's office to the White House and that they did not believe it had required the approval" of either Ashcroft or his deputy.[46] For his part, Yoo maintained that, in the words of one press account, "OLC kept the attorney general or his staff fully informed of all its work in the war on terrorism."[47]

Although some later would maintain that the memorandum on torture did not have, in the words of one observer, "the rhetoric of detachment" that normally characterized OLC opinions, the ruling appeared to have generated little controversy while it was being drafted. No one who reviewed it urged "significant changes" in the document, according to Yoo, nor did he recall any disagreements over its conclusions.[48]

Last Stop. After the memorandum on interrogation had been vetted, it was ready for Assistant Attorney General Jay Bybee, the head of the Office of Legal Counsel, to sign. Bybee's role in the drafting of the opinion was unclear; his name did not come up in descriptions of the "inner circle" of lawyers surrounding Addington or their discussions on the handling of detainees. Bybee had come to OLC relatively recently—he was appointed head of the office in October 2001, one month after the terrorist attacks—and he seemed likely to follow soon in the judicial footsteps of some of his predecessors. In May 2002, the Bush administration had nominated him to the Ninth Circuit Court of Appeals; his appointment was awaiting confirmation in the Senate. Bybee was described by those who knew him as "a pretty gentle soul," in the words of one, and as a "reflective" and undominating type. But he was "not an autopen machine" either, as another put it, who simply rubber-stamped opinions written by others.[49]

Whatever his involvement in the drafting process, Bybee would know that interest in the memo and in the issue of interrogation was strong among administration officials who worried about the nation's vulnerability to terrorists. At a White House meeting in July—reportedly attended by Yoo—to discuss interrogation techniques, one participant recalled that Gonzales, who had convened the gathering, was concerned to stay within the law, but equally concerned to forestall another attack on Americans. "Are we forward-leaning enough on this?" Gonzales was reported to have asked many times. "And the second part of that statement," the participant told the *Post*, "was always, 'Prevent an attack, save lives.' If Gonzales had any role in this, it was to be the fair arbiter of 'Are we doing enough?' "[50]

Once signed by Bybee, the memorandum would provide legal protections to CIA agents who sought to be "forward-leaning" in their interrogation of terror suspects abroad. An OLC opinion had "the weight of law," in the words of one report.[51] This meant essentially that if OLC determined that an act was legal, it would be difficult for the government later to prosecute someone who had relied on that determination. In view of the sense of urgency in the White House, there could be little doubt that it would exercise whatever legal authority it was given to the fullest extent. "We're going to live on the edge," General Michael Hayden, then Deputy Director of National Intelligence, was reported to say in describing the administration's counterterrorism philosophy. "My spikes will have chalk on them....We're pretty aggressive within the law. As a professional, I'm troubled if I'm not using the full authority allowed by law."[52]

15

Weighing Intangibles, Questioning Assumptions

Before looking at Bybee's decision and its consequences, we should pause to look at the ingredients of the decision. Its proponents were successful in getting the decision they (either White House Counsel Gonzalez or his superiors) wanted: a legal judgment that no one could be prosecuted even for torture, let alone for anything less. That political dimension of policy choice has been the subject of the first three parts of this book. But the decisions made would turn out to be mammoth failures in terms of taking account of predictable consequences and enjoying the staying power that a more legitimate process could bestow. Let us examine, first, what effort was made to identify all important classes of consequences and then to predict and assess them. I will begin with the overall government choice and, after that, look specifically at the decision by the Office of Legal Counsel (OLC).

What Was Omitted from the Broader Government Decision Process

Nowhere in the process leading up to the Bybee memo, nor in the series of discussions after that, does anyone seem to have carefully considered the categories of cost, or the doubts about benefits, associated with the decision the White House seems to have wanted.

Costs

The administration could readily have identified five types of costs. Even if they did not have the information to weigh each category accurately, each category had to be incorporated into the decision, with as much weight as it seemed to deserve. None seems to have been taken seriously.

- Stories about mistreatment would plainly make new enemies of the United States, strengthen the support among Islamic groups for terrorism, and embolden new terrorist recruits. That had been true during the Palestinian intifada against Israel.
- Coercive interrogation would also undermine the support we need at home for U.S. foreign policy objectives. Within the U.S. population, Bybee could anticipate a contest between support for our policies, generated by trust in the President or by the hope for democracy in Iraq, and opposition to these policies, generated not only by their cost in dollars and lives but also by the cost in national self-respect accompanying tales of cruel or degrading practices. A similar array of moral embarrassments had cost President Lyndon Johnson dearly in terms of support for a continued war in Vietnam. President Bush would later say we had made no greater mistake than Abu Ghraib.
- Highly coercive interrogation would be costly to our foreign relations with our closest allies. It would predictably alienate allies in Western democracies, making it, at a minimum, far harder to find coalition partners. Extradition and other exchanges would be inhibited.

  Inequality compounded this. There was much to be said for insisting that American citizens be subject to the same risks that would apply to foreigners abroad—no more and no less. This would minimize foreign resentment. But it would undermine support at home. The Bush administration decided to distinguish broadly between alien suspects from abroad and U.S. suspects and others within the United States. Except for two or three Americans, no American would be detained except for trial and, almost without exception, no American would be subjected to torture or, perhaps, any treatment that would be considered cruel, inhuman, and degrading. That would be manifestly untrue of our practices with regard to non-U.S. persons abroad, whether the subject was detention (of thousands) or highly coercive interrogation (of tens or hundreds).

- The practice would also eliminate U.S. capacity to criticize brutality by others in the world, and to play the role of moral

leader. We could hardly continue to lecture Egypt and/or Saudi
Arabia on brutality.
- Such interrogation might well endanger our soldiers in enemy
  hands now or in the future. The traditional military commitment to
  interpreting broadly, and then complying with, our legal obligations
  under the Geneva Conventions had been largely motivated by this.

Benefits

The advantages of authorizing highly coercive interrogation in any situation depend upon: how often it obtains the truth; whether we can tell
the truth from lies; if it works at all, how quickly it works; and how much
this technique can add to a variety of other ways of getting information
from an unwilling individual. Even if the information is only in the hands
of a particular individual—probably a rare occasion—there are a number
of alternatives to coercive interrogation.

No real effort was made until five years later, to determine whether
there were any reliable studies, or even accounts, of the efficacy of highly
coercive interrogation, let alone of its marginal benefits over alternatives.
(There were not.) Britain and Israel doubted the reliability of what each
had obtained from coercive interrogation (as opposed to results gained
from fear itself), but no one seems to have asked either ally.

In the absence of more solid evidence, a useful four-step check on the
benefits of particular tactics and strategies in the fight against terrorism is:
First, specify the benefits we anticipate from the actions we are thinking
of taking. Then, second, list the most important assumptions on which
the belief in those likely benefits is based. Third, ask if there are alternative assumptions that are also plausible and which, if true, would lead to
different consequences. If so, we must probe further into the particular
choice of actions. If there are—and there often will be—alternative plausible assumptions under which the benefits sought would not materialize, we must then, fourth, look for evidence that bears on the likelihood
of one or another of the competing assumptions being correct. If the
evidence starts to point in the direction of an alternative assumption that
would undermine the reasons for the actions we are considering taking,
we must reject the proposed actions.

Taking such steps with regard to highly coercive interrogation would
not have been reassuring. The practice would, in all likelihood, produce
some spoken answer to questions, but the assumption that the person

interrogated would generally tell the truth was no more likely than that he would provide a lie intended to mislead, or would say whatever he thought would please the interrogator. The alternatives were at least as plausible.

Even regarding the "ticking bomb," the strongest case, nobody questioned the assumptions underlying the belief that coercive interrogation would be helpful. How frequently would we have the wrong person? Even if we had the right person, would he be likely to hold out until the information he had was no longer useful? Was he likely to lie, perhaps in a clever way developed and taught by his organization? Even if a particular plan was stopped, wouldn't his colleagues change the plan and substitute another?

Finally, nobody assessed the marginal advantage of coercive interrogation in various situations. Federal law enforcement relies on recruiting informants, electronic surveillance, and placing law enforcement agents undercover within an organization to obtain information from individuals who would not willingly disclose it without being deceived in one of these ways. Physical surveillance could be added to that list. Even when U.S. law enforcement wants to extract information from an individual disinclined to talk, it relies on relatively noncoercive interrogation (after Miranda rights have been waived) or the threat of far longer sentences for an individual who does not cooperate in furnishing information. If the practices that OLC approved were likely to be very costly—as they were—it was important to assess how much the power to engage in coercive interrogation would add to our store of information in light of the available alternatives. The FBI thought little would be added.

What Was Omitted from Even the Narrowest of OLC Roles

Even if a wise decision would have required a much more farsighted and inclusive look at the consequences of the government's options on highly coercive interrogation, perhaps many of the types of consequences should have been addressed outside the Office of Legal Counsel. A legal judgment might have been sought only to define the outer bounds of decisions whose contours would later be set by others. But, from what we know after the release of this and many other memos, the legal definitions of outer bounds seem to have, almost mechanically, defined the administration's choice of wise actions. Recognizing this might well have demanded that Bybee take a broader view of his responsibilities.

Even with the relatively constrained role of looking only to the legal implications of highly coercive interrogation, OLC should have considered the costs of lost respect for U.S. legality. This concern alone was powerful enough to cause the Senate in September 2006 to repudiate, overwhelmingly, one of OLC's positions: that Common Article 3 of the Geneva Conventions did not apply in the war against terror. Our national pride in the rule of law and the tendency of other nations to judge us by that self-proclaimed standard should have cautioned against very strained interpretations of our obligations—interpretations difficult for others to accept as adopted in good faith. Yet, the interpretations were very strained indeed.

Much has been written about the exceedingly narrow definition of torture, the careful development for the CIA of defenses to even that narrow definition, and of the claim that neither treaties nor statutes could bind the President if he claimed to be acting in the name of national security. Less well known was the secret interpretation of the words of our reservation to the Torture Convention, which set limits on our understanding of a second prohibition in the Convention against "cruel, inhuman, and degrading" treatment. We agreed to prohibit only conduct forbidden by three Amendments to our Constitution—mainly conduct that would "shock the conscience"—and not lesser forms of interrogation. We could easily live with that.[1] Instead, an opinion of the Department of Justice decided that, since these Constitutional provisions do not generally apply to aliens abroad, our apparent acceptance of a reasonable treaty obligation not to do anything shocking to an American conscience was largely illusory; it applied only to interrogators within the United States and not in Abu Ghraib or Guantanamo or Afghanistan.

We do not know the precise effects of adopting such an implausibly narrow interpretation of our treaty obligations. We do know that it is of great value to us as a nation that we can make promises that can be taken as reliable in the form they are likely to be understood by the recipient states. This commitment to our promises is not inspired by a fear that the United States will be sanctioned for violating a treaty obligation; there may be such a sanction, but that would be rare, and its use and practice would be even rarer. International agreements are far more frequently supported by the mutual benefits of compliance with promises. We enter into them because we care about other nations complying. If we ignore our commitments, or interpret them in an unreasonably narrow manner, we can expect to receive less from the commitments that were made in exchange for our promises.

More broadly, nations develop reputational value from being law-abiding and promise-keeping. That a loss to that reputation would be an area of potential cost from ignoring either the Geneva Conventions or the Convention Against Torture and Other Cruel, Inhuman or Degrading Treatment or Punishment was clear, but what weight it should be given was far less clear. What is clear is that it was the obligation of OLC to raise that issue. In the area of these particular treaties, and perhaps more generally of human rights agreements, the subject matter may be sufficiently distinct and isolated as not to bear on some of our other commitments in, for example, the fields of trade or national security. If so, then we would have to know how much we had to gain from others' compliance with treaties in the area of human rights or the humanitarian laws of war; and we would have to assess whether there was some reason to think that the extent of compliance by others would be affected by our actions.

Our early interpretations of the Geneva Conventions and the Convention Against Torture and Other Cruel, Inhuman or Degrading Treatment or Punishment were stretched beyond what others would believe were good faith interpretations of our promises. That applied to the severity the administration said was required if something was to be considered torture. It applied to the administration's interpretation of cruel, inhuman, and degrading punishment, the effect of which was to make our promise applicable only within the United States (where the Constitution already forbade what we agreed to forbid) and not outside the United States. This interpretation would have seemed implausible to any state entering into the treaty in partial reliance on the benefits to be realized from U.S. promises. Although we cannot easily weigh the costs of this loss of credibility, we cannot safely ignore it.

On a domestic stage, Bybee had to consider the effect of a highly implausible secret interpretation of the law, responsive to a request of the White House, on the legitimacy of future opinions of OLC. He was undermining the capacity of any future President or Attorney General to assert persuasively the legality of an activity not subject to judicial review.

Even a constrained sense of his responsibilities should have caused Bybee to address these likely consequences. Even without being able to weigh them with any precision, OLC could try to reduce them by carefully specifying the circumstances in which highly coercive interrogation could be used. But that creates still another cost, which is the most difficult of all to measure: the risk that whatever highly coercive interrogation they approved for the CIA would spread from the limited area in which it was to be permitted to broader and broader areas: from ticking bombs to strategic intelligence; from foreigners to resident aliens to American citizens; and from use against terrorism to criminal drug trafficking and then to ordinary crimes. We know how to write standards and how to allocate responsibility for decisions and even how to monitor those decisions with devices of legislative or judicial oversight. OLC never considered such possibilities. That we cannot know how these efforts to control and direct discretion would apply when an administration believes we are at war and can keep what it does secret, does not, in the cold light of history, justify the costs we bore from that omission.

With a process that ignored major categories of consequences, the outcome was not promising.

Defining Torture in the War on Terror: The Trail of the "Torture Memo" A Case History by Esther Scott

On August 1, 2002, the Justice Department's Office of Legal Counsel (OLC) issued a memorandum to Alberto Gonzales, then White House counsel to President George W. Bush, on "standards of interrogation" under U.S. law.[2] The OLC opinion was signed by the head of the office, Assistant Attorney General Jay Bybee, though it was widely believed to have been authored by Deputy Assistant Attorney General John Yoo. The ruling had, as we have seen, been sought at the request of the Central Intelligence Agency (CIA), which was conducting interrogations of detainees captured on the battlefields of Afghanistan and elsewhere and held in secret detention centers overseas. As a signatory to the Convention against Torture and Other Cruel, Inhuman or Degrading Treatment or Punishment, the United States had enacted legislation in 1994 criminalizing the use of torture outside the country and imposing stiff penalties on offenders. The CIA was concerned that its agents would face prosecution under the law for using "enhanced interrogation techniques" on suspected members of the Al Qaeda terrorist organization, the perpetrators of the September 11, 2001 attacks on the United States.

In essence, the August 1 opinion—later dubbed the "torture memo"—narrowly defined torture to encompass only extreme acts that inflicted physical pain at a level associated with "death, organ failure, or serious impairment of body functions," or mental pain or suffering that caused "significant psychological harm" lasting "for months or even years."

Moreover, the memorandum concluded that enforcement of the 1994 anti-torture statute, "in the circumstances of the current war against al Qaeda and its allies," could represent an "unconstitutional infringement" on the President's broad wartime powers as commander-in-chief.

Once issued, the OLC opinion, which was then kept secret, provided legal protection to CIA agents who would be employing—or, as was later reported in the press, had already employed—coercive interrogation techniques ranging from hooding to sleep deprivation to waterboarding (or simulated drowning) on "high-value" detainees who refused to reveal what they knew about Al Qaeda's terrorist network. But while the OLC memorandum on torture was written specifically to address the concerns of the CIA, its findings would prove to have a wider influence. Over time, the legal rationale it provided for questioning by CIA agents would be applied to military interrogations conducted at the U.S. naval base in Guantanamo Bay, Cuba, where some high-value detainees were also being held. From there, some would later argue, the aggressive techniques sanctioned by the OLC opinion "migrated" to military facilities in Afghanistan and later in Iraq, where revelations about the abusive treatment of detainees in the Abu Ghraib prison would become an international embarrassment for the United States.

The Abu Ghraib scandal in April 2004, and the subsequent public release of administration memos and OLC rulings, sparked debate in the United States and outrage abroad over the handling of detainees suspected of aiding Al Qaeda's violent anti-U.S. agenda. Those who opposed the administration's espousal of enhanced interrogation techniques deplored what they saw as gross violations of international treaties—the Geneva Conventions as well as the Convention against Torture—and the domestic legislation that enforced their terms. Those who supported it pointed to what they viewed as important intelligence gains—particularly in identifying Al Qaeda leaders and disrupting the organization's operations. Ultimately, the debate made its way to the halls of Congress, where an influential Senator faced off against the administration over the treatment of prisoners captured in the "war on terror."

Military Interrogations at Guantanamo

The detention center at Guantanamo opened in January 2002, and by that fall its population had swelled to over 600 detainees, "culled," as the *New York Times* put it, from roughly 10,000 prisoners captured during the war in Afghanistan. Later, there would be some dispute over how dangerous or important the Guantanamo detainees were; while administration officials labeled them as "the worst of a very bad lot," in Vice President Richard Cheney's words, others characterized them as mostly "low-level militants" or, in some cases, "simply innocents in the wrong place at the wrong time."³ Nevertheless, the Guantanamo detainee population did include some high-value Al Qaeda operatives, most notably Mohammed al-Kahtani, the so-called "twentieth hijacker," who had been refused entry into the United States and therefore prevented from participating in the September 11 attacks. It was, according to some accounts, frustration with al-Kahtani's reticence that prompted the military to seek permission to use rougher methods to make him talk.

The Rules. Normally, interrogations conducted by military intelligence officers were expected to adhere to guidelines laid down in Army Field Manual 34–52, "Intelligence Interrogation," which had last been revised in 1992. The manual listed seventeen "interrogation techniques" that could be used in questioning detainees—such as "emotional love" and "emotional hate," "fear up (harsh)" and "fear up (mild)," and "pride and ego up" and "pride and ego down." Although the techniques were "described in broad terms," as one report put it, and left "room for creativity in their implementation,"⁴ the field manual stipulated that interrogators must comply with the principles of both the Geneva Conventions and U.S. policy, which "expressly prohibit acts of violence or intimidation, including physical or mental torture, threats, insults, or exposure to inhuman treatment as a means or aid to interrogation." Those who violated these strictures were liable to punishment under the Uniform Code of Military Justice.

The methods listed in the manual, however, proved ineffective with al-Kahtani. When, late in 2002, there was, according to General James Hill, commander of the U.S. Southern Command (SOUTHCOM), "a spike in a lot of intel [i.e., intelligence] that we were picking up in terms of more attacks" on the United States, military interrogators grew impatient with al-Kahtani's silence.⁵ The concern over possible attacks and pressure to provide the administration with useful intelligence led officers at Guantanamo to request a loosening of the rules for questioning recalcitrant detainees like al-Kahtani. "We'd been at this for a year-plus and got nothing out of them," one remarked, and "we need[ed] to have a less-cramped view of what torture is and is not."⁶

The Quest for New Interrogation Techniques. On October 11, 2002, the head of Joint Task Force 170, an intelligence unit at Guantanamo, forwarded to General Hill of SOUTHCOM a memo requesting approval of new interrogation procedures to "counter advanced resistance" from detainees. The memo outlined eighteen different techniques, organized into three categories. Category I comprised two relatively mild techniques—yelling and various forms of deception. By contrast, there were twelve Category II techniques, including stress positions, such as standing, for a maximum of four hours; isolation for up to thirty days; hooding; removal of clothing; and using detainees' "individual phobias" to "induce stress." There were only four Category III techniques, which were intended only for "the most uncooperative detainees": the use of "scenarios" to convince a detainee that "death or severely painful consequences are imminent for him and/or his family"; exposure to cold weather or water; waterboarding, here defined as use of a "wet towel and dripping water" to induce a sense of suffocation; and use of "mild, non-injurious physical contact such as grabbing, poking in the chest with the finger, and light pushing." Interrogators would need permission from their superiors to use either Category II or III techniques.

Two weeks later, Hill sent the memo, along with a legal analysis by a staff judge advocate at Guantanamo, to the chairman of the Joint Chiefs of Staff. In his cover memo, Hill noted that "despite our best efforts, some detainees have tenaciously resisted our current interrogation methods." While acknowledging concern about the legality of the Category III techniques, particularly the death threats to detainees or their families, Hill also wrote of the need to "provide our interrogators with as many legally permissible tools as possible" in order to "maximize the value of our intelligence collection mission."

In the end, military interrogators got some, but not all, of what they sought. On November 27, William Haynes, general counsel at the Department of Defense (DOD), sent a memo to Defense Secretary Donald Rumsfeld recommending that he authorize the use of all of the Category I and II techniques, but only one of the Category III—the "mild, non-injurious physical contact." While the other techniques in that category might be "legally available," Haynes wrote, "we believe that, as a matter of policy, a blanket approval of Category III techniques is not warranted at this time. Our Armed Forces are trained to a standard of interrogation that reflects a tradition of restraint." Several days later, on December 2, 2002, Rumsfeld approved Haynes's recommendations.[7]

Objections. Though the memos on military interrogation were kept secret, it did not take long for word of the new techniques and their effects to percolate up from Guantanamo. It reached the ears of Alberto Mora, then the Navy general counsel, on December 17, when a colleague told him that some detainees were, as he wrote in a July 2004 memo, "being subjected to physical abuse and degrading treatment." The logs of al-Kahtani's interrogation revealed that, among other things, he had been isolated for 160 days in a room that was lit artificially around the clock; subjected to interrogations that lasted from 18–20 hours at a stretch; stripped naked; straddled by female guards; forced to wear women's underwear on his head; and threatened by dogs. He was also reported to have been made to wear a leash and bark like a dog, deprived of sleep, and kept in a cold room.[8]

Eventually, Mora was shown copies of the memos on the new interrogation techniques, which he quickly concluded "should not have been authorized because some (but not all) of them, whether applied singly or in combination, could produce effects reaching the level of torture...." Even if they did not reach that level, he noted in his July 2004 memo, "they almost certainly would constitute 'cruel, inhuman, or degrading treatment,' another class of unlawful treatment."[9]

Mora took his objections to Haynes, and, at least initially, it did appear that his concerns were heard. On January 15, 2003, Rumsfeld issued a memorandum rescinding the use of Category II and III techniques at Guantanamo. At the same time, he ordered the establishment of a "working group" within DOD to "assess the legal, policy, and operational issues relating to the interrogations of detainees held by the US Armed Forces in the war on terrorism." As it would turn out, the Office of Legal Counsel would play a key role in the group's deliberations.

The Working Group. The group—chiefly composed of representatives from various legal units within DOD and headed by Air Force General Counsel Mary Walker—began meeting in January 2003 and was almost immediately engulfed in "sometimes contentious debate," in the words of a March 2005 report to Rumsfeld on detainee operations and interrogations written by Vice Admiral A. T. Church. The source of the controversy appeared to be a draft legal memorandum prepared by OLC and first circulated among group members sometime in late January. While the OLC memo was never made public, it was reported to track closely—"virtually word for word," according to one later account[10]—the legal arguments of the August 1, 2002, memorandum on torture. Its principal author, it turned out, was John Yoo.

The OLC draft memo met with strong objections from some members of the DOD legal community. Mora, for example, wrote that he found it "profoundly in error," first in holding that cruel, inhuman or degrading treatment was "authorized with few restrictions or conditions," and second, in espousing "an extreme and virtually unlimited theory" of the President's powers as commander-in-chief. Also worrisome to Mora and others, the opinion appeared to shape the findings of the working group. Contributions from its members, Mora noted in his July 2004 memo, "began to be rejected if they did not conform to the OLC guidance."

A number of judge advocates general[11] and other lawyers at DOD detailed their concerns with OLC's analysis, as well as with the working group's draft reports based on it, in a series of memoranda; but once the final version of the OLC opinion—entitled, "Military Interrogation of Alien Unlawful Combatants Held Outside the United States"—was issued on March 14, 2003, internal debate appeared to come to a halt. Later, during a July 2005 Senate hearing, Senator Carl Levin, D-Mich., quoting an apparently classified section of the report by Admiral Church, said that the March 14 memo became the "controlling authority" on all legal issues addressed by the group.[12] This was confirmed by a DOD deputy general counsel, who told a Senate hearing that the March 14 memorandum was a "binding legal document" that governed Defense Department policy on interrogations.[13]

The Report. On April 14, 2003, the working group issued its final report. Unlike earlier drafts, which had been circulated within DOD, the final version, over seventy pages long, was given only to Rumsfeld. In it, the group provided a lengthy legal analysis, modeled on the OLC opinion—and, in some instances, directly incorporating language from the original torture memo. After a discussion of various "considerations" affecting policy determinations, the report enumerated a total of thirty-five interrogation techniques "believed to be effective but with varying degrees of utility." The first seventeen were largely the same as those contained in the Army field manual on interrogation. The next nine offered a variety of harsher techniques, including hooding, mild physical contact, dietary and environmental manipulation, and "sleep adjustment." The remaining nine were described as "more aggressive counter-resistance techniques that may be appropriate for detainees who are extremely resistant" to the first twenty-six. These included isolation, prolonged interrogations, prolonged standing, sleep deprivation, removal of clothing, and "increasing anxiety by use of aversion." Reportedly, an earlier version of the working group report, dated March 6, had listed a thirty-sixth technique—waterboarding—but that was later dropped.

The working group recommended that all thirty-five methods be approved for use with "unlawful combatants," but added that the last nine "exceptional" techniques should be hedged around with "specific limitations"—they should, for example, be used only by specially trained interrogators who had received senior-level approval and were appropriately supervised. Rumsfeld, however, chose to pare down the options for interrogators. In an April 16 memorandum to the commander of SOUTHCOM, he authorized twenty-four techniques, omitting all nine in the "exceptional" group, as well as hooding and mild physical contact in the middle group. Use of the techniques was limited to unlawful combatants at Guantanamo; and four of them—incentive/incentive removed, pride and ego down, "mutt and jeff" (i.e., a harsh interrogator paired with a friendly one), and isolation—would require a determination of "military necessity" and notification of Rumsfeld himself in advance (see Figure 15.1).[14]

Rumsfeld's memo—like the final report of the working group—was not shown to critics in the Department of Defense.[15] Internal debate over detainee treatment largely subsided, as military interrogators—and their CIA counterparts—proceeded with their work at Guantanamo and at overseas detention centers, respectively. The public knew little of what went on at these facilities or who was being detained there. Aside from scattered stories in the press, which aroused little outcry outside of the human rights community, the treatment of detainees did not command the attention of a nation preoccupied with the prosecution of the war in Iraq. It was not until the end of April 2004, when the first photographs of Abu Ghraib prisoners surfaced, that the issue of torture came under strong scrutiny from the media and the public.

Abu Ghraib and Its Repercussions. On April 24, 2004, the CBS program *60 Minutes II* aired photographs of naked Iraqi prisoners at Abu Ghraib being forced by their military guards into a variety of humiliating positions: stacked in human pyramids, simulating sex, being menaced by dogs.

UNCLASSIFIED

~~SECRET//NOFORN~~

THE SECRETARY OF DEFENSE
1000 DEFENSE PENTAGON
WASHINGTON, DC 20301-1000

APR 1 6 2003

MEMORANDUM FOR THE COMMANDER, US SOUTHERN COMMAND

SUBJECT: Counter-Resistance Techniques in the War on Terrorism (S)

(U) I have considered the report of the Working Group that I directed be established on January 15, 2003.

(U) I approve the use of specified counter-resistance techniques, subject to the following:

(U) a. The techniques I authorize are those lettered A-X, set out at Tab A.

(U) b. These techniques must be used with all the safeguards described at Tab B.

(U) c. Use of these techniques is limited to interrogations of unlawful combatants held at Guantanamo Bay, Cuba.

(U) d. Prior to the use of these techniques, the Chairman of the Working Group on Detainee Interrogations in the Global War on Terrorism must brief you and your staff.

(U) I reiterate that US Armed Forces shall continue to treat detainees humanely and, to the extent appropriate and consistent with military necessity, in a manner consistent with the principles of the Geneva Conventions. In addition, if you intend to use techniques B, I, O, or X, you must specifically determine that military necessity requires its use and notify me in advance.

(U) If, in your view, you require additional interrogation techniques for a particular detainee, you should provide me, via the Chairman of the Joint Chiefs of Staff, a written request describing the proposed technique, recommended safeguards, and the rationale for applying it with an identified detainee.

(U) Nothing in this memorandum in any way restricts your existing authority to maintain good order and discipline among detainees.

Attachments:
As stated

classified Under Authority of Executive Order 12958
Executive Secretary, Office of the Secretary of Defense
lliam P. Marriott, CAPT, USN
e 18, 2004

NOT RELEASABLE TO
FOREIGN NATIONALS

UNCLASSIFIED

Classified By: Secretary of
Defense
Reason: 1.5(a)
Declassify On: 2 April 2013

Figure 15.1. A

TAB A

INTERROGATION TECHNIQUES

(U) The use of techniques A - X is subject to the general safeguards as provided below as well as specific implementation guidelines to be provided by the appropriate authority. Specific implementation guidance with respect to techniques A - Q is provided in Army Field Manual 34-52. Further implementation guidance with respect to techniques R - X will need to be developed by the appropriate authority.

(U) Of the techniques set forth below, the policy aspects of certain techniques should be considered to the extent those policy aspects reflect the views of other major U.S. partner nations. Where applicable, the description of the technique is annotated to include a summary of the policy issues that should be considered before application of the technique.

A. (U) Direct: Asking straightforward questions.

B. (U) Incentive/Removal of Incentive: Providing a reward or removing a privilege, above and beyond those that are required by the Geneva Convention, from detainees. [Caution: Other nations that believe that detainees are entitled to POW protections may consider that provision and retention of religious items (e.g., the Koran) are protected under international law (see, Geneva III, Article 34). Although the provisions of the Geneva Convention are not applicable to the interrogation of unlawful combatants, consideration should be given to these views prior to application of the technique.]

C. (U) Emotional Love: Playing on the love a detainee has for an individual or group.

D. (U) Emotional Hate: Playing on the hatred a detainee has for an individual or group.

E. (U) Fear Up Harsh: Significantly increasing the fear level in a detainee.

F. (U) Fear Up Mild: Moderately increasing the fear level in a detainee.

G. (U) Reduced Fear: Reducing the fear level in a detainee.

H. (U) Pride and Ego Up: Boosting the ego of a detainee.

Classified By:	Secretary of Defense
Reason:	1.5(a)
Declassify On:	2 April 2013

Tab A

Figure 15.1. B

I. (U) Pride and Ego Down: Attacking or insulting the ego of a detainee, not beyond the limits that would apply to a POW. [Caution: Article 17 of Geneva III provides, "Prisoners of war who refuse to answer may not be threatened, insulted, or exposed to any unpleasant or disadvantageous treatment of any kind." *Other nations that believe that detainees are entitled to* POW protections may consider this technique inconsistent with the provisions of Geneva. Although the provisions of Geneva are not applicable to the interrogation of unlawful combatants, consideration should be given to these views prior to application of the technique.]

J. (U) Futility: Invoking the feeling of futility of a detainee.

K. (U) We Know All: Convincing the detainee that the interrogator knows the answer to questions he asks the detainee.

L. (U) Establish Your Identity: Convincing the detainee that the interrogator has mistaken the detainee for someone else.

M. (U) Repetition Approach: Continuously repeating the same question to the detainee within interrogation periods of normal duration.

N. (U) File and Dossier: Convincing detainee that the interrogator has a damning and inaccurate file, which must be fixed.

O. (U) *Mutt and Jeff: A team consisting of a friendly and harsh* interrogator. The harsh interrogator might employ the Pride and Ego Down technique. [Caution: Other nations that believe that POW protections apply to detainees may view this technique as inconsistent with Geneva III, Article 13 which provides that POWs must be protected against acts of intimidation. Although the provisions of Geneva are not applicable to the interrogation of unlawful combatants, consideration should be given to these views prior to application of the technique.]

P. (U) Rapid Fire: Questioning in rapid succession without allowing detainee to answer.

Q. (U) Silence: Staring at the detainee to encourage discomfort.

R. (U) Change of Scenery Up: Removing the detainee from the standard interrogation setting (generally to a location more pleasant, but no worse).

S. (U) Change of Scenery Down: Removing the detainee from the standard interrogation setting and placing him in a setting that may be less comfortable; would not constitute a substantial change in environmental quality.

T. (U) Dietary Manipulation: Changing the diet of a detainee; no intended deprivation of food or water; no adverse medical or cultural effect and without intent to deprive subject of food or water, e.g., hot rations to MREs.

Figure 15.1. C

U. (U) Environmental Manipulation: Altering the environment to create moderate discomfort (e.g., adjusting temperature or introducing an unpleasant smell). Conditions would not be such that they would injure the detainee. Detainee would be accompanied by interrogator at all times. [Caution: Based on court cases in other countries, some nations may view application of this technique in certain circumstances to be inhumane. Consideration of these views should be given prior to use of this technique.]

V. (U) Sleep Adjustment: Adjusting the sleeping times of the detainee (e.g., reversing sleep cycles from night to day.) This technique is NOT sleep deprivation.

W. (U) False Flag: Convincing the detainee that individuals from a country other than the United States are interrogating him.

X. (U) Isolation: Isolating the detainee from other detainees while still complying with basic standards of treatment. [Caution: The use of isolation as an interrogation technique requires detailed implementation instructions, including specific guidelines regarding the length of isolation, medical and psychological review, and approval for extensions of the length of isolation by the appropriate level in the chain of command. This technique is not known to have been generally used for interrogation purposes for longer than 30 days. Those nations that believe detainees are subject to POW protections may view use of this technique as inconsistent with the requirements of Geneva III, Article 13 which provides that POWs must be protected against acts of intimidation; Article 14 which provides that POWs are entitled to respect for their person; Article 34 which prohibits coercion and Article 126 which ensures access and basic standards of treatment. Although the provisions of Geneva are not applicable to the interrogation of unlawful combatants, consideration should be given to these views prior to application of the technique.]

Tab A

Figure 15.1. D

TAB B

GENERAL SAFEGUARDS

(U) Application of these interrogation techniques is subject to the following general safeguards: (i) limited to use only at strategic interrogation facilities; (ii) there is a good basis to believe that the detainee possesses critical intelligence; (iii) the detainee is medically and operationally evaluated as suitable (considering all techniques to be used in combination); (iv) interrogators are specifically trained for the technique(s); (v) a specific interrogation plan (including reasonable safeguards, limits on duration, intervals between applications, termination criteria and the presence or availability of qualified medical personnel) has been developed; (vi) there is appropriate supervision; and, (vii) there is appropriate specified senior approval for use with any specific detainee (after considering the foregoing and receiving legal advice).

(U) The purpose of all interviews and interrogations is to get the most information from a detainee with the least intrusive method, always applied in a humane and lawful manner with sufficient oversight by trained investigators or interrogators. Operating instructions must be developed based on command policies to insure uniform, careful, and safe application of any interrogations of detainees.

(U) Interrogations must always be planned, deliberate actions that take into account numerous, often interlocking factors such as a detainee's current and past performance in both detention and interrogation, a detainee's emotional and physical strengths and weaknesses, an assessment of possible approaches that may work on a certain detainee in an effort to gain the trust of the detainee, strengths and weaknesses of interrogators, and augmentation by other personnel for a certain detainee based on other factors.

(U) Interrogation approaches are designed to manipulate the detainee's emotions and weaknesses to gain his willing cooperation. Interrogation operations are never conducted in a vacuum; they are conducted in close cooperation with the units detaining the individuals. The policies established by the detaining units that pertain to searching, silencing, and segregating also play a role in the interrogation of a detainee. Detainee interrogation involves developing a plan tailored to an individual and approved by senior interrogators. Strict adherence to policies/standard operating procedures governing the administration of interrogation techniques and oversight is essential.

Classified By: Secretary of Defense
Reason: 1.5(a)
Declassify On: 2 April 2013

Tab B

Figure 15.1. E

Other graphic images on television and in the press soon followed. One much-reprinted photo showed a hooded man standing on a box with wires attached to his body—he had been told that if he fell off the box, he would be electrocuted—and another, a man being dragged on a leash by a female guard; many featured American soldiers grinning and giving thumbs-up signs next to their victims.

The ugly photographs and the harrowing narratives of abuse that accompanied them—widely carried in the media—shocked the nation and the world, and unleashed a torrent of criticism at home and abroad. Overseas, the image of the United States took a battering, as first the pictures from Abu Ghraib and, later, stories of secret CIA detention centers in foreign nations appeared in the press. Coupled with the growing unpopularity of the war in Iraq in many countries, these revelations took their toll abroad. A June 2006 study by the Pew Research Center showed steady erosion in "favorable opinions" of the United States in most of the nations surveyed (see Figure 15.2).

Further revelations followed the Abu Ghraib scandal. In June 2004, press stories appeared on two secret documents—the March 6, 2003, draft of the Pentagon working group's report, portions of which were

Favorable Opinions of the U.S.

	1999/2000 %	2002 %	2003 %	2004 %	2005 %	2006 %
Great Britain	83	75	70	58	55	56
France	62	63	43	37	43	39
Germany	78	61	45	38	41	37
Spain	50	—	38	—	41	23
Russia	37	61	36	47	52	43
Indonesia	75	61	15	—	38	30
Egypt	—	—	—	—	—	30
Pakistan	23	10	13	21	23	27
Jordan	—	25	1	5	21	15
Turkey	52	30	15	30	23	12
Nigeria	46	—	61	—	—	62
Japan	77	72	—	—	—	63
India	—	54	—	—	71	56
China	—	—	—	—	42	47

1999/2000 survey trends provided by the Office of Research, U.S. Department of State

Figure 15.2

leaked to the *Wall Street Journal*, and OLC's seminal memo on torture, leaked to the *Washington Post*. In addition, the *Post* reported on June 12 that Lieutenant General Ricardo Sanchez, the senior military officer in Iraq, had "borrowed heavily from a list of high-pressure tactics" approved for use at Guantanamo and had permitted "senior officials" at Abu Ghraib to employ them. They comprised a mix of techniques, including some that Rumsfeld had initially okayed and then rescinded his approval in January 2003 after objections were raised.[16]

The leaked documents further stoked the furor over Abu Ghraib and raised the question of whether they had led to the abuse of Iraqi detainees—who were, unlike the "unlawful combatants" captured in Afghanistan and elsewhere, considered by the administration to be protected under the terms of the Geneva Conventions. While there was little argument that some of the techniques used at Guantanamo had migrated to military detention facilities in Afghanistan and Iraq, there was disagreement over their connection to events at Abu Ghraib specifically. Military and administration officials generally maintained that the abuses there were aberrations, the handiwork of a few "bad apples," or the result of terrible conditions at the prison, confusion over the proper conduct of interrogations, and a breakdown of military discipline. Critics, however, believed they could trace a direct line from the findings of the OLC torture memo to the harsher interrogation methods used first by the CIA overseas and then by the military at Guantanamo, and from there to the brutal treatment of detainees at Abu Ghraib.

Whatever the true cause of the abuses at Abu Ghraib, the photographs and the subsequent leaks had the effect of prying open the door to the Bush administration's internal deliberations on the handling of detainees in the war on terror. On June 22, the White House abruptly released hundreds of pages of previously classified documents—fourteen documents in all, including the torture memo. Administration officials maintained that the documents would demonstrate that the President had "never authorized torture against detainees," the *Post* reported. "All interrogation techniques actually authorized," White House Counsel Alberto Gonzales declared, "have been carefully vetted, are lawful and do not constitute torture."[17]

The Torture Issue. The document release served to shine a spotlight, uncomfortably, on the torture memo in particular. In a White House briefing the day the documents were made public, Gonzales appeared to distance himself from the OLC opinion. The administration's internal debate on interrogation policy had included, he said, "unnecessary, overbroad discussions." The OLC memo and "a related Pentagon memo" had been meant, Gonzales explained, to "explore the limits of the legal landscape" and had "never made it to the hands of the soldiers in the field, nor to the president." The Justice Department was more blunt. The OLC opinion, said one "senior" Justice official, was "overbroad and irrelevant" and would be rewritten.[18]

By this time, both Jay Bybee and John Yoo had left the Office of Legal Counsel—Bybee in March 2003 to take a seat on the Federal Appeals Court, and Yoo that summer to resume teaching law at the University of California at Berkeley.[19] Bybee's replacement, Jack Goldsmith—who had worked in the general counsel's office at DOD before assuming the OLC post in October 2003—had, it would later emerge, already taken aim at another opinion written by Yoo: the March 14, 2003, memorandum, still unreleased, that had been the "controlling authority" for the Pentagon working group's deliberations. In December 2003, months before the Abu Ghraib scandal broke, Goldsmith had advised DOD General Counsel William Haynes that, in the words of one account, the March 14 memorandum "was under review by [OLC] and should not be relied upon for any purpose."[20] It was, *Newsweek* asserted, "almost unheard-of for an administration to overturn its own OLC opinions."[21]

While the general public knew little about the March 14 opinion, the August 1, 2002, memo was widely quoted in the media and became the subject of intense debate. Among other things, it raised the question of whether the use of enhanced interrogation techniques was effective, and therefore perhaps justified. Although the public seemed troubled by the use of torture, or techniques that approached it, there appeared to be some willingness to resort to it if it would protect the nation from further attack. According to one *Newsweek* poll, 51 percent of respondents said that torture was "rarely or never justified," while 44 percent said that torture was "often or sometimes justified as a way to obtain important information...." However, 58 percent said they would support torture if it would "thwart a terrorist attack."[22]

Proponents of coercive interrogation argued that it had in fact proven successful in extracting information that aided the administration's efforts to uncover terrorist plots. As examples, they offered the case of Ibn al-Shaykh al-Libi, a Libyan detainee captured in November 2001, who had "pointed officials in the direction" of Abu Zubaida, a top Al

Qaeda lieutenant; Zubaida, in turn, had helped identify Khalid Sheikh Mohammed, believed to be the mastermind of the September 11 attacks, as well as José Padilla, who was alleged to have been involved in a conspiracy to detonate a radioactive "dirty bomb" in the United States.[23] Both al-Libi and Zubaida had been subjected to more aggressive techniques by the CIA—and, in al-Libi's case, by Egyptian interrogators, to whom he was handed over for questioning. Military officials also reported achieving "solid intelligence gains" from their interrogation of al-Kahtani at Guantanamo.[24]

But critics questioned the value—and the credibility—of the information obtained through enhanced interrogation techniques. "These tactics," one FBI agent complained in 2003, "have produced no intelligence of a threat neutralization nature to date."[25] Moreover, prisoners subjected to harsh treatment would, skeptics argued, say anything to gain relief. Perhaps the most notorious example of this was al-Libi's confession that Al Qaeda terrorists had, in the words of one account, "gone to Iraq to learn about chemical and biological weapons." Later, when Secretary of State Colin Powell went before the UN in February 2003 to make the case for invading Iraq, he cited al-Libi's statement, attributing it to a "senior Al Qaeda terrorist." Subsequently, al-Libi recanted, asserting that he had been coerced.[26]

The Lawyer's Role. The memorandum on torture also gave rise to an impassioned debate in the press and within the legal community over how well the Office of Legal Counsel had acquitted itself of its responsibilities as legal advisor and, more fundamentally, what those responsibilities consisted of. Critics viewed the OLC ruling as an abdication of a lawyer's duty to provide objective advice that did not pander to a client's wishes. Writing in the Wall Street Journal, Professor Ruth Wedgwood of the Johns Hopkins School of Advanced International Studies and former CIA director R. James Woolsey maintained that the "president's need for wise counsel is not well served by arguments that bend and twist to avoid any legal restrictions."[27] The "stunning legal contortions" of the opinion, in the words of two commentators, suggested that OLC was being "disingenuous" in its reading of the law in order to justify the use of coercive interrogation techniques. When advising a client in an "opinion letter," they maintained, lawyers were "ethically bound to be frank." Those who "tell their clients what they want to hear—rather than the advice they need—are sometimes rewarded with advancement," they added.[28]

Others decried what they saw as OLC's limited interpretation of the lawyer's duty to a client—specifically, its failure to address the moral and ethical questions implicit in any attempt to define a term as problematic as torture. The memorandum on interrogation, and others like it, was, in the words of one critic, a "hyper-technical legal analysis detached from underlying moral and pragmatic considerations"—the result, he asserted, of "the law of war becoming 'overlawyered.' "[30]

OLC had its defenders as well. The August 1 opinion's arguments, wrote University of Chicago Law School professors Eric Posner and Adrian Vermeule, were "standard lawyerly fare, routine stuff" produced by an office that was traditionally "both defender and advisor of the executive branch...." Whether or not one agreed with the conclusions of the memorandum, they fell "well within the bounds of professionally respectable argument." Moreover, Posner and Vermeule maintained, OLC had not failed its clients by shying away from the moral or ethical ramifications of coercive interrogations. OLC lawyers were "not asked for moral or political advice; they were asked about the legal limits on interrogation," they wrote. "They provided reasonable legal advice and no more, trusting that their political superiors would make the right call....[W]e find it hard to understand why people think that legal technicians in the Justice Department are likely to have more insight into the morality of torture than their political superiors or even the man in the street."[31]

Although Bybee refused any comment, Yoo mounted a vigorous defense of both the arguments that OLC had put forward and those it had not. He asserted that the new kind of war being waged by "terrorist organizations and rogue nations" demanded new "laws of war," and that the President's constitutional powers in wartime allowed him to override international treaties and the will of Congress. Members of Congress did not have the authority to "tie the President's hands in regard to torture as an interrogation technique," he said provocatively. "They can't prevent the President from ordering torture."[32]

As for the moral arguments the memorandum did not make, Yoo contended that a legal memorandum was not the place to take up such considerations. In interviews and articles, he repeatedly drew a distinction between law and policy, the former being the province of the lawyer, the latter of "elected and appointed officials." There was, he maintained, "a clear and necessary difference between law and policy. The memo did not advocate or recommend torture....Rather, [it] sought to answer a discrete question: What is the meaning of 'torture' under the federal law?

What the law permits and what policymakers [choose] to do are entirely different things." A lawyer, Yoo wrote, "must not read the law to be more restrictive than it is just to satisfy his own moral goals, to prevent diplomatic backlash or to advance the cause of international human rights law. However valid those considerations, they simply do not rest within the province of the lawyer who must make sure the government understands what the law permits before it decides what it should do."[32]

The Torture Memo Revisited

Yoo's spirited defense notwithstanding, the memorandum on torture was officially withdrawn in June 2004. It was not until December 30, however, that a revised version appeared, unannounced, on the Justice Department's web site—just days before confirmation hearings for White House Counsel Alberto Gonzales, who had been nominated to replace John Ashcroft as Attorney General, were slated to begin. The memorandum—a slim seventeen pages, compared to its bulky fifty-page predecessor—was addressed to Deputy Attorney General James Comey (the original had been addressed to Gonzales) and signed by Daniel Levin, acting head of OLC. Goldsmith had resigned on July 31, after serving nine months as OLC chief, but, according to the *Wall Street Journal*, he, as well as Levin, had had a hand in drafting it.[33]

The new memo began strikingly, with a declaration that torture "is abhorrent both to American law and values and to international norms." Referring to the August 1, 2002, memorandum, it noted that questions had arisen about its "non-statutory discussion" (i.e., of the President's constitutional powers) and "various aspects" of its "statutory analysis," in particular its definition of "severe" pain. "This memorandum," the December 30 opinion crisply stated, "supercedes the August 2002 Memorandum in its entirety."

The chief reason for the revised memorandum's relative brevity was that it dispensed altogether with the August 1 opinion's argument that anti-torture laws could not infringe on the President's wartime powers. It cited the President's own words—issued in a July 5, 2004, statement honoring UN International Day in Support of Victims of Torture—to explain the decision to omit that portion of the original. "Because the discussion in that memorandum concerning the President's Commander-in-Chief power and the potential defense to liability [i.e., defendants could claim "necessity" or "self-defense" when charged with violations of the law] was—and remains—unnecessary," the revised memo stated, "it has been eliminated from the analysis that follows. Consideration of the bounds of any such authority would be inconsistent with the President's unequivocal directive that United States personnel not engage in torture."[34]

The bulk of the new memorandum was devoted to an analysis of the meaning of "severe," as applied to "physical or mental pain or suffering" in the Convention against Torture and the Senate's "understanding" of the treaty at the time of ratification. It did not agree with the August 1 opinion's conclusion that severe pain should be equal in intensity to "organ failure, impairment of bodily functions, or even death," or equivalent to "excruciating and agonizing" pain or suffering. But the memo was less clear on what "severe" did mean, other than signifying a more intense degree or form of cruel, inhuman, or degrading treatment. The new opinion also distinguished between "severe physical suffering" and "severe physical pain"—which the original memo had lumped together— concluding that severe physical suffering "may constitute torture," even if severe physical pain was not involved. Finally, the December 30 memorandum declined to assign a "precise meaning" to the term "specific intent," as its predecessor had, arguing that in view of the President's "directive" against engaging in torture, "it would not be appropriate to rely on parsing the specific intent element of the statute to approve as lawful conduct that might otherwise amount to torture."[35]

Despite its repudiation of much of the torture memo's analysis, it was not entirely clear what difference, if any, the revised memorandum would have on the conduct of interrogations. In what the *New York Times* called a "cryptic footnote," the memo stated that "[w]hile we have identified various disagreements with the August 2002 Memorandum, we have reviewed this Office's prior opinions addressing issues involving treatment of detainees and do not believe that any of their conclusions would be different under the standards set forth in this memorandum." This meant, officials told the Times, that "coercive techniques approved by the Justice Department under the looser interpretation of the torture statutes were still lawful even under the new, more restrictive standards."[36]

Meanwhile, there were other developments related to the Convention against Torture. In addition to banning torture, the treaty required signatory nations to "undertake to prevent" cruel, inhuman, or degrading treatment or punishment. When the United States originally ratified the treaty in 1994, it defined such treatment as "the cruel, unusual, and inhumane treatment or punishment prohibited by the Fifth, Eighth, and/or Fourteenth Amendments" (loosely defined by the courts as conduct that "shocks the conscience"). But in a written response to a Senate Judiciary Committee inquiry in January 2005, Gonzales maintained that there was "no legal prohibition" on the use of cruel, inhuman or degrading treatment in the case of "aliens overseas," because they were not protected by the U.S. Constitution.[37] It was this "loophole" in the law that Republican Senator John McCain of Arizona—whom the *New York Times* called the nation's "most famous former prisoner of war"—sought to close through legislation, against strong opposition from the White House.

The McCain Amendment

On October 5, 2005, the Senate voted on McCain's amendment to a military spending bill, which would prohibit cruel, inhuman, or degrading treatment of detainees in U.S. custody anywhere in the world. The measure would also restrict military interrogators to using only those tactics described in the Army field manual, which was then being revised; though it set no similar limits on the CIA, the agency would, like the military, be required to abide by the ban on cruel and inhuman treatment. The amendment did not, however, include any provisions that would make violators liable to criminal prosecution or civil suit.

Despite strong pressure from Vice President Cheney and the threat of a presidential veto, the amendment passed resoundingly, on a 90–9 vote. In response, the administration launched a vigorous campaign to limit its reach. Arguing that the President needed "maximum flexibility" to prosecute the global war on terror, Cheney pressed McCain to add language to the measure that would specifically exempt the CIA's "clandestine counterterrorism operations" overseas "if the president determines that such operations are vital to the protection of the United States or its citizens from terrorist attack."[38] McCain refused.

A little over two months later, on December 14, the House voted to endorse the McCain amendment in its upcoming negotiations with the Senate on the military spending bill. Like the Senate vote, the House tally was lopsided—308 to 122—giving McCain veto-proof margins in both chambers. Reluctantly, President Bush agreed to support the measure. In a joint appearance with McCain the following day, he told reporters, "We've been happy to work with him to achieve a common objective, and that is to make it clear to the world that this government does not torture and that we adhere to the international conventions [on] torture, whether it be here at home or abroad."[39]

But when Bush signed the military spending bill, with the McCain amendment—now called the Detainee Treatment Act[40]—on December 30, 2005, he appended a "signing statement" (i.e., a document articulating his interpretation of the law) to it. "The executive branch," it declared, "shall construe [the law] in a manner consistent with the constitutional authority of the President...as Commander-in-Chief...which will assist in achieving the shared objective of the Congress and the President...of protecting the American people from further terrorist attacks." This meant that the White House could waive the restrictions of the new law at its discretion, when it concluded that national security was at stake. With the signing statement, argued one disgruntled observer, the President had "re-opened the loophole" that the amendment was intended to close. A White House spokesman, however, insisted that the administration was "not going to ignore this law," although he acknowledged that there were circumstances—such as a "ticking bomb" scenario, when a detainee was suspected to have information about an imminent terrorist attack—in which it could be set aside. "Of course the president has the obligation to follow the law," the official said, but "he also has the obligation to defend and protect the country as the commander-in-chief, and he will have to square those two responsibilities in each case...."[41]

16

The Effect of Process on Results

Introduction

The Bush decision makers handling the issue of torture and other highly coercive interrogation made choices that divided the administration, weakened U.S. support for the administration's national security policies, undermined foreign support, became a rallying cry for terrorists, and lasted only so long as the decisions could be kept secret from Congress and the press. These and other undesired consequences seem less surprising when there is little indication in the history that has emerged so voluminously since 2002 that any serious attention was given to:

- what was known and, more to the point, wholly unknown about the usefulness of highly coercive interrogation
- what would be the effect of information or, far worse, inflammatory pictures, on the extent and passion of opposition to our policies in Muslim and Arab nations
- what would be the effect of our policies on the badly needed cooperation from Western allies
- what would be the effect of the memo on U.S. efforts to further rule-of-law values and human-rights values in the world
- what would the effects be in terms of the safety of those in the military service faced with reciprocal treatment and in terms of the mental health of U.S. interrogators
- what would the effects be on U.S. citizens' pride in our morality as a nation and thus on needed public support for an unpopular war in Iraq.

This criticism is not unfairly biased by hindsight. Of course, the starting place of any criticism of a lack of foresight is to make sure that our expectations are reasonable. Many of the results of some major decisions, like invading Iraq in 2003, are bound to be largely unforeseeable. Predictions and probabilities are likely to be speculative. Marginal policies have far more predictable consequences than major changes in direction. They also have the advantage of allowing adjustment based on trial and error. Still, sometimes events require major and abrupt changes in direction.

Whether the decision is large or small, direction-changing or marginal, we cannot expect the full understanding of causes and effects that comes with time and hindsight. At best, we can only ask that decision-making processes give serious attention to possibilities that might have been foreseen and that the structure of roles in the organization and the decision processes make as much as possible foreseeable.[1] Still, even with expectations reduced to a realistic level, we can and should expect much better than the performance of the Bush administration in its efforts to define "torture" and "cruel, inhuman, and degrading" treatment. As dramatic and motivating as was the national danger in the background of these decisions about interrogation shortly after 9/11, that danger was neither necessary nor sufficient to explain the failure to see intangible concerns and the ready acceptance of unexamined assumptions as to how the source of fear and danger could best be handled.

A comparison of the administration's decisions on highly coercive interrogation with the recommendations of Georgetown University's Daniel Byman on an equally inflammatory subject, targeted killings, is startling.[2] Byman draws on what experience is available (largely from Israel), carefully assesses benefits and costs, including powerful intangibles as well as lives saved, rigorously examines the possible differences between the United States and Israel, proposes a range of protections, and develops the conditions under which any recourse to targeted killings would be considered legitimate by the American people. That "grown-up" analysis should inform actual decisions and, as we shall see, often has.

The problems in the OLC case were rooted in the process of decision. Without intelligent management and structure, the politics of policy choice that I have described leave our national decisions locked into a process that combines a short-term time horizon with a narrow focus that misses uncertain and intangible consequences, and that accepts unexamined assumptions. The Stinger missile case, when the danger and fear were far less, provided another striking example.

There is often something about the politics of choosing policies that disadvantages the consideration of long-term or intangible results. It also privileges unqualified certainty; think of CIA Director Tenet's erroneous assurance that the existence of an Iraqi nuclear program was a "slam dunk." We pay a high price for this short-sightedness and narrowed vision in the policy realm—high enough to make it worth considering the causes of this frequent weakness. That is the subject of this chapter.

Classifying the Weaknesses in Decision-Making Process and Structure

A starting point is to identify several possible explanations for the failure to fully consider consequences. Either missing skills or skewed incentives may be the problem, and the causes of those conditions may be very hard to remedy.

1. At the level of the individual, a lack of skills, experience, or knowledge, or a perceived need to posture by a show of excessive confidence can be the source of the problem. Any bureaucracy works by allocating responsibility for different types of decisions to people with different skills, who are expected to focus their attention in particular areas and on specific concerns. The individual may have little experience with or training in the subject matter for which he has been made responsible. No one in the OLC process had any experience with interrogations, Islam, or alliances. No one asked anyone who did. And it is rare that an organization hires people trained to think about the interaction of their own decisions with the decisions of outsiders who are pursuing different goals and objectives. At an extreme, Bin Laden's decision to attack the World Trade Center may well have been intended to cause the type of U.S. decision—an invasion of two Muslim countries—that would be helpful to Al Qaeda. Similarly, our turning to abusive interrogations would help Bin Laden meet his pressing need to recruit.

An appointee may, at the same time, be too insecure to take advice from better informed subordinates or colleagues, or he may believe that showing decisiveness and confidence is critical to exercising the influence that his position invites, and is therefore more important than deliberation. Professional training—as an economist, soldier, lawyer, and so on—may also blind an official to aspects of the decision that his particular professional lens does not highlight. This, too, was a fault in the process.

2. A distorted incentive structure can be an important part of the problem. Few of the individuals responsible for making the decisions with regard to highly coercive interrogation were still in their positions when the most important negative consequences began to appear. The short tenure of most political appointees tends to mean being account-able only for results that accrue during that period, not long after one has left the job.

Short tenure is not the only problem. Incentives may be askew in other ways. A structure that divides up responsibility for different facets of decisions that affect multiple areas of delegated authority—in order to prevent unintentional interference with another's responsibilities—dif-fuses any individual sense of overall responsibility. Inevitably, it will also lead to a failure to consider any aspect of the decision that has not been assigned as the specific responsibility of a particular individual and unit. The President and the Attorney General repeatedly declared that their policy was to minimize the damage that terrorists would do by pressing forward with whatever their chosen attorneys said was legal. Who mean-ingfully represented the other concerns—long run and intangible—in this framework of choice?

Providing some types of incentives is particularly difficult. The orga-nization must find a way of maintaining attention on important risks that only occasionally materialize. Before September 11, 2001, the risk of attacks by Al Qaeda fell into this category and was given little atten-tion. Unusual dangers (such as the risk of collapse of the New Orleans levees that occurred at the time of Hurricane Katrina or of a bridge in Minneapolis) surrounded by long periods of safety rarely seem worth the very real costs of attention to officials and bureaucracies with demanding daily responsibilities.

3. Limited skills and distorted individual incentives may themselves be symptoms of a prior problem. As the last example begins to demon-strate, institutional weaknesses may create either type of failure.

Take, first, limited skills. If we have no one in the government who speaks Arabic or who understands an Islamic revival, or is familiar with Shia and Sunni conflicts, a decision to invade Iraq will miss important variables.

So knowing what skills and understanding will be needed in the future is necessary to develop better predictions of long-term outcomes. But hiring and training for the future competes with immediate operational needs as well as with hiring and training for the present; and every official knows that he is more likely to be held accountable for a small failure soon than to be criticized for a larger failure later. Similarly, if the process or the structure skews incentives by rewarding boldness and not also carefulness, actors will take foolish risks to look bold. John Yoo at OLC must have looked like just the sort of thinker the administration wanted in its response to terrorism. The cautionary advice from the Secretary of State and his Legal Advisor was hardly encouraged.

4. The difficulty in making long-term intelligent decisions may be traceable to the fact that constituent concerns may themselves be narrow or, perhaps, are assumed erroneously to be narrow. Democracy adjusts to public reactions, which may themselves be based on immediate responses and narrow predictions. Public opinion and interest-group influence matter to elected officials, who in response pressure appointed decision makers. This pressure can often play a major role.

Take the congressional battle in 2006 to alter a very traditional habeas corpus right for those individuals, including resident aliens, detained because they were suspected of providing support to terrorism. Carefully designed to occur just before the congressional elections, the decision in the Senate (as well as in the House of Representatives) resulted from the majority of members believing that a majority of the voters in the imminent election would, when stimulated by frightening appeals on both sides of the issue and from both parties, be more fearful of terrorist attack than of uninhibited presidential powers, and that they would care far less about national self-image and pride in our protection of human rights than fearful of terrorist attack. Soon after the election, congressional attitudes changed.[3]

The effect of electoral politics works in other ways as well. The electoral advantages of appearing tough in the face of terrorism or of appearing decisive, determined, and certain may require a less deliberative approach, more focused on appearances and ideology. Our decision to invade Iraq had something of that about it, explained as it was by a new presidential doctrine of preemption. The effect of electoral politics may often be to force an elected official to adjust to the more symbolic, necessarily less considered, impressions of voters who are very likely to put much greater weight on an appearance of confident control than on long-term demands and long-term consequences. The long-term consequences will be a matter for later elections, not for this one.

5. Finally, even without electoral politics, a bureaucratic or legislative contest for control of a decision—the core subject of this book—operates in two ways to disadvantage consideration of long-term possibilities.

The tactics for horizontal, clearance-based decision making in a bureaucracy obviously include efforts to minimize the role of those who reject a proposal, or to exclude them completely. Before the invasion of Iraq, the view of the State Department's Bureau of Intelligence and Research, arguing that the evidence for Hussein's possession of weapons of mass destruction was weak, appeared only in a footnote to a long intelligence estimate. In contrast, false and widely criticized "evidence" of Iraqi efforts to buy "yellow cake" uranium appeared prominently in a presidential address to Congress. More broadly, sharing information, which is necessary for intelligent choice, has bureaucratic costs, as the run-up to the September 11 attacks has reminded us dramatically. Protecting "turf" is a powerful motivation limiting interagency cooperation.

These ways of disarming the arguments of dissenters and thereby filtering the range of considerations brought to the attention of a higher-level decision maker are not conducive to enlightening the choice. Even when a decision is unanimous, each player must make a decision as to how much of her time and the time of her staff shall be allotted to thinking about the long-term consequences of a policy choice and how much should be concentrated on bargaining in a contest over policy. Time spent winning the contest, or even coordinating for a desirable outcome, is time that has not been spent examining outcomes in depth.

The Ultimate Choice: Prediction and Legitimacy or Presumptions and Ideologies

For any of the reasons I have described, a player can totally fail to see important long-range considerations or, perhaps more likely, can see such considerations but find them outweighed by political concerns of electoral, bureaucratic, or legislative politics. What he cannot do, if he even remotely foresees long-range effects, is put them totally out of his mind. He needs a substitute, even if less adequate, for the capacities to analyze a whole range of possible intangible as well as tangible consequences of several options for action. Ideology and strongly held presumptions are the only available alternatives.

The final part of any description of the weakness of our decision processes in considering long-term effects is thus that a necessary background condition of unconsidered choice is having available presumptions and ideology to substitute for careful deliberation about the uncertainties of the future. Ideology—believing in a set of policy preferences that can be applied to choice without carefully predicting outcomes—provides the most important part of the answer. It can be full blown, like a preference for market outcomes or for democratic political choice for private incentives or for social safety nets. Substitutes for evidence can also be created by far more limited and partial beliefs, like a presumption that a wide range of others will always take advantage of us if they can, or a contrary belief that it is only suspicion and hostility about other players that generate deceit or aggressiveness.

Each of these substitutes for skepticism and for a need for evidence operates as a presumption—like the presumption of innocence unless proven guilty—that gives general answers to compensate for the unavailability of time, energy, or ability to predict specific consequences of a particular policy or action. When, immediately after our military triumph over Saddam Hussein and our occupation of Iraq, the administration of George W. Bush had to staff an occupation force that was to rebuild Iraq on a democratic and capitalist model, it chose people largely on the basis of conservative economic and social beliefs, even though they knew nothing about Iraq. The reliance on ideology as a source of presumptions, rather than seeking more specific knowledge and more careful predictions of consequences, was doubtless reassuring, but it was a serious mistake.

Of course, no decision maker can claim to foresee all the consequences of her choices. That is where we began. At some point she must stop efforts at predicting and must evaluate the options in terms of what has already been predicted for each. Presumptions about how things work, such as "generosity will inspire reciprocal good faith" or its opposite, "generosity will be taken as indulgence or weakness," then must take over to substitute for more detailed predictions. The substitutes may take the form of values. The first presumption about generosity could be expressed as a liberal value of reciprocal concern and the second as conservative values of responsibility and independence. The problem arises when we too quickly move to these substitutes for the hard work of predicting consequences.

Legitimacy and its Alternatives. Finally, a wise decision in a democracy requires something more than a process well designed to develop, as far as reasonably possible, the likely and less likely consequences of choice along a number of dimensions that may be important. I have emphasized that the substitution of ideology for prediction too quickly is dangerous. But, no less important if a decision is to endure for even a reasonable period of time, the process that creates it must reflect whatever democratic values are essential for legitimacy: the set of conditions that command deference, even to decisions with which one may disagree (and perhaps made by others with whose more ultimate values or presumptions one disagrees). Legitimacy, too, must determine what process is used.

Legitimacy is not easily measured. Still, there is no way to make even a moderately responsible decision without considering it, and the agreement of a handful of like-thinking officials cannot create legitimacy. A strained and largely unpersuasive argument by carefully chosen lawyers that the President had "legal power" to torture where he thought it wise was no substitute for legitimacy.

Consider the failure to use a legislative process that could create legitimacy. Seeing the value of public debate and legislative involvement even at the height of President Bush's re-election popularity, the thoughtful legal counsel to the Department of Defense, Jim Haynes, took me to meet the recently appointed Attorney General, Alberto Gonzales, to make my case for substituting public and legislative involvement for the secret and closed processes by which these decisions had been made. Mr. Gonzales had no interest. He explained that any legislative involvement would risk the administration's present unconstrained capacity to shape the policy as it wished. Of course he was right, but there were also grave risks in the alternative he chose. When the costly consequences of its policy emerged, the secret and controlled processes by which decisions were reached greatly increased those costs and the resulting outrage. Nothing in the process had tied anyone outside the administration to a set of decisions that the Congress and courts soon rejected. A great deal about the secrecy of the process aroused suspicions that would be difficult to overcome.

An Example of a Farsighted and Legitimate Process of Decision

There is nothing inevitable about the style of governmental decision making illustrated by the case of the torture memos. There may be unusual circumstances in which that style is even wise (for example, in reacting immediately to an imminent danger), but for most situations, it invites serious mistakes in decisions that should be made far more deliberately, like those about invading Iraq and about authorizing the

President to delegate the power to torture. Consider an example of a far better political and deliberative process used to handle a decision just as difficult as these.

Soon after South Africa's President and National Party leader Frederik Willem ("F. W.") deKlerk decided to release Nelson Mandela from his prolonged detention on Robin Island and then to negotiate a new constitution with Mandela's African National Congress based on equality of races and ethnic groups in South Africa, it became apparent to Mandela and deKlerk that the needed public support for their plans for creating a new South Africa could be effectively undermined by those who wanted to maintain the old, cruel, and radically unequal relationships. In discussing the case "Dancing with the Devil," we saw the inherent vulnerabilities of negotiations between two coalitions, each of which contains a group adamantly opposed to compromise; Mandela and deKlerk could see that something very similar threatened their negotiations.

A sometimes violent struggle for power within the African community between the ANC and the largely Zulu Inkatha Party provided an opportunity to be exploited by those parts of the still dominant white population who wanted to resist changes that would empower the African populations and the ANC. The security forces loyal to the old National Party and its apartheid traditions could themselves kill members of the ANC, or even of the negotiating team of the National Party. Or they could more secretly stimulate Inkatha forces to engage in massacres of ANC supporters, hoping to encourage violent ANC responses. The advantages of using proxies in order to maintain secrecy about their involvement were clear; open opposition by security forces would not demonstrate spontaneous and uncontrollable dangers in a post-apartheid South Africa. Open opposition would also invite measures to counter such violence.

As the preamble to the National Peace Accord of September 14, 1991, documents, the participants in the peace negotiations (all the parties and other political organizations in South Africa) could see that:

> The current prevalence of political violence in the country…now jeopardizes the very process of peaceful political transformation and threatens to leave a legacy of insurmountable division and deep bitterness in our country….In order to effectively eradicate intimidation and violence, mechanisms need to be created which shall…deal with the investigation of incidents and the causes of violence and intimidation….

Mandela and deKlerk could not depend on the security forces of the old South Africa to prevent violent disruption or to make its sources obvious. Even if they had been trustworthy, these forces would have no credibility with the ANC, whom they had been brutally suppressing for decades. Only the old state apparatus was authorized to investigate and impose punishment, but it had earned the suspicion and hostility of the ANC by extreme brutality and bias. To deal with violence that was often intended to disrupt negotiations and undermine the trust upon which successful negotiations would depend, Mandela and deKlerk needed a widely trusted body to use public hearings to place responsibility for any attacks or massacres during the four years that it would take to produce a new interim constitution. Mandela and deKlerk hoped that merely placing responsibility credibly, publicly, and legitimately would, at a time of competition for both public and international support, provide a substantial deterrent to attacks and an incentive to avoid reprisals. It did.

Together they created a five-member Commission of Inquiry Regarding the Prevention of Public Violence and Intimidation (the "Goldstone Commission") to place responsibility for ongoing violence. Its membership was acceptable to both the ANC and President deKlerk. Its chair, Judge (later Justice) Richard Goldstone, enjoyed the considerable confidence of both the National Party government (because of his reputation as a jurist) and of the ANC, because of his courageous opposition over the years to callous treatment of black South Africans.

The politics of one particular action of the Goldstone commission shows the possibility of using and benefiting from wise processes. It contrasts in every particular with the initial development of the U.S. position on highly coercive interrogation, including torture.

Besides determining the responsibility for massacres and other political violence, the Goldstone Commission turned its attention to a particular problem that had long plagued South Africa: the mishandling of demonstrations and parades—important forms of expression for the black South African population which was, until 1994, denied the right to vote. A demonstration typically elicited a government reaction that "public order" was dangerously threatened, requiring highly repressive control of any large crowd, but particularly of a massing of black South Africans. The head-on collision between demands to be heard and fears of mass disorder were producing dangers and deaths. In Soweto in 1976, hundreds of black youth were killed by police and the army. In the Western Cape in 1980, many black school children lost their lives in protests designed to obtain an elected student representative council. In the Vaal Triangle, 142 people were killed in the black townships in the course of a United Black Democratic Front campaign against proposed new political institutions. In Uitenhige in 1985, twenty people were killed fleeing from the police. In Athlone, a number of black youths were killed when police opened fire on a crowd of demonstrators from their hiding place in the back of a truck. In Bophutatswana in 1986, eleven people were killed at an open air meeting. In Sebokeng in 1990, police fired on a march of 50,000 organized by the United Democratic Front to protest housing and educational shortages. Five people were killed and 160 were wounded. In Bishio in 1992, twenty-nine people were shot dead at an ANC protest march (Storey and Rauch).

To defuse this dangerous issue and to save lives, Judge Goldstone decided he had to develop a new agreement on the responsibilities of demonstrators and of the police, overcoming both deep traditions of state fear and hostility toward demonstrations and parades and deep suspicions of the police on the part of demonstrators. Stated differently, he could see that he had to create a new set of conditions of legitimacy for marching, an important freedom and an essential form of political expression, and for policing a demonstration in the name of maintaining order. Let me describe what Goldstone did to create that legitimacy so that I can contrast it with the Bush administration's effort to legitimate torture and "cruel, inhuman, and degrading" forms of interrogations.

Judge Goldstone and his commission defined the problems to be addressed. If the issue had been sent to him by a party interested in vindicating actions that had been taken, such as the South African police, the setting would have been far less legitimate from its beginning. There was a great deal of law surrounding demonstrations, but he did not limit consideration of the issues to the legal definition of government powers or to exploring the extent of formal liberties to demonstrate. He sought a policy that might be within those outer bounds or might change them, if that was necessary to generate broad public acceptance of a solution.

In part because of the pressures of the workload the Goldstone Commission had already assumed, but more importantly for reasons of legitimacy, he decided to appoint a committee that could both develop needed recommendations and give credibility to the conclusions of his commission. For legitimacy, the composition of the committee would be critical. It had to, and did, include individuals from a broad political spectrum of the public supporting peace in South Africa. He decided to add experts from outside South Africa, recognizing that their support, based on their experience of countries that South Africans admired, would add legitimacy and tend to make less sharp any divisions that might otherwise develop among the South African representatives. At the same time, the six individuals from outside South Africa would have an effect on world opinion, which would also add to the legitimacy before Parliament of whatever the Goldstone Commission would ultimately propose. The Goldstone Commission remained free to reject the views of the committee of five South Africans and six outsiders, but the price of his strategy was to somewhat increase the costs of that course. Unlike Attorney General Gonzales, Judge Goldstone was willing to pay that price in exchange for heightened legitimacy. He asked me to chair the committee.

I and several of my colleagues began by meeting with police leaders from several continents and asking them what they had learned about policing demonstrations and parades. I visited a number of U.S. police departments. A Belgian expert could report on continental systems. Another of our members knew how the London Metropolitan Police handle demonstrations, and still another could speak about related experiences in Australia and Canada. The "foreign" members and one of the South Africans distilled that experience into a first draft of recommendations for review by the South African participants, who would bring to bear whatever they considered unique or special about South African demonstrations. Then we sat down as a group of eleven for a week of solid negotiation to develop a penultimate draft of our recommendations. That process, drawing on multiple viewpoints, was not likely to miss any significant issues or perspectives.

Judge Goldstone saw that ultimately the legitimacy of what we recommended to him and what his commission would recommend to the South African Parliament would depend on public understanding. It would depend on respect for the viewpoints of the important stakeholders (the protestors and the order maintainers) as well as on broad public understanding and acceptance of a new form of public-order policing. For the former, he had me solicit and carefully consider the views of the South African police and of each of the major political parties likely to be involved. For the legitimacy that could come with public consideration of the matter, Goldstone arranged an open and widely reported hearing at which the Goldstone Commission formally received the proposals of the committee it had appointed and the responses of the other stakeholders. After that hearing, the committee was directed to make such changes as it felt warranted as a result of the stakeholders' submissions. Then there was a final public hearing, with much media present, where the ultimate judgment of the committee was presented to the commission for such actions as it considered appropriate.

David Storey and Jeanine Rauch produced a summary of these events which notes that:

> After finalizing its deliberations, the Goldstone Commission proposed a draft Bill to address the civil liability of organizers of gatherings, the prevention and prohibitions of gatherings, and demonstrations near courts, Parliament and the Union Buildings. The Bill incorporated most of the policy recommendations made by the multinational panel and was seen as legitimate by most of the political parties since they had all participated in the drafting process by way of submissions and hearings.
>
> The Commission said that legislation was desirable even before the elections, because mass demonstrations and marches were matters of urgency....The Goldstone bill became the Regulation of Gatherings Act...enacted after the election in November, 1996....

A Comparison in Terms of Process

A quick comparison of the Goldstone Commission's handling of demonstrations to the work of Gonzales, Addington, Bybee, and Yoo on highly coercive interrogation is instructive. One process created legitimacy; the other did not. One process reached out to incorporate the array of information and the multiplicity of viewpoints needed for a trustworthy position. The other was calculated to avoid the risk of disagreement that would come with unexpected evidence or widening participation.

From the beginning, the White House sacrificed credibility by shaping when and who would address the issue of highly coercive interrogation. No one could have had faith in the objectivity of a process that began with a request for an after-the-fact justification of what had already been done by the CIA. Within the Justice Department's Office of the Legal Counsel, the request was promptly routed to trusted loyalists. Career attorneys were excluded. The role of the Department of State was carefully minimized.

Only by taking the risk of a recommendation he did not want was Goldstone able to claim objectivity for the recommendations he would get. His process was designed to require the resolution of multiple viewpoints by negotiation instead of eliminating, as the OLC process did, all who might disagree. Goldstone assured that the committee's recommendation would be exposed to public criticism as well. The OLC recommendation would be kept secret and thus without the restraint that would have been imposed by anticipating public reaction.

Either Gonzales directed, or Bybee and Yoo assumed, that the only considerations would be technical ones, leaving questions of policy to somehow be incorporated at some other stage. Even within these constraints, Bybee could have envisaged his responsibility in any of several ways. He chose—or accepted—the narrowest of visions. Policy concerns got lost; for the President and his Attorneys General had repeatedly announced that they would do everything that was found legal to produce security. Goldstone invited his committee to address policy as well as law. Only by their addressing all aspects of the problem could he prevent confusion at later stages about whether its recommendations had omitted critical concerns from any field.

Goldstone's committee sought out expert knowledge about the handling of demonstrations; the office of Legal Council avoided any research or expert judgment as to effectiveness of the techniques that they were straining to authorize. Goldstone's committee invited its members to consider world opinion. The Office of Legal Council gave no thought, even within the narrow constraints of discussion of lawfulness, as to how needed allies and others would react to its conclusions. Having built multiplicity of viewpoints into his structure, Goldstone expected the committee's members to negotiate or reason to shared conclusions. With minor exceptions they did. There are few if any signs of open negotiation of competing viewpoints in the process leading to the President's positions on interrogation. Nor does any such working out of differences seem to have been desired.

Goldstone provided and announced opportunities for the stakeholders to comment on the committee's suggestions, and those comments were made publicly at open hearings before the commission. The Office of Legal Council contemplated that the results be kept secret. Goldstone demanded that his committee consider the stakeholders' comments and make revisions where they seemed justified on this basis. Nothing could have been further from the process in the OLC. Goldstone received the final recommendations, and his commission only then took responsibility for accepting and rejecting all or any part of the committee's work. The OLC had developed the habit of allowing the White House secretly to urge changes in its opinions.

It is fair to say that in every respect Goldstone's project was designed to develop legitimacy, and it did. The decisions of the Bush administration on highly coercive interrogation—ultimately unpalatable to a great majority in both houses of Congress—had been developed in a way that would minimize their claim to credibility or legitimacy.

A Past Not Really Lost

It is worth recalling that U.S. leaders have shown similar wisdom in simultaneously developing processes well designed to protect legitimacy and to critically explore a wide range of even intangible consequences. That history should not be lost if we are to avoid a full-scale retreat from a willingness to trust government with great responsibilities. I began Chapter 14 with a very partial list of momentous choices we handled carefully and got just about "right." Let me conclude by illustrating with only a few, generally less momentous, decisions that are therefore more easily described. In each, concerns for legitimacy or recognition of other intangible concerns, overrode more immediate governmental interests.

Protecting Legitimacy

President Ford's Attorney General, Ed Levi, inherited an FBI whose post-Watergate legacy was major distrust along two fronts: legality (e.g., it had secretly conducted illegal "black bag" break-ins); and partisanship (e.g., its Director had destroyed the records of illegal wiretaps requested by the White House at the urging of the White House). A valuable intangible—the capacity to elicit citizen support for law enforcement and citizen trust in legal control of the FBI—was at stake, not just the immediate extent of government power. Moreover, Levi could foresee that an angry Congress might respond by legislating reforms more restrictive than necessary of intelligence-seeking searches and wiretaps.

So Levi charged a group of attorneys and investigators with the responsibility for cabining the most sensitive investigative powers within a set of guidelines he would issue—guidelines dealing with the most contested issues in a wholly transparent way. These guidelines, with some amendments and supplemented to deal with additional issues, remain in place several decades later, bolstering the legitimacy the FBI needs in exercising otherwise frightening law enforcement powers.

A few years later, President Carter's Attorney General, Griffin Bell, addressed the fears of partisanship in prosecution that Watergate had engendered and that have resurfaced periodically—most recently in 2007 with White House involvement in an unprecedented firing of a half-dozen U.S. Attorneys. Foreseeing such fears, Bell forbade direct contact by anyone in the White House or anyone in the Congress with U.S. prosecutors about a pending case. Any questions or comments were to go to him and his deputy, Ben Civiletti, who never passed them along to the prosecutors.

Strategy, including plans to maintain legitimacy, involves how you handle decisions that come to you as well as those you initiate. Thus later, when President Carter, outraged by a brutal shooting of a Hispanic youth in a patrol car (and by the minimal sentence it received in a Texas court), announced that the United States would try the police officer again, Bell and Civiletti publicly rejected the quasi-directive to prosecute, insisting on applying established Justice Department guidelines regarding retrials. They saw that the credibility of the Department for independence of political influences—a critical intangible—was more important than compliance with a very public presidential directive, even though some of the President's closest aides felt that, in the next election, this might well cost the President the electoral votes of Texas.

In the field of foreign affairs, examples of thoughtfully protecting legitimacy are also readily available. President George H. W. Bush initiated "Desert Storm" only after obtaining the support of Arab allies. President Clinton acted in Kosovo only under the umbrella of NATO.

Critically Exploring a Wide Range of Intangibles

Nor has concern for predicting a wide range of consequences always or regularly been lacking in decisions of the United States. President Richard Nixon could see that, despite our scientific lead in the field, both self-interest and concern for citizens throughout the world dictated our joining a convention against biological weapons. The interest of the United States was not in having the most weapons of mass destruction but in having as few as possible rivals with such weapons. Nuclear bombs were difficult and expensive to make; biological weapons were not. The United States could only gain by pressing for the intangible benefit of a worldwide rejection of biological weapons.

More recently, the judgment of Colin Powell about the lessons of Vietnam for a nation that could not long be held in a land war of choice—one without high and visible national stakes—served President George H. W. Bush and President Clinton well in the first Iraq war and then, again, in Kosovo. In particular, it showed extraordinary restraint and remarkable wisdom to have quickly won the "Desert Storm" war against Saddam Hussein and then not sought to occupy the country.

In foreign trade, the United States resisted the temptation to engage in competitive bribery in sales to foreign nations, recognizing not only the immorality of the practice and the demoralizing effects on pride in our businesses, but also the long-range disadvantage to American businesses whose employees might learn to take as well as give bribes, and to a country, the United States, better situated to compete on its merits than by bribery. After many years of competing at some disadvantage because of a self-imposed prohibition on foreign bribery, the United States was finally able to negotiate an agreement that bound, more or less, its primary competitors as well and invented a workable system for monitoring that compliance.

Nor are domestic examples of farsightedness lacking, although the force of politics and domestic constituencies make careful, deliberative processes rarer. Having promised in 1943 that World War II veterans would not return to the economic devastation that many of their World War I predecessors had faced, President Roosevelt signed the GI Bill of Rights eleven months later. At a cost estimated to be a small fraction of even its economic benefits, the new law transformed America: its social structure, its level of inequality, its educational and housing systems, and its creativity. Twenty years later, President Johnson's Civil Rights Acts of 1964 and 1965 without violence marked the end of centuries of widespread acceptance of racially based, privately and governmentally enforced, social and political inequality.

We have also learned to regulate capital markets to maintain investment and have adjusted fairly quickly to new devices for fooling investors, recognizing the central importance for the long run of an intangible: maintaining the trust of investors. We have managed with some success the issues of smoking and are prepared to trade more home runs for less steroids in a commitment to maintaining the long-term value of role models. None of these involve perfect devices, but they all involve thoughtful departures from immediate self-interest.

Decision processes that create both wisdom and legitimacy have been an American tradition since our remarkable Constitution was written well over two hundred years ago. But only if the American public demands processes that embody a concerted effort to predict intangible as well as tangible consequences and to design answers that accommodate as much as possible not only of our concerns but also of our values will we get wise decisions. If we demand that leaders choose policies in a way that builds, not consumes, legitimacy, we will get that too.

Appendix to Chapter 1

The Caulkins Matrix

To assist a group of experts on drug policy in addressing the issues of law enforcement on the streets of American cities, Dr. Jonathan Caulkins of Carnegie Mellon University produced a matrix combining options or alternatives along one dimension (the rows) and pertinent value variables or policy concerns along the other (the columns). The matrix appears in Appendix Figure 1.1.

A fuller description of Caulkins's simplified options is provided in Appendix Figure 1.2. Nothing much simpler than Caulkins's matrix

Illustrative Matrix of Sentencing Options and Outcomes

Positively or Negatively Valued Outcomes

	Public Outcomes					CJS Effects			Justice
	Use by Current Users and Related Problems	Initiation of New Users	Harm to Dealers and their Families	Drug-related Crime and Violence	Community Effects (Other than Crime and Violence)	Cost of Enforcement/ Prison	Number of Trials	Ability to Prosecute Higher Level Dealers	Public Sense of Justice about System
B1 Status Quo									
B2 Status Quo w/ Half as Many Areas									
B3 More Certain but Shorter Sentences									
B4 More Certain and More Severe									
B5 Focus on Recidivists									
B6 Focus on Amount Sold									
B7 Focus on Context of Dealing									

(Row label group, left side: **Policy Options**)

Appendix Figure 1.1.

could capture the major options when the only two alternatives were as simple as more or less police and more or less punishment (leaving out options of treatment or prevention). Without need of further explanation, the values or concerns of possible decision makers are clear from the column headings in the matrix. None of these could be eliminated, to simplify

---

Descriptions of Sentencing Options

B1: Status Quo. A mixture of sentences from zero (if the case is not prosecuted or the sentence is probation) to five years or more, depending largely on prior drug convictions and the amount of drugs possessed at the same time of arrest. Currently, half of those arrested are convicted. Of those, 27.4 percent received a sentence of probation, 22.5 percent jail, and 51 percent prison.

B2: Status Quo with Half as Many Drug Arrests. Cut enforcement in half by reducing all types of drug arrests by 50 percent. No change in the type of arrests made, the probability of prosecution given arrest, the probability of conviction given prosecution, or the distribution of sanctions given conviction.

B3: More Certain but Shorter Sentences. Increase by 50 percent the number of people incarcerated by increasing prosecution given arrest and reducing the probability of probation given conviction. Reduce length of longer sentences by enough to hold constant the number of people incarcerated.

B4: More Certain and More Severe. Two- to five-year sentences for everyone convicted of drug selling who does not offer substantial assistance in developing a case against someone else.

B5: Focus on Recidivists. First-time offenders would receive probation, a suspended sentence, or a diversionary punishment that does not create a criminal record. Subsequent convictions would lead to sentences comparable to those given today, with longer sentences for those with the longest records.

B6: Focus on Amount Sold. Sentences would increase sharply in the amount possessed and/or amount found to have been sold previously. For example, sanctions for cocaine might be one week for a gram or less, two months for 1–10 grams, one year for 10–100 grams, five years for 100–1,000 grams, and more than five years for more than a kilogram.

B7: Focus on Context of Dealing. The base sentence for drug dealing would be no more than six months for low-level selling, but there would be significant (e.g., five-year) add-ons for selling while in possession of a firearm; employing a minor in the drug trade; exercising violence in the course of drug dealing; selling within a certain distance of a school or drug treatment clinic; open and notorious taking over of a neighborhood; and so on.

Appendix Figure 1.2.

the problem, without losing values that would be very significant to many people.

Now consider the problem of delegating this choice by conveying the manager's preference. For a manager to convey what she wanted done on each of a number of occasions by developing a formula that would value each of the seven options in each frequently encountered situation, it would not be adequate simply to give a weight to each column heading conveying how seriously she took that variable. The importance of, for example, the fourth column heading—drug-related crime and violence—would depend on the particular situation confronting one of her subordinates. She would want to convey her appraisal of the likely effects of each option in terms of that value in each situation. If gang warfare suddenly became a major problem in a formerly peaceful neighborhood, stopping drug-related violence might immediately take on a far greater importance or weight, and more policing might look like a more promising strategy.

The manager would have to convey how she would value each of the alternatives in terms of each of her types of concerns, depending on the situation the subordinate was facing. That would require her to be able to imagine the important situations and how they would affect the weights of her concerns. The complexity of the task of her creating a formula and conveying it and of her subordinates applying it would be overwhelming. The skills needed would be rare; the costs immense.

Appendix to Case Studies

Cast of Characters

Abramowitz, Morton—Director of the Bureau of Intelligence and Research (INR) at the State Department. He vigorously pushed to have Stingers sent to the Afghan rebels.

Addington, David—General counsel for Vice President Richard Cheney during the case about Defining Torture in the War on Terror. John C. Yoo was regarded as his protégé. Numerous press accounts reported that he had a hand in drafting the memo that defined torture.

Akhtar Abdul Rahman Khan (General Akhtar)—Director of the Pakistani military intelligence service, the Inter-Services Intelligence Directorate (ISI). In a meeting with Undersecretary of Defense Fred Iklé and his deputy Michael Pillsbury, General Akhtar was enthusiastic about receiving Stinger missiles for distribution.

al-Kahtani, Mohammed—The "twentieth hijacker" who had been refused entry into the United States and therefore prevented from participating in the September 11, 2001, attacks. He was held at Guantanamo during the case about Defining Torture in the War on Terror. The initial interrogation tactics that U.S. operatives used on him did not work.

al-Libi, Ibn Sheikh—Al Qaeda member who had run its training camps in Afghanistan. The United States captured him in Afghanistan in November 2001, sparking a disagreement between the FBI and CIA about how to interrogate him. He apparently provided information that was useful in the capture of Abu Zubaida.

Anderson, Frank—An officer in the CIA's Directorate of Operations during the Stinger missile case.

Anderson, Tommy—A tobacco lobbyist during the "Dealing with the Devil" case. He and John Sears made clear to different state officials that the tobacco industry was interested in a comprehensive settlement.

Armacost, Michael—Undersecretary of State for Political Affairs during the Stinger missile case and the Iran-Contra case. In the Stinger missile case, he was impressed by Morton Abramowitz's support for providing Stingers to the rebels, and he therefore supported the move.

Armitage, Richard—An official at the Department of Defense during the Stinger missile case.

Ashcroft, John—Republican senator from Missouri and a presidential hopeful at the time of President Clinton's needle exchange controversy. He condemned Donna Shalala's support for needle exchange programs as sending a bad message about drug use.

Bible, Geoffrey—CEO of Philip Morris during the "Dealing with the Devil" case.

Bliley, Thomas—A Republican Congressman from Virginia during the "Taking On Big Tobacco" case. He was a supporter of the tobacco industry.

Brzezinski, Zbigniew—National Security Advisor during the Stinger missile case. He met with Pakistani President Muhammad Zia-ul-Haq to formalize the U.S.-Pakistani collaboration in transferring weapons to the Afghan rebels. He also reached an agreement with the Saudis that they would match U.S. contributions to the Afghan resistance.

Bybee, Jay—Former Assistant Attorney General. In 2002 he was asked by White House Counsel Alberto Gonzales what the laws permitted and prohibited in terms of coercive interrogation. This likely affected interrogation techniques the United States has used in its war on terror. As head of the Office of Legal Counsel (OLC) in the case about Defining Torture in the War on Terror, he signed off on the OLC's memo defining torture.

Cannistraro, Vince—A CIA officer seconded to the NSC staff as Director of Intelligence during the Stinger missile case.

Carlton, Phil—A tobacco industry intermediary in negotiations to reach a settlement during the "Dealing with the Devil" case.

Carol, Julia—An anti-smoking activist who was especially adept at community organizing. She ran Americans for Nonsmokers' Rights. She opposed compromise with the tobacco industry.

Casey, William—Director of the CIA during the Stinger missile case and the Iran-Contra case. In the Stinger missile case, he enthusiastically supported the supply of weapons to Afghan rebels. He was fond of covert operations. He developed a strong relationship with Mohammad Zia-ul-Haq. He did not, however, support the supply of Stingers to the rebels. In the Iran-Contra case, he favored selling arms to Iran.

Cogan, Charles—Near East/South Asia chief for the CIA's Directorate of Operations during the Stinger missile case.

DeLay, Tom—A Republican Congressman from Texas. He became House Majority Whip in 1994, during the "Taking On Big Tobacco" case. He strongly opposed regulation.

Fortier, Don—Deputy National Security Advisor during the Stinger missile case.

Gardner, Norman—Deputy to Clair George, who was the CIA's liaison with Congress and who later became the Head of the CIA's Directorate of Operations during the Stinger missile case.

Gates, Robert—William Casey's deputy in 1981, and later the Director of Central Intelligence.

George, Clair—Head of the CIA's Directorate of Operations during the Stinger missile case, and the CIA's liaison with Congress before that. He thought that giving the Afghan rebels Stinger missiles was an alluring option.

Glantz, Stanton—Founder of a small grassroots organization, Californians for Nonsmokers' Rights, which focused its efforts on pushing for smoke-free public places in cities and towns. He opposed compromise with the tobacco industry.

Goldsmith, Jack—Head of the Office of Legal Counsel from October 2003 through July 2004. He reversed some of the opinions written by John C. Yoo during the case about Defining Torture in the War on Terror.

Goldstone, Steven—CEO of R. J. Reynolds during the "Dealing with the Devil" case. He had been a lawyer with a Wall Street law firm and he often attempted to settle cases before going to court.

Goldwater, Barry—Republican Senator from Arizona during the Stinger missile case. He chaired the Senate Intelligence Committee. He originally resisted Rep. Charlie Wilson's efforts to fund Oerlikon guns for the Afghans, but he relented after John McMahon of the CIA asked him to change his position.

Gonzales, Alberto—White House counsel during the case about Defining Torture in the War on Terror. He referred the CIA's questions about interrogation techniques to the Justice Department's Office of Legal Counsel.

Hafner, Dudley—CEO of the American Heart Association during the "Dealing with the Devil" case.

Hart, Howard—The CIA station chief in Islamabad at the end of 1983. He deemed the Oerlikon an unsuitable weapon for the Afghan rebels.

Hatch, Orrin—Republican Senator from Utah, and a member of the Senate Select Committee on Intelligence during the Stinger missile case. He had strong ties to Michael Pillsbury.

Haynes, William—General counsel at the Department of Defense during the case about Defining Torture in the War on Terror. He recommended to Defense Secretary Donald Rumsfeld that not all of the severest interrogation techniques be authorized.

Hitt, Scott—Chair of President Clinton's Advisory Council on HIV/AIDS. He strongly opposed Clinton's decision not to fund needle exchange programs, saying, "At best, it's hypocrisy, and at worst, it's immoral."

Humphrey, Gordon J.—Republican Senator from New Hampshire during the Stinger missile case. To the media he voiced support for the Afghan rebels.

Iklé, Fred—Undersecretary of Defense during the Stinger missile case. He favored giving the Afghan rebels U.S.-made Stinger missiles. His Office of Policy and Planning originally floated the idea, which drew opposition from the CIA. During the Reagan administration, he engineered the change of U.S. policy toward Afghanistan, by which the U.S. acknowledged that it was attempting to challenge the Soviets "by all means possible." This was an escalation from the United States' previous stance that it would assist in efforts of "harassment" against the Soviets.

Kessler, David—Administrator of the Food and Drug Administration in the "Taking On Big Tobacco" case. He attempted to regulate the tobacco industry. In the "Dealing with the Devil" case, he and C. Everett Koop sat on a committee that reported to Congress on the outcome of the tobacco settlement negotiations.

Khan, Akhtar Abdul Rahman—(*see* Akhtar Abdul Rahman Khan)

Khan, Riaz—Pakistani diplomat who was involved in the Afghan proximity peace talks in Geneva during the Stinger missile case.

Koop, C. Everett—Former Surgeon General and a hero of the tobacco control movement for his strong stand on such issues as the addictiveness of nicotine and the dangers of secondhand smoke. In the "Dealing with the Devil" case, he was publicly critical of the tobacco industry settlement. With David Kessler, he sat on a committee that reported to Congress on the outcome of the settlement negotiations.

Lindsey, Bruce—White House advisor during the "Dealing with the Devil" case. President Clinton made him a facilitator of talks to reach a tobacco settlement.

Long, Clarence D.—A Democratic Congressman from Maryland during the Stinger missile case. He served as chair of the foreign operations subcommittee of the House Appropriations Committee. He led a delegation to Asia, where they analyzed the Afghan-Soviet conflict. He supported Rep. Charlie Wilson's amendment to shift money from the Defense Department to the CIA for its Afghan operation.

McCaffrey, General Barry—President Clinton's drug czar, who was appointed in 1996. He was chosen because he was a stern and tough military man, which would send a message about the war on drugs. He opposed needle exchange programs because he felt they would send a mixed message about the wrongness of drug use. Although he disagreed on this issue with Sandra

Thurman, the AIDS czar, he agreed to hold off on making any decisions until scientific evidence was gathered about the effectiveness of the programs.

McCain, John—A Republican Senator from Arizona and chair of the Senate Commerce Committee during the "Dealing with the Devil" case. His committee was responsible for a bill formalizing the tobacco industry settlement.

McDonough, Jim—Director of Strategy at the Office of National Drug Control Policy (ONDCP) under President Clinton. General Barry McCaffrey was McDonough's superior. McDonough backed McCaffrey's opposition to needle exchange programs. McDonough first received word from a reporter that the Clinton administration would go ahead with funding needle exchange programs, even though one day earlier McCaffrey believed he had made progress in convincing President Clinton to do just the opposite.

McFarlane, Robert—National Security Advisor to President Reagan. In the Iran-Contra case, he advocated using Israel as a go-between in selling arms to a hostile Iran on the understanding that the Iranians would use their influence to secure the release of U.S. hostages taken prisoner in Lebanon by Iranian-directed terrorists.

McMahon, John—A career CIA employee who became the agency's number-two official in 1982. He wrote a letter to Senator Barry Goldwater, convincing him to change his stance and support the funding of Oerlikon guns for the Afghan rebels. He opposed sending Stingers to Pakistan and the Afghan rebels, but eventually gave in and allowed the proposal to go forward.

Meese, Edwin, III—Attorney General during the Iran-Contra case. He approved direct sales of U.S. arms to Iran.

Mikva, Abner—White House Counsel during the Clinton Administration and in the "Taking On Big Tobacco" case.

Moore, Mike—Attorney General of Mississippi during the "Dealing with the Devil" case. He filed suit against cigarette makers, seeking to recover $940 million in Medicaid expenditures on smoking-related illnesses.

Mora, Alberto—Navy General Counsel during the case about Defining Torture in the War on Terror, who expressed concerns about the interrogation methods being used on Guantanamo detainees.

Morris, Dick—President Clinton's political advisor during the "Taking On Big Tobacco" case.

Myers, Matthew—Executive vice president of the National Center for Tobacco-Free Kids during the "Dealing with the Devil" case. He was the sole representative of the "tobacco control movement" at meetings that sought to limit the monetary damages that the tobacco industry would have to pay, in exchange for some concessions from the industry.

North, Oliver—Assistant to National Security Advisor Robert McFarland during the Iran-Contra case. He spearheaded the effort to use the proceeds from arms sales to Iran and send the funds to the Contras in Nicaragua.

Novelli, Bill—Matthew Myers's boss in the "Dealing with the Devil" case. He strongly favored reaching a settlement with the tobacco industry.

Nussbaum, Bernie—White House Counsel at the time of Vince Foster's death in 1993.

Panetta, Leon—White House Chief of Staff to President Clinton during the "Taking On Big Tobacco" case.

Peck, Robert—Deputy to Arnold Raphel at the Department of State. Like Raphel, he opposed providing Stinger missiles to the Afghan rebels.

Pertschuk, Michael—The chair of the Federal Trade Commission who unsuccessfully attempted to ban advertisements on Saturday morning television programs for sugar-coated cereals and other products addressed to very young children.

Piekney, William—The CIA's senior intelligence advisor in Islamabad from 1984 to 1986. He strongly opposed providing Stingers to the Afghan rebels.

Pillsbury, Michael—Deputy to Undersecretary of Defense Fred Iklé during the Stinger missile case. Like Iklé, he favored giving the Afghan rebels U.S.-made Stinger missiles. He did not believe it was important for the United States to maintain plausible deniability of involvement in the conflict.

Poindexter, John—National Security Advisor during the Iran-Contra case. He succeeded Robert McFarlane.

Powell, Colin—Assistant to Secretary of Defense Caspar Weinberger during the Stinger missile case. He ascertained that the Joint Chiefs of Staff were opposed to the Stinger program. As Secretary of State in the case about Defining Torture in the War on Terror, he objected to the decision that the Third Geneva Convention did not apply to Al Qaeda and the Taliban.

Raphel, Arnold—Senior Deputy Assistant Secretary of State for Near East and South Asian Affairs. He opposed providing Stinger missiles to the Afghan rebels; he worried that it could expose Pakistan to Soviet reprisals. Raphel headed the U.S. team monitoring the Afghan proximity peace talks in Geneva, and he felt the time was wrong to escalate U.S. involvement.

Regan, Donald—President Reagan's chief of staff during the Iran-Contra case.

Scruggs, Richard—A trial lawyer who handled the litigation against cigarette makers for the state of Mississippi during the "Dealing with the Devil" case.

Sears, John—A tobacco lobbyist during the "Dealing with the Devil" case. He and Tommy Anderson made clear to different state officials that the tobacco industry was interested in a comprehensive settlement.

Seffrin, John—CEO of the American Cancer Society during the "Dealing with the Devil" case.

Shalala, Donna—Secretary of Health and Human Services under President Clinton. She strongly favored needle exchange programs, contending that they would reduce the spread of HIV. She opposed General Barry McCaffrey's stance on this issue.

Shultz, George—Secretary of State during the Stinger missile case and Iran-Contra case. He vehemently opposed selling arms to Iran in order to win the release of U.S. hostages.

Simmons, Robert R.—Former Chief of Staff for the Senate Select Committee on Intelligence.

Synar, Mike—A former Democratic Congressman from Oklahoma. He was a friend of President Clinton. In an effort to win support for regulation of tobacco, David Kessler approached him after Synar was no longer in office; he wanted Synar to use his friendship with Clinton to pitch the proposal to those in the White House.

Thurman, Sandra—President Clinton's AIDS czar. She favored needle exchange programs and opposed General Barry McCaffrey's stance on this issue, though she agreed with McCaffrey to hold off on making any decisions until scientific evidence was gathered about the effectiveness of the programs.

Twetten, Thomas—From 1983 to 1986, deputy chief of the CIA Directorate of Operations' Near East/South Asia Division. He adamantly opposed providing Stingers to the Afghan rebels.

Wallop, Malcolm—A Republican Senator from Wyoming during the Stinger missile case. He served as chair of the Senate Intelligence Committee's budget subcommittee. He successfully requested greater funding to the Afghan rebels.

Waxman, Henry—A Democratic Congressman from California in the "Taking On Big Tobacco" case. He chaired the Energy and Commerce Subcommittee on Health and the Environment. He was a tobacco foe.

Weinberger, Caspar—Secretary of Defense during the Stinger missile case and the Iran-Contra case. He opposed the sale of weapons to Iran in the latter case.

Wickham, John, Jr.—Army General and member of the Joint Chiefs of Staff. He opposed the provision of Stinger missiles to the Afghan rebels.

Wilson, Charles (Charlie)—A Democratic Congressman from Texas during the Stinger missile case. He sat on the Subcommittee for Defense Appropriations of the House Appropriations Committee, where he was a senior Democrat. He strongly disliked the Soviets and fervently supported efforts to aid the Afghan rebels. In 1983 he sponsored a secret amendment to the annual appropriations bill that would shift $40 million from the Defense Department to the CIA's

364   APPENDIX TO CASE STUDIES

budget for the Afghan effort. He then lobbied hard to provide Oerlikon guns to the Afghans.

Yoo, John C.—Professor of law at the University of California at Berkeley who had been appointed Deputy Assistant Attorney General of the Office of Legal Counsel (OLC) in July 2001. In the case about Defining Torture in the War on Terror, he construed extremely narrowly the statutory and treaty obligations of U.S. interrogators and authored the OLC's opinion that the Constitution vested the President with plenary authority to use such military force abroad during grave national emergencies. He also wrote that detainees held at the U.S. Navy base on Guantanamo Bay in Cuba would be beyond the jurisdiction of U.S. federal courts, and that the provisions of the Geneva Convention should not be extended to members of Al Qaeda and their Taliban supporters being held by the U.S. military.

Yousaf, Mohammad—An official in the Pakistani military intelligence service, the Inter-Services Intelligence Directorate (ISI), who ran the day-to-day operation of the pipeline of weapons from Pakistan to the Afghan rebels from 1983 to 1987.

Zia-ul-Haq, Mohammad (President Zia)—President of Pakistan during the Stinger missile case. He worked with the United States to coordinate the transfer of weapons to the Afghan rebels. He did not want this link to the United States to become known to the anti-American population of Pakistan. He developed a strong relationship with William Casey.

Zubaida, Abu—A top aide of Osama bin Laden who was captured by the United States in Pakistan in March 2002.

Suggested Readings

Allison, Graham T., and Philip Zelikow. *Essence of Decision: Explaining the Cuban Missile Crisis.* New York: Longman, 1999. This splendid book offers three models for interpreting the Cuban Missile Crisis, and these models serve as a helpful way to consider all government decisions.

Haass, Richard N. *The Bureaucratic Entrepreneur: How to be Effective in any Unruly Organization.* Washington, D.C.: Brookings Institution Press, 1999. This handbook provides guidance on how to work well within bureaucracies, and in the process offers valuable insights on the intricacies of government decision making.

Halperin, Morton H., Priscilla Clapp, and Arnold Kanter. *Bureaucratic Politics and Foreign Policy.* Washington, D.C.: Brookings Institution Press, 2006. No one has shown the distorting effects of systematic flows of partial information in a government (or any) bureaucracy better than Mort Halperin did in this book.

Heclo, Hugh. *A Government of Strangers: Executive Politics in Washington.* Washington, D.C.: Brookings Institution Press, 1977. In this interesting book, Heclo considers the nature of career civil servants and political appointees and finds that their relations have a large impact on many government decisions.

Heymann, Philip B. *The Politics of Public Management.* New Haven, Conn.: Yale University Press, 1987. In this book, I consider how political appointees chosen to head government agencies deal with the powerful political forces that surround them.

Janis, Irving L. and Leon Mann. *Decision Making: A Psychological Analysis of Conflict, Choice, and Commitment.* New York: Free Press, 1977. Using a psychological model that envisions a decision maker as beset by internal doubts, this interesting book relies upon scientific experiments to consider a wide array of factors in decision making.

Kingdon, John W. *Agendas, Alternatives, and Public Policies*. New York: Addison-Wesley, 2003. Kingdon's work, which was first published in 1984, remains an authoritative study on how issues land on government officials' agendas.

Moore, Mark H. *Creating Public Value: Strategic Management in Government*. Cambridge, Mass.: Harvard University Press, 1995. Moore argues that public managers should do more to seek out creative ways to benefit the public. He illustrates his argument with numerous detailed case studies showing how public managers have tried to do this.

Neustadt, Richard E. *Presidential Power and the Modern Presidents*. New York: Free Press, 1990. Neustadt's book, one of the most important studies of the American presidency, explores how the President's ability to influence policy comes not from the Constitution, but from his ability to negotiate effectively with other decision makers.

Porter, Roger B. *Presidential Decision Making: The Economic Policy Board*. Cambridge, U.K.: Cambridge University Press, 1982. Porter, a White House veteran, uses case studies from 1970s economic policy to analyze how the President receives advice and makes decisions. The appendix is an especially readable and valuable essay.

Notes

PREFACE

1. A new edition by Morton Halperin, Priscilla Clapp, Arnold Kanter has been published by Brookings Institution Press in 2006.

CHAPTER 1

1. The Appendix to this chapter demonstrates the extreme difficulty of any effort to restrict the delegation in terms of creating, conveying, and applying a cost/benefit calculation. The example shows the difficulty even if people do not have diverse responsibilities and even in the case of one of most familiar and straightforward of issues.
2. "1998 Needle-Exchange Decision: The McCaffrey-Shalala Confrontation." This case (C-15–98–1466.0) was written by John Buntin for Professor Philip Heymann, for use at the John F. Kennedy School of Government, Harvard University (0798).
3. "Ban on Funding for Needle Swap Expected to End, White House Decision Is Imminent, Sources Say," *San Francisco Chronicle*, April 11, 1998, p. A1.
4. Julie Bruneau and Martin T. Schechter, "The Politics of Needles and AIDS," *New York Times*, April 9, 1998, p. A27.
5. After spending several days with the President in Chile, McCaffrey had gone on to the interior of Brazil, where ONDCP had no secure line to McCaffrey.
6. "US Decision against Funding Needle Plan Draws Fire: Administration Agrees Exchange Program Cuts AIDS Spread, Doesn't Foster Illegal Drug Use, but Will Leave Financing to State, Local Groups," *Los Angeles Times*, April 21, 1998, p. A18.

7. "Clinton Supports Needle Exchanges But Not Funding," *Washington Post*, April 21, 1998, p. A1

8. "US Drug Czar's Ouster Demanded," *The Sacramento Bee*, April 25, 1998, p. A6.

9. Ibid.

10. "Drug Policy Chief Is Facing New Foes; McCaffrey's 'Tactics' on Needle Exchange Program Prompt Anger among Advocates,'" *Washington Post*, May 18, 1998, p. A15.

11. "Puncturing an AIDS Initiative: At Last Minute, White House Political Fears Killed Needle Funding," *Washington Post*, April 23, 1998, p. A1.

CHAPTER 2

1. "After the Soviet troops left, fears grew that loose Stingers would be bought by terrorists or hostile governments. Once the weapons reached Afghanistan they proved to be beyond auditing. President George H. W. Bush and later President Bill Clinton authorized a highly classified program that directed the CIA to buy back as many Stingers as it could from anyone who possessed them at a going rate of between $80,000 and $150,000 per missile. Pakistan's intelligence service handled most of the purchases on a subcontract basis. The total amount spent by the CIA on repurchases from Afghan warlords during the mid-1990s was about the same amount as the U.S. spent on humanitarian assistance during the same years. By the time the Taliban took Kabul, an estimated 600 missiles remained missing. There was an active market for the missiles across central Asia and the Middle East, with the Iranians buying as many as they could, perhaps as many as 100. The CIA made a direct offer to the Taliban's leader, Mullah Omar, for the 53 missiles they were thought to possess, even though this would provide the Taliban an instant cash infusion of between $5 and 8 million, or twice the amount provided by Bin Laden. When the CIA team arrived in Kandihar in February 1997, the Taliban said they had no desire to sell the missiles, fearing that they might need them for use against the Iranians" (Steve Coll, *Ghost Wars*, New York: Penguin Books 2004, pp. 11–12, 337–338).

2. "The Politics of a Covert Action: The U.S., the Mujahideen, and the Stinger Missile." This case study (C15–99–1546.0) was written by Kirsten Lundberg for Professors Philip Zelikow and Ernest May, under the auspices of the Harvard Intelligence and Policy Project, with support from the Central Intelligence Agency. The John F. Kennedy School of Government, Harvard University, takes sole responsibility for the content of this case. (1999.)

3. The Afghan leader who invited in the Soviets, Hafizullah Amin, died December 27 when Soviet and Afghan Army troops stormed his palace. His replacement was Babrak Karmal.

4. In an interview with ABC-TV after the invasion, Carter said "My opinion of the Russians has changed most [more] drastically in the last week than even the previous 2½ years before that." Republicans seized on the statement as an example of naivete. Peter W. Rodman, *More Precious Than Peace* (New York: Charles Scribner's Sons, 1994), p. 217.

5. Carter's Cabinet had also heeded CIA warnings in the autumn of 1979 of a possible Soviet invasion of Afghanistan and discussed contingency plans.

6. Robert Gates, *From the Shadows* (New York: Simon & Schuster, 1996), p. 146.

7. Stephen Coll, "Anatomy of a Victory: CIA's Covert Afghan War; $2 Billion Program Reversed Tide for Rebels," *Washington Post*, July 19, 1992.

8. The Brezhnev Doctrine was a concept that the West believed existed, but the Soviets refused to name or acknowledge it.

9. Gates, p. 148.

10. Milton Bearden interview with author, Washington D.C., October 6, 1998. All further quotes from Bearden, unless otherwise attributed, are from this interview.

11. For a full description of the ISI operation, see Yousaf and Adkin, *The Bear Trap*.

12. John McMahon telephone interview with author, October 19, 1998. All further quotes from McMahon, unless otherwise attributed, are from this interview.

13. Indulging in a bit of melodrama, Brzezinski on February 3 posed for the world press on the Khyber Pass holding a Chinese submachine gun pointed at the Soviet Union.

14. Gates, p. 148.

15. The Directorate of Intelligence (DI) is the other principal branch of the CIA. The DI provides policy makers with intelligence assessments: written analysis of global trends and events.

16. Senator Robert R. Simmons interview with author, Hartford, Conn., September 30, 1998. All further quotes from Simmons, unless otherwise attributed, are from this interview. Simmons was staff director for the Senate Select Committee on Intelligence (SSCI) from November 1981 to February 1985 under Chairman Senator Barry Goldwater (R-AZ) and vice chair Senator Daniel Patrick Moynihan (D-NY).

17. William Piekney interview with author, McLean, Va., October 26, 1998. All further quotes from Piekney, unless otherwise attributed, are from this interview.

18. The volume grew from some 10,000 tons of arms in 1983 to 65,000 tons by 1987. Yousaf, p. 83.

19. The Soviets apparently quickly learned that the U.S. was buying SA-7s in Poland, so they set in motion their own program to sabotage the weapons before the CIA bought them. It was the Mujahideen, of course, who suffered the consequences. John Walcott, Tim Carrington. "Role Reversal: CIA Resisted Proposal to Give Afghan Rebels US Stinger Missiles," *Wall Street Journal*, February 16, 1988. Vincent Cannistraro, at the time on the National Security Council staff, confirms that "they were all sabotaged by the Soviets."

20. Unbeknownst, presumably, to the CIA buyers, a significant proportion of the Egyptian arms were rusty—and unusable—World War II weaponry.

21. Yousaf and Adkin, pp. 97–102. Most of the details of the ISI operation are taken from this book.

22. Even the Pakistanis considered the North-West Territory a wild and lawless place. It held a quasi-independent status dating back to the days of British rule. The North-West Territory was self-administered, and considered technically outside the legal jurisdiction of the Pakistani government.

23. Yousaf and Adkin, p. 102. Yousaf was quick to note, however, that the CIA-controlled part of the pipeline was "riddled with opportunities for fraud."

24. Cogan, "Partners in Time," p. 79. To keep the comment in context, however, one must add that corruption was commonly known to be widespread in Pakistan.

25. Gates, p. 321. Contemporary press accounts put the annual appropriation through 1983 at $30 million, but Gates gives the higher figure.

26. Cordovez and Harrison, pp. 66–67. Harrison adds (p. 70) that Saudi Arabia, still matching U.S. contributions to the Afghans as agreed with Brzezinski, also exacted its pound of flesh from the new Administration. In the fall of 1981, after a bitter congressional debate, the US agreed to sell Saudi Arabia five Airborne Warning and Control Systems (AWAC) airplanes in an $8.5 billion deal.

27. However, most of the dismissed DO officials found employment in other branches of the Agency.

28. David B. Ottoway and Patrick E. Tyler, "US Sends New Arms to Rebels; Afghans, Angolans Get Stinger Missiles in Change of Policy," *Washington Post*, March 30, 1986. p. A1.

29. Coll, "Anatomy of a Victory," July 19, 1992, quoting Mohammad Yousaf.

30. Graham Fuller interview with author, Rockville, Md., October 7, 1998. All further quotes from Fuller, unless otherwise attributed, are from this interview.

31. Gates, p. 251.
32. Charles Cogan interview with author, Cambridge, Mass., September 21, 1998. All further quotes from Cogan, unless otherwise attributed, are from this interview.
33. Woodward, p. 312.
34. For a useful table tracking progress on these items from 1982 to 1988, see Riaz M. Khan, *Untying the Afghan Knot* (Durham, N.C.: Duke University Press, 1991), pp. 110–111.
35. For a discussion of General Secretary Yuri Andropov's views on a withdrawal from Afghanistan, see Sarah E. Mendelson, *Changing Course* (Princeton, N.J.: Princeton University Press, 1998), pp. 73–76. Mendelson says "much evidence suggests that Andropov was aware a military solution to the war was not possible, but that he was politically unable to initiate a withdrawal." p. 73.
36. Charlie Wilson interview with author, Washington, D.C., October 27, 1998. All further quotes from Wilson, unless otherwise attributed, are from this interview.
37. Gates, p. 320.
38. Bob Woodward and Charles Babcock, "US Covert Aid to Afghans on the Rise; Rep. Wilson Spurs Drive for New Funds, Antiaircraft Cannon for the Insurgents," *Washington Post*, January 13, 1985, p. A1.
39. Wilson later explained that he had great admiration for the Pakistanis, in part because he "always despised the Indians with a visceral hatred, the Nehrus and the Gandhis," and Pakistan was an enemy of India. Cordovez and Harrison, p. 158.
40. Bob Woodward and Charles R. Babcock, "US Covert Aid to Afghans on the Rise," *Washington Post*, January 13, 1985, p. A1.
41. Asked subsequently where the $40 million figure came from, Wilson said he pulled the number "right out of the sky." Woodward and Babcock.
42. Cordovez and Harrison, p. 158.
43. Cordovez and Harrison, p. 104.
44. Richard Whittle and George Kuempel, "Afghan Arms Inquiry Targets Friend of Ex-Rep. Wilson," *Dallas Morning News*, October 21, 1997, p. 1A.
45. In a 1997 interview (Whittle and Kuempel), McMahon remembered his surprise at Wilson's insistence on the weapon—"We used to make comments like 'It must be Charlie's uncle who owns Oerlikon.'" The DO's Thomas Twetten confirms that "we were a little worried that Charlie, because he was pushing that so hard, might have a financial interest."
46. In congressional parlance, intelligence committees *authorized* funding, appropriations committees *appropriated* the actual dollars.

47. Whittle and Kuempel.

48. Woodward and Babcock.

49. Margaret Shapiro, "$50 Million for Covert Arms, More Aid Voted for Afghan Rebels," *Washington Post*, July 28, 1984, p. A1.

50. Woodward, *Veil*, p. 372.

51. In 1984, a major public battle erupted when it was reported that the CIA had been behind the mining of Nicaraguan harbors. This was well before the much wider contours of the Iran-Contra scandal became visible.

52. Margaret Shapiro, "Domestic-Spending Bill Is Approved Minus Aid for Nicaraguan 'Contras.'" *Washington Post*, June 27, 1984, p. A19.

53. Woodward and Babcock.

54. Mendelson says that "what appears to have happened in 1985 was a decision to escalate involvement and to postpone any kind of serious reappraisal of the war." p. 102.

55. From December 1980 to May 1981, Pillsbury had served as acting director of the Arms Control and Disarmament Agency. His first job in Washington was as a staff member on the Senate Budget Committee in 1978.

56. Lee Roderick, *Leading the Charge: Orrin Hatch and 20 Years of America* (Carson City, Nev.: Gold Leaf Press, 1994), pp. 218–219. Roderick says Hatch personally asked Secretary Weinberger to give Pillsbury a job at the Pentagon.

57. Simpson, p. 62. NSDD 32 is still classified, as are NSDD 66 and 70, discussed below. NSDD 75 is published in Simpson, p. 255.

58. E-mail from Pillsbury to author, May 6, 1999.

59. For details of what the U.S. knew about the Soviet plans, see Peter Schweizer, *Victory* (New York: Atlantic Monthly Press, 1994), pp. 212–213. Schweizer says the National Security Planning Group discussed this intelligence in a meeting in late January 1985. "The intelligence," writes Schweizer, "came largely from the CIA source on the Soviet General Staff. It was detailed, direct, and substantial.... The goal was an outright military victory in two years."

60. NSDD 166, including its annex, remains classified. See Simpson, p. 446, for a description of what is known about it.

61. Raymond L. Garthoff, *The Great Transition: American-Soviet Relations and the End of the Cold War* (Washington, D.C.: The Brookings Institution, 1994), p. 712.

62. Coll, "Anatomy of a Victory."

63. Vince Cannistraro interview.

64. Coll, "Anatomy of a Victory."

65. Michael Pillsbury interview.

66. Alan J. Kuperman, "The Stinger Revisited; Lessons of the US Intervention in Afghanistan," *Political Science Quarterly* (Summer 1999): 219–263. The article is also included in *The New American Interventionism: Lessons from Successes and Failures* (New York: Columbia University Press, 1999), pp. 159–203.

67. David B. Ottaway, "What Is 'Afghan Lesson' for Superpowers?" *Washington Post*, February 12, 1989, p. A1.

68. Kuperman.

69. Except for the secret annex, which would have been considered separately.

70. There is considerable and understandable confusion, even among committee members, over who was on which committee. This account draws from interviews with Armacost, Pillsbury, Armitage, Iklé, Cannistraro, and Twetten.

71. Cannistraro interview.

72. David B. Ottaway and Patrick E. Tyler, "US Sends New Arms to Rebels; Afghans, Angolans Get Stinger Missiles in Change of Policy," *Washington Post*, March 30, 1986, p. A1.

73. Simpson, p. 496.

74. Kuperman.

75. Twetten interview.

76. Simpson, p. 495.

77. Armacost and Iklé usually accompanied their bosses to these breakfasts.

78. The trip also took them to Rome, Israel, and New Delhi.

79. Kuperman.

80. Pillsbury himself refused to name Piekney, referring to him as the chief of station only.

81. Walcott and Carrington (*Wall Street Journal*) reported that the CIA had in Islamabad "three officers, none of them paramilitary experts." A former CIA official, while declining to give a correct number, says Islamabad was always "a major station," relatively speaking, and that two officers is "flat wrong." Yousaf (p. 91) says, "CIA had two officers on post in 1983, but these increased to five by the time I left [1987]."

82. E-mail from Piekney to author, May 27, 1999.

83. Cordovez and Harrison, p. 195.

84. Kuperman.

85. Cordovez and Harrison, p. 103.

86. Rodman, p. 326.

87. Ambassador Arnold Raphel died tragically on August 17, 1988, a passenger on the aircraft carrying Zia Ul-Haq, which blew up in mid-air. The causes of the explosion have never been conclusively determined. Robert Peck is also deceased. Their views expressed here are recalled by

various former colleagues and counterparts, as well as in several books, the most detailed being Selig Harrison and Diego Cordovez's *Out of Afghanistan.*

88. Kuperman.

89. Philip Geyelin, "US Leaks and the Afghan Resistance," *Washington Post,* August 9, 1984, p. A23.

90. Editorial, "Getting Too Close." *Los Angeles Times,* February 4, 1985, Metro, p. 4.

91. Kuperman. Pillsbury, however, gives considerable credit to Powell—as Weinberger's gatekeeper—for allowing the Stinger issue to be introduced and re-introduced at the top policy level as new facts emerged. Says Pillsbury: "The Stinger issue would have stayed dead had it not been for his role as honest broker." E-mail to author, May 6, 1999.

CHAPTER 4

1. "The Politics of a Covert Action: The U.S., the Mujahideen, and the Stinger Missile" by Kirsten Lundberg appears courtesy of the Kennedy School of Government Case Program (C15–99–1546.0).

2. Pillsbury had secured the Vice President's Air Force 2 airplane when he discovered that all other military aircraft used for official trips were already reserved. Kuperman.

3. E-mail from Pillsbury to author, May 6, 1999.

4. E-mail from Piekney to author, February 24, 2001.

5. Pillsbury says Piekney made the decision to ban Pillsbury and was overruled after Hatch contacted Casey. The whole incident, he says, "was presented as a very minor administrative oversight." E-mail from Pillsbury to author, March 8, 1999.

6. Cordovez and Harrison, p. 195.

7. Ibid., p. 190.

8. Ibid.

9. Abramowitz took over as head of INR in February 1985.

10. Cordovez and Harrison, p. 196.

11. David B. Ottaway and Patrick E. Tyler, "The CIA in Transition: New Era of Mistrust Marks Congress' Role," *Washington Post,* May 19, 1986, p. A1.

12. Cordovez and Harrison, p. 202. The authors cite Anatoliy S. Chernyayev, *Shest let s Gorbachevym: po dnevnikovym zapisyam* [Six Years with Gorbachev: According to Diary Notes] (Moscow: Progress-Kultura Publishing Group, 1993), pp. 57–59.

13. Ibid, p. 191. The authors cite an interview with Iklé in Washington, D.C., January 22, 1993.

14. Others, including Rodman, give Armacost credit for convincing Shultz. Armacost himself says "I don't remember George having to be brought around."

15. George Shultz, *Turmoil and Triumph* (New York: Charles Scribner's Sons, 1993), p. 692.

16. The NSC had been effectively neutralized as a decision-making body by the resignation on December 4, 1985, of National Security Advisor Robert "Bud" McFarlane—reportedly out of frustration at his inability to produce a good national security working team. Admiral John Poindexter would take over a month later, on January 6, 1986. In the interim, Donald Fortier was acting NSA.

17. Pillsbury's memo to author, May 6, 1999.

18. E-mail from Pillsbury to author, February 17, 1999.

19. David B. Ottaway and Patrick E. Tyler, "The CIA in Transition: Casey Strengthens Role under 'Reagan Doctrine,'" *Washington Post*, March 31, 1986, p. A1. Also Ottaway and Tyler, "The CIA in Transition," May 19, 1986.

20. Patrick E. Tyler and David B. Ottaway, "Casey Enforces 'Reagan Doctrine' with Reinvigorated Covert Action," *Washington Post*, March 9, 1986, p. A1.

21. David B. Ottaway, "Rebels' Backers on Hill Press Aid Issue; Administration Accused of Ambiguity in Military Efforts," *Washington Post*, January 16, 1986, p. A1.

22. Iklé indicates he does not recall McMahon's new willingness to accept Stingers. Army Chief of Staff Gen. John Wickham says the JCS would have defended its own opinions in interagency meetings, although McMahon may have expressed the military's views in public forums. Says Wickham: "I don't think he was carrying water, though that may be an apt phrase. I think John was trying to reflect as accurately as he could the concerns that he was privy to."

23. Gates, pp. 349–350.

24. Pillsbury says the anti-McMahon campaign was orchestrated by Cannistraro, CIA's liaison to the NSC for intelligence matters. Cannistraro had been reprimanded and transferred out of the CIA to NSC after an investigation, led by McMahon, into a controversial CIA manual that Cannistraro and others approved for the Contras.

25. Kuperman.

26. Gardner adds that Cannistraro was opposed to Gardner's going because "he never liked me. He wanted to be the center on this trip."

27. Steven Coll, "In CIA's Covert Afghan War, Where to Draw the Line Was Key," *Washington Post*, July 20, 1992, p. A1.

28. Cordovez and Harrison, p. 196.

29. Kuperman. The PSQ article does not give a date for the tank meeting. It does provide the following quote from a 1986 Defense Investigative Service report.

30. Cordovez and Harrison, p. 197.

31. David Wise, "The Spy Who Wouldn't Die," *Gentlemen's Quarterly (GQ)*, July 1998, pp. 148–155, 183–186. The GRU agent, Sergei Bokhan, made his Stinger report in 1984. Bokhan eventually escaped from Greece with CIA assistance, one of the few double agents who survived exposure by Aldrich Ames, the Soviet mole inside the CIA.

32. Iklé considers it one of the great mysteries of the Afghan conflict that the Soviets had the Stinger plans, but never developed effective countermeasures against it. They did, however, manufacture a similar weapon, the SA-14, and sold it worldwide.

33. Cordovez and Harrison, p. 197.

34. Pillsbury interview, February 3, 1999. Most of the details of this meeting come from this interview.

35. Kuperman. Kuperman's article does not name Twetten, but it does describe this incident.

36. Twetten says in an e-mail to the author, February 16, 1999, that "I do not recall the first [there would be a second on Feb. 26] PCG meeting. If Abramowitz does, I would trust his memory." Abramowitz says in a telephone conversation with the author, May 26, 1999, that "I believe the incident is correct."

37. David Ottaway of the *Washington Post* ("US Sends New Arms to Rebels") dates this meeting on February 25. Harrison and Cordovez say February 26. The principals say they cannot recall meetings that took place so long ago. There is no declassified record.

38. Rodman, p. 277.

39. Ibid.

40. McMahon elaborates that he did not resign over Afghanistan specifically, but over his disagreements with the NSC across the board: "I had found myself at loggerheads with the NSC staff. I was not impressed by their acumen." Armitage adds that McFarlane and Poindexter "were frustrated at the fights in and among the agencies, yet were not strong enough themselves to resolve them at the table. So they did a lot of these things in the dead of night."

41. There is a lively and ongoing debate as to the influence of the Stinger deployment on the outcome of the war in Afghanistan. For a discussion, see Mendelson, *Changing Course*. Mendelson concludes that the Stinger had a marginal effect: "Many inside the leadership believed in the necessity of withdrawal long before the Mujahideen received the Stingers" (p. 99). See also Kuperman article.

42. See the excerpt from the records of the Politburo meeting of November 13, 1986, published in the *Cold War International History Project Bulletin*, nos. 8–9 (Winter 1996/1997): 178–181. Also Mendelson, who says the Politburo minutes are not conclusive regarding a decision to withdraw, leaving it unclear even whether this was the first time Gorbachev urged withdrawal. But, she says, "policy began to change substantially after this meeting and a serious debate on withdrawal ensued."

CHAPTER 6

1. John Kingdon, *Agendas, Alternatives, and Public Policies,* 2nd ed. (New York: Pearson Education, 1997).

CHAPTER 7

1. In the description that follows I am borrowing heavily from Chapter 10 of my earlier book, *The Politics of Public Management.*

CHAPTER 8

1. The facts that follow are largely based on the *New Yorker* article by Elsa Walsh, "Annals of Politics: Louis Freeh's Last Case," May 21, 2002.
2. Abraham Rabinovitz, *The Yom Kippur War: The Epic Encounter That Transformed the Middle East* (New York: Schocken Books, 2004).

CHAPTER 9

1. "Telling the Boss He's Wrong: George Shultz and Iran/Contra." This case study (C16–94–1254.0) was written by Kirsten Lundberg at the request of Philip Heymann for use in the Program for Senior Managers in Government at the John F. Kennedy School of Government, Harvard University. (1194) by Kirsten Lundberg appears courtesy of the Kennedy School of Government Case Program (C16–94–1254.0).
2. Secretary of Defense Caspar Weinberger also disliked the idea.
3. The commission, convened by order of President Reagan and led by former Texas Senator John Tower, was charged with conducting a "comprehensive study" of the NSC's role in foreign and national security policymaking.
4. George P. Shultz, *Turmoil and Triumph* (New York: Charles Scribner's Sons, 1993), p. 807. Emphasis in original.
5. Don Lippincott, "George Shultz and the Polygraph Test," Kennedy School of Government, Case C16–86–681.0.

6. The NSC includes, by statute, the President, Vice President, and Secretaries of State and Defense, with the head of the CIA and chairman of the Joint Chiefs of Staff acting as advisors. Other members can be appointed at will by the President.

7. This section relies heavily on the account of events presented in the *Final Report of the Independent Counsel for Iran/Contra Matters*, Aug. 4, 1993, Vol. 1, pp. 11–24.

8. Apparently, due to problems with the delivery, only 18 of the planned shipment of 80 HAWKs actually made it to Iran. Eventually, Iran rejected the shipment and returned 17 of the missiles.

9. Shultz, p. 804.

10. That is, instead of selling U.S.-made arms from Israeli stockpiles, the CIA would buy them directly from the Defense Department and, with help from Israel, have them shipped to Iran.

11. In his memoirs, however, Shultz indicates that he was unaware of the diversion of funds to the Contras.

12. It is important to note here that there are two versions of Shultz's actions from mid-1985 to December 1986. They differ on the degree to which Shultz knew what was going on. Shultz in his memoirs, and in the testimony he gave during successive investigations into Iran-Contra, said he knew very little and indeed complained of being left "out of the loop" on U.S. policy toward Iran. Another picture emerges, however, from detailed, handwritten notes compiled by Shultz's executive assistant, Charlie Hill, and obtained by the Independent Counsel late (1990) in its investigation into Iran-Contra. These indicate that Shultz was kept well informed, though orally, of developments in the arms-for-hostages operation. Even if Shultz knew more than he testified, however, both versions of events agree that he frequently spoke out against the policy within top administration circles.

13. Shultz, p. 794.

14. Shultz, p. 796.

15. Independent Counsel Report, vol. 1, p. 335.

16. Shultz, p. 798.

17. In fact, 18 HAWKs did arrive in Tehran. Moreover, the Independent Counsel report documents notes which indicate Shultz did have forewarning of the November shipment, including "the flight plan, the need for over-flight clearances, the delay in the shipment and the reasons the Iranians eventually returned the missiles." Independent Counsel Report, vol. 1, p. 337.

18. Shultz, p. 799.

19. Ibid, p. 803.

20. Ibid.

21. Ibid, p. 804.

22. As quoted in the *New York Times*, December 9, 1986.

23. The Independent Counsel investigation found reference to the timeline in detailed notes taken by Weinberger at the luncheon. Independent Counsel Report, p. 339.

24. Ibid.

25. Shultz, p. 806.

26. Independent Counsel Report, p. 341. Shultz's assistant, Charles Hill, gave Oliver North the moniker "Polecat" in his private notes.

27. Ibid, p. 343.

28. Shultz, p. 816. Reagan had considered Philippine leader Ferdinand Marcos a friend and loyal ally and always regretted that his administration had not found a way to save Marcos's regime, p. 639.

29. As quoted in the *New York Times*, May 23, 1987.

30. Independent Counsel Report, p. 343.

31. Shultz, p. 811.

32. Ibid, p. 816.

33. As quoted in the *New York Times*, June 25, 1987.

34. Ibid.

35. Independent Counsel Report, p. 359.

36. "At an Army School for Officers, Blunt Talks About Iraq Strategy," Elizabeth Bumiller, New York Times, October 14, 2007.

37. The account given here is largely taken from Ron Suskind, *The Price of Loyalty* (New York: Simon and Schuster, 2004).

CHAPTER 10

1. "Taking on Big Tobacco: David Kessler and the Food and Drug Administration." This case study (C120–96–1349.0) was written by Esther Scott for Professor Philip B. Heymann, for use at the John F. Kennedy School of Government, Harvard University (1996).

2. The law stipulated that the agency would complete review of new drug applications within six months of their submission; but if the agency failed to meet the deadline, new drugs could nevertheless not be put on the market.

3. The statutory definition of a device closely paralleled that of a drug: it was an instrument or other article "intended for use in the cure, mitigation, treatment or prevention of disease," or "intended to affect the structure or any function of the body."

4. As a result of a reorganization in the mid-1990s, the FDA chief now reports directly to the HHS secretary. The FDA was for many years part of the Department of Agriculture; in 1940, it was transferred to the

Federal Security Agency, the forerunner of the Department of Health, Education and Welfare and, later, HHS.

5. *New York Times*, February 27, 1991, p. B7.

6. Joshua Wolf Shenk, "Warning: Cutting the FDA Could be Hazardous to Your Health," *Washington Monthly*, January 1996, p. 17.

7. *New York Times*, April 11, 1991, p. 1.

8. As a result of intense lobbying, the FDA did agree to speed up the approval process for drugs used against AIDS (*New York Times*, June 30, 1991).

9. *New York Times*, June 8, 1991, p. 10.

10. Herbert Burkholz, "A Shot in the Arm for the FDA," *New York Times Magazine*, June 30, 1991.

11. Ibid.

12. Ibid.

13. *Wall Street Journal*, April 4, 1996, p. A12. Kessler sought to prevent pharmaceutical firms from advertising or distributing information about uses for which a drug had not been originally approved, until it had undergone clinical trials for the new applications.

14. *New York Times*, April 17, 1992, p. 1.

15. *New York Times*, June 18, 1992, p. 21.

16. *Business Week*, July 31, 1995, p. 40.

17. *Government Executive*, April 1995.

18. *Science*, August 25, 1995, p. 1038.

19. Ibid.

20. Shenk, *Washington Monthly*, January 1966. The other was NASA chief, Daniel Goldin.

21. *Time*, April 18, 1994, p. 58. Over 400,000 deaths each year in the U.S. were attributed to tobacco products. According to one FDA document, cigarettes killed more Americans annually than AIDS, alcohol, car accidents, murders, suicides, illegal drugs, and fires combined.

22. In fact, according to Kessler, the Food, Drug and Cosmetic Act was one of the few health and safety acts passed by Congress that did not specifically exempt tobacco.

23. *Journal of the American Medical Association*, April 24, 1996, p. 1258.

24. *Washington Post*, April 15, 1994, p. A1.

25. The FDA also regulated nicotine products, such as the skin patch and chewing gum, that were developed specifically to help smokers quit.

26. *Washington Post*, May 31, 1994, p. A1.

27. Ibid.

28. Philip J. Hilts, *Smokescreen* (Reading, Mass.: Addison-Wesley, 1996), p. 110.

29. *Washington Post*, May 31, 1994.

30. *The Nation*, April 25, 1994, p. 555.

31. Hilts, pp. 200–201.
32. *Business Week*, April 11, 1994, p. 58.
33. *Washington Post*, May 29, 1994, p. A1.
34. *New York Times*, April 18, 1994, p. 10.
35. Essentially, the industry maintained that nicotine effects did not meet the "traditional scientific definition" of addiction, including intoxication. Tobacco firms typically likened the effects of nicotine to substances such as caffeine or sugar.
36. "Taking on Big Tobacco: David Kessler and the Food and Drug Administration." This case study (C120–96–1349.0) was written by Esther Scott for Professor Philip B. Heymann, for use at the John F. Kennedy School of Government, Harvard University (1996).
37. "Foreseeability," in a legal sense, refers to consequences that "reasonable person" could be expected to foresee. Under this argument, the FDA could assert that the foreseeability of addiction to nicotine constituted legal intent on the part of tobacco companies. The tobacco industry disputed the validity of this interpretation of intent.
38. Hilts, p. 141.
39. *Science*, August 25, 1995, p. 1038.
40. *Time*, January 8, 1996, p. 60.
41. *Washington Post*, January 21, 1995, p. A7.
42. Over a year later, the *Journal* was still pressing its point. An April 4, 1996, op-ed article, entitled, "Why Kessler Must Go," offered a critical view of the drug approval process, among other things, at the FDA.
43. *Washington Post*, November 11, 1994, p. A1. According to a Common Cause study, Bliley headed the list of "top tobacco PAC recipients" in Congress, receiving a total of almost $124,000 from 1986 to 1995; next in line was Rep. Charlie Rose (D-NC), with roughly $105,000.

CHAPTER 11

1. "Taking on Big Tobacco: David Kessler and the Food and Drug Administration." This case study (120–96–1349.0) was written by Esther Scott for Professor Philip B. Heymann, for use at the John F. Kennedy School of Government, Harvard University (1996).
2. While the proposed rule did not directly address the issue of congressional intent, which Kessler's predecessors had invoked in part to justify their decision not to exercise jurisdiction over tobacco, it did consider the issue of whether earlier legislation—in particular, the Cigarette Labeling and Advertising Act and the Smokeless Tobacco Health Education Act—precluded FDA regulation, and concluded that it did not.

3. When the 1976 Medical Device Amendments were passed, they contained grandfathering provisions that allowed existing products to remain on the market without premarket approval for safety and effectiveness until such time as the FDA would formally require premarket applications (Allison M. Zieve and Alan B. Morrison, "Comments of Public Citizen, Inc., Regarding the FDA's Proposal to Regulate the Sale and Promotion of Tobacco Products to Minors," January 2, 1996, pp. 11–12).

4. The rule would not, however, affect advertising in publications with "primarily adult readership."

5. "Taking on Big Tobacco: David Kessler and the Food and Drug Administration." This case study (C120–96–1349.0) was written by Esther Scott for Professor Philip B. Heymann, for use at the John F. Kennedy School of Government, Harvard University (1996).

6. *New York Times*, July 13, 1995, p. 18.

7. *New York Times*, July 16, 1995, Section 4, p. 18.

8. *Newsweek*, August 21, 1995, p. 25.

9. *Washington Post*, July 25, 1995, p. A1.

10. Ibid.

11. Philip J. Hilts, *Smokescreen* (Reading, Mass.: Addison-Wesley, 1996), p. 193.

12. Ibid.

13. *American Medical News*, August 28, 1995, p. 1.

14. *Washington Post*, August 11, 1995, p. A15.

15. *Bergen Record*, March 20, 1995, p. A13.

16. *New York Times*, August 11, 1995, p. 18.

17. *Washington Post*, August 11, 1995, p. A1.

18. As quoted in *American Medical News*, August 28, 1995.

19. Jill Wechlser, "Going Up in Smoke?" *Pharmaceutical Executive*, October 1995, pp. 20–24.

20. As quoted in *US News and World Report*, July 24, 1995, p. 20.

21. *Business Week*, July 27, 1995.

22. Wechsler, *Pharmaceutical Executive*.

23. *Washington Post*, January 3, 1996, p. A20.

24. *New York Times*, August 11, 1995.

25. *Washington Post*, May 18, 1996, p. A1. Tobacco executives and PACs, the *Post* reported, had donated over $100,000 to Dole's campaigns over the past decade. Dole's party as a whole had benefited as well, especially in recent times: in 1995, the tobacco industry contributed almost $2.8 million in "soft money," 85 percent of which went to Republicans.

26. *Boston Globe*, June 14, 1996, p. 21.

27. *Boston Globe*, June 15, 1996, p. 21.

28. *New York Times*, August 24, 1996, p. 1.

CHAPTER 12

1. *Coyne Beahm, et al. v. FDA, et al.*, 966 F. Supp. 1374 (M.D.N.C. 1997)
2. *Brown and Williamson Tobacco Corporation, et al. v. FDA, et al.*, 153 F.3d 155 (4th Cir. 1998)
3. *FDA, et al. v. Brown and Williamson Tobacco Corporation, et al.*, 529 US 120 (2000)
4. "'Dealing with the Devil': The Tobacco Control Negotiations of 1997–1998." This case study (CR14–04–1737.0) was prepared for Professor Philip Heymann for use at the John F. Kennedy School of Government, Harvard University. It is adapted, with the permission of Michael Pertschuk and Vanderbilt University Press, from *Smoke in Their Eyes: Lessons in Movement Leadership from the Tobacco Wars*, by Michael Pertschuk, copyright © 2001 Vanderbilt University Press. Unless otherwise indicated, all quotations in this case are taken from Pertschuk's book. Pertschuk Funds for the case were provided in part by the Center for Public Leadership at the John F. Kennedy School of Government, Harvard University (0304).
5. It was not until 1988 that the Surgeon General, Dr. C. Everett Koop, officially declared the nicotine in tobacco to be addictive.
6. Georgia Levenson, "Tobacco Negotiations," Harvard Business School Case No. 9–899–049, Rev. April 17, 2002, p. 5. The top three corporate contributors to the Republican Party, the case reports, were tobacco companies: Philip Morris, R. J. Reynolds, and Brown and Williamson. Of roughly $12.9 million in "soft money" given to national parties by "tobacco interests" between 1987–96, according to Common Cause, Republicans received about $10.4 million and Democrats, a little less than $2.5 million.
7. The industry appealed the case to the Supreme Court, whose complex decision, in 1992, would have obliged the family to sue again. Faced with the prospect of another expensive trial, the family chose not to pursue the case Philip J. Hilts, *Smokescreen: The Truth behind the Tobacco Industry Cover-Up* (Reading, Mass.: Addison-Wesley Publishing Company, 1996), p. 201.
8. Levenson, p. 9.
9. Ibid., p. 13.
10. Ibid., p. 17.
11. Ibid., p. 13.
12. Ibid., p. 21. Philip Morris, for example, owned Kraft Foods and Miller Brewing. Lorillard's parent company, Loew's Corporation, was in the hotel and insurance business, among other things.
13. Ibid., p. 14.

14. Levenson, p. 20.
15. Ibid., p. 20, p. 18.
16. Ibid., pp. 17–18.
17. Ibid., p. 21.
18. Ibid., p. 17.
19. Ibid.
20. The FDA's authority to regulate tobacco was ambiguous. In the past, the FDA itself had argued that Congress had made clear its intent that the agency's jurisdiction should not extend to tobacco. It was unclear whether Congress would have to approve an extension of its regulatory powers to include tobacco products.
21. Funds from the sale of these cigarettes, Glantz envisioned, would go to helping tobacco farmers re-tool and to funding anti-smoking campaigns "to reduce smoking as quickly as possible."
22. The one exception to the general euphoria was John Garrison, head of the American Lung Association, who expressed less enthusiasm for the opportunities a global settlement might offer. But, according to Myers, he appeared not so much opposed to a settlement as "fundamentally uninterested."
23. Levenson, p. 18.
24. Initially, the industry sought liability protection from criminal and civil litigation, but the attorneys general would agree to consider only civil liability.
25. However, the regulation of nicotine—particularly its elimination altogether from cigarettes—continued to be a source of contention in the settlement talks.
26. Unlike ordinary, or compensatory, damages, which are limited to the calculated cost of an injury, punitive damages are left to the discretion of the jury, and are often set significantly higher than compensatory damages.
27. Levenson, p. 2.
28. Glantz later apologized to Myers for calling him a fool, but in a June 1997 interview with the *New York Times*, he described Myers as a "tragic figure. He's spent the last 15 years working on this issue and he's going to go down in history as the guy who allows the industry to slime off the hook again."
29. The language in question, which had escaped Myers's notice, would have required the FDA to institute formal rule-making proceedings for any nicotine-removal initiative; this would have given the industry leverage to overturn such an action in the courts. According to Myers, industry negotiators acknowledged that formal rule-making procedures had not been agreed to in settlement talks and promised to change the language.

Kessler was not entirely critical of the settlement; he told the *Wall Street Journal* on June 23 that "[s]ome of the elements [of the settlement] are wonderful and I support them, but other elements have to be rewritten."

30. The bill authorized the FDA to regulate tobacco under a "separate chapter" created especially for the purpose, which the industry preferred; others argued for the agency to regulate tobacco under its existing "drug" and "drug device" authority, which they felt would be stronger.

CHAPTER 14

1. "Defining Torture in the War on Terror (A)." This case study (1853.0) was written by Esther Scott for Professor Philip B. Heymann, for use at the John F. Kennedy School of Government, Harvard University (2006).

2. Dana Priest and Barton Gellman, "US Decries Abuse, but Defends Interrogations," *Washington Post*, December 26, 2002, p. A1.

3. Richard Schmitt, "Senators Quiz Gonzales on Torture Policy," *Los Angeles Times*, January 7, 2005, p. A1.

4. Peter Slevin, "Scholar Stands by Post 9/11 Writings on Torture, Domestic Eavesdropping," *Washington Post*, December 26, 2005, p. A3.

5. Daniel Klaidman, Stuart Taylor Jr., and Evan Thomas, "Palace Revolt," *Newsweek*, February 6, 2006, p. 34.

6. Jane Mayer, "The Memo," *The New Yorker*, February 27, 2006, p. 36.

7. From the OLC homepage: http://www.usdoj.gov/olc/index.html.

8. Klaidman et al., February 6, 2006.

9. John McGinnis, "Models of the Opinion Function of the Attorney General: A Normative, Descriptive and Historical Prolegomenon," *Cardozo Law Review* 15 (1993): 422.

10. Nancy V. Baker, *Conflicting Loyalties: Law and Politics in the Attorney General's Office* (Lawrence: University Press of Kansas, 1992), p. 11.

11. Ibid.

12. Toni Locy and Joan Biskupic, "Interrogation Memo to Be Replaced," *USA Today*, June 23, 2004, p. 2A.

13. McGinnis, p. 442.

14. Chitra Ragavan, "Cheney's Guy," *US News and World Report*, May 29, 2006, pp. 32–38; Eric Posner and Adrian Vermeule, "A 'Torture' Memo and Its Torturous Critics," *Wall Street Journal*, July 6, 2004, p. A22.

15. Adam Liptak, "Author of '02 Memo on Torture: 'Gentle' Soul for a Harsh Topic," *New York Times*, June 24, 2004, p. A1; Adam Liptak, "How Far Can a Government Lawyer Go?" *New York Times*, June 27, 2004, section 4, p. 3.

16. Posner and Vermeule, July 6, 2004.

17. Liptak, June 27, 2004.

18. The perpetrators of the anthrax letters were not identified and, five years later, the crime remained unsolved.

19. Jane Mayer, "Outsourcing Torture," *The New Yorker,* February 14, 2005.

20. Mike Allen and Dana Priest, "Memo on Torture Draws Focus to Bush," *Washington Post,* June 9, 2004, p. A3.

21. Michael Hirsh, John Barry and Daniel Klaidman, "A Tortured Debate," *Newsweek,* June 21, 2004, p. 50.

22. Dana Priest, "CIA Puts Harsh Tactics on Hold," *Washington Post,* June 27, 2004, p. A1.

23. Hirsh et al., June 21, 2004. Renditions began under the Clinton administration, but the practice expanded after September 11.

24. Priest, June 27, 2004.

25. David Johnston and James Risen, "Aides Say Memo Backed Coercion Already in Use," *New York Times,* June 27, 2004, section 1, p. 1.

26. Susan Schmidt, "Disclosure of Authorized Interrogation Tactics Urged," *Washington Post,* July 3, 2004, p. A3.

27. Mayer, February 14, 2005.

28. Accounts of exactly how waterboarding was done varied. Some described it as immersing the subject directly in water; others as wrapping the subject's face in a wet towel or plastic wrapping and dripping water on it; yet another, as forcing a wet rag down a subject's throat. The one thing all the descriptions had in common was that the technique created a sense of drowning and suffocation.

29. Priest and Gellman, December 26, 2002; Michael Isikoff, Daniel Klaidman and Michael Hirsh, "Torture's Path," *Newsweek,*" December 27, 2004, p. 54.

30. Isikoff et al., December 27, 2004.

31. Memorandum for William J. Haynes, Department of Defense, from John Yoo, Department of Justice, January 9, 2002. Some of the conventions dated back to the 19th and early 20th centuries, but all were updated at the time of the 1949 conference.

32. House Committee on the Judiciary, Report on H.R. 3680, War Crimes Act of 1996, July 24, 1996.

33. R. Jeffrey Smith, "Detainee Abuse Charges Feared," *Washington Post,* July 28, 2006, p. A1.

34. Michael Isikoff, "2001 Memo Reveals Push for Broader Presidential Powers," *Newsweek,* December 18, 2004.

35. Ragavan, May 29, 2006.

36. R. Jeffrey Smith and Dan Eggen, "Gonzales Helped Set the Course for Detainees," *Washington Post,* January 5, 2005, p. A1; Richard Serrano, "Prison Interrogators' Gloves Came Off Before Abu Graib," *Los Angeles Times,* June 9, 2004, p. A1.

37. Powell did suggest that the President could determine that the Geneva Conventions applied to the conflict, but that "members of al Qaeda as a group and the Taliban individually or as a group" were not entitled to POW status; all detainees would, however, be treated "consistent with the principles of the [Third Convention]."

38. The OLC memorandum cited the use of the term "severe pain" in earlier statutes "defining an emergency medical condition for the purpose of providing health benefits."

39. Johnston and Risen, June 27, 2004.

40. The memorandum also provided "certain justification defenses"—i.e., "necessity" and "self-defense"—which a defendant could use in the event that an interrogation method "might arguably cross the line" and application of the anti-torture law was "not held to be an unconstitutional infringement" on presidential authority.

41. John Yoo, "Behind the 'Torture Memo,'" *San Jose Mercury News*, January 2, 2005, p. 1P.

42. Keeping some OLC memos out of the public eye was not unusual. According to Walter Dellinger, head of OLC during the Clinton administration, about 20 percent of OLC memoranda were typically unpublished. (Jeffrey Rosen, "The Struggle over the Torture Memo," *New York Times*, August 15, 2004, section 4, p. 5.]

43. Ragavan, May 29, 2006; Dana Milbank, "In Cheney's Shadow, Counsel Pushes the Conservative Cause," *Washington Post*, October 11, 2004, p. A21.

44. John Yoo, *War by Other Means* (New York: Atlantic Monthly Press, 2006), p. 170.

45. Ibid.

46. Liptak, June 24, 2004.

47. Klaidman et al., February 6, 2006. *The New Yorker* reported, in its July 3, 2006. issue, that Ashcroft's relations with the administration were "strained, and he was left out of the inner circle" that was working on legal strategies for the war on terror.

48. Yoo, p. 170.

49. Liptak, June 24, 2004.

50. Isikoff et al., December 27, 2004.

51. Mayer, February 27, 2006, p. 39.

52. Dana Priest, "Covert CIA Program Withstands New Furor," *Washington Post*, December 30, 2005, p. A1.

CHAPTER 15

1. Our obligations would, of course, be far greater if this were a war against the army of a signator to the Geneva Conventions or a militia whose troops wore uniforms and were under firm command. The latter wasn't true of

al Qaeda but, as to soldiers of the Taliban, an argument that Afghanistan, a signatory, was no longer really a state was too stretched and self-serving to be acceptable to any but the most unquestioningly loyal of parties. *Cf.* arguments made by the administration that the Geneva Conventions do not apply to either al Qaeda or the Taliban. Memorandum from John Yoo, Deputy Assistant Attorney General, and Robert J. Delahunty, Special Counsel, on Application of Treaties and Laws to al-Qaeda and Taliban Detainees, to William J. Haynes II, General Counsel DOD (January 9, 2002) available at http://www.gwu.edu/~nsarchiv/NSAEBBIN/NSAEBB127/02/01/09.pdf.

2. "Defining Torture in the War on Terror (B)." This case study (1854.0) was written by Esther Scott for Professor Philip B. Heymann, for use at the John F. Kennedy School of Government, Harvard University (2006). For a more detailed account of the torture memo and its genesis, see Part A of this case, "Defining Torture in the War on Terror: 'Checking with the Professionals.'"

3. Tim Golden and Don Van Natta Jr., "US Said to Overstate Value of Guantanamo Detainees," *New York Times,* June 21, 2004, p. A1.

4. Vice Admiral A. T. Church, "Review of Department of Defense Detention Operations and Detainee Interrogation Techniques," memorandum for the Secretary of Defense, March 5, 2005, p. 34.

5. Michael Hirsh, John Barry and Daniel Klaidman, "A Tortured Debate, *Newsweek,* June 21, 2004, p. 50.

6. Jess Bravin, "Pentagon Report Set Framework for Use of Torture," *The Wall Street Journal,* June 7, 2004, p. A1.

7. In a handwritten note below his signature, Rumsfeld added, apparently intending to be jocular, "However, I stand for 8–10 hours a day. Why is standing limited to 4 hours?"

8. Jane Mayer, "The Memo," *The New Yorker,* February 27, 2006, p. 34, p. 37.

9. Both the Convention against Torture and the Geneva Conventions barred cruel treatment of prisoners, as well as torture.

10. Senator Carl Levin, opening statement at the Personnel Subcommittee hearing on military commissions, detainees and interrogation procedures, July 14, 2005. Levin cited the Church report as his source.

11. Judge advocates general are the chief legal officers of the armed services.

12. Levin, July 14, 2005.

13. http://balkin.blogspot.com/2005/07/graham-hearing-on-detainees-progress.html.

14. Each of these four techniques, Rumsfeld noted in his memo, could be seen as violations of provisions of the Geneva Conventions by those nations that believed the detainees were entitled to protection as prisoners of war. Although, he wrote, those provisions were "not applicable to the interrogation of unlawful combatants, consideration should be given to these views prior to application of the technique."

15. Mayer, p. 39.

16. R. Jeffrey Smith and Josh White, "General Granted Latitude at Prison," *Washington Post*, June 12, 2004, p. A1.

17. Mike Allen and Susan Schmidt, "Memo on Interrogation Tactics is Dismissed," *Washington Post*, June 23, 2004, p. A1; Richard Stevenson, "White House Says Prisoner Policy Set Humane Tone," *New York Times*, June 23, 2004, p. A1.

18. Allen and Schmidt, June 23, 2004; Stevenson, June 23, 2004.

19. According to an account in *Newsweek*, Gonzales and David Addington, then Vice President Cheney's influential general counsel, had wanted Yoo to succeed Bybee as head of OLC, but Attorney General John Ashcroft had "balked." (Daniel Klaidman, Stuart Taylor Jr., and Evan Thomas, "Palace Revolt," *Newsweek*, February 6, 2006, p. 34.)

20. Letter from Acting Assistant Attorney General Daniel Levin to William Haynes, February 4, 2005.

21. Klaidman et al., February 6, 2006.

22. Evan Thomas and Michael Hirsh, "The Debate over Torture," *Newsweek*, November 21, 2005. A November 2005 survey by the Pew Research Center reported that 48 percent of respondents believed torture was either "often" or "sometimes" justified.

23. Dana Priest, "CIA Puts Harsh Tactics on Hold," *Washington Post*, June 27, 2004, p. A1; Eric Lichtblau with Adam Liptak, "Questioning to Be Legal, Humane and Aggressive, the White House Says," *New York Times*, March 4, 2003, p. A13.

24. Josh White, "Abu Ghraib Tactics Were First Used at Guantanamo," *Washington Post*, July 14, 2005, p. A1.

25. Eric Lichtblau, "Bush Nominee Plans to Stand Firm on War-Captive Memo," *New York Times*, January 6, 2005, p. A25.

26. Thomas and Hirsh, November 21, 2005.

27. Ruth Wedgwood and R. James Woolsey, "Law and Torture," *Wall Street Journal*, June 28, 2004, p. A10.

28. Kathleen Clark and Julie Mertus, "Torturing the Law," *Washington Post*, June 20, 2004, p. B3.

29. Lt. Col. Geoffrey Corn, as quoted in the *Los Angeles Times*, "In Wartime, This Lawyer Has Got Bush's Back," by Anne-Marie O'Connor, December 12, 2005, p. E1.

30. Eric Posner and Adrian Vermeule, "A 'Torture' Memo and Its Tortuous Critics," *The Wall Street Journal*, July 6, 2004, p. A22.

31. John Yoo, "Rewriting the Laws of War for a New Enemy," *Los Angeles Times*, February 1, 2005; Mayer, February 14, 2005.

32. John Yoo, "A Crucial Look at Torture Law," *Los Angeles Times*, July 6, 2004.

33. Jess Bravin, "US Revamps Policy on Torture of War Prisoners," *Wall Street Journal*, December 31, 2004, p. A1. Some press accounts reported that Goldsmith's departure was hastened by frequent clashes with David Addington, then Cheney's general counsel, who opposed Goldsmith's decision to withdraw both the torture memo and the March 14 memo.

34. The memorandum quoted the statement, in which Bush declared that "America stands against and will not tolerate torture. We will investigate and prosecute all acts of torture…in all territory under our jurisdiction.…Torture is wrong no matter where it occurs, and the United States will continue to lead the fight to eliminate it everywhere."

35. The federal anti-torture law defined torture as an act "specifically intended" to cause severe physical or mental pain or suffering.

36. Douglas Jehl and David Johnston, "White House Fought New Curbs on Interrogation, Officials Say," *New York Times*, November 13, 2005, p. A1. The *Times* reported that the Justice Department, in "still-secret documents," had approved "specific interrogation methods"—including waterboarding—for use by the CIA in questioning high-value detainees.

37. Jackson Diehl, "Inhuman: Yes or No," *Washington Post*, September 12, 2005, p. A19.

38. Eric Schmitt, "Exception Sought in Detainee Abuse Ban," *New York Times*, October 25, 2005, p. A16.

39. Josh White, "President Relents, Backs Torture Ban," *Washington Post*, December 12, 2005, p. A1.

40. Another amendment attached to the military spending bill—this one sponsored by Republican Senator Lindsey Graham of South Carolina—dealt with legal rights of foreign detainees; among other things, it barred new detainees at Guantanamo from challenging their detention in federal court. The two amendments together comprised the Detainee Treatment Act.

41. Charlie Savage, "Bush Could Bypass New Torture Ban," *Boston Globe*, January 4, 2006, p. A1. Nine months later, Congress demanded a public statement of how our interrogation policies fit with the requirements of "Common Article 3" of the Geneva Conventions. The President's Executive Order of July 20, 2007, now forbids not only torture and cruel, inhuman, and degrading treatment as defined by the 2005 statute, but also such humiliating or degrading acts as occurred at Abu Ghraib.

CHAPTER 16

1. Even then, if a decision is to be made at a high level, we have to recognize the limiting effects of the length of any realistic allotment

of the time by an extremely busy individual or organization charged with making the decision. And we can't even expect that much unless something about the decision makes the decision makers aware that it is worth careful, though costly, attention.

2. "Do Targeted Killings Work," *Foreign Affairs,* March/April 2006.

3. This is not solely a self-interested, ambition-based set of decisions. All the influence and power that comes with holding a majority in the Senate or House of Representatives had to be balanced against the benefits of defending the habeas corpus jurisdiction. A member could easily conclude, even if looking only at societal effects, that the former effects outweighed the latter.

Index

problems in decision process, 336
September 25 opinion after destruction
  of Twin Towers, 297–299
"standards of interrogation" memo,
  314–315
torture definitions, 298f, 299f
torture memo, 302–307
Office of National Drug Control Policy,
  needle exchange program, 7, 8–10,
  12, 13
Office of Secretary of Defense (OSD),
  71, 72
O'Neill, Paul (Secretary of Treasury),
  165–169
opinions, favorable, of U.S., 326t
opportunity. See windows of opportunity
opposition, levels of support or, for
  proposal, 101–102
organization, loyalty, 128
organizational resources, 58–60, 129–130,
  193–195
organizational self-interest, 91
overconfidence, leadership, 143
oversight hearings, precedent or principle
  for, 94–95

Pakistan. See also Stinger missiles
  Abramowitz to, 67–68
  agreeing to no nuclear weapons, 29
  CIA supplying Afghans through,
    41–42
  Geneva talks with Afghanistan, 32–33
  mutual interests with United States,
    25–26
  Stingers for own use by United
    States, 66
  U.S.-funded arms shipment, 25
Pakistani President Zia
  access and crowded agenda, 104
  Hatch assuring Casey of Zia's support
    for Stinger, 77
  helping Afghan rebels, 25
  influences for Stinger missile case,
    123–124
  leaving different impressions, 64–65
  risk taking, 117
  Senator Orrin Hatch visits, 64, 76–77
  Stinger request, 65
  Stingers for Afghanistan needing
    approval of, 46–47
  Zia–Casey relationship, 31
partisanship, protecting legitimacy,
  349–350
Pentagon, position on Stinger missiles, 47

personal interests, concerns of decision
  makers, 60
personal liberty, smoking, 208–209
personal relationships, influence, 121
personal resources of influence
  concerns of decision makers, 57–58
  FBI Louis Freeh, 133
  loyalty, 129–130
  persuasion, 114–117
Pertschuk, Michael, regulation or legislation,
  189–191
pet proposals, windows of opportunity, 105
Philip Morris
  attacking Kessler and smoking
    regulation, 222
  campaign to prevent smoking by kids,
    174
  new leadership, 235–236
  predicting influence with Congress, 196
  tobacco company and influence, 232
Pillsbury, Michael
  access to Zia and his crowded agenda,
    104
  angry over CIA influence on national
    policy, 71
  assistant undersecretary for policy
    planning, 39
  confusion over Stinger request, 65
  discovery of espionage Stinger leak, 79
  finding support for missile issue,
    101–102
  influence in Stinger missile, 110–111,
    117, 123–124
  meeting with Pakistani President Zia, 47
  National Security Decision Directive,
    39–41
  persuasion with Senator Hatch, 114
  reaction to Stinger denial, 51
  rules of policy makers, 52, 53–55
  steps defining political strategy, 266
  understanding Stinger missile case, 90
  vagueness of process rules, 88
  ways to convince other players, 100
Planning and Coordination Group, 44–45,
  79–80
plausible deniability
  dismissing Stingers as a violation of, 42–43
  Pakistan and United States, 23, 27
  shift to open support, 53
  U.S. role in Afghan–Soviet conflict, 89
players. See also understanding significance
  of occasion (USO)
  chains of influence, 123–124
  demands of time and influence, 103–104

Yellowface

CREATING THE CHINESE IN AMERICAN POPULAR MUSIC AND PERFORMANCE, 1850s–1920s

KRYSTYN R. MOON

RUTGERS UNIVERSITY PRESS
New Brunswick, New Jersey, and London

LIBRARY OF CONGRESS CATALOGING-IN-PUBLICATION DATA

Moon, Krystyn R., 1974–
    Yellowface : creating the Chinese in American popular music and performance,
1850s–1920s / Krystyn R. Moon.
        p.   cm.
    Includes bibliographical references and index.
    ISBN 0–8135–3506–9 (hardcover : alk. paper) — ISBN 0–8135–3507–7 (pbk. :
alk. paper)
    1. Popular music—United States—History and criticism.   2. Chinese
Americans—Music—History and criticism.   I. Title.
    ML3477.M66 2005
    780′.89′951073—dc22

                                                                                2004007534

    A British Cataloging-in-Publication record for this book is available
                            from the British Library.

Copyright © 2005 by Krystyn R. Moon

Manufactured in the United States of America